Caesarea Philippi

CAESAREA PHILIPPI

BANIAS, THE LOST CITY OF PAN

John Francis Wilson

I.B. TAURIS

LONDON · NEW YORK

Published in 2004 by I.B.Tauris & Co Ltd
6 Salem Road, London W2 4BU
175 Fifth Avenue, New York NY 10010
www.ibtauris.com

In the United States and Canada distributed by Palgrave Macmillan,
a division of St. Martin's Press, 175 Fifth Avenue, New York NY 10010

ISBN 1 85043 440 9
EAN 978 1 85043 440 5

A full CIP record for this book is available from the British Library
A full CIP record for this book is available from the Library of Congress
Library of Congress catalog card: available

Typeset in Minion by Dexter Haven Associates Ltd, London
Printed and bound in Great Britain by MPG Books Ltd, Bodmin

CONTENTS

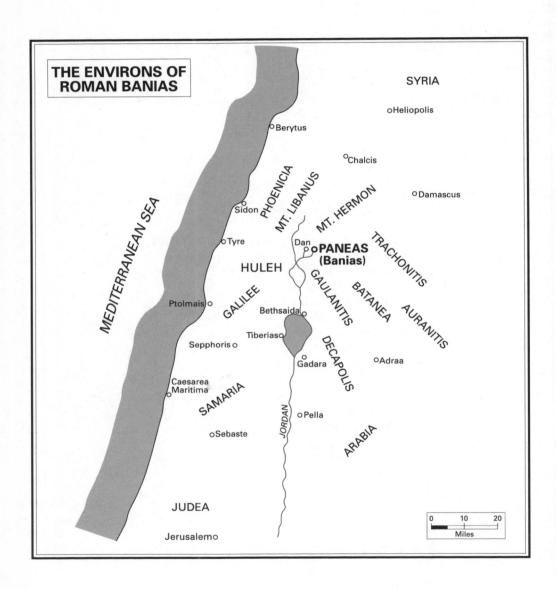

THE ENVIRONS OF ROMAN BANIAS

SYRIA

oHeliopolis

oBerytus

oChalcis

PHOENICIA

MT. LIBANUS

MT. HERMON

oDamascus

MEDITERRANEAN SEA

oSidon

oTyre

Dan
o**PANEAS**
(Banias)

TRACHONITIS

HULEH

GALILEE

GAULANITIS

BATANEA

AURANITIS

Ptolmais o

Bethsaida o

Tiberiaso

DECAPOLIS

Sepphoris o

Gadara o

oAdraa

Caesarea
Maritima o

SAMARIA

JORDAN

oPella

oSebaste

ARABIA

JUDEA

Jerusalemo

0   10   20
Miles

ILLUSTRATIONS

Photograph and illustration credits:

Preface

S ome time in 1997 the ancient city of Banias passed its two thousandth anniversary. There was no celebration. Although almost continuously inhabited for two long millennia, on its anniversary year not one permanent inhabitant remained. All that remained to memorialise the innumerable hosts who lived out their lives in this place were scattered stones within the archaeological squares, picnic tables set under a stand of old poplar trees to serve the ever-present hoards of tourists and schoolchildren, and the ancient sounds of nature – roaring waters and rustling leaves. This book has grown out of many years of association with the site of Banias as a part of the archaeological effort to open windows into the long and wonderfully eventful history of the place. It is not an archaeological report, though it makes use of the growing amount of archaeological data revealed over the last two decades and increasing yearly to the present day. It has been written mostly at Banias itself, over a period of more than a decade, after days of working in the archaeological squares, or walking along the banks of the river, or tramping through the Hellenistic, or Crusader, or twentieth-century battlefields (with careful attention to still-lethal fields of landmines!). It has taken form during quiet moments before the cave of Pan, or after looking down on the site from the heights of Subaybah, attempting to recreate in the mind a Roman city, or a medieval Islamic fortress, or a tiny nineteenth-century village. To these experiences has been added an 'archaeology of books', undertaken in great libraries such as those at the University of California at Los Angeles, the British Library, the Library of the Institute for Classical Studies at the University of London, and the tiny but historic rooms of the Palestine Exploration Fund. One chapter was drafted among the redwoods of California.

This is a book of history, with an emphasis on 'story'. I have attempted to let the story itself provide the agenda. In order to look at a very long story, encompassing two millennia, I have painted with a broad brush on a very small canvas. Or, to alter the metaphor, I have sought to trace one small, multi-hued thread as it winds its way through the massive tapestry of the history of the Middle East – through empires, religions, languages and cultures, partaking of each, but also contributing its own colours and textures to the whole. There are obvious risks in such an exercise in broad synthesis, not the least of which is the appearance of impudence in moving so often and so far outside one's own disciplinary boundaries. The broader the brushwork the more necessary are certain bold theoretic leaps across wide and deep chasms of uncertainty, and thus the more susceptible is the picture to learned criticism.

The subject of this story is the city itself, but cities without people are desolate and ultimately meaningless. I have tried to introduce the reader to more than the historical currents, or the geographical, social, or architectural aspects of Banias. History is story, and so is this account: the story of a city, and the stories of those who gave it life. It is a matter of wonder that so many names have survived. Some survived, of course, because they were famous and powerful in their day, and left their names wherever they went: Antiochus III, Herod the Great and his sons (especially Philip and Agrippa II), Jesus of Nazareth, Vespasian and Titus, Constantine and Julian 'the Apostate', Nūr ed-Dîn and Saladin, even Samuel Clemens (Mark Twain). But dozens of others somehow escaped the anonymity that is the usual fate of the not-so-famous-and-powerful, and this is also their story: Victor, son of Lysimachos, priest of Pan (second century AD); Rabbi Jose ben Kisma (second century AD); Bishop Philokalos, participant in the Council of Nicea (fourth century AD); Husayn ben Hillel, who signed a legal document at Banias on 11 July 1056 AD; Ibn al-Nabûlusi, Sunni ascetic and rebel (eleventh century AD); Bahrâm, the Assassin (twelfth century AD); Renier Brus, Crusader Lord of Banias and his ill-fated wife, whose name, unfortunately, we do not know (twelfth century); Fakhr al-Dîn Jahârkas, friend of Saladin and Lord of Banias (thirteenth century); Fakhr al-Dîn ('the Second'), the diminutive Druze and friend of the Medicis of Florence (seventeenth century); 'Ismā'îl, the genial village sheikh (nineteenth century) – the list goes on and on.

There is a tendency in the West to restrict research and discussion of Middle Eastern historical and archaeological sites to a rather limited and predetermined timeline (the Iron Age, perhaps, or the Greco-Roman or Byzantine periods) and thus to neglect the long centuries of Islamic superiority, the Middle Ages, and modern times. Banias's story does not end in the ancient world; it is a place caught in the currents of Middle Eastern history as recent as today's newspapers. As these words are written, discussions continue about the fate of the site in our own day and age. Its story furnishes a unique opportunity to learn something about the whole saga of the human habitation of this place and in a way, to reveal a microcosm of the story of the Middle East itself. I have been particularly interested in the transitional points – those moments when one culture is transformed into another. After all, our artificial charts of 'historical periods' (Roman, Byzantine, Islamic, Modern etc.), fail to account for the linkages between one 'period' and another that characterise real history, and it is precisely those linkages that sometimes provide the most interesting and useful insights into human experience.

A list of all those persons and institutions that have made this work possible would be excessively long. Mention can be made only of my academic home, Pepperdine University, steadfast in support; Dr Vassilios Tzaferis and the Israel Antiquities Authority, along with all those colleagues in the field who are bringing the ancient city and its environs to light once again; friends and professional colleagues such as Professor James Russell, who provided many helpful suggestions and criticisms, and Claudette – whose support has been constant and ubiquitous.

And now, the story of Banias.

1 The Beginnings

CANAANITE TIMES

Crowning the southern extremity of the range of mountains known as the Anti-Lebanon stands Hermon, the Mountain of Snow, its pinnacle rising near the mid-point of a line stretched between the cities of Tyre and Damascus (Fig. 3). Hermon forms a formidable natural barrier between the homelands of the ancient cultures of the Phoenician coast and the Syrian hinterland. To the east, melting snows water the territory of Abilene and the plains of Damascus. To the west, the waters pass down the mountains and are caught in the valley between the Lebanon and Anti-Lebanon ranges. There, instead of flowing on to Phoenicia and the Mediterranean, they turn southward. Soon they intermingle with other waters. First they join the springs that gush up out of the earth at ancient Dan, in the northern Huleh Valley. Then they connect with the cold, clear waters of springs originating further up the foothills of the snowy mountain, at a place of many names, which we will call by its modern name, Banias.

The springs of Banias pour from the foot of an imposing red-rock bluff (Fig. 4). They are abundant enough to be called a river at their very source. From a spot a few yards south of a large natural cave, they rush away rapidly, swirling through a jungle of trees and vines. Soon they roar over another bluff, creating a beautiful waterfall. Finally, at least in ancient times, they disperse into the marshes and swamps of the Huleh Valley. At the southern end of the Huleh the confluent waters of many streams, including those of Banias, emerge as the nascent River Jordan.

Banias looks down on the Huleh Valley, commanding a view all the way across it to the mountains of Napthali on the west. Behind Banias the ancient road from the Phoenician coast to Damascus winds its way upward, and then down again into the Damascene plain. This road, which was to secure for Banias a place in the history of one successive empire after another, has continued to be used, and its control contested, until our own times. Countless generals have marched their troops past the springs of Banias on their way to or from the Mediterranean coast. Among them, no doubt, was the mighty Tiglath-pileser of Assyria, on his way to a rendezvous with his Tyrian representative, in preparation for the destruction of nearby Dan, and the famous siege of the mound city of Hazor, for this was none other than the fabled 'Way of the Sea' mentioned by the prophet Isaiah (Isaiah 9:1).[1]

There followed the Assyrian conquest of the cities and the exile of the peoples of the region (733–32 BC).[2] This catastrophe befell the people of the Kingdom of Israel, asserts the author of II Kings, because of 'the sins of Jeroboam the son of Nebat, which he made Israel to sin'.[3] The most notorious of these sins was the institution of the cult of the 'golden calf' at Dan (biblical Laish), barely three miles from Banias, where additional springs broke forth. Extensive archaeological work at Dan has revealed the site of this cult,[4] which no doubt had its origins in the simple nature worship of the local Canaanites: the golden calf is highly reminiscent of the bulls upon which the Canaanite Ba'als can be seen in surviving stelae. The amalgamation of the Canaanite deity with Israel's Yahweh, so highly offensive to the biblical writer, was but one example of a process common to the history of religion in this region. And beyond the fact of the amalgamation stands the remarkable persistence of the earliest forms of religious awe practised at such sites. It is the primeval gods of nature that form the chain binding the succeeding procession of deities, whose cultural identity and names tended to survive only so long as their cultural sponsors controlled the sites where the cults were practised. Thus, the ancient Ba'al cults of Hermon continued to flourish throughout the entire history of the Kingdoms of Israel and Judah[5] and, as we shall see, survived in one form or another through a succession of historical vicissitudes reaching into modern times.

From the very earliest times the Phoenicians, Syrians and nomadic peoples of the region knew the cave and springs of Banias well. Travellers on the 'Way of the Sea' must have often paused to stand and watch the waters pour forth, marvelling at the beauty and power of nature exhibited so dramatically before them. This was surely a place of special holiness, a place where one could sense the presence and the power of the Ba'als, the primeval lords of nature. Long ago, René Dussaud noticed significant similarities between Aliyan, son of Ba'al, the 'god of the sources' mentioned in the Ras Shamra tablets, and the sites and cults of Dan and Banias. There are striking similarities between the two deities. Aliyan's duty was to watch over and control the springs and underground waters, for example. Dussaud suggests that the Phoenicians had made this connection long before Banias became associated with the Greek god Pan, who, also a 'god of the sources', became for the Greeks the logical successor to the ancient Semitic deity.[6]

THE ARRIVAL OF THE GREEK GOD PAN

Alexander the Great may not have passed directly by this place on his way to Egyptian triumphs. We do know, however, that sometime after Alexander's march of conquest, during the time when his successors set about to Hellenise the East, the Canaanite god who was honoured at Banias merged with the Greek god Pan.[7] There were sufficient reasons to connect the two based on no more than the similarities of their mythological attributes.[8] Banias was certainly not the only place where such syncretism occurred. There is good evidence for the introduction of Pan-worship at other existing holy places in the Hellenised East. In Egypt, from where the Ptolemaic successors of Alexander ruled the regions around Banias, Pan was identified with Khem, and worshiped at the latter's ancient temples in the desert. A town there even took upon itself the name Panopolis, as the centre of a district giving special honour to the god, and his goat-like image could be found in the Egyptian temples.[9] At this stage, however, such syncretism was often quite superficial. The Greeks began the process of interpreting the local deities in terms of their own theological understanding, while the local population continued to think in traditional terms, despite the new names that the Greeks might have imposed on their pantheons.[10] This process of syncretism may also be observed on the coinage of Phoenician cities of Canaanite heritage. To judge by the coins alone, we might conclude that the Canaanite gods had given way to those of the Greeks. In fact, however, in the minds and hearts of the Canaanite population, very little had changed, and in fact, the local traditional theology remained as a strong undercurrent even after many generations of Hellenism.[11]

But it was not simply the personal characteristics of the local deity and Hellenic Pan that led to their amalgamation at Banias. To the Hellene, the place may well have been a more relevant factor. Pan was, after all, the god of forests and deserted places, of shepherds and of flocks. Originating in Arcadia, he had suddenly appeared to help the Greeks in their victory at Marathon, using his special talent for generating 'pan-ic' in an opposing army.[12] For this service he received a cave on the Acropolis of Athens itself, where his cult could be maintained.[13] So ugly was he, according to the traditions,[14] that his own parents abandoned him and a series of gentle maidens resoundingly rejected his advances, among them Selene (the moon), Echo, whose voice may be heard in his haunts, Syrinx, from whom came his reed pipe, which one may hear him playing sadly in the forests, and Pitys, whose symbol is the pine cone. Thus rejected, he turned to the grossest kinds of sexual adventures, forcing himself indiscriminately on maidens, young boys and even animals with amoral abandon. He is commonly depicted as a leering, bestial freak, though often in the company of beautiful forest nymphs.

Despite his distasteful appearance and habits, Pan lived in places of great beauty. The lush and bucolic imagery of his habitat is already present in Plato's *Phaedrus*, with its prayer to Pan,[15] and continues to be repeated in Hellenistic and Roman times. The Homeric Hymn 19 speaks thus of him:

> Muse, tell me about Pan, the dear son of Hermes, with his goat's feet and two horns – a lover of merry noise. Through wooded glades he wanders with dancing nymphs who foot it on some sheer cliff's edge, calling upon Pan, the shepherd – god, long-haired, unkempt. He has every snowy crest and the mountain peaks and rocky crests for his domain; hither and thither he goes through the close thickets, now lured by soft streams, and now he presses on amongst towering crags and climbs up to the highest peak that overlooks the flocks. Often he courses through the glistening high mountains, and often on the shouldered hills he speeds along slaying wild beasts, this keen-eyed god. Only at evening, as he returns from the chase, he sounds his note, playing sweet and low on his pipes of reed ... At that hour the clear-voiced nymphs are with him and move with nimble feet, singing by some spring of dark water, while Echo wails about the

mountain-top…On his back he wears a spotted lynx-pelt, and he delights in high-pitched songs in a soft meadow where crocuses and sweet-smelling hyacinths bloom at random in the grass.[16]

This language, undoubtedly originally describing some Arcadian landscape, fits the setting of Banias perfectly. The 'dark-watered spring' brings quite naturally to mind the lovely river Banias, and the 'mountain's top', of course, snowy Hermon. In addition, this hymn introduces us to Pan's circle: his father Hermes, and grandfather Zeus, the nymphs, and Dionysus – all of whom will eventually enter the story of the cult centre at Banias.

At this stage, however, the cult of Pan at Banias seems to have been relatively undeveloped, certainly not to be compared to that of Alexandria, where, according to Strabo, Ptolemy II Philadelphus built a Paneion for the god (identified with the Egyptian Min) in order to include him within his dynastic cult of Dionysus.[17] The evidence for this conclusion regarding Banias is archaeological. Excavations of the extensive group of sanctuaries that eventually lined the base of the red cliff beside the cave produced no buildings that can dated to the Hellenistic period. There were definite signs of cultic activity, however. Small bowls and saucers, locally made, indicated a very modest attempt to offer honour to the deity, perhaps by the local peasants (Fig. 5). By the later second century BC the dedicatory vessels became 'abundant, varied in type, and quite sophisticated' and in some cases showed connections with the Phoenician coast, as might be predicted. The presence of a large number of cooking vessels from the same period suggests that ritual dining also took place at the site by this time.[18] Ma'oz, the excavator, has made the interesting suggestion that a road may have run along the terrace and that 'at that time the site was merely a road-side sanctuary with activities focused around the natural grotto'.[19]

THE BATTLE OF THE PANEION AND SELEUCID DOMINATION

The first reference to Banias specifically, and by its Greek name, is in the work of the Greek historian Polybius. In the division of Alexander's empire, Ptolemy of Egypt and his successors controlled Palestine for a long time. As we have suggested, it was most likely during this period that the cave and spring at Banias, and the area around them, were first identified with the Greek as well as the Canaanite religion, just as the establishment of Panopolis and the Paneion at Alexandria in Egypt can certainly be attributed to Ptolemaic times.

Polybius describes in detail a battle between Scopas, an Aetolian officer serving as chief of staff in the Ptolemaic army, and Antiochus III ('the Great') of Syria. This battle took place, he says, at the 'Panium in Coele-Syria'.[20] It may be dated approximately 200 BC.[21] Since Polybius wrote his account after the events he describes, it is impossible to draw any firm conclusions as to whether the name he gives for the site was already attached to it before the battle. It has even been suggested that the attribution of the power of Pan here came as a direct consequence of the battle, since the elephants of the Syrian army caused panic among the Egyptians.[22] Even if, as seems probable, the grotto were already dedicated to Pan before the battle by the Ptolemaic Egyptians, nothing is likely to have existed at the cave-spring site besides a simple altar, consistent with the tradition that this god was usually worshipped in unaltered caves in out-of-the-way places.[23]

Polybius's account of this decisive battle mentions a number of geographical details about the battle site. The task of identifying them is made difficult, however, by the fact that his purpose in giving the account is to show the carelessness of his source, Zeno. Nevertheless, Bar-Kochva, in his work on the Seleucid army, has provided an interesting, if not entirely definitive, reconstruction of the battle that takes into account the topography of the area and provides a logical sequence of events (see map below). He suggests that since neither Polybius nor Zeno knew the topography, they both confused certain aspects of what happened and that the event should be reconstructed as follows:

Antiochus III occupied Palestine in 202 BC. In the winter of 200 BC, however, Scopas moved north and reoccupied Coele-Syria. Antiochus counterattacked in the following summer and Scopas, in an attempt to stop this incursion at the northern frontier of Palestine, advanced his troops toward what Polybius calls 'the Panium'. Before he arrived, however, Antiochus, accompanied by his two sons, took the old 'Way of the Sea' from Damascus and established himself near the spring of Banias, camping beside its waters. To the southwest of Antiochus's camp lay the crescent-shaped plain or 'platform' some 1.5 km wide that would eventually be the site of residential quarters belonging to Roman and Byzantine Banias. The area now serves as agricultural land associated with the Israeli settlement Senir. On the west, this 'Banias Plateau' descends rapidly into the Huleh Valley.

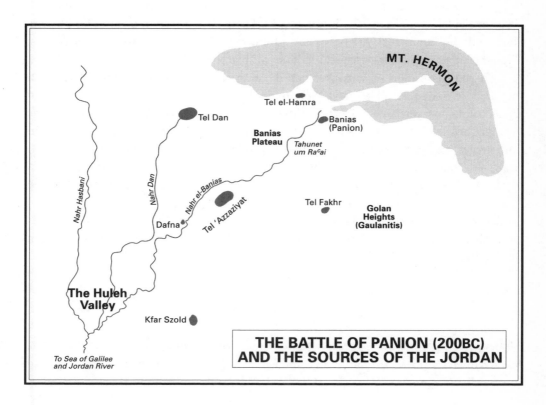

THE BATTLE OF PANION (200BC) AND THE SOURCES OF THE JORDAN

On the east, it extends to the banks of the Banias river, which may be easily forded any-where from its source to a spot some 1.5 km below called Tahunet um Ra'ai. At that point the river enters a deep ravine, too steep for armies to cross. To the north of the plateau Tel Hamra, a foothill of Mount Hermon, dominates the landscape. South of the river lies another more extensive, very uneven plateau dominated by two hills, Tel 'Azzaziyāt on the west and Tel Fakhr on the east. Zeno's 'level ground' may thus be identified as the Banias Plateau, his 'river' with the Nahr El-Banyas, the 'commanding hill' with Tel Hamra, and the 'lowest slopes of the mountain' with Tel 'Azzaziyāt.[24]

Zeno says that Scopas placed the right wing of the phalanx, with a few horsemen, 'on the hills' and the left wing and most of the cavalry 'on the level ground'. Part of the other army, under the command of Antiochus the Younger, the son of King Antiochus, occupied 'the parts of the hill which commanded the enemy'. At daylight the king took the rest of his army 'across the river which separated the two camps and drew it up on the plain'. The Syrian army thus had its phalanx in one line opposite the enemy's centre with some of the cavalry to its left and some to its right.[25] Thus, the main Seleucid army, including elephants and a phalanx, left their camp, crossed the river and took up a position on the plateau, facing the Ptolemaic forces, who were stretched from the plateau on the left to the lowest slopes of Tel 'Azzaziyāt on the right, divided by the river. Part of the Seleucid army on the plateau, consisting of heavy cavalry, under at least the nominal command of Antiochus the Younger, only about fifteen years old at the time, positioned itself on Tel Hamra.

Zeno next describes the actions of King Antiochus, who sent a contingent including a corps of elephants to occupy Tel Fakhr (Fig. 7). These were placed in front of his phalanx along with the Tarantines, with bowmen and slingers in the spaces between the elephants. Then the king and his horsemen and foot guards placed themselves behind the elephants. Now the younger Antiochus with his armoured cavalry charged down from the hill on which they were stationed, attacking the Egyptian Aetolian cavalry which had been stationed to the left of its own phalanx and north of the river. Then, as he saw his son winning in the northern area, the elder Antiochus also charged the Ptolemaic forces south of the river. In both arenas the Syrian elephants played a large role in their victory, perhaps, some have suggested, creating such a Pan-ic in the Egyptian army that the grateful Syrians identified, or at least confirmed the place as the domain of the goat-footed god. At any rate, the Ptolemaic forces fled toward the coast in defeat.[26]

Regardless of the difficulties in reconstructing the details of the battle, its result was clear enough. Seleucid Syria would dominant Palestine and the region of Banias, from that time until the revolt of the Maccabees.[27]

THE ITUREANS

After the Battle of Panium, the Syrians controlled the territory from Damascus to the Mediterranean and all of Palestine.[28] But within a few decades their power began to recede. Challenges came from the Jews of Palestine, summoned to independence by the

Maccabees, the Arab Nabateans further to the south, and the Aramaic-speaking Itureans centred to the west of Hermon in the Beka'a Valley. Far to the northeast the Parthians were putting on their own pressure, and by the first century BC Tigranes, the king of Armenia, dominated much of northern Lebanon.[29]

The Itureans, known for their military prowess, shared with the Jewish kings an interest in weakening the Seleucid hold on the area. They were also competitors at times, since they shared a common border. References to Itureans can be confusing in the ancient sources, since the term may describe either an ethnic entity or a political one. Recent archaeological work has identified distinctive pottery, now designated 'Iturean', over a wide area stretching from the Beka'a Valley across the Anti-Lebanon, and throughout the district surrounding Banias.[30] The finds are consistent with the theory that the Itureans were Aramaic tribes who had ranged over a large area for many centuries and who seemed originally to be nomadic or semi-nomadic for the most part.[31] The Iturean principality, on the other hand, developed during Seleucid times under the guidance of a series of indigenous, but Hellenised, petty dynasts who ruled over only a part of the territories inhabited by ethnic Itureans.[32] The situation was remarkably parallel to the relationship of the Jews, also a wide-ranging ethnic group, and the Hellenised Hasmoneans, who took advantage of Seleucid weakness to form an independent principality whose boundaries were constantly changing.[33]

The founder of the Iturean dynasty was Ptolemy, son of Mennaeus (ca. 85–40 BC).[34] His capital seems to have been at Chalcis, possibly modern Anjar, overlooking the Beka'a Valley in Lebanon.[35] Already, before he came to power, the Itureans had lost parts of northern Galilee to the Jewish king Aristobulus I.[36] According to Timagenes (first century BC), Aristobulus I conquered 'a portion of the Iturean nation, whom he joined to them [i.e. the Jews] by the bond of circumcision' (104–3 BC). Josephus, who preserved Timagenes's account, does not say that an Iturean kingdom was conquered, but only that some of the territory inhabited by Itureans was taken over and united with Judaea, and that its inhabitants converted to Judaism.[37] At least some of these converts may have resided in the Banias area.

At the death of Antiochus XII (84 BC), who had succeeded to the Seleucid throne ca. 97 BC, the power vacuum created by Seleucid weakness reached a stage of crisis. Ptolemy, son of Mennaeus apparently took advantage of the situation to make himself ruler of the Itureans, and perhaps other local tribes, and thus began his long reign of over forty years (ca. 85–40 BC).[38] Initially there was a clash with the Jewish king Alexander Jannaeus (103–76 BC) who seems to have grabbed the Huleh Valley and perhaps the region of Banias as well, areas that had been increasingly under local control as the Seleucid power base deteriorated.[39] As so often its lot in consequent history, the area around Banias represented a disputed frontier – this time between the Iturean territories and Jewish state. The presence of a major Iturean cult centre only four kilometres north of Banias at Senaim suggests, however, that the area remained more Iturean than Jewish. This centre served local settlements as the Itureans' main cult place, according to its excavator.[40] It featured an impressive temenos with architectural features and inscriptions dating from the third and second centuries BC to the fourth century AD. Coins found in the excavation parallel these dates as well.[41] Ptolemy's coins proclaim him to be 'ΑΡΧΙΕΡΕΥΣ' ('high priest' – a title also held by his neighbour and rival Alexander Jannaeus). But his priesthood was probably exercised at Baalbek, near his capital, rather than in the mountains of Banias.[42] Since ceramic finds at Banias indicate at least modest cultic activity there during this period as well, we might attribute such activity to the remnants of the old Canaanite population who still inhabited the area and the Greek settlers who worshipped at the cave of Banias, while the Itureans established their own cult centre a short distance away.

Relations between the two rulers, Alexander Jannaeus and Ptolemy, were generally cordial, particularly as both watched warily the Roman advance to the east.[43] Ptolemy even got directly involved in the dynastic struggles of the Hasmonean family. When the Roman general Pompey appeared on his mission to pacify the area and organise the series of petty Eastern states according to Roman interests, he killed the father of the Hasmonaean prince Mattathias Antigonus, who fled with his two sisters to Askelon. Ptolemy sent for them and gave Mattathias Antigonus protection within his own principality, even marrying Alexandra, one of the sisters. This action got him in trouble with Pompey, who undoubtedly saw it as provocative.[44] Pompey reduced Ptolemy's territories and forced him to pay a huge bribe for his life.[45] Apparently he did clarify the situation regarding control of Banias in Ptolemy's favour, however,[46] and allowed him to use the titles 'tetrarch' and 'high priest' but not 'king'. He was also allowed to continue to mint coins in his own name. These coins were thoroughly Hellenised – featuring portraits of Artemis, Hermes, the Dioscuri, Zeus and Athena.[47]

Rome understandably took great interest in the Anti-Lebanon region, in particular its southeastern end, stretching from the Beka'a Valley to Damascus, and reaching southward to the Golan Heights, the headwaters of the Jordan, and the hills of Galilee. This was, in the words of Millar, 'an inner "frontier" [between Rome and the east] possibly more real than that which lay along the fringes of the steppe'.[48] It was populated, even high into the mountains, by people who valued their independence and could be a potential source of difficulties for the Romans. Indeed, some seventy years after the founding of the Roman province of Syria, in the early part of the first century, it was still necessary to conduct large military operations in the area against the rebellious mountaineers.[49]

Under Ptolemy and his successor, Lysanias (40–34 BC), who bore the same titles as his father, the fortunes of his tetrarchy declined even further. Lysanias issued coins soon after his reign began, in the year in which he helped Antigonus take the Jewish throne. Antigonus's rival, Herod, was forced to flee the area. One of these coins depicted Nike (Victory), holding a wreath and palm branch.[50] However, Lysanias was then held culpable for his support of the Persians during their invasion of the Levant, and executed by Mark Anthony. His territory was divided into four parts – a considerable portion going to Cleopatra.[51]

Cleopatra leased the principality, presumably including the Paneion, to a man named Zenodorus, who was most likely also Lysanias's rightful heir.[52] Though at least one inscription calls Zenodorus the son of Lysanias, extant coin portraits of the two show little resemblance and Josephus does not make such a connection. He may have been a more distant relative. Coins of Chalcis minted during this period feature portraits of Cleopatra and Mark Antony.[53] However, shortly after the defeat and subsequent deaths of these two at Actium on 2 September 31 BC, an anonymous coin was minted depicting Nike – most likely a not-so-subtle celebration of this turn of events.[54] Upon Cleopatra's death, Zenodorus assumed the titles of his predecessors, as seen on his coins: 'ΤΕΤΡΑΡΧΟΥ ΚΑΙ ΑΡΧΙΕΡΕΩΣ' ('tetrarch and high priest').[55] These coins feature portraits of Zenodorus on the reverse and Octavian on the obverse – clearly placing the Iturean principality within the sphere of Rome's new 'first citizen' (Fig. 8).

Included in Zenodorus's territory was Trachonitis, where a primitive and unruly population made its living in banditry, preying on the people of Damascus and, according to Strabo, 'robbing the merchants of Arabia Felix', who were forced to travel through their bailiwick.[56] Zenodorus encouraged the Trachonitines in this activity and took his share of the spoils. For this complicity the Romans deprived him of Trachonitis, and of Batanaea and Auranitis as well, and turned these territories over to his rival, Herod, who was by this time (23 BC)[57] secure in his place as Rome's client ruler over Palestine.[58] Herod's assignment from Rome was not only to suppress the brigands, but also to provide a system of consistent order and security to the whole area. Having long served as a battleground between the Ptolemies and Seleucids, the Golan, Trachonitis and Batanea were only sparsely settled prior to Herod's reign. These regions were subject to the disorder and violence characteristic of nomadic cultures unchecked by the discipline of strong external control. Under his patronage, however, they would now flourish.[59] Although Strabo attributes the pacification of the area to 'the good government established by the Romans' and 'the security established by the Roman soldiers that are kept in Syria', it is obvious that the major agent in this process was Herod himself.[60]

When Zenodorus died in 20 BC his remaining lands were also bestowed upon Herod by the emperor Augustus.[61] This was, Josephus says, a 'substantial piece of good fortune' for Herod, for Zenodorus's remaining territory was extensive. It lay between Trachonitis and Galilee 'and contained Ulatha and Paneas[62] and the surrounding country'.[63] Ulatha designates the marshy lowland region known also as the Huleh[64] and Paneas refers to the nearby territory at higher elevation that derived its name from the cultic site at the cave of Pan, the Paneion of Polybius and the other Greeks. These territories were to remain more or less under the control of Herod's family for more than a century.[65]

HEROD THE GREAT (37–4 BC)

Herod was one of the dominant personalities not only of the East, but also of the empire. Through skilful and diplomatic machinations, and considerable luck, he ingratiated himself to Augustus and gradually gained more and more power, territory, wealth and glory for himself. The territories north and east of Palestine came under his control, as we have seen, as a reward for pacifying the robber bands of Trachonitis and then as the heir to the territories of Zenodorus. The latter came to a tragic end in Antioch of Syria, bleeding to death in consequence of a ruptured intestine.[66] Augustus, who happened to be in the East at the time, seems to have made the presentation of Zenodorus's domain to Herod personally. Thus Herod's triumph over his old rival was complete. By this time he was well into his second decade as king and enjoying Augustus's warm support. 'There was no one after Agrippa whom Caesar held in greater esteem than Herod,' says Josephus.[67]

These were the circumstances under which Roman Banias enters history. Having escorted Augustus back to the sea, Herod returned home and 'erected to him a very beautiful temple of white stone in the territory of Zenodorus, near the place called Paneion'.[68] In the mountains here Josephus continues,

> there is a beautiful cave, and below it the earth slopes steeply to a precipitous and inaccessible depth, which is filled with still water, while above it is a very high mountain. Below the cave rise the sources of the river Jordan. It was this most celebrated place that Herod further adorned the temple which he consecrated to Caesar.[69]

Josephus provides a second description of the place in *The Jewish War*:

> When, later on, through [Augustus] Caesar's bounty he received additional territory, Herod there too dedicated to him a temple of white marble near the sources of the Jordan, at a place called Paneion. At this spot a mountain rears its summit to an immense height aloft; at the base of the cliff is an opening into an overgrown cavern; within this, plunging down to an immeasurable depth, is a yawning chasm, enclosing a volume of still water, the bottom of which no sounding-line has been found long enough to reach. Outside and from beneath the cavern well up the springs from which, as some think, the Jordan takes its rise...[70]

Josephus's account is, as usual, both illuminating and somewhat confusing, partially due to his proclivity toward colourful and exaggerated, rather than precise language. The Paneion, in the *Antiquities*, seems surely to refer to an entire district. In *The Jewish War* the term is applied quite specifically to the Pan cave itself and the spring before it. Josephus's insistence in both accounts that within the cave there is a very deep pool of still water is problematic to anyone who has visited the site, since today the floor of the cave seems quite solid and shows no evidence of such a limitless chasm. There is little or no water in the floor of the cave today, and the spring emits from the ground several metres down the hillside from the cave opening. Josephus says that the waters originated partially outside and partially from 'beneath the cavern'. Allowing for some exaggeration in the matter of depth, it is quite possible that the cave contained a pool that communicated in some way with the spring outside. When the American missionary William Thomson visited the site in 1843 he speculated that the water did in fact originate inside the cave and that the Romans had constructed an arched passageway, now covered with ruins and debris, through which the waters flowed.[71] Modern excavations seem so far at least partially to confirm Thomson's theory.[72] It is likely that the waters flowing from the cave via the arched passageway were captured in some sort of 'sacred pool' outside the cave as well, situated approximately where the springs burst forth today.[73] An illustrative parallel is the Pool of Siloam in Jerusalem, created by waters that flowed from a cave (in this case, actually the famous 'Hezekiah's Tunnel'). Another is the cave spring, channel and collecting pool at Sataf.[74]

Josephus's assertion that the temple was built of 'white marble' has been questioned. At the most, some decorative elements and facings may have been of marble. More likely the basic construction material was 'white' limestone, such as the elaborately carved architectural fragments that have been found in considerable numbers at the site, reused in later buildings.[75]

We have no specific evidence that Josephus himself ever visited Banias, though it is hard to imagine that he had not done so, given its fame and the fact that he had served as governor of nearby Galilee. What he would have seen on such a visit was the imposing city of Caesarea Philippi built in Hellenistic style as it existed before and during the Jewish Revolt (64–70 AD), almost a century after the construction of Herod's temple to Augustus. It is noteworthy that even so he refers to the cavern of Pan as 'overgrown'. Apparently, despite elaborate ornamentation of the area by a series of Herodian rulers, the cave itself was left in a natural state, as befitted a sanctuary of the god Pan. Josephus mentions no other buildings or installations of any kind at the Paneion, in this case a term referring specifically to the immediate area of the cave and spring. Nor does he allude to an active cult of Pan there. Since Pan grottos were traditionally left in a natural state, this omission by Josephus might lend credence to the possibility that in his time the area immediately around the grotto was still a relatively untouched site, albeit it a 'celebrated' one.[76]

THE TEMPLE OF AUGUSTUS

Josephus's terse reference to the structure as a 'temple to Augustus' must be placed in the context of contemporary developments, particularly the rise of the cult of Augustus and Roma, and more particularly the Eastern manifestations of the cult. The Paneion temple could not, by Augustus's own decree, be dedicated to himself alone, but only to himself alongside the goddess Roma.[77] This duality is explicitly mentioned in the case of the temple Herod built at Caesarea Maritima,[78] and must be presumed in all references to 'Augustus temples' in the East during the emperor's lifetime. In this connection, a marble helmeted head, found among a cache of smashed statuary from the sanctuary at Banias, has been interpreted as possibly representing Roma.[79]

Why did Herod build a temple in honour of Augustus 'near the Paneion'? Certainly this project was consistent with his general policy of giving 'flattering attention' to Caesar and other influential Romans. Josephus complains that Herod ran roughshod over the customs and sensitivities of his Jewish subjects and 'founded cities and erected temples – not in Jewish territory, for the Jews would not have put up with this, since we are forbidden such things, including the honouring of statues and sculptured forms in the manner of the Greeks – but these he built in foreign and surrounding territory'.[80]

But the motives behind the construction of this temple extend beyond an act of obeisance to the imperial family.[81] This project should also be seen as part of a strategy in the political and economic development of the area. As Urman suggests, the site provides an 'axis connecting Herod's territories in the northern sections of Western Palestine with the new territories given him by Augustus in Batanaea and Trachonitis'. Thus the Paneion becomes both a symbolic and an actual keystone for a geographic and economic arch stretching from northern Transjordan to the Galilee.[82] Archaeological surveys of the area, particularly the Golan to the south, indicate a dramatic increase in the number of settlements during this early period of Roman supremacy. The uncertainties and dangers created by the struggles between the Ptolemies and the Seleucids, and the resulting lawlessness in the region, disappeared. Herod sponsored and supported the establishment of many new settlements by introducing an influx of immigrants, many of them Jewish. The area known as the Paneion, with its central location and reputation as a cult site, and now with its dramatic white Augusteum, was the ideal symbol for the changes wrought by Rome through its vassal Herod.[83]

Herod's temple to Augustus at Banias was one of a series of three such structures that he caused to be erected, all well north of the concentration of Jewish cultural and religious conservatism in the province of Judaea, all during approximately the same period (ca. 25–10 BC), and all with clearly political implications. Indeed, the cities that grew up around the three temples were all named after the Roman emperor: Caesarea Maritima, with its port of Sebastos; Samaria-Sebaste; and Caesarea Philippi or Paneas.[84] Since the Augusteum of Caesarea Maritima and that of Samaria-Sebaste have been thoroughly excavated and studied, it is useful to examine these, hoping by this means to learn something of the situation in Banias by analogy.

The most prominent of the Augustan temples was the centrepiece of Herod's magnificent window to the west, the port of Caesarea Maritima. Rivalling the famous ports of Alexandria and Carthage, Herod's artificial harbour on the Mediterranean was a marvel of engineering and an aesthetic *tour de force*. There, rising above a line of marble buildings tracing the harbour, 'was a mound on which there stood a temple of Caesar, visible a great way off to those sailing into the harbor, which had a statue of Rome and also one of Caesar'.[85] The statue of Augustus was modelled after the Olympian Zeus, and the goddess Roma was depicted as Hera of Argos, for, as we have seen, according to Suetonius, Augustus would only allow himself to be worshipped in combination with Roma. Fragments of this building have been excavated and are now on display at the site.[86]

The second in the series of Augustus temples was erected in Samaria-Sebaste. Herod had completely rebuilt this ancient site, once the capital of the Northern Kingdom of Israel, and populated it with his veterans and other (pagan) supporters. He renamed the city Sebaste in honour of Caesar. 'Within it, at its centre, he consecrated a precinct of one and a half stades (in circumference), which was adorned in a variety of ways, and in it he erected a temple which in size and beauty was among the most renowned.'[87] The general character of this temple is well known.[88] It was built on a great platform with massive retaining walls at the highest point on the western end of the city's summit. In order to construct this platform, Herod's architects levelled old Israelite and Hellenistic buildings, as well as newer houses standing on the site. The temple was thus provided with a large forecourt (approximately 50 metres wide by 70 metres long). An altar stood in the centre of the southern side of the forecourt. Behind the altar were 24 steps leading up to a colonnaded portico that was equal in width to the temple's facade. The Corinthian-style columns continued down the side of the temple on the east and west. Next to the temple stood an apsidal building with three rooms that apparently had some use in connection with the imperial cult.[89]

Since their characteristics have up to now been far better known than the one in Banias, the temples at Caesarea and Sebaste may provide some idea of the form, style, placement and environment of the Banias temple. So may other temples dedicated to Augustus that were constructed throughout the empire during the same period (Fig.10),[90] and, to a lesser extent, other temples associated with Herod.[91] Significant information may also be found via the series of coins minted in Banias over a period of more than three decades by Herod's son and heir in the region, Herod Philip II.[92] The series is widely understood by numismatists to depict the very temple mentioned by Josephus (Fig.9). The temple always appears as the reverse on coins either featuring members of Augustus's family: Augustus, his wife Livia, his adopted son Tiberius, or else Philip himself. No better symbol than the Banias temple could be found to associate Philip with his father's favoured status in the imperial household, and to remind both his subjects and the Romans of his own loyalty as a client of the imperial family.

The same temple is obviously depicted on many of the coins of Philip, though they differ in some minor decorative details.[93] This consistency argues against the idea that the building depicted is a symbol only, that is that it does not represent the actual structure.[94] There is nothing particularly remarkable in its design; it is a simple tetrastyle building (that is having four columns in its facade), standing on a high platform with steps leading up, having capitals and bases consistent with, if not certainly identifiable as, the Corinthian style. An altar stood in front of the temple, in a prominent position at the foot of the stairs.[95] No cult object or statue appears between the central columns, as is often the case with coins depicting temples, but only the dates of issue, interspersed between the columns.[96] This omission may have been a gesture to the large Jewish community in Banias during Philip's reign, though the existence of the temple itself was certainly scandal enough from their point of view.

Herod's strategy in erecting this temple extended far beyond the symbolism represented by the structure itself. He was among the first of all provincial rulers in the empire to commit to the cult of Augustus. His Augustan temples, and the elaborate priesthood they required, may even have been influential in setting the course of imperial worship throughout the Eastern empire. While ostensibly the act of erecting these temples represented loyalty and commitment to Rome, it also furnished a basis for the social and political organisation of diverse populations such as those in Herod's kingdom. At the same time, because the new cult left the traditional local cults intact, it represented no threat to them. In fact, it symbolised an interest in protecting the local culture. In following this policy Herod was likely accepting the advice of his friend and counsellor Nicolaus of Damascus, a strong advocate of loyalty to Rome and a clever strategist.[97] The aristocracy thus created was, of course, solidly pagan and, as we shall see, since the Jewish population of the area seems to have had its own independent governmental system, the stage was set for the dramatic conflicts between the 'Syrians of Caesarea' and the 'Jews of Caesarea' during the Jewish Revolt almost a century later.[98] The Jews would certainly have balked at repeating the loyalty oath required of those who attended the ceremonies at the Augusteum: 'I swear by Zeus, Ge, Helios, all the gods and goddesses and the Sebastos himself to be loyal to Caesar Sebastos and his children and his descendants'.[99]

The question of the location of the temple at Banias is not settled. The excavator of the Pan sanctuary complex believes it stood directly in front of the cave.[100] This conclusion is based primarily on an Augustan analogy in Rome, namely the Lupercal or Lycaeum described by Dionysius of Halicarnassas. The analogy is in fact an intriguing one. Dionysius of Halicarnassas claims that the ancient Arcadians established a Pan cult in archaic Rome at 'a large cave under the hill overarched by a dense wood' and that 'deep springs issued from beneath the rocks, and the glen adjoining the cliffs was shaded by thick and lofty trees. In this place they raised an altar to the god and performed the traditional sacrifice, which the Romans have continued to offer up to this day in the month of February.'[101] Here, according to legend, Romulus and Remus were suckled by the wolf. 'The grove, to be sure, no longer remains,' Dionysius says, 'but the cave from which the spring flows is still pointed out, built up against the side of the Palatine hill on the road that leads to the Circus, and near it is a sacred precinct in which there is a statue commemorating the incident'.[102] This site received some sort of architectural adornment – at least a dignified entrance, and is listed in the Monumentum Ancyranum (19.1) among the public buildings repaired by Augustus.

At first sight this passage appears to be valuable in establishing a point of contact between the Hellenistic and Roman worlds where the worship of Pan is concerned. Physically the sites were strikingly similar. Since earliest Banias was essentially a Roman city, not a Greek one, this story shows how a Hellenistic shrine to Pan could be quickly assimilated into a Roman context, the city of Rome itself purportedly having done precisely the same thing. The interesting similarities do not provide sufficient basis for locating the Herodian Augusteum in Banias in front of the cave of Pan, however. The Lupercal carried important dynastic meaning in Rome that did not exist in Banias. Augustus had strong reasons for placing his 'mark' on the ancient site in the centre of Rome, not because of its ties to the Arcadian Pan, but rather because of its mythic connection to Romulus and Remus. There is no obvious connection to be made between Pan and Augustus, and so the cave at Banias carried none of the political significance associated with the one in Rome. There seems to be little motivation for literally covering a time-honoured and celebrated local cult site with a cult to the Roman emperor. To do so would invite local hostility and imply a sort of suppression of the ancient cult of Pan, both of which would contradict the Roman and Herodian strategy. The Herodian dynasty not only refrained from suppressing the worship of Pan, it eventually even seems to have encouraged it.[103]

Furthermore, the archaeological remains in front of the cave at Banias, while impressive, are not consistent with those of a temple facade. The excavations in front of the cave revealed two parallel walls running north–south, perpendicular to the rock scarp, standing approximately 10.5 metres apart. Almost nothing remains of the Eastern wall, but the western one is described as 18 metres long, 2 metres thick, at least 4 metres high and built of *opus quadratum*, rubble and concrete faced with limestone ashlars. Incorporated into this wall were five alternating semi-circular and rectangular niches that had originally been lined with marble. These walls may be dated to the late first century BC, and thus might well have been commissioned by Herod.[104] But the archaeological evidence points to their belonging to some sort of monumental entrance to the cave, perhaps even a passageway open to the sky, along which various statues were placed in niches, rather than to a Roman-style temple with a raised podium approached by a staircase, such as that depicted on the coins of Banias. Such an entrance way, built on arches spanning the prodigious water flow coming from inside or in front of the cave, would have provided worshippers with a way of approaching the sacred pool inside the cave without having to wade through cold and turbulent waters. It would also have preserved the cave entrance in such a way that Josephus could describe it as 'an overgrown cavern'.

Herod's other temples to Augustus stood on high ground, visible from a great distance, and were each surrounded by an impressive temenos and, most likely, a complex of related structures. Finding a place to fit such an arrangement into the area in front of the Banias cave is awkward to say the least, as speculative artists' conceptions of such an arrangement show.[105] Nor do Herod's other temples replace or infringe on earlier cult sites as this one would seem to do if it stood in front of the Pan Cave.[106] A careful reading of Josephus reveals that he does not say that the temple stood in front of the cave, but rather simply at a spot 'near the sources of the Jordan'.[107] We have already noted how his use of the word Paneion included more than simply the cult site itself. His language allows the possibility of locating the temple at a variety of sites within what became the city centre of Roman Banias, or even somewhere outside the city. Some of these sites seem more appropriate than the area in front of the cave, particularly in that they allow for a temple complex more consistent with those at Caesarea Maritima and Sebaste.

In cities possessing well-developed centres, one might expect the temple to the emperor to be constructed in the most prominent location possible. Indeed, given the political nature of the emperor cult, such a location would normally be absolutely necessary.[108] If a site for the temple were to be sought within what eventually became the city centre, one might suggest the area later occupied by a large Byzantine church some 250 metres southwest of the cave entrance. Tzaferis, the principal excavator of the church, believes it was built on the ruins of a Roman structure, possibly a Nymphaeum. It is even possible that the apse of the church is an *in situ* remnant of that structure. The church, described in detail below, was obviously built upon the ruins of Herodian-period buildings, parts of which were incorporated into the construction. Many of these reused stones exhibit elaborate decoration, and are very light coloured – thus possibly originally belonging to the 'white' Augusteum. The practice of building churches at the site of earlier temples is relatively common. The placement is appropriate and logical, since the building would have stood along the long ceremonial way (Cardo Maximus) that ran from the southern gate of the city to the cave of Pan, opening onto the cardo itself. Between the temple and the cave would have been the large ceremonial pool mentioned above, created by collecting the spring waters flowing from inside and below the cave. This thesis, like that proposing to identify 'Herod's Palace' as actually the temple site (see below), remains to be tested by excavation.

But the situation in this case may be exceptional. Unlike the old cities of Asia Minor, for example, this was not a situation in which there was an existing civic leadership wishing to express its loyalty to the emperor. Rather, this Augusteum was the expression of the loyalty of a despotic local client king. Nor is there presently any evidence of a 'city centre' at this point in the history of the site; at most, the existence of a village near the cave and springs might be hypothesised. The remains of a temple that seem to fit Josephus's description have recently been found at Omrit, a site a short distance south of the city (Fig. 11). These may in fact be the remains of the famous Herodian Augusteum. The excavators found a podium on which a temple stood, rising 9 feet above the ancient street level. Inside this podium was an earlier one, belonging to an earlier temple – a 'perfectly drafted, mortarless structure made of ashlars – a signature of Herod's grand building projects'. This earlier temple measured 75 × 48 feet and was tetrastyle (i.e. had four columns on the front, as does the temple on the coins of Philip). Ceramic evidence suggests that the first temple at Omrit be dated to the last quarter of the first century BC, and that the second, larger temple built over it be dated to the late first or early second century. If this dating is sustained, it fits well with the chronology of the city developed below.[109]

'HEROD'S PALACE' AT BANIAS

Herod's other temples to Augustus featured auxiliary structures adjacent or nearby the sanctuary itself. One structure of this type at Banias was studied by Netzer in 1977.[110] He examined the remains of walls of a building that stood on the ridge above and 100 metres southwest of the cave. These walls were constructed in an *opus reticulatum* style so similar to walls in the Herodian palace at Jericho that Netzer concluded they were likely built at the same time (Fig. 6). He concluded that they are either 'remains of the temple which was built here in honour of Augustus, or remains of other buildings built here by Herod which Josephus did not mention at all'.[111] Excavations revealed, to the north of these walls, remains of a large hall (11 by 16 metres, at least) partially cut into the rock that seems to be related to the *opus reticulatum* walls. Holes chiselled into the rock proved that this building had once been decorated with marble. The site is dramatic, providing a panoramic view of the surrounding countryside and itself visible from miles away and thus reminiscent of the temple sites at Caesarea Maritima and Sebaste. Because they also might be interpreted as belonging to some palatial structure these remains are sometimes called 'Herod's Palace'. Further excavation is needed to settle the question of their identity. Until the matter is settled, this site remains a candidate for the location of the Augusteum as well.[112]

Whatever the original purpose of this building, it provides evidence that Herod's building programme at Banias, while centred on the Augusteum, was not limited to the temple itself. A major centre for emperor worship would necessitate an accompanying bureaucracy, priests and other personnel, and thus we cannot think of some isolated shrine, standing alone and empty in the oak forest at Banias. And given the larger political purpose of the temple, it is quite likely that Banias was in some sense an administrative centre as well as a cult centre. In addition to the temple, we might expect the construction of buildings necessary for administering Herod's northern territories (including a 'palace'). Josephus's emphasis on the most impressive building, the temple itself, does not preclude the possibility of other structures as well, though whether we can describe the complex as a 'town' at this point remains problematic.

2 Herodian Banias

HEROD PHILIP (4BC–34AD)

When Herod died, his extensive hegemony was divided between three of his sons: Archelaus, Antipas and Philip.[1] Historians ancient and modern have neglected Philip in favour of his dynamic father, his more famous brothers and his successors the two Agrippas (his nephew and grand-nephew). In this he suffered the fate that a mischievous history often assigns to those who quietly do the work assigned to them with skill and wisdom, in a time and place where relative tranquility prevails.[2] In this case, Philip's assignment from the Romans was to maintain peace and security along a very important 'frontier' between the East and West, while keeping the vital trade routes open and safe. From the Roman point of view Philip was an important man indeed. Nevertheless, biographical details are hard to come by. He was born *ca.* 26 BC, the son of Cleopatra the 'Jerusalemite'.[3] Around 14 BC he was sent to Rome, where he received a good education and formed the same intimate relationships with the empire's ruling elite as had his more famous relatives. Josephus says that he had a brother ('Herod') and that he married Salome, the daughter of Herodias (the wife of his brother Antipas).[4]

Philip's territories consisted of that group of diverse geographical entities that constituted the northeastern part of Herod's kingdom. These territories, with populations equally diverse, had been hammered into a single administrative unit through the administrative skills of Herod I, serving as an agent of Roman policy.[5] The temple complex at the Paneion was, as we have seen, the keystone of these diverse territories, both figuratively, through the presence of the Augusteum, and literally, through its geographical location. But this area was a relatively small part of Herod's kingdom. By separating it and placing it under the tetrarchy of Philip (except for Galilee, which went to his brother Antipas), the Romans recognised the area as a political entity. And in point of fact, though *de facto* no more than a subdivision of the province of Syria, and despite its ethnic diversity, Philip's 'kingdom' hung together with enough integrity to survive for another century.

It is no surprise then, that Philip established his capital at Banias. He could hardly have done otherwise.

THE FOUNDING OF 'CAESAREA PHILIPPI'

Dates on coins minted in the city of Banias during the second and third centuries AD, when compared to the regnal dates of the rulers depicted on them, suggest that the era of Philip's capital began in 3 BC, during the second year of his reign.[6] Among the coins which Philip himself minted in the city is one (dated 'Year 34', that is 30/31 AD) which calls him 'ΚΤΙΣ[ΤΗΣ]', 'founder'. This title might be understood to refer to the founding of Banias, and to suggest that Philip created a city near the Paneion where none had existed before. Josephus had asserted, after all, that 'Philip built ['κτίζει', founded] Caesarea near the sources of the Jordan, in the district of Paneas'.[7] At first glance, these facts would seem to furnish sufficient evidence that the city beside the fountain of the Jordan near the cave of Pan did not exist prior to the beginning of Philip's tetrarchy.

In fact, however, this evidence is not entirely conclusive. The title 'founder' was often used by rulers in reference to cities which they had enlarged, or reorganised, or embellished, but which already had long histories. So-called 'founder coins' showing the Roman emperor following a plough, the symbol of 'ground breaking', often appear more than once in the history of a city. Nero is called 'founder' on a coin of Ptolemais-Akko,[8] for example, Jerusalem, was 'founded' in this sense by Hadrian, and named Aelia Capitolina, despite the fact that these cities had already existed for centuries.[9] Caesarea Maritima was likewise 'founded' more than once,[10] as were many other cities in the Roman Empire, though admittedly the practice became more common from the second century forward than during the Julio-Claudian period.

Josephus's testimony regarding the foundation of Banias, or 'Caesarea Philippi' is ambiguous to say the least. The quotation above is in the context of the accession of Tiberius to the throne, following the death of Augustus: 'On his accession, Herod (Antipas) and Philip continued to hold their tetrarchies and respectively founded cities: Philip built Caesarea near the sources of the Jordan, in the district of Paneas, and Julias in lower Gaulanitis; Herod built Tiberias in Galilee and a city which also took the name Julia, in Perea'.[11]

The city of Tiberias was indeed apparently founded at that time. The situation with Banias is somewhat more complicated. Philip minted a number of coins featuring the Augusteum and carrying dates during the reign of Augustus, whose portrait prominently appears on them. These coins were certainly minted before the accession of Tiberius and the founding of the city of Tiberias.[12] If, as is usually assumed, these coins are attributed to the mint of Banias, the city must have existed prior to 14 AD. The city coins of Banias, minted from the mid-second century AD forward, use the same era as the coins of Philip. This would seem to suggest that the city considered its founding to have taken place in 3 BC. In a parallel passage in the *Antiquities*, Josephus remains ambiguous. Antipas fortified

Sepphoris to be the ornament of all Galilee, he says, while Philip 'made improvements at Paneas', and called the city Caesarea. In addition, he 'raised the village of Bethsaida on Lake Gennesaritis to the status of city by adding residents and strengthening the fortifications. He named it after Julia, the emperor's daughter.'[13] This is a summary statement and not a chronologically precise one. It should not be taken to mean that work on these cities took place at the same time, though it does seem likely from this statement that all three existed prior to Tiberius's accession. Sepphoris was 'fortified', Bethsaida was 'raised in status', and Paneas was 'improved' and named Caesarea. The naming of the city probably had already occurred at the beginning of Philip's tetrarchy, and thus the era of Banias/Caesarea Philippi coincided with the era of Philip. Josephus's imprecise statements may be understood to imply that on the accession of Tiberius, Philip 'improved' what he had 'founded' earlier.

Meshorer has suggested that Philip issued a series of three coins in 29/30 AD, the purpose of which was to commemorate the founding of the city of Caesarea Philippi.[14] The largest of these depicts Tiberius on the obverse and the inscription 'under Philip the Tetrarch, Founder' on the reverse. The middle denomination depicts Livia on the obverse, a hand holding ears of grain on the reverse, along with the inscription 'fruitbearing' ('ΚΑΡΠΟΦΟΡΟC'). This may be a reference to the prosperity of the capital city and of the kingdom in general. The smallest denomination has a portrait of Philip himself on the obverse and the date on the reverse.[15] If this attribution of purpose is correct, it further strengthens the theory that the city was founded in 3 BC.[16]

Although Josephus gives no hint of a city existing near where Herod build his temple of 'white marble', neither does he mention the city of Caesarea Philippi when he describes the cave and spring as they appeared in his own day. Since a city certainly stood on the site in the latter case, there is at least the possibility that the same is true in the former case. Temples such as the one Herod had built near the Paneion required extensive staffing – priests, custodians etc. Civic councils generally administered them, and the presiding priest was an important figure in local society.[17] In fact, the construction of temples connected with emperor worship was often preceded by the formation of local cults dedicated to the Caesars. At Samaria-Sebaste, the large population of pagan veterans formed a natural constituency for the Augusteum there. Nevertheless, in that city the presence of the temple and 'the superficially religious paraphernalia of an imperial cult in no way interfered with the exercise of those native instincts which found their true expression in the solemnities of the Kore ritual or the abracadabra of a Simon Magus'.[18] We might imagine a similar situation at Banias, where the venerable local traditions of Pan-worship could continue to exist among the resident populace and thrive side-by-side with the imperial cult.

In the immediate vicinity of Banias one would expect to find at least some of the descendants of the Greek military colonists who had settled there during the days of Seleucid control. Itureans, by now rather thoroughly Hellenised, and various other groups of Bedouin origins, would have been present as well, along with Syrians and Phoenicians of old local stock. Within a generation Banias had a large Jewish community, and we may presume that the forebears of this community were already in the area at the time of

Herod's death. Some of these may have been immigrants from Judaea, and many others from among those brought from 'Babylonia' and resettled by Herod himself.[19] It is consistent with his known policies to suppose that the king introduced numbers of his own (pagan) supporters, veterans of his armies etc., into this more or less indigenous population, and that he appointed a clergy for the care of the temple and the performance of its rites. This certainly seems to be the case in regard to the other two Augustus temples built by Herod at Sebaste and Caesarea Maritima.[20] Thus, whether, and to what extent, similar settlers were gathered into an urban setting before Philip's 'founding' of Caesarea Philippi remains an open question.

The creation of the city of Caesarea Philippi most likely took the form of a common process called synoecism, literally 'wedlock' or 'dwelling in the same house', that is the gathering of the inhabitants of surrounding villages and the introduction of other groups such as colonists and retiring veterans into a single unit by order of the sovereign.[21] The *polis* itself represented the primary unifying factor for the new entity's citizens without requiring that the various ethnic or socio-economic subgroups disappear into the whole. A similar process may be observed in the founding of the city of Tiberias.[22] Thus, one could still speak of the 'villages of Caesarea Philippi'[23] as being more than simply individual communities subservient to the capital, and explain the existence and relative independence of communities such as the 'Syrians of Caesarea Philippi' and the 'Jews of Caesarea Philippi' described by Josephus.[24]

The literary sources do not settle the question of the origins of the city of Banias. The cumulative evidence leans toward the conclusion that some sort of settlement pre-dated Philip's 'founding'. An intriguing, but problematic, piece of additional evidence for this conclusion is found in one of the epigrams of the poet Meleager. Meleager's early life was spent in the vicinity of the Paneion. He was born *ca.* 140 BC at Gadara, a few miles to the south and east. He grew up and was educated at Tyre. Though he spent his later life on the island of Kos, where he died *ca.* 70 BC, his poetry is usually thought to be heavily influenced by memories of his homeland. In the epigram, the only purely mythological one among Meleager's works, the poet imagines a conversation with a statue of Pan, asking why it stands in a city and not in the mountains beloved by the god. The statue replies that grief over the death of his beloved Daphnis had driven Pan into the town: 'No longer do I, goat-footed Pan, want to spend my life among the goat kids, or inhabit the peaks of mountains. What is sweet to me, what desirable in the mountains? Daphnis is dead, Daphnis who gave birth to a fire in my heart. I'll make my home in this town; let someone else set out to hunt wild beasts. His former [ways] are no longer dear to Pan.'[25] The epigraphist Louis Robert suggests that 'one might ask whether Meleager of Gadara did not write this epideictic poem for a neighbouring town, for Panian, the future Caesarea Panias, of which Pan was the city divinity'.[26] If this were the case, the town existed as early as the late second century BC. But this isolated piece of evidence is thin and inconclusive.[27] Thus far, the archaeological evidence provides nothing earlier than the architectural efforts of Herod I and some Hellenistic shards. The matter will hopefully be settled one day through further excavation of the site.[28]

Caesarea Philippi was certainly 'founded' in some sense in 3 BC, shortly after Philip was given his inheritance by the Romans. Whether this is the occasion when the process of synoecism was ordered by the tetrarch, and whether or not an earlier community situated in front of the cave formed the basis for the new entity, cannot yet be determined. It remains possible, though unproved, that a settlement called 'Paneas', or something similar, existed at or near the site selected by Philip for his administrative capital. In any case, Caesarea Philippi now joined a list of Herodian cities, all of which bore the names or titles of Roman emperors – cities that represented the triumph of Rome in the East rather than advance of Hellenism. These were, after all, not so much Greek cities as Greco-Roman ones.[29]

PHILIP'S REIGN AT BANIAS

As we have noted, when their sibling Archelaus lost his position as the ruler of Judaea and Samaria in 10 AD, Philip and his brother Antipas managed to retain their tetrarchies.[30] The death of Augustus, after a reign of over fifty-seven years, and the accession of Tiberius was a crucial moment both for Banias and its ruler. That Philip once again survived is further evidence of his competence and his close ties with the power elite of the empire. In order to express his gratitude to the new emperor for retaining him in power, Philip 'made improvements' at Banias and 'raised the village of Bethsaida on Lake Gennesaritis to the status of city by adding residents and strengthening the fortifications'.[31]

Though we lack extensive literary references to this period, the coinage of Philip's mint at Banias provides some additional insights into his reign. We have already taken note of the recurring depiction of the Augusteum, and of numerous portraits of the imperial family, drawn numismatically into close association with Philip himself. Despite Jewish sensitivities, Philip did not hesitate to put portraits of himself on coins. The first of these portraits appeared on two coins issued shortly after his reign began (1/2 AD), one showing Augustus on the obverse and the other featuring Philip's portrait on the obverse and the Augusteum on the reverse (Fig. 9). The issue seems to follow the numismatic tradition of the Iturean tetrarchs Lysanias and Zenodorus, who had ruled the same area two or three decades before. Zenodorus, for example, placed his own portrait on the reverse of an issue depicting Octavian (Augustus) between the years of 30 and 27 BC (Fig. 8). The similarity in style between this type and the early coins of Philip even raises the possibility that the mint of Banias had its roots somehow in the time of Zenodorus. Philip's portrait soon disappeared from the coinage, but not, as Kindler suggests, because the Romans forbade its use, since it reappeared in the 30s AD.[32]

Philip not only made improvements on his capital city; he also apparently took a personal interest in the geology of the region. Josephus credits him with the 'discovery' that the real source of the Jordan was not at the Paneion ('where the ancients believed that the stream had its origin') but rather

the pool called Phiale from which it passes by an unseen subterranean channel to Paneion. Phiale will be found at a distance of a hundred and twenty furlongs from Caesarea, on the right of and not far from the road ascending to Trachonitis; the pool derives its name Phiale from its circular form; the water always fills the basin to the brim without ever subsiding or overflowing.

After passing underground, the water issues from the Paneion grotto, Josephus assures us, its course now becoming visible. Then the river 'intersects the marshes and lagoons of Lake Semechonitis... and below the town of Julias cuts across the Lake of Gennesar, from which, after meandering through a long desert region, it ends by falling into the Lake Asphaltitis'.[33]

The Jordan's course from Banias, through the swamps of the Huleh (Semechonitis), into the Sea of Galilee (Gennesarat) and finally the Dead Sea (Asphaltitis), is of course accurately traced. But it is geologically impossible for water to run from the Phiale (now called Birkat Ram) to Banias. Nevertheless, Josephus says that Philip, whom he calls 'tetrarch of Trachonitis',[34] himself made this gravity-defying discovery by means of a scientific experiment. The king 'had chaff thrown into the pool of Phiale and found it cast up at Panion'. Since this result is physically impossible, given the geological relationship of the two sites,[35] we can only speculate that Philip's assistants in this experiment, eager to please, manipulated the evidence to match the king's theory.

The coins present a picture of tranquility and prosperity during Philip's last years, of good government and good times for the inhabitants of the land. This picture is for the most part an accurate one. Josephus describes the tetrarch as 'a person of moderation and quietness in the conduct of his life and government'. He notes his custom of staying within his territories throughout his long reign (in striking contrast to his Herodian successors), serving as an itinerant judge.

> He used to make his progress with a few chosen friends; his tribunal also, on which he sat in judgment, followed him in his progress; and when any one met him who wanted his assistance, he made no delay, but had his tribunal set down immediately, wheresoever he happened to be, and sat down upon it, and heard his complaint: he there ordered the guilty that were convicted to be punished, and absolved those that had been accused unjustly.[36]

The description brings to mind the retinue of an itinerant Bedouin chieftain.

Philip died in the city of Julias in the fall of 33 AD,[37] in the twentieth year of the reign of Tiberius, and the thirty-seventh year of his own. He left no heirs, and so his territory, including Banias, was annexed to the province of Syria, but with the right to administer its own revenues.[38] This latter provision probably indicates that the Romans still regarded the region as having an independent integrity and this arrangement nothing more than a sort of *interregnum*. Josephus says that his body was 'carried to that monument which he had already erected for himself beforehand' and that he was 'buried with great pomp'. It is usually presumed that this monument was located in Bethsaida-Julias, but excavations there show the place to be very modest at best, and besides, Philip's capital and home were at Banias. It seems more reasonable to understand Josephus to mean that a sad procession carried the remains of this successful ruler, respected by both the Romans and his own subjects, northward along the banks of the nascent Jordan's cool waters to the springs of Banias. There, somewhere, he was laid to rest.[39]

AGRIPPA I (37–44 AD)

Agrippa, the grandson of Herod the Great, was in no position to rise to power at the time of his uncle Philip's death. He was, in fact, imprisoned in Rome, having fallen out of favour with Tiberius. When the latter died, however, on 16 March, 37 AD, Agrippa's friend Caligula became emperor. Caligula not only gave the young man his freedom, but also bestowed on him the territories of Philip, centred, of course, in Banias, along with the title 'king'. Neither Augustus nor Tiberius had allowed the sons of Herod to assume this title.

We have no record of any particular attention paid by Agrippa to the city of Banias, even though during Caligula's reign it was his one and only capital city. He did, however, mint some coins there, no doubt in order to establish the fact of his royal status and publicly to set the tone for his regime. These date from the very earliest years of his reign and thus they are presumed to come from the Banias mint established by his uncle Philip.[40] The first issues, dated LB (Year 2=38/39 AD) were obviously meant to celebrate Agrippa's inaugural. The coins appear to be adaptations of Roman sestertii and dupondii struck in Rome just the year before, and quite likely were ordered by the new king before he had even left Italy to claim his throne.[41] They are obviously a part of his strategy in establishing his authority and his close relationship with the imperial family at the very outset of his reign. Thus, they were timed to coincide with his arrival in Banias.

Every coin in the four-coin series reveals some facet of the new king's strategy for maintaining himself in power. The first features the portrait of his benefactor Caligula and Caligula's three sisters, Julia Livilla, Drusilla[42] and Agrippina the Younger.[43] The next two feature not only Agrippa's portrait, but also members of his family, an entirely new phenomenon on Herodian coins. On one of these we see the king's young son, Agrippa II, riding a horse.[44] There is no doubt about the identification, or its motivation. The inscription reads 'ΑΓΡΙΠΠΑ ΥΙΟ[Υ] ΒΑΣΙΛΕΩΣ' ('Agrippa, son of the king'). Thus Agrippa emphasises the dynastic nature of his rule. The second type features a bust of Cypros, Agrippa's wife. The reverse depicts a hand holding ears of grain and a vine branch.[45] Finally, another type, also dated 'Year Two', depicts an inscription within a wreath that reads 'ΑΓ[ΡΙΠΠΑ] ΒΑ[ΣΙΛΕΥΣ]' ('King Agrippa') on one side and the familiar image of the four-columned temple of Augustus on the other.[46] These four coins sum up the various themes of importance to the new king's success: his close personal relationship to the imperial family, his own family (son/heir and queen), the fruitfulness and prosperity of his kingdom, and the importance of Banias itself as the site of the temple dedicated to the imperial majesty.

But Agrippa's ambition lay far beyond the rather pastoral realm he had inherited from his uncle Philip. In 39 AD Caligula once again rewarded his loyalty by giving him the territories of another uncle, Antipas, who was sent off into exile along with his wife Herodias.[47] Once again Agrippa responded to this show of imperial confidence with a series of coins having the same purpose and design as the earlier one. The first of the series is dated LE (Year 5=41/42 AD) and pictures Caligula in what turned out to be the year of his death. The reverse has a standard Roman numismatic scene of a figure in a chariot with four horses and the inscription 'ΒΑΣΙΛΕΩΣ ΑΓΡΙΠΠΑ'. The second depicts Caligula's wife Caesonia and his daughter Drusilla. The third mirrors the second, but with Agrippa's own portrait and that of his wife, Cypros. The fourth features a bust of the heir apparent, a youthful Agrippa II (Fig. 12).[48] The ties between the Roman imperial family and that of Agrippa could not be more vividly emphasised. This series also seems to have been minted in Banias[49] just prior to Agrippa's moving his capital to Tiberias, a city more conveniently located now that he was also ruler of Galilee.

Agrippa continued to have immense influence in Rome, where he spent much of his time. When Caligula was assassinated he was able to help Claudius gain the throne and for this was rewarded with territory equal to that of his grandfather.[50] At this point he once again moved his capital – to Caesarea Maritima.[51] From now on his strategy for survival became even more complex, as he attempted to ingratiate himself with his Jewish subjects in his new territory of Judaea. Thus, says Josephus, he 'enjoyed residing in Jerusalem and did so constantly'[52] – no doubt in order to keep the necessary fences mended there. Thus, despite his close ties with Rome, Agrippa I became a champion and defender of the Jews and was generally disliked by his gentile subjects. In the meantime, Banias fell into the background, no doubt entrusted to local officials or political appointees of the absent king.

Agrippa was now in a position to follow in the steps of his famous grandfather, for he controlled the entire extent of Herod the Great's hegemony, had a huge income and enjoyed, if anything, an even more intimate relationship with the emperor and his family. But fate intervened to dash his ambitions. He died in 44 AD, a relatively young man still, to the great sorrow of the Jews and delight of his gentile subjects.[53] The writer of the New Testament book of the Acts of the Apostles shared in the decidedly negative opinion of the gentile contingent of the king's subjects, since Agrippa had persecuted the fledgling messianic movement of the followers of Jesus of Nazareth, especially in Jerusalem.[54]

ANOTHER INTERREGNUM (44–53 AD)

During the next near-decade, Roman policy toward both the principality of Banias and the Herodian family became clear. Judaea was not presumed to be a part of the Herodian heritage; Banias, however, was. Agrippa I's heir (born in Rome in 27/28 AD), whom he had so carefully been preparing to succeed him, was still living in the imperial capital. Claudius wanted to turn Agrippa I's kingdom over to the young man immediately, but was dissuaded by his advisors, who thought 'that it was hazardous to entrust so important a kingdom to one who was quite young and had not even passed out of boyhood'.[55] Behind the diplomatic language we can see the conviction that trouble was ahead in Judaea, and that Rome had better handle the situation directly, especially in view of the strong undercurrents of opposition to a continuing Herodian dynasty.

Banias, on the other hand, while it was also placed under direct Roman provincial administration, seems to have been considered more or less permanently Herodian. The same was true of the little principality of Chalcis, whose ties with Banias extended back into the days of the Iturean Ptolemy and his successors and which was now ruled by Herod, Agrippa I's brother. Chalcis was presented to Agrippa II, still not twenty years old, when his uncle Herod of Chalcis died in 48 AD – this in spite of the fact that Herod of Chalcis had three sons. Two of these were the children of his second wife (also his niece), Berenice, the reigning queen of Chalcis, who was Agrippa's sister.[56] Thus began a lifelong brother-sister partnership between Agrippa and Berenice that was to amaze and scandalise Rome itself. Berenice, who wore the title 'queen' for the rest of her life, was one of the most interesting characters of the age and is of particular importance to Banias, where she played the role of 'queen' longer than anywhere else.

We know nothing about events at Banias during the *interregnum* except that the mint apparently continued to function. Another series of coins appeared during this period, which, though bearing the name of neither Agrippa nor the town itself, are attributed to the Banias mint, primarily because they are usually found in the area. The inscriptions on these coins are in Latin rather than the usual Greek. All honour the emperor Claudius and his family – in particular his designated heir Britannicus.[57] Why would the Banias mint, which had served so transparently as an instrument of propaganda for the Herodian family, continue to function even though the throne was unoccupied? The existence and design of these coins suggest that a form of local government continued in the absence of a king that maintained control over the mint. This government may in turn have been controlled by the priests of the emperor cult (themselves under the watchful eye of the legate of Syria, of course).[58] Thus continued the strong tradition of honouring the imperial family by means of coin issues.

AGRIPPA II, KING OF BANIAS

About five years later (in 53/54 AD), Claudius took Chalcis from Agrippa and gave him the territory of Philip instead. Banias was once again under the direct control of the Herodian dynasty. The youthful king received not only his uncle Philip's tetrarchy, which included Banias, but also the territories of Lysanias (Abila) and of Varus, themselves remnants of the old Iturean kingdom of Ptolemy, son of Mennaeus.[59] Presumably Agrippa had proven himself a sufficiently capable ruler and politician during this 'internship' in Chalcis. There is reason to believe that the Romans did not give him full power immediately, however, despite his title. An interesting series of coins, obviously dating from the early days of the reign of Nero, though they are almost universally thought to be issued by the Banias mint, make no mention of Agrippa at all. They extol the family of Nero and seem to have the same origin as the series just discussed above, that is, local (temple?) authorities under the general supervision of the Legate of Syria. One of the coins depicts Agrippina II, Nero's mother, and his wife Octavia, both as priestesses.[60] The second depicts two female figures, each in a small temple or shrine, with an inscription mentioning Nero's second wife Poppaea.[61]

Agrippa arrived in Banias in 53/54 AD, bringing with him an entourage that included his three sisters Berenice, Drusilla and Mariamme. These young women were all available as candidates for politically and financially advantageous marriages. Agrippa would need help from whatever quarter it was available. His father's policy of favouring the Jewish population in Judaea had created great dissatisfaction in Caesarea and Sebaste, where his sister's statues were abused by the resident soldiers when news of Agrippa I's death reached them.[62] There was reason to expect a certain amount of trouble at Banias as well, whose history and population shared some similarities with these two Herodian cities. Drusilla married Azizus, King of Emesa, a neighbour to the north. The marriage did not last, the Agrippan sisters all being known for their marital 'irregularities'. Drusilla divorced Azizus and married the Roman procurator of Judaea, Felix, a somewhat scandalous alliance that actually served Agrippa's interests better than her previous one.[63] Like his father, he would attempt to sustain his reign by clinging tightly to the Romans on one hand, and seeing after the interests of the Jewish population on the other. This would mean that the pagan population, both the indigenous groups and those who had colonised the Hellenistic cities of the region, would continue to be a problem for him.

It was his sister Berenice, however, who would play the most prominent role in succeeding events. Though still quite young, she had been twice widowed, and was the mother of two young children by her second husband, Herod of Chalcis. She was, by virtue of her second husband's status as king, 'Queen Berenice' – a title that stayed with her throughout her life. She also became, in a very literal sense, the 'Queen of Banias' – as we shall see.

In 54 AD Nero granted Agrippa additional territory that included portions of Galilee, including Tiberias, Tarichaeae and Julias – all important sites around the lake.[64] Two years later, at the age of 28, he was apparently awarded a yet higher level of independent power, for this became the year 1 of his first era. Later, he adopted a second era as well, dated from 61 AD. Our knowledge of this period is limited, but it is apparent that Agrippa, presumably with Berenice by his side, was busy organising his new kingdom and its capital city. He not only made great improvements in the city materially – 'the natural beauties of Panion have been enhanced by royal munificence', notes Josephus, 'the place having been embellished by Agrippa at great expense'[65] – but also reorganised Banias's social, governmental and even religious institutions.

Mindful of his Jewish heritage and position as protector of Jewish interests, the king took care to clarify or confirm the status and rights of the large Jewish community in the city. The Jewish community seems to have been recognised as a *politeuma*, while the non-Jewish community was designated a *polis*, a system similar to that documented in such contemporary cities as Caesarea Maritima, Antioch and Alexandria.[66] Since he was absent from the city almost constantly during the early years of his reign, Agrippa appointed an official (a 'viceroy') to administer the city's affairs in his absence. This system continued through the period of the Jewish Revolt.[67] In addition, Berenice was active and very visible in representing the political interests of her brother.[68]

Agrippa may also have been responsible for certain changes in the nature of the imperial cult as practised in Banias. Consistent with normal practice, the Augusteum, so prominently pictured on the coins of Herod Philip, was no longer limited to the cult of Augustus, becoming instead the sanctuary for the worship of each successive reigning emperor. In this way the cult of Augustus was transformed into a more general cult of the Imperator.[69] It seems likely, however, that this change took place even earlier, and that the series of coins discussed above which honoured the succeeding imperial families of Rome were produced by the temple authorities during the *interregnum*.

Josephus does not specify precisely the nature of the 'expensive embellishments' that Agrippa provided for the city, except to say that they enhanced the natural beauties of the site. The fact that he carried out similar 'embellishments' in other cities, suggests that in addition to simply enhancing the glory of his capital, he had political aims in mind. The nature of the embellishments at Berytus, for example, suggests an attempt to ingratiate the pagan population of the Phoenician coast, which served as his window to the Mediterranean world. Josephus is much more explicit in describing Agrippa's embellishment of Berytus than of Banias, but it would seem reasonable to assume that he 'improved' both cities in a similar fashion. In Berytus he 'built at great expense a theatre for the people … and presented them with annual spectacles, spending many tens of thousands of drachmas upon this project … He also adorned the whole city by erecting statues, as well as replicas of ancient sculptures.' This created much ill will among his own pagan subjects, however, since 'he almost transferred all that was most ornamental in his own kingdom' to these favoured cities, and 'took those things away that belonged to them to adorn a foreign city'.[70] The subjects referred to here, who 'more than ordinarily hated him' for these actions, would seem to be those who had already declared against him in cities like Caesarea Maritima and Sebaste. Banias, on the other hand, as his capital, received special beneficence, receiving various public buildings and monuments and, presumably, many statues as well.[71]

In the year 58 AD a remarkable meeting took place, according to the author of the New Testament book of Acts, between Agrippa and Berenice and the Apostle Paul. The couple, on a welcoming visit to the new procurator Porcius Festus at Caesarea Maritima, heard Paul's defence of his activities as a leader in the new Jewish sect of followers of Jesus of Nazareth.[72] Agrippa appears in the story to be a rather sympathetic character who, unlike his father, might be more tolerant toward the development of this new movement within his own territories. It is highly likely, in fact, that followers of Jesus were already to be found in considerable numbers in his kingdom.

In 61 AD Agrippa took a dramatic step, formally refounding his capital city and renaming it Neronias, in honour of his patron on the imperial throne.[73] This action may have been part of a larger celebration, carried on in Rome and elsewhere, in honour of the first shaving of Nero's beard.[74] Whatever may have been his motives for this action, beyond the obvious attempt to ingratiate himself even further to the emperor, the name change would rid his capital city of its identification with his great-uncle, which adhered to its common name: Caesarea Philippi. Not long after this (63 AD), apparently in an attempt to deal with what would today be called a 'public relations' problem, Berenice temporarily left Banias and Agrippa's side to become the wife of Polemon, king of Cilicia. This marriage, Josephus tells us, was designed to quiet the rising rumours about the relationship between Berenice and Agrippa, widely thought to be incestuous. The strategy was unsuccessful. Even after their deaths the rumour continued to titillate Rome. The couple was satirised by Juvenal in his satire on women. A certain woman will, he says, 'carry off... a diamond of great renown, made precious by the finger of Berenice. It was given as a present long ago by the barbarian Agrippa to his incestuous sister, in that country where kings celebrate festal Sabbaths with bare feet, and where a long established clemency suffers pigs to attain old age.'[75]

Not surprisingly, this marriage was also unsuccessful. Being a matter of pure convenience for both parties – for Berenice a salve for scandal and for Polemon a shameless interest in the young queen's considerable wealth[76] – it ended in less than two years. Berenice returned to her brother's side at Banias.

BANIAS AND THE FIRST REVOLT OF THE JEWS (66–70 AD)

As war clouds began to gather in Judaea and Galilee, Agrippa and Berenice were about to undergo a fiery test of their political skills. Agrippa had identified himself emphatically with his Jewish subjects. Now he watched in apprehension as radical elements among those subjects moved closer and closer to open revolt against the power that served as the very foundation of his kingship – the Roman Empire. Prudence dictated that he stay close to his Roman sponsors, and thus he was seldom in his capital during the years just before the revolt broke out. More often he was in Jerusalem, where he had a palace, or, when hostilities began in Galilee, travelling with the Roman troops. This meant that the government in Banias was in the hands of a 'viceroy'.

Agrippa's choice for this post (in collaboration with Berenice) turned out to be a poor one. Varus, to whom he entrusted his kingdom[77] during his absences, was a descendant of King Soaemus of Lebanon and thus a member of the old Iturean royal family. Relations were obviously not good between the two major segments of the population in Banias, identified by Josephus as 'the Syrians of Caesarea' and 'the Jews of Caesarea'.[78] The former, a mixture of descendants of Hellenised Iturean tribes and pagan descendents of Hellenistic military retirees from pre-Roman times, found their champion in Agrippa's viceroy, Varus, and their hope in his royal credentials. The 'Syrians of Caesarea', like the gentile pagan inhabitants of all the Hellenistic cities of the area, hated the imposition of the Jewish Herodian dynasty upon them, despite the many compromises the dynasty made with local culture and religion.

But Banias, though predominantly pagan, also had a large and influential Jewish community numbering, if we may believe Josephus, 'many thousands'.[79] Because of Agrippa's patronage, this community, as noted above, enjoyed privileges that included a kind of quasi-autonomous government. The champion of this community was not the local governor Varus, but Philip, son of Jacimus, an energetic Jewish military commander of the 'Babylonian Jews' – descendants of soldiers settled to the east of Banias by Herod the Great in an earlier generation. Philip and his family had enjoyed a long and close relationship with the Herodians, and Philip had in fact trained local troops for Agrippa and served as 'his general'.[80]

Varus and his supporters saw the situation as an opportunity to return the principality of Banias to its Iturean roots, and to restore the monarchy of Ptolemy, son of Menelaus, and his descendants, which had, from their point of view, been usurped by the Herodians. When the revolt broke out in Palestine, Varus saw his chance. The time seemed right to overthrow the king. Surely, as Varus reasoned, before the revolt was over Agrippa, caught between his responsibilities to the Jews and his suzerainty to the Romans, would lose his crown and most likely his life.[81] Varus boldly sealed off the town, allowing no communication between its citizens and Agrippa himself. He then proceeded to move against the Jewish community, ordering many executions, presumably on the charge that the Jews of Banias were rebels against Rome.[82]

Next Varus hatched an elaborate scheme designed to eliminate the Jewish leadership, both in Banias and in Ecbatana,[83] the centre for the 'Babylonian Jews' who, because they had an organised military force, might thwart his plans to seize independent power. The idea was to cause the indigenous population of Trachonitis in Batanaea, which traditionally had been a part of the tetrarchy of Herod Philip and his successors, to rise up against the 'Babylonian Jews' in their midst and massacre them. As the revolt progressed in Palestine, such massacres of local Jewish populations were to become commonplace.

Varus thus summoned 'twelve of the most esteemed of the Caesarean Jews' and ordered them to travel to Ecbatana to urge the Jews there to lay down their arms and to send back a delegation to answer charges of insurrection against them. While Josephus, who records the incident, does not specifically say so, these 12 leaders were most likely the ruling council of Banias's Jewish *politeuma*. They departed, not knowing that Varus had marked them for death.

Arriving in Ecbatana, the 12 Jewish leaders from Banias found that in fact the Jews there had no intention of joining the revolt in Palestine. Following Varus's orders, the 12 urged the ruling council of 70 of the Babylonian Jews to return with them to prove their loyalty to Rome. Not realising the trap that had been set for both groups by Varus, secretly planning his own revolt, certainly against Agrippa and possibly even against Rome itself, the two groups travelled together back to Banias. There they were met by the royal troops under Varus who had them all killed without a hearing. Then he ordered the troops to march against the Jews of Ecbatana.[84]

The scheme failed, however, on three accounts. First, the threatened community of Ecbatana fled south to Gamala. At that mountain fortress-city near the Sea of Galilee, some of them would indeed meet a terrible fate later in the struggle with Rome. Second, Agrippa, finally receiving intelligence on the situation, recalled Varus and replaced him with a new governor for the city, Aequus Modius. Third, the presence of Babylonian Jewish military units at Gamala, commanded by Philip, son of Jacimus, and the latter's skilful diplomacy, dissuaded the gentile citizens of Caesarea Philippi from carrying out the massacre and thus causing all-out war between Jews and gentiles throughout the principality. Philip's intervention saved the lives of thousands of Caesarean Jews who had been marked for complete annihilation by Varus and his allies, the Syrians of Caesarea.[85] Had Varus succeeded, Banias might have become an autonomous *polis*, like the neighbouring Decapolis cities, or even a small Iturean state like the one that had disappeared during the days of Lysanias and Zenodorus.[86] As it was, the Jewish community survived, and was able to establish itself as loyal both to its own religious traditions and to Agrippa and the Romans.

It was, in fact, the community's loyalty to Jewish tradition that set the stage for a 'knavish trick' by John of Gischala, Josephus's rival during the time when both were local leaders of the Jewish rebels in Galilee. Modius, Agrippa's new viceroy in the city, had 'shut up' Caesarea Philippi's Jewish inhabitants after the trouble with Varus.[87] At first glance this seems an action hostile to the Jews. But, as Kasher notes, Josephus's word may as well be translated 'shut themselves up' (i.e. middle voice), implying that Modius in fact assisted them in barricading themselves into their quarter of the city for their own protection.[88] However, isolated in this way, the Caesarean Jews lost access to 'pure oil', that is oil produced according to Jewish law. So, says Josephus, they 'sent a request to him [John of Gischala] to see that they were supplied with this commodity, lest they should be driven to violate their legal ordinances by resort to Grecian oil'.[89]

Josephus, always ready to excuse himself and to show his enemies in the worst possible light, asserts that John of Gischala agreed to help the Jews of Caesarea Philippi – motivated not by piety, but by

> profiteering of the most barefaced description; for he knew that at Caesarea two pints were sold for one drachm, whereas at Gischala eighty pints could be had for four drachms. So he sent off all the oil in the place, having ostensibly obtained my authority to do so. My permission I gave reluctantly, from fear of being stoned by the mob if I withheld it. Thus, having gained my consent, John by this sharp practice made an enormous profit.[90]

Whatever we may think of Josephus's assertions about John's motives and his own, the incident shows that the Jewish community at Banias enjoyed official protection, else they could not have made such an arrangement with John at all. Further, they must have lived in a defensible quarter of the city, and thus could 'shut themselves up', where they exercised the kind of control necessary to maintain their traditions in an orderly fashion.[91]

At some point during the revolt, the Romans gave Agrippa the culminating and most significant prerogative of kings: the right to mint coins in his own name. This was most likely a reward for his loyalty to Rome during very difficult circumstances.[92] Several coins were minted by Agrippa that provide almost the only material evidence for the short-lived name change of his capital city. Two of these exhibit a curious system of dating by two eras: 'The year 11, which is also the year 6', that is 66/67 AD.[93] This indicates that Agrippa had adopted a new era for his reign that coincided closely with his refounding and renaming of Banias, and is further evidence that he had by this time been vested with full royal power by Rome, a process which had stretched over almost a decade.[94] This series may have been minted both to commemorate and to facilitate the visit of the Roman army described below. These coins could thus provide the small change necessary for both the local merchants and visiting soldiers during the latters' periods of rest at Banias, and serve as propaganda as well. Despite their appearance in the midst of the clouds of death and destruction that hung heavily over the area, these coins display an optimistic iconography that speaks of prosperity and fecundity. The first features a head of Tyche, the city goddess, inscribed 'ΝΕΡΟΝΙΑΔΙ ΚΑΙCΑΡΙ ΑΓΡΙΠΠΑ', with a double cornucopia and caduceus on the reverse.[95] The second has a hand holding ears of corn, inscribed 'ΒΑCΙΛΕΟC ΜΑΡΚΟΥ ΑΓΡΙΠΠΟΥ'.[96] Undated, though probably from the same issue, is a type displaying Agrippa's portrait and an anchor.[97]

The second series is the subject of debate among numismatists since the ambiguous inscription permits a date of either the 'Year 5' or the 'Year 15', or perhaps more likely, no date at all (Fig. 13). Three different denominations in this series are known, each with the same designs and inscriptions. The coins feature Nero's portrait on the obverse and the reverse inscription clearly places them 'ΕΠΙ ΒΑΣΙΛΕ[ΩC] ΑΓΡΙΠΠ[Α]' ('under' or 'in the time of King Agrippa'). The inscription continues with these two lines: 'ΝΕΡΩ ΝΙΕ'. The letters 'ΝΕΡΩΝ' are presumed by numismatists to refer to the city's new name Neronias. The last letter in the inscription might be a date ('Ε', 5). But the intervening letter ('Ι') may either be a part of the abbreviation for 'Neronias' or may stand for the number 10, thus dating the coins 'Year 15'.[98] The coins give no hint as to which of Agrippa's eras has been utilised. Until these issues are settled in some way, it is difficult to say precisely what event generated these impressive coins.

THE ROMAN ARMY COMES TO BANIAS

Agrippa managed to walk the fine diplomatic line necessary in order to prove his loyalty to Rome in the midst of the revolt of his Jewish brothers. In the summer of 67 AD the Roman general, Vespasian, sent by Rome to put down the revolt, accepted Agrippa's invitation to visit Banias and to bring along his army. Agrippa's motives were mixed. He was intent, Josephus says, on 'entertaining the general and his troops with all the wealth of his royal household'. Such a project would have been immensely expensive and it is not unlikely that Agrippa was risking his entire fortune on such a lavish gesture.[99] His second objective indicates why he must have felt the risk necessary. He had hopes, with the aid of Vespasian's army, of 'quelling the disorders within his realm'. Obviously the disturbances spilling over from the revolt in Galilee and Judaea had not been laid to rest following the conflict between the Syrians of Caesarea and the Jews of Caesarea. Agrippa continued to have serious internal opposition. He was willing to 'entertain' Vespasian and the troops, even at excessive expense, in order to use the Roman presence to intimidate those who might have designs on his kingdom, be they rebellious Jews or local pagans inimical to his own rule.

'Leaving Caesarea-on-Sea,' Josephus continues, 'Vespasian accordingly repaired to the other Caesarea called Caesarea Philippi. There for twenty days he rested his troops, while he was being feted himself and rendering thank offerings to God for the successes which he had obtained.'[100] This report provides an insight into the nature of the city at this point in its history. Situated in a place of great natural beauty, with dozens of cool mountain springs and a great oak forest in which to camp, the Roman legions would find delightful opportunities for rest and relaxation. But the city itself must have had substantial facilities to host such a gathering, providing urban delights as well as bucolic ones. The 'feting' of the mighty Roman general was in itself a formidable challenge for the city of Banias. We can imagine almost three weeks of lavish entertainment such as special productions in the local theatre, afternoons in the baths and great evening banquets in the royal palace.

Equally revealing is Josephus's reference to the religious activities of the general while in Banias. The city was, after all, a place of religious pilgrimage, not only for devotees of Pan, but also for those who wished to give homage, and thus show loyalty, to the imperial house of Rome. Josephus, as a Jew, has obscured and softened the obvious pagan implications of the visit by simply stating that Vespasian 'rendered thank offerings to God'. He neglects to tell us which god. Perhaps Vespasian made his sacrifice to Zeus, the head of the pantheon of Hellenism, long syncretised with the Roman Jupiter, and because of his predominate position perhaps appropriately called 'the God'. A temple to Zeus certainly existed in Banias in the second century AD, and almost certainly earlier.[101] Or Vespasian's worship may have been directed toward Pan. One of Pan's most prominent activities throughout history had, after all, been assistance in battle. Moreover, as we shall see, in some quarters Pan had already begun to be thought of as a universal god, and it was not uncommon for gentiles even to syncretise Pan with the God of the Jews.[102] It is most likely, however, that Vespasian's devotions centred on the Augusteum, now dedicated to the ruling emperor, Nero. Such homage would have been politically expedient for both Agrippa and Vespasian for, after all, the cult of the emperor was first and foremost a matter of political loyalty and social piety. There is a certain irony in the situation, because not long thereafter Vespasian himself would be the emperor and, presumably, the cultus in this very temple would be directed toward him.

Nero died on 9 June 68 AD, and the Roman Senate officially condemned his memory. Agrippa's attempt to ingratiate himself to Nero by renaming Banias Neronias now became an embarrassment, and the name was no doubt suppressed as quickly and quietly as possible. Other moves had to be made as well, and quickly. Agrippa left for Rome, along with Titus, to pay homage to the new emperor, Galba. In his absence, his sister Berenice, along with the governors of Egypt and Syria, seems actively to have plotted to raise Vespasian to the throne.[103] Titus, says the Roman historian Tacitus, when he heard that Galba was dead, 'hovered uneasily between hope and fear. Finally, hope triumphed.' He left Agrippa, who continued on to Rome, and returned to his father's side. 'Some,' Tacitus adds, 'have held that his passion for Queen Berenice made him turn back.'[104] That passion was by now a widely known fact, and the Queen of Banias would remain in the very centre of Roman politics, perhaps the most powerful woman in the world, for the next several years.

Vespasian was proclaimed emperor in Syria as well as Egypt, and Agrippa hurried back home to secure his relationship with the new sovereign. 'Equal enthusiasm marked the support given to the cause by Queen Berenice,' adds Tacitus. 'She was in her best years and at the height of her beauty, while even the elderly Vespasian appreciated her generosity.' Now forty years old, she seems to have totally captivated the much younger Titus, who had been put in command of the Roman legions in Palestine. Thus it was he who presided over the fall and destruction of Jerusalem and the disintegration of the Jewish rebel state (August, 70 AD). Leaving Jerusalem in ruins, Titus first moved his victorious troops and thousands of Jewish captives to Caesarea Maritima. Then, following the lead of his father, he brought them to Banias. His choice of Banias had much to commend it as the site for what was to be primarily an orgy of celebration and of revenge against the Jewish prisoners in the army's custody. No doubt the Roman troops remembered fondly their previous days of rest and relaxation at Banias earlier in the war. The population of the city had remained loyal to Rome, Jew and gentile alike, throughout the duration of the war, making the place particularly hospitable to the legions. The facilities for the celebrations, including an arena for simulated battles and combat with beasts, were no doubt especially well appointed. And of course it was the home of one of the empire's most interesting and beautiful women, Queen Berenice – whose affair with Titus was now a matter of public record. Thus it was that Titus, 'removing his troops from Caesarea Maritima, now passed to Caesarea Philippi so called, where he remained for a considerable time, exhibiting all kinds of spectacles. Here many of the prisoners perished, some being thrown to wild beasts, others compelled in opposing masses to engage one another in combat.'[105]

The ostensible purpose of the festivities at Banias, including the gruesome display of blood revenge, was the celebration of the birthday of Titus's younger brother, Domitian, (born 24 October 51 AD).

> During his stay at Caesarea, Titus celebrated his brother's birthday with great splendour, reserving in his honour for this festival much of the punishment of his Jewish captives. For the number of those destroyed in contests with wild beasts or with one another or in the flames exceeded two thousand five hundred. Yet to the Romans, notwithstanding the myriad forms in which their victims perished, all this seemed too light a penalty.[106]

It must have been a spectacle to both titillate and horrify the local citizenry and thousands of spectators who streamed in from the Hellenised cities of the area: Damascus, the Decapolis, and coastal cities such as Tyre, Sidon, Berytus etc. Kasher suggests that 'the rejoicing and celebration characterising these events must certainly have included a considerable component of *Schadenfreude*, not to mention the libertine debauchery common at such occasions'.[107] Watching all of these things transpire must have evoked complex and contradictory feelings within the local Jewish community, and especially within Agrippa II himself. Ironically, the Jewish king found himself 'rejoicing as a Roman in the defeat of his people'.[108]

POST-WAR BANIAS

We know little about life in Banias during the final decades of the first century AD, after those events connected with the Jewish Revolt. The city did come to the attention of Pliny the Elder (23/24–79 AD), who comments in his *Natural History*: 'The source of the river Jordan is the spring of Panias from which Caesarea described later takes its second name. It is a delightful stream…'[109] Palestine was put under direct Roman administration, except for Agrippa's kingdom. In fact, he seems to have been awarded additional territory as well.[110] Berenice did not accompany Titus back to Rome when he became emperor, though their relationship remained strong. This delay was necessary due to considerable opposition to the relationship in Rome itself. Titus and Berenice, it has been suggested, evoked unpleasant images of Anthony and of Cleopatra. The possibility of yet another Eastern temptress, intent on dominating Rome through seduction of its leaders, was an exceedingly unpopular concept. But in 75 AD, after Titus was well-established in power, Berenice appeared in Rome with her brother, accompanied by considerable fanfare.[111] Agrippa was given the rank of praetor, and Berenice moved into the imperial palace with Titus. She was, says Dio, 'at the very height of her power' and fully expected to marry the emperor. She was, he says, 'behaving in every respect as if she were his wife'.[112] A Cynic philosopher who publicly spoke out against the relationship was beheaded for doing so. The opposition was intense, however, and when Vespasian's health began to fail, some even started to question whether Titus should succeed him. Berenice left the city in order to maintain a lower profile. She returned at the time of Titus's accession as emperor in 80 AD. She had high hopes, but it was no use. Rome simply would not accept this 'barbarian' Jewish woman as its empress. With deep disappointment and profound reluctance from both, the couple broke off their relationship. Titus's willingness to concede to this popular sentiment was seen as strength of character on his part[113] though Suetonius says that the decision was made 'against her will and against his own'.[114]

Agrippa's mint at Banias remained active during this time. Many coins were issued, beginning at the time of the fall of Masada and continuing throughout the AD 70s and 80s. These issues featured portraits of Vespasian, Titus, and Domitian, with reverses depicting Tyche and Nike. A series dated 'Year 19' (79/80) – just at the time of the final attempt to make Berenice empress of Rome – seem connected to that campaign. Two of these depict Titus on the obverse and a ship on the reverse, possibly suggesting Berenice's trip to Rome (Fig. 14).[115] The third is even more provocative, having a veiled female bust on the obverse with the inscription 'ΣΕΒΑΣΤΗ', and an anchor on the reverse. One might understand the female to be the empress Livia. But, as Maltiel-Gerstenfeld has said, 'It is tempting to identify the veiled woman on the obverse as Berenice and conjecture that the coin was issued in anticipation of the forthcoming marriage and elevation of Berenice to the status of ΣΕΒΑΣΤΗ. One may further conjecture that the anchor of the reverse hints at Berenice's voyage by sea to Rome' (Figs 14, 16).[116]

Titus died in 81 AD and the dreams of grandeur entertained by the king and queen of Banias died with him. Berenice left Rome and, we may presume, returned to the town beside the springs of Pan to live out her days as the trusted colleague of her brother. She was 53 years old.[117] She was the daughter and great-granddaughter of kings, the sister of a king, the wife of two kings, and, very nearly, the empress of Rome. She was certainly one of the best-known and most powerful women of her age. But we never hear from her again.[118]

Banias in the 80s is known only through its coins, most of which are based on Roman prototypes. The mint itself, now approaching a century of existence, may be honoured on one of the coins of a series dated 'Year 25' (85–86 AD) which depicts the goddess Moneta. It is more likely, however, that this coin and others of the series, which depict an altar, have no local connections, but simply copy their Roman prototypes.[119]

Two coins of Agrippa, however, both dated 'Year 27', do present an insight into the life of the city. They testify to Agrippa's continuing attempt to ingratiate himself to the pagan population there. The coins depict Pan and the Tyche of Banias. Meshorer suggests that these coins depict two statues dedicated by Agrippa II to the local temples of these two deities.[120] The first of the two is the most interesting since it depicts Pan himself (Fig. 15). The obverse of the coin pictures facing busts of Titus and Domitian. On the reverse, Pan is shown, walking left, playing the syrinx and holding a pedum over his shoulder. To his right is a tree trunk.[121] This Pan is quite different from the one we will encounter on the coins of the second and third centuries, who plays the pipes, not a syrinx, is standing, not walking etc. It was a familiar image in its own time, however. It may be seen to this day, though reversed, as a bas-relief cut in the rock above the cave of Pan in Athens, providing a further indication of the connection between the cult of Pan at Banias and the ancient Greek traditions upon which it was based.[122] Of this coin, Meshorer comments,

> It would not be overly daring to suggest that among the many gifts granted by Agrippa II to his non-Jewish constituency was a new statue of Pan for the local sanctuary at Caesarea Paneas. This dedication may have been made either before or after his extensive investments in the city…The figure depicted on the coin may therefore represent a statue of the god given to the city by Agrippa II. The dedication of the statue may even have provided the impetus for this coin. Because the design is not repeated on later coins, it was probably struck to commemorate such a singular event.[123]

This coin is unique among those minted by Jewish rulers in that it unquestionably depicts a pagan deity. It is true that figures such as Tyche (Fortune) and Nike appear on Herodian family coins, but these might be interpreted as nothing more than symbols or personifications of abstract concepts. The rabbis had decreed that only those images that bear some object like a staff or bird or orb in their hands are truly idols. The Pan appearing on this coin of Agrippa II does have a staff in his hand, and thus this Jewish ruler, in minting it, had crossed the line, in rabbinic terms, separating Judaism from paganism and idolatry.[124]

The second coin features the bust of Vespasian and, on the reverse, the Tyche, or City-Goddess of Banias. She holds a rudder and cornucopia, and is dressed in military fashion.[125] Meshorer suggests that this is another depiction of an actual cult statue presented to the city by Agrippa II.[126] Unlike the image of Pan, this Tyche appears on several coins, in several forms, during the second and early third centuries (cf. Fig. 24). There are some differences, though relatively minor, between the figure depicted on Agrippa's coin and those seen later on some of the imperial city coins, but it is at least possible that one of the statues of the city goddess venerated later was originally presented to the city by Agrippa.[127]

A massive building (over 100 metres in length) discovered and partially excavated during the recent excavation of the city centre of Banias seems to be a sumptuous but heavily fortified palace (Figs 17, 18). The building is constructed of huge, expertly crafted stones fitted together without any use of mortar. No expense seems to have been spared in creating this architectural masterpiece. The great circular towers at the southern entrance to the structure, and the elaborate system of 'blind corners' in the hallways which led to the now-missing upper story (and thus presumably to the royal apartments), point to a builder who was somewhat uneasy about the loyalty of his subjects – certainly bringing to mind the strained relations between Agrippa I and the 'Syrians of Caesarea'. The building was probably erected in the 80s, perhaps after Berenice's humiliation (a token of regret from Titus?). It was magnificently built, apparently by the empire's finest architects and engineers, and was extensively decorated with mosaics, painted stucco and marble veneering and detailing. The latter is unusual in Herodian structures, but feasible in this case, since the ports of Tyre, Berytus etc., were only a few miles away and we know that Agrippa and Berenice decorated buildings in similar style there.[128] The eastern side of the building consisted of a series of massive arched rooms that have survived intact, due to their incorporation into a medieval citadel. These rooms led into a magnificent apsidal basilica, which may have served as the audience hall or throne room of the king. An elaborate system of expertly constructed channels brought water from the springs directly into the palace to supply the many pools and fountains in its internal courtyards. Some of this system still carries water today. Portions of this structure, which surely is one of the most impressive buildings of the early empire, are remarkably well preserved. Further excavation will undoubtedly provide further revelations and delights to those who seek to understand this period in the history of the eastern provinces of the empire of Rome.

As the 90s dawned, Agrippa's kingdom was apparently gradually dismantled, though our evidence is most ambiguous and circumstantial.[129] He seems to have lost his eastern territories during the early 90s, so that by the end of his life he ruled only Paneas, Ulatha, part of northern Galilee and perhaps some other areas. The date of Agrippa's death has been widely debated, and various dates have been proposed. After centuries of doubt, the date given by Photius (*Bibliotheca* 33),[130] namely, the third year of the emperor Trajan (i.e. 100 AD) seems now to be generally recognised as correct.[131] Numismatic evidence (coins may have been minted until at least 95/96 AD),[132] and the discovery of some relevant inscriptions[133] and other artifacts[134] have all contributed to this conclusion.[135] The matter is not yet definitely settled.

In any event, by the time of the death of Agrippa the little principality of Banias was absorbed into the larger Roman world as a part of the Province of Syria.[136] This time there was no *interregnum*. The long-standing policy of allowing client kings to rule small principalities on the edges of the empire in the East was itself coming to an end.[137] That the principality lasted so long is as much a credit to its ruler as to larger Roman policy. Agrippa had maintained his kingship through the reigns of Claudius, Nero, Otho, Galba, Vitellius, Vespasian, Titus, Domitian and presumably also Nerva and Trajan. Over and over again he had played the dangerous game of imperial politics with the instinct of a crafty survivor. And because of his skills as an administrator, and his proven loyalty to Rome he, along with his great-uncle Philip, enabled the little principality of Banias to enjoy over a century of independent existence. With their passing, the 'pre-provincial phase' in southern Syria ended.[138]

3 Roman Banias

During the last few decades more and more of the Hellenistic cities of Syria-Palestine have been systematically excavated. When these excavations are compared a rather consistent pattern of urban development begins to surface. Without significant exception, these cities exhibit growth and prosperity beginning in the second and extending into at least part of the third century. During this period Rome's governing policies in the Middle East underwent a major change. The days of client princes such as those of the Herodian dynasty were gone. Rome now ruled the area directly through governors sent out from the imperial capital to administer the generally well-governed provincial capitals. Peace and economic good times allowed the construction of countless architectural amenities: forums, amphitheatres, colonnaded streets, nymphaea, temples, stadia, gymnasiums, baths etc. Paganism, responding to a more sophisticated age, and reacting to a growing threat from Christianity, began to think of its gods in more comprehensive terms. Local divinities were syncretised into a smaller and smaller circle of universal deities, though the local population remained fiercely loyal to traditional belief in oracles, divinations, dreams, visions, spiritual possession, miraculous cures, astrology etc. The strength of this combination of popular and state-supported paganism can be seen in the many temples, festivals, games and cultic observances characteristic of urban life during the period. These were also the days of severe, but sporadic, persecutions against the Christians, a people now numerous enough in Syria-Palestine to draw considerable official attention.

The nature of the evidence by which the historian reconstructs life in Banias changes as well. We long for a contemporary historian like Josephus to reveal to us in detail the political and cultural currents of the times, and to give us names and dates. But we have no such informant. Instead, we find that we must piece together a synthesis based on bits of disconnected data from various sources – a jigsaw puzzle of fragments. References to Banias by contemporary authors during these centuries are few and far between, though what little we have certainly confirms the fact that the city was well known in the empire and sheds at least some light on events there. Gaius Julius Solinus, writing at the beginning of the third century knows that the river Jordan 'is of extraordinary pleasantness', and that 'it derives from the spring Paneas, and flows past the most delightful regions'.[1] And Porphyry (232 AD – *ca.* 300 AD), recounting the decisive battle fought between Antiochus and Scopas (see Chapter 1), adds a significant phrase: 'Antiochus joined battle with Scopas, Ptolemy's general, near the sources of the Jordan where the city now called Paneas was founded'.[2]

The old mint at Banias, which provides valuable historical and cultural information for the Herodian period, fell curiously silent for three quarters of a century – from the death of Agrippa II to the beginning of the reign of Marcus Aurelius as sole emperor (169 AD). The absence of coinage during the reigns of Trajan and Hadrian is particularly strange, since other evidence indicates that the city continued to have a certain importance at that time, and other cities in the area were certainly minting coins. It may be that the right to mint coins belonged personally to Agrippa and was not granted to the city *qua* city until long after his death. Once the mint was reactivated, however, it became an important source of information. Numerous dated coins are known from 169 AD to 220 AD, issued under the authority of most of the emperors and many members of their families during that period.[3] These coins feature an array of temples, including detailed depictions of the Pan sanctuary, and a number of deities, and thus suggest that the city had become an important pagan cult site by this time.

A modest corpus of inscriptions from or about the city, and dating from these two centuries, is beginning to surface.[4] One of the first things noticed by European explorers during the period of the 'rediscovery' of Banias in the nineteenth century were the inscriptions carved on the red-rock cliff near the cave of Pan, several of which were easily decipherable. To these have now been added inscriptions and fragments of sculpture[5] found during recent excavations, and inscriptions mentioning Banias scattered here and there around the empire, several of which we will describe.

Finally, we are immensely assisted by the emerging data provided by excavation at the site. The work of Tzaferis, Ma'oz, Hartal and others over the past decade is beginning to reveal something about the city plan, economic life and cultural context of Roman Banias. This information, when added to the other kinds of evidence noted above, makes an historical synthesis much more plausible than it would have been only a few years ago. We will first lay out a chronological outline of life in Banias under Rome, then investigate some aspects of urban life in Banias thematically, and in succeeding chapters deal with the question of the nature of the religions – Pagan, Jewish, and Christian – which were practised in the Roman city.

BANIAS IN THE REIGNS OF TRAJAN (98–117 AD) AND HADRIAN (117–38 AD)

The disappearance of the Herodian dynasts in Banias meant that the Romans had to take direct responsibility for policing the area, keeping the nomads to the east and south under control, protecting the vital routes from Syria to the coast, and keeping a watchful eye on the Jewish population, where rumblings of revolt were never far beneath the surface. The emperor Trajan (98–117 AD) might therefore have been expected to replace the armies of Agrippa II with troops of his own, and even to consider Banias a place of some strategic importance. There are some intriguing hints in the archaeological record that this was in fact the case.

To the east of the shrine of Pan, which itself stood east of the natural cave, Zvi Ma'oz found the remains of a large ashlar building facing the city centre that extended approximately 17 metres from the cliffside, including a front porch with four columns measuring 11 metres by 4.15 metres. The building was approached by a broad stairway. Because the pottery found in the foundations dates to the late first century AD, and two inscriptions found nearby mention Zeus,[6] and because a temple to Zeus almost certainly stood in the city, as indicated by second- and third-century coins, he dubbed the building 'the Temple of Zeus'.[7] This identification is, of course, speculative. The pottery found in the foundation fill of the porch seems consistently to date to the late first and early second centuries, and so it is not unreasonable to suppose that the building existed at least from the reign of Trajan. This is further confirmed by the content of one of the inscriptions. Apparently once attached to an altar, this inscription was found in a destruction layer of the northwest corner of the ashlar building. It reads: 'To Heliopolitan Zeus and to the god Pan who brings victory, for the salvation of our lord Trajan Caesar, with his entire house Maronas son of Publius Aristo has dedicated this holy altar'.[8] The reference to Pan 'who brings victory' continues the long tradition of connection between the military and the goat-god who can 'panic' the troops of whichever side he pleases.[9] Furthermore, Heliopolitan Zeus is well-known as a god of soldiers.[10] The dedicant, who has an Aramaic name, and whose father has a Greek name and a Latin name, was almost certainly a soldier from Trajan's army, stationed at or near Banias. Another inscription, found on a bas-relief in Syria and dating from the beginning of the second century, identifies an officer in similar circumstances, whose military service bridged the transition from client kingdom to direct Roman rule. Archieus is described as 'having served eighteen years under King Agrippa and ten years under Trajan'.[11]

Benjamin Isaac's analysis of another recently discovered inscription provides further evidence of a military presence in the city during Trajan's reign. A centurion, whose name is missing from the inscription, makes a dedication to his patron, L[ucius] Nonius, son of Marcus, who is described as 'tribune of the millinary cohort of Thracians'.[12] The centurion himself also belonged to this cohort. The *Cohors (I) Miliaria Thracum* is known to have been in Syria in 88 and 91 AD. It seems to have been transferred to Judaea in 117 AD as a part of a much larger movement of troops to that area at that time.[13] Its presence in the area of Caesarea Philippi, as indicated by the inscription, can thus be dated somewhere between 91 AD and 117 AD – precisely the period during which Agrippa II died and his territories fell under the direct supervision of the governor of Syria. It seems reasonable to conclude that the Herodian army, after maintaining order in the region of Banias for over a century, was replaced by Trajan, in accordance with his larger policy toward the East, with Roman units such as the *Cohors I Miliaria Thracum*. Then, as trouble began to brew in Judaea, at least some of these troops were sent south by Trajan's successor Hadrian.

Other changes certainly occurred as Banias moved from its status as a royal capital to a more modest standing within the empire. We have suggested, for example, that the Augusteum, so closely identified with the relationship between the Herodian dynasty and the Julio-Claudian and Flavian imperial families, might have been transformed into something else – a temple of Zeus or Tyche perhaps? The temple discovered at Omrit was in fact rebuilt and enlarged sometime in the late first or early second century AD, according to its excavators, and so the intriguing possibility arises that specific archaeological evidence may eventually throw light on this period of transition.[14] The royal palace of Agrippa would now be redundant, and was certainly altered in purpose and plan a few decades after his death. Archaeological evidence makes it clear that the complex was transformed into a huge public bathhouse (Fig. 19).[15]

Hadrian (117–38 AD), that consummate imperial traveller, if he did not visit Banias, at least made a circuit around the city, leaving distinct, if sometimes faint, footprints behind him in the area. In the autumn of 129 AD, the emperor left Antioch for Berytus, en route to Palmyra. From the coast, he probably went east to Damascus, conceivably through Banias, but more likely by way of Heliopolis (Baalbek) and then straight through the mountains. Before leaving Antioch he rewarded both Damascus and Tyre by conferring metropolitan status upon them, and proposed that each rule a province, though this did not actually come about until eighty years later. In Berytus the citizens dedicated an offering to him in the temple of Balal Marqod at Deir al-Qala, and at Damascus coins were minted calling that city by its new title of 'metropolis' and hailing Hadrian as a god. Several cities seem to have held games in his honour. Hadrian continued southward from Damascus to Arabia (Petra), then up to Jerash in the Decapolis and, in early 130 AD, entered Palestine (Jerusalem). At this point he probably set in motion the 'refounding' of Jerusalem under the new name Aelia Capitolina.[16] His itinerary then carried him via Gaza to Egypt, where his 'favourite' Antinous drowned, and finally back westward to Greece. Shortly after his visit to Judaea the so-called Second Revolt of the Jews broke out (132 AD) and Hadrian returned to the area, though he was back in Rome by 134 AD. The revolt had been crushed by the end of 135 AD.[17]

Into this general historical context we may insert a number of intriguing clues as to what was happening in Banias. First, there is the beautiful and well-preserved bust of Antinous that was discovered in the mid-1800s in Banias by M. Pétretié, Chancellor of the French Consulate in Beirut. It should be dated somewhere between 130 and 138 AD.[18] Inscribed 'To the hero Antinous', this sculpture suggests strong Hadrianic connections in Banias. The dedicant, one 'M[arcus] Lucius Flaccus', is otherwise unknown. If the imperial cult was still centred in Herod's Augusteum, the bust may have stood in some place of honour in that temple. If not, it must have been located at some place within the growing cult complex near the cave and springs or among the monuments of the city centre.

There is reason to believe that a statue of Hadrian himself stood in a prominent place near the cult complex. This statue, which eventually was buried beneath earth washed down from higher ground, was rediscovered in the fourth century. At that time it was identified by the growing Christian community in Banias as being nothing less than a statue of Jesus himself. A second statue, situated in front of this one, depicted a woman kneeling in supplication. This, the Christians believed, was the woman whom Jesus had healed of chronic haemorrhaging (Luke 8:43–44). We will investigate the fascinating story of this statue in a later chapter, and present there the reasons for identifying it as a depiction of Hadrian. At this point we are concerned only with what its existence tells us about early-second-century Banias. The story of the rediscovery we owe to Philostorgius (*ca.*386–*ca.*439), the Christian historian, writing in the early fifth century. He says that the locals told him that the statue had long stood 'exposed to the open air', and that 'a great part of it was covered over by the earth' that washed down against the base of the statue, 'especially during seasons of heavy rain'. Significantly, he adds that the statue 'was placed near the fountain in the city among other statues, and presented a pleasant and agreeable sight to the passers-by'. Because of the 'lapse of time' all memory of the erection of the statue had been forgotten, he says, and 'it was even forgotten whose statue it was'.[19] It seems clear that the statue was not only located near the cave and spring, but was also close enough to the cliff that it was subject to partial burial by mud washed down from above.

Another Christian historian, Eusebius of Caesarea, also saw this statue in its original place in the early fourth century, before it was moved inside the local Christian basilica. On a tall stone base, he says, there '... stood a bronze statue of a woman, resting on one knee and resembling a suppliant with arms outstretched. Facing was another of the same material, an upright figure of a man with a double cloak neatly draped over his shoulders and his hand stretched out to the woman.'[20] The coinage of Hadrian is characterised by numerous issues depicting the emperor reaching out benevolently toward supplicating women, who represent the provinces he visited or upon which he bestowed great favours. Among these so-called 'restorer' type coins there exists a rare sestertius with the legend IUDAEA depicting the emperor standing, dressed in Greek style, and a woman representing the province kneeling before him (Fig.31).[21] The depiction exactly fits Eusebius's description of the two statues he saw in Banias. This coin clearly commemorates the 'restoration' of Judaea that Hadrian accomplished through the establishment of Aelia Capitolina, thus providing a new centre for life and culture in the Roman manner. And the woman, her himation drawn over her head to form a veil, is meant to show the great sense of gratitude that the province had for this magnanimous gesture on the emperor's part.

Of course, Banias was not technically in the province of Judaea, and it is unlikely that the statue that was erected there commemorated events in Judaea. Rather, it is more likely that it was one of many 'restorer'-type statues that were produced in some workshop outside of Palestine and shipped to various cities throughout the empire in connection with the travels of the emperor. It is curious that thus far no coins have been discovered in the Hadrianic series depicting either the provinces of Syria or Phoenicia, the areas to which Banias belonged, despite Hadrian's great favour shown them mentioned above. Figures on commemorative coins often represent real statues and indeed often commemorate the erection of those statues. It would not seem unreasonable to suggest that statues of the 'restorer' type were erected in many places, such as Damascus and Tyre – and in Banias as well – which for one reason or another did not also mint coins to commemorate the event.[22]

The existence of two statues in Banias intimately connected with Hadrian, along with evidence of a strongly 'pro-Roman' position taken by the city during the Bar Kochba Revolt (see below), makes it extremely tempting to theorise that the emperor did indeed visit the city on some unrecorded part of his journeys in the area.

THE GOLDEN AGE OF PAGAN BANIAS: THE ANTONINES

Two of the famous inscriptions cut into the red-rock cliffside next to the cave of Pan may be confidently dated to the reign of Hadrian's successor, Antoninus Pius (138–61 AD).[23] They were meant to be associated with two niches cut into the rock to hold statues as part of an expansion of the cult site constructed east of the 'Temple of Zeus' in Trajan's time. Both statues were gifts of the same man, one Victor, son of Lysimachos. Victor is described in the second of the inscriptions as a priest.[24] The statues apparently depicted Hermes and Echo. These installations illustrate the process of developing and expanding the Pan sanctuary, which involved not only the addition of altars, shrines and temples, but also the introduction of additional deities traditionally associated with Pan. This process continued throughout the second century (Fig. 29).

Under Antoninus Pius's successor, Marcus Aurelius (161–80 AD), the Banias mint reopened. An impressive series of coins was produced which were to set the typology of Panian numismatics for almost a century. The largest coin of the series depicts Zeus standing, nude, holding a sceptre in one hand and a *patera* with the other. At his feet stands an altar, no doubt the altar before the sanctum of the Zeus temple in which the cult statue depicted on the coin stood (Fig. 22).[25] This figure, sometimes shown in the temple itself, recurs on coins of Banias for the next half-century.[26] The second coin in the series depicts Pan, standing nude beside a tree trunk, and playing on his pipe. This image also occurs over and over on coins of Banias for the next half-century and is by far the most prevalent theme shown on the coins of the city (Fig. 32). A third type appears in the same series, picturing a sort of 'generic' bust of Tyche, the protector goddess of the city, a depiction which is replaced in the coinage of later rulers by a Tyche specific to Banias (Fig. 24). The iconography of this series of coins will be analysed below in the context of our discussion of religion in Banias. At this point we simply note the potential significance of the reopening of the mint, and the appearance of Zeus, Pan and Tyche as the dominant deities of the city, in the year 169 AD, a date that featured prominently on the coins. Tzaferis has suggested that the beginnings of the Zeus cult in Banias should be placed within the context of the religious reforms of Marcus Aurelius. These gave prominence to Zeus-Jupiter in Rome and elsewhere, and at the same time syncretistically incorporated Zeus within the emperor's stoic worldview.[27] While it is likely that a syncretistic Zeus was already worshiped in Banias (one inscription found there dated 'Year 65', i.e. 63 AD, is dedicated to 'Heliopolitan Zeus'), the appearance of the coin series we have described seems to mark a major moment in the history of religious practice at Banias, as the sophisticated philosophies of Marcus Aurelius found their place in everyday provincial practice.

It is worth noting that the Augusteum never again appears on the coinage of Banias. However, a tetrastyle temple with a pediment and acroteria, and an 'old-style' roof that very much resembles the one pictured on the coins of Philip[28] appears on imperial issues of 217 AD (Macrinus and Diadumenian) as a temple of Zeus. The cult statue described above can be clearly seen inside the building.[29] This raises yet another interesting possibility as to the fate of Herod's old temple, namely that after a period of usage as a temple to each of the succeeding Julio-Claudian and, perhaps, Flavian emperors, it was eventually transformed by Hadrian's successors into a temple of Zeus, as a part of a major development of the worship of Pan and his associates.[30]

A few years after the issuance of the coins described above, one of the most interesting of all the inscriptions on the red-rock cliffside appeared, dedicating a shrine and a statue to 'the Lady Nemesis'. The inscription, dated 178 AD, reads as follows:

> For the preservation of our lords the Emperors, Valerios Hispanos, priest of the god Pan [dedicated] the Lady Nemesis and her shrine which was made by cutting away the rock underneath, with an iron fence. Year 180 in the month of Apellaios.[31]

The niche in which the statue stood has survived, as well as the mortises that were designed to hold the iron grill that separated the worshippers from the cult object. These grills were a feature of several of the shrines and temples in Banias. The Nemesis shrine is located just to the east of the ashlar building (the so-called 'Temple of Zeus'), where it could be reached by an ashlar pavement that lay between the building and the niche, from the south, by means of a street and broad staircase. The pavement formed a narrow (16.5 metres by 4.3 metres) court by which worshippers could approach the open-air shrine.[32]

Leaving aside for the moment the significance of this shrine within the religious development of the city, we draw upon Hornum's exhaustive study of this goddess, looking for further clues about Banias in the second century.[33] Hornum found that Nemesis was often associated with the emperor and was also a protector of cities, perhaps even sometimes being conflated with Tyche. 'It seems clear,' he says, 'that Nemesis had some role in the Roman period as a guardian of municipal bodies as well as individuals.'[34] But her most distinctive association was with theatres, amphitheatres and stadia,[35] and particularly with gladiatorial contests or violent games featuring condemned criminals or young men engaged in hunts or mock fights.[36] As the goddess of Justice, whom Zeus had commissioned to distribute to men what each one deserved, whether reward or punishment, she became the personification of moral standards and decency. She was thus particularly at home in the games, where she not only watched to see that the rules were followed, but also 'manifested in a special way her power over those who exceeded what was proper, specifically over those who violated or threatened what was deemed proper within the Roman State'.[37] Thus, she was also at home with those displays in the amphitheatre involving 'the slaughter of military enemies, criminals, insolent slaves and wild animals', since these are all offensive to proper order in society.[38]

All this is highly reminiscent of Josephus's account of the slaughter of the Jewish rebels in Banias following the fall of Jerusalem, almost a century before the dedication of the Nemesis shrine by Valerios Hispanos:

During his stay at Caesarea, Titus celebrated his brother's birthday with great splendour, reserving in his honour for this festival much of the punishment of his Jewish captives. For the number of those destroyed in contests with wild beasts or with one another or in the flames exceeded two thousand five hundred. Yet to the Romans, notwithstanding the myriad forms in which their victims perished, all this seemed too light a penalty.[39]

This event may have been repeated over the years. In addition to the usual athletic events, a particular characteristic of these spectacles may have been the punishment of prisoners of war, given the strong military presence in or near the city that we have already noted. It is important to remember, however, that the cult of Nemesis was common in the area in other cities, so perhaps there was no special circumstance in Banias to call for the shrine there.[40] We will return to these issues in a later discussion of religion in Banias.

THE SEVERAN DYNASTY

There are signs of a burst of energy in Banias beginning with the ascendancy of Septimius Severus (193–211 AD) that even exceeds that of the reign of Marcus Aurelius.[41] This is not surprising, given the fact that the new Emperor married a Syrian woman and thus inaugurated what has been called the 'Syro-Lebanese Dynasty' in Rome. The Empress Julia Domna was from Emesa, Banias's neighbour not far to the north (Fig. 24). The dynasty showed great interest in the region in various ways. Soon after his reign began, Septimius Severus completed the reorganisation that had been promised by Hadrian, partitioning the province of Syria into an eastern half, called Coele-Syria, and a western half, called Syro-Phoenicia. Banias came under a new administration, being assigned a place in the province of Phoenicia.

Banias's location between the two provincial capitals, Damascus and Tyre, increased the city's importance and enhanced its already-considerable fame, not to mention its economic prosperity as a key stage on the trade routes north, east, south and west. An analysis of a large number of bronze coins (mostly from the early third century) found near an entrance into the public basilica in the former palace of Agrippa II illustrates the important web of trade connections. Of the identifiable coins, five were minted in Banias itself, six in Tyre, two in Damascus and one each in Sidon, Heliopolis, Petra and Nysa-Scythopolis. The pattern of trade is clear, even in this small sample. The local mint at Banias reached its peak, both in number of issues and creativity of design, during the days of the Severan Dynasty. The religious interests of the dynasty, and particularly its interest in the Syrian cults, are well known. The coins, along with inscriptions and archaeological finds, suggest a strong upsurge of interest in Pan in the city, beginning in the days of Marcus Aurelius, but reaching its climax under Elagabalus (218–22 AD), whose assumed name proclaimed his identification with Syrian religious traditions.

Septimius Severus visited Palestine in 199 AD and passed from Egypt to Coele-Syria in 200/1 AD.[42] He may well have personally visited Banias during this time, but even if he did not, his tour seems to coincide with a flurry of coin issues depicting members of his family, and dated during the years of his travels.[43] In 217 AD, during the short reign of Macrinus and Diadumenian, the mint became active again, issuing coins showing the cult statue of Zeus standing in his temple.[44] When the Severans returned to the throne, in the person of Elagabalus, the minting continued yearly, and in 220 AD there was a veritable explosion of coin types. These depicted not only the emperor, but also several female members of his family (his mother Julia Soaemus, his grandmother Julia Maesa and two of his wives, Aquilia Severa and Annia Faustina, both of whom he married in that year). Many of these coins feature Pan, but place him in impressive new surroundings. He is seen in a niche, usually identified as the one above the artificial grotto next to the cave, but more likely located in the westernmost shrine along the cliff base, in what Ma'oz calls 'The Temple of Pan and the Goats',[45] or standing inside a semi-circular colonnade,[46] or perhaps even within the natural cave.[47] Several of the coins depict what appear to be grill fences, reminiscent of the iron grillwork mentioned on the inscription at the shrine of Nemesis. It is especially significant that a particular reverse design may be found from this same year (220 AD) on coins having the portraits of every one of the family members of Elagabalus mentioned above. On these coins the usual cult statue of Pan is shown, but on either side of the figure there are flags or decorated standards.[48]

The cumulative impression that all this numismatic activity produces is that major events were occurring in Banias during these years which had to do with the cult of Pan, and which had a strong feminine quality to them. New female deities related to Pan appear; women of the imperial household are featured on the coins; and the Pan sanctuary is enlarged and beautified. More will be said about the direct religious implications of this activity in the next chapter. Here we only note that the city of Banias has obviously come strongly to the attention of the imperial family, particularly the women in that family, and that this attention climaxes in the year 220 AD. We are led to seek a reason. The answer may lie in the nature of the Pan cult itself, with its strong connections with fertility and sexuality. It is most likely that the cult of Pan (in his aspect as a god of nature, flocks and fecundity) was of particular interest to women.[49] To this fact we add the special 'problem' the imperial family had at this time, namely the need for an heir to the throne. Elagabalus, whose sexual orientation was ambiguous to say the least, and who appears to have been totally uninterested in women, was married to a series of wives, two of whom appear on the coins of Banias, in hopes of producing an heir. Could it be that a huge 'Pan Festival' was held during the year 220/221 AD in an attempt to invoke the god's assistance in dealing with the family's delicate problem?

Certain building activities revealed in the archaeological excavations may have taken place at the Pan sanctuary as a part of this general 'Pan Festival'. To the east of the Nemesis shrine Ma'oz found what he calls the 'Tripartite Building' or 'The Tomb-Temple of the Sacred Goats'.[50] This building featured three adjacent halls, bounded by a paved street. The red-rock cliff served as the back wall of the structure. A niche had been carved into the cliffside at that point with a series of small compartments along a walkway leading to it. Within these compartments were found a large number of goat bones. A coin of Julia Maesa was found in the foundation, proving that the building was built in 220 AD or later.

Just south of the Tripartite Building, Ma'oz found an 'Apsidal Court' which opens to the west, facing toward the emerging waters of the spring. He thinks this might be the structure with a semi-circular colonnade depicted on the coins.[51] Ceramic evidence is consistent with a date after 220 AD. These two structures seem to be associated; perhaps offerings made in the Apsidal Court were deposited in the compartments of the Tripartite Building.[52]

Though these activities may primarily have been inspired by concerns associated with the imperial family, they were supported by the locals as well. High above the court dedicated to Nemesis there is an inscription on the face of the cliffside beside a small niche that has been carved into the rock. It is so high that it could only have been reached by climbing up onto the roof of the 'Temple of Zeus' next door, which perhaps had some sort of terrace to be used for this purpose. The inscription seems to announce the dedication of a small statue of the goddess Echo by the archon (chief magistrate) of the city, whose name is Agrippas, son of Markos. He is joined in this act by his wife Agrippias and (presumably) their kinsmen Agrippinos, Markos and Agrippas, who are *bouleutai* (town councillors), and their children, Agrippine and Domne.[53] Agrippas says that he was led to make this gift after having 'received divine instructions in a dream'. Although this phrase is rather common on inscriptions of this type, it may indicate a particular religious fervour in the town at this time, during which the ancient cult received new life and the gods worshipped there become active in the lives of the citizens, appearing to them in dreams etc. The discovery of other fragments of inscriptions and altars dedicated to Elagabalus and possibly to Caracalla, show that other citizens were moved to participate in this activity as well.[54]

After the reign of Elagabalus, the relative wealth of data regarding Banias disappears. Other than a milestone bearing the name of Gordian III (238–44 AD),[55] the record falls silent as the empire itself began to descend into economic and political chaos. There is one possible exception to this pattern of silence. The map of Palestine depicted in the famous Peutinger Table calls Banias 'Cesareapaneas'. There is no consensus concerning the dating of the various recensions of this map; it seems to have been based on a first-century original and a fourth-century edition.[56] The depiction of Jerusalem, however, is far less prominent than one would expect in the fourth century, and an explanation that it was previously called Jerusalem but at the time was called Aelia Capitolina suggests the political and religious situation during the intervening centuries, and thus the possibility of a recension during that time.[57] The name used for Banias, Cesareapanias, is consistent with the one found on coins of the second and third centuries. Several other names on the map are pre-Constantinian, but later than the first century. This seems to be the case with Banias as well. On the map it is no longer Caesarea or Caesarea Philippi, but Caesarea Paneas – a name that disappears in favour of simply 'Paneas' later. Bowersock suggests that the treatment of Banias on the map is, then, 'transitional'.[58]

The people of Banias, whether they belonged to the substantial Jewish community, one of the various growing Christian sects, or even the city's solid pagan majority, began to experience an increasing burden of taxes during the middle and waning days of the third century.[59] But it is the literary record of the Jewish community that provides the only glimpse into the nature of the times, especially during the reign of Diocletian (284–305 AD).

BANIAS AND THE EMPEROR DIOCLETIAN (284–305 AD)

Much of what has been preserved in the rabbinical literature concerning Diocletian is clearly legendary. Still, something of the spirit of the times survives. We do not know what special relationship Diocletian had with Banias, but it is curious that several rabbinical stories tie the emperor to the city, even claiming that he lived there while he was emperor of Rome. The memories of his interest in the city are not pleasant ones. Apparently his empire-wide programme of heavy taxation was particularly vexing to the people of Caesarea Paneas, and his relationship with the rabbis in the area less than congenial. The following strange story appears in the *Midrash Rabbah*:

> The emperor Diocletian was [originally] a swineherd near Tiberias. Whenever he came near a school, children would come out and beat him. Later he became emperor, and went and stayed at Paneas, and sent letters to Tiberias just before the even of the Sabbath, with the order: 'I command the Rabbis of the Jews to appear before me on Sunday morning.' He further instructed the messenger not to give them the message until just before Friday evening. When R. Samuel b. Nahman went down to bathe, he saw a Rabbi standing before his academy with his face all pale. On inquiring why he was so pale he told him of the letters sent him by the emperor. 'Go and bathe,' he told him, 'for God will perform a miracle for you.' So he went in to bathe, and there Arginitun [a bath sprite?] came jesting and dancing toward him. Rabbi wished to scold him, but R. Samuel b. Nahman said to him: 'Leave him alone, for sometimes his coming heralds a miracle… Go home, eat and keep the Sabbath with good cheer, for your Creator will perform a miracle for you and I will set you Sunday morning where you desire.' At the termination of the Sabbath, after the Service, he [the sprite] took them and set them before the gates of Paneas. He [the emperor] was informed, 'Lo, they are standing before the gates. Then let the gates be closed, he ordered. Thereupon he [the sprite] took them and set them upon the rampart of the town. On being apprised of this he [Diocletian] exclaimed: 'I command that the baths be heated for three days, then let them go and bathe therein and then appear before me.' The baths accordingly were heated for three days, but the sprite went and tempered the heat for them, after which they entered, bathed, and appeared before him. 'Because you know that your God performs miracles on your behalf you insult the emperor', he upbraided them. 'Diocletian the swineherd we did indeed insult, but to Diocletian the emperor we are loyal subjects,' they answered. 'Even so,' he replied, 'you must not insult the humblest Roman or the meanest soldier.[60]

The 'rabbi' in this story is apparently the Patriarch Judah III (265–320 AD).[61] He is summoned from his home in Tiberias, where 'the children' (probably the students in his academy there) had mistreated Diocletian the swineherd. Having now become the emperor, and living in Paneas, the emperor summons the rabbi, intent on exacting vengeance. But each attempt, first to force the rabbi to break the Sabbath, and then to harm him by overheating the baths, is foiled due to the intercession of a supernatural being, an 'Arginitun'.

There is very little in the story that adds to historical knowledge. Banias is described as a fortified city, with ramparts and gates, but these may be no more than literary devices.[62] The reference to the baths seems to indicate some knowledge of the huge bath complex that recent excavations have found in the city centre. At the most, there may be here the dim memory of a visit to Banias by the emperor Diocletian, and of some altercation that occurred between him and the local Jewish community during that visit. There are other hints of trouble between Diocletian and the citizenry of Banias, Jew and gentile alike. The *Midrash Rabbah* proposes this interpretation of Numbers 11:5 ('The Lord bless thee and guard thee'): 'The Lord bless thee with wealth and guard thee that thou not be compelled to take office in the province of Paneas and that no fine be imposed upon the district as a result of which they should say to you: "Give gold!"'[63] The implication of this statement is either that such a fate had already befallen the people of Banias, or that there was a strong threat that it would do so. In fact, another rabbinical text, this time in the *Palestinian Talmud*, recalls just such a misfortune, and at the hands of this same Emperor Diocletian:

> Diocletian oppressed the inhabitants of Paneas. They said to him, 'We are going' [i.e. running away from there to escape the burdens of taxation]. A wise counsellor said to him, 'They will not go, and if they do they'll come back. And should you wish to test [this, my statement], take some deer and send them away to a far-off land, and in the end they will return to their place.' He [Diocletian] did this. He brought deer and coated their horns with silver and sent them off to Africa, and at the end of 30 years they returned to their place.[64]

Although Diocletian apparently had his differences with the Jewish community, there is no reason to think that this excessive taxation was directed exclusively or even primarily toward them. In fact, the emperor attempted to impose very heavy taxes on a number of Palestinian communities, some of which presented him with petitions that threatened abandonment of those towns by the whole population.[65] The situation is one in which small landowners are put under severe pressures by a system of high taxation. That a crisis of considerable proportions was created by this policy in Banias tells us something of the economic structure of the town, and indicates the presence of large numbers of small landowners, or what might today be thought of as 'middle-class' citizens.[66] Archaeological evidence of this situation is seen in the discovery of a number of boundary stones in the Banias area. These had apparently been erected to mark the territories of the villages as a part of Diocletian's campaign to survey and register lands and property for purposes of taxation. Many such stones are known, six of them naming a certain Aelius Statutus as 'διασημότατος' (provincial governor).[67] Since Banias belonged to the Province of Syro-Phoenicia, Aelius Statutus seems to have been governor of that province during the time when the policy was instituted.[68] Several of the inscriptions are dated precisely to the year when the survey was made, that is 297 AD. That they are found only in the Golan Heights, and not in Galilee proper or Judaea, suggests that the citizens of the territory of Banias received 'special treatment' in the form of especially oppressive taxation under Diocletian.[69] Whether they had done something that caused the emperor to react in this way we cannot know, though the rabbinic tradition had its own interpretation of his reasons, as the fanciful story recounted above indicates.

LIFE IN ROMAN BANIAS

Before continuing in a chronological treatment, it will be helpful now to synthesise what can be known of Roman Banias[70] as a city – its topography, city plan, and infrastructure, its economy and the nature of its population. Although archaeological work on the site is still only in its initial stages, and the literary evidence is sketchy to say the least, we are nevertheless able to know a good deal about the nature of the city and the life of its inhabitants during the second and third centuries.

It is important to remember that while we may describe Banias as 'Greco-Roman', far greater stress must be placed on the second element in this designation than the first. The Hellenism we see here is a Hellenism tightly sandwiched between the old Phoenician and Syrian cultures that preceded it, and the heavy and pervasive overlay of Imperial Rome. The civic institutions, architecture, cultural and religious life of Banias reflect the Roman way of being 'Greek'. The city had little or no 'history' during Hellenistic times. It was essentially a Roman foundation. At the same time, most of the citizens of the city, whether old stock or recent immigrants, were neither Roman nor Greek. It is true that many of those citizens mentioned on votive inscriptions at the sanctuary of Pan or elsewhere had Greek or Roman names. But quite often they also had relatives, particularly parents, with Semitic names, indicating families in cultural transition.[71] A relatively large number of inscriptions appear in Latin, something usually seen in the East only in Roman colonies. Isaac suggests that this probably indicates the presence of 'men from the region, who also served in the Roman army and had undergone a measure of Latinization'. It is possible that some army veterans from elsewhere, or who were serving in Syria or Palestine at the time of their discharge, retired to Banias following their term of service as well, having enjoyed the beauties of the locality during one of several periods when armies were camped in the area. Most were likely, however, to have been Itureans recruited from the area to serve in auxiliary units of the military. Thus, the Latinisation is not very deep, and results from the somewhat superficial transfer of cultural elements among and between soldiers.[72] The continuing presence of a strong Iturean element in the population is also indicated by the existence of a major Iturean cult site no more than 4 kilometres north of Banias at Senaim on Mount Hermon. This sanctuary has rock-cut worship niches reminiscent of those at Banias itself, as well as a temenos, a temple and a number of inscriptions. The inscriptions seem to date mostly from the second century and are thus contemporary with the development of the romanised Pan cult under the Antonines. Here the local population could continue to practise their ancient religious rites without having to cope with the Greco-Roman 'innovations' at Banias – if they wished to do so.[73]

The Pan sanctuary has been characterised as 'highly Hellenized' and the pantheon worshiped there as of 'entirely Hellenistic, as opposed to Semitic or mixed character'.[74] The deities represented by the fragments of sculpture found at the site 'were not read by their patrons and viewers as Semitic deities dressed in Hellenistic iconography and style'.[75] And thus, 'the Sanctuary of Pan seems to have been a centre of Hellenistic pagan worship situated within the Semitic Levant'.[76] But such conclusions can be accepted only in the context of the definition of 'Hellenistic' noted above, and even then in a limited sort of way. The cult of Pan at Banias during this period, discussed at length below, insofar as it was a cult of the people, was essentially a Roman cult being practised by a mostly Semitic population.

The local aristocracy of the second and third centuries was not likely to have had Seleucid origins, but rather to have consisted of 'friends' of the Herodian dynasty and then of the Roman Imperial bureaucracy. Most often these were probably of local ancestry as well. Two extant inscriptions refer to the city's ruling class. Both imply the existence of forms of local government common in the period in provincial cities, namely a 'council' made of up local persons of wealth, headed by a chief magistrate or mayor. These not only administered day-to-day affairs, but also were themselves financially responsible for maintaining the municipal infrastructure.[77] We have already referred to the early third-century inscription on the red-rock cliff[78] that identifies the archon or chief magistrate of Banias at that time as 'Agrippas, son of Markos'. Additionally, three members of the town council are listed: Agrippinos, Markos and Agrippas. These are all obviously members of the same family and their names suggest that the local ruling class maintained its loyalty to the Herodian family. The same phenomenon may be observed in another, earlier inscription[79] in which the town council commemorates the erection of statues honouring a father, Philippos son of Antipatros, and his son, Antipatros (Fig. 28). The father is particularly commended for having served as Gymnasiarch and priest 'by his own will'. This means that he bore the considerable expenses connected with the municipal religious rites, including games. His contribution is noteworthy because, unlike so many contemporary cases, he did this without being forced to do so.[80] It cannot be coincidence that the names that have survived of local aristocrats in Banias are without exception Herodian family names: Antipater, Philip, Agrippa and Mark. This suggests that the 'friends' of Herod and his descendants remained at the top of the social and political system throughout the Roman period, long after the kingdom was dismantled.[81]

We must also take into account the presence of another strongly Semitic influence in the cultural life of the city: the Jewish community. After all, this was a community that had enjoyed the patronage of the Herodian family, refused to join in the Bar Kochba Revolt,[82] and that had enjoyed relatively close ties with the Antonine and Severan Dynasties.[83] Thus, while Banias must be thought of as both Hellenistic and Roman in many significant ways, particularly at the highest levels of society, it was nevertheless primarily a city of Itureans, Syro-Phoenicians and Jews.

THE CITY PLAN (FIGS 1, 2)

Archaeological and survey work at Banias reveals the extent to which topography determined the city's development. The traditional Roman style of city centre was in this case severely restricted. The rapidly flowing mountain streams that cut deep ravines on two sides (south and west), and the sheer cliff that stretched across its northern side, left only the eastern approach on more or less level ground. But even there the terrain worked against urban expansion. There was simply no room in the centre of the city for a residential population. Rather, one found at the centre two public complexes, each with its own distinctive character. The 'Sacred District' with its host of temples, chapels and altars stretched across the north along the base of the cliff. This district was apparently bounded on the south by a 'sacred pool' that momentarily captured the cold waters gushing up from the spring before the cave of Pan. Here, lining the base of the red-rock cliff to the east of the cave stood the sanctuary of Pan, the 'Temple of Zeus', chapels to the Lady Nemesis and the Nymph Maia, the so-called 'Tripartite Building' and probably other similar religious installations as well. South of the lake, the other structures in the city centre, all in one way or another public buildings, were organised along a typical Roman street grid, insofar as the terrain would allow. The Cardo Maximus, which has been discovered and partly excavated, reveals a flair for the dramatic on the part of the city planners (Fig. 26). The paved and colonnaded street began at the point where one entered the city centre by means of a bridge on the south across the Wâdî Sa'âr. The paving stones were made of fine-cut black basalt, providing a dramatic contrast to the white columns lining either side of the street.[84] Proceeding across the bridge and entering the city, the visitor's eye was directed along majestic rows of columns towards the cave of Pan at the other end of the street. On the left loomed the high walls of the royal palace (transformed into a magnificent public bath in the second century), which stretched from the Cardo to the high banks of the river on the west. This much can be known. The identification of other structures within the centre awaits further excavation. Still to be discovered are the amphitheatre, which must have existed to host the 'Panian Games', a formal *agora* (marketplace) where trade could take place, and the Augusteum[85] itself (unless it was located elsewhere in the area such as at Omrit).

The second major street in the Roman system of town-planning, the Decumanus, crossed the Cardo Maximus at right angles, and the crossing point was often a central feature of the town centre. Approaching Banias from the west, the visitor first encountered a bridge across the Nahal Hermon.[86] Crossing, one found oneself alongside the northern wall of the royal palace, and then at the crossroads with the Cardo Maximus. Since this was also the main thoroughfare of the Tyre–Damascus highway, the flow of traffic most likely turned south onto the Cardo Maximus and from thence left the city across the Wâdî Sa'âr bridge.[87] Thus far no signs of the extension of the Decumanus to the east have been found.[88]

The impression that the city centre left on travellers must have been immensely dramatic. Ma'oz has plausibly suggested that the waters from the spring were first gathered in a large artificial pool created by restraining the waters on the natural terraces.[89] The circular colonnade depicted on several coins of Banias may in fact have surrounded this pool, providing a dramatic backdrop for the view of the sanctuary from the city centre.[90] This pool, as we have suggested, would also have served to divide the religious district from the administrative buildings to the south. The Beth Ussishkin Museum, Kibbutz Dan, has an inscribed limestone block designating the boundary between lands belonging to the sanctuary of Pan and those belonging to the city, probably dating to the time of

Diocletian. Unfortunately, the original find spot for this stone is unknown, so it is not possible to know precisely where the boundary was located.[91] Leaving the pool, the river itself was further domesticated within the city centre by means of massive ashlar walls that continued for some 180 metres from the 'sacred pool' to the place where the water pours into a deep canyon south of the centre. This artificial channel was 4.6–6.3 metres wide.[92] Elaborate underground water channels with connecting pipe systems, some of which have been found,[93] and some of which still carry water, fanned out from the spring and pool in all directions, delivering water to the buildings, pools, and fountains of the city and depositing the residue into the canyons. The roar of the river, and the splashing sounds of the fountains and water channels would have created an overwhelming impression of grandeur – one which undoubtedly equalled the wonder of the gleaming temples, innumerable statues and ornately decorated and columned public buildings on all sides.

We cannot yet know where the city's primary *agora* is located, though it is very probable that it was within the city centre, east and south of the intersection of the Cardo Maximus and the Decumanus. The city's strategic location along the Tyre–Damascus highway, and its position as a crossroads for north–south routes as well, meant that goods from east and west passed through the city. Indeed, the road system required that goods pass through, since the highway carried traffic directly into the city centre. In addition to goods brought in from far away, locally made pottery[94] and produce would have been found for sale. The economy of the district of Banias depended heavily on agriculture. Blessed with abundant water and an excellent climate, crops like wheat were suited to the area, and a distinctive red-coloured rice grew well in the Huleh Valley.[95] Sheep and goats thrived on the grasses of the Golan, and the fields and mountainsides produced walnuts, sesame seeds and 'early-ripening Damascene plums'.[96]

Evidence of the existence of supervised markets comes to us in the form of two inscribed weights that were found in the western part of the site in 1988. The first of these reads 'A Third of a Local Libra' and carries the name 'Marinou', a Semitic name. The object is similar in weight to the 'light mina' used in other Syrian cities of the time (550–600 grams). The other weight has a palm branch with X-shaped characters on the sides and two letters on the back 'L H' (probably signifying 'Unit of Weight 8').[97]

THE VILLAS

Roman Banias had significant upper- and upper-middle classes, some of whose members were landowners, some businessmen, and some civil servants. (Banias had been, after all, first a royal capital, then a district administrative centre.) Ground surveys of the areas around the city centre show that on the east, west and south there stood numerous fine villas decorated with marble-coloured plaster walls, and mosaic floors in black and white patterns.[98] Particularly to the west, as one approached the city centre, one would have encountered elaborate villas along the approach road. Remains of these are clearly visible even today. To the south, across Wâdî Sa'âr, the residential district had its own wall in late

Roman/Byzantine times. Residences did not exist to the north of the centre, where neither topography nor the sacred nature of the area would permit such use.

Ironically, despite the abundant waters of the spring, the owners of these villas were forced to go to tremendous expense to have an adequate water supply. This is because most of these aristocratic neighbourhoods stood on land higher in elevation than the spring. To the east, the problem could be partially solved by means of a large stone-lined cistern.[99] But to the west more elaborate measures were taken. A long aqueduct brought water from distant springs up on Hermon, running along the high ground to the north of the city on top of the ridge above the red-rock cliff. Hartal excavated much of this interesting system in 1992–94.[100] The water was carried through a covered channel past various industrial areas, pottery kilns etc., and even through a cemetery before reaching the city proper. Along it Hartal found five settling pools and seventeen distribution pools. The latter were connected to the channel by perforations or by means of ceramic pipe. Conical lead pipes then controlled the amount of water allotted to each villa, and ceramic pipe carried the water to individual users. Filters were installed at the mouth of the pipes to keep dirt and debris from entering. Thus, Banias had a 'public utility' designed so that individual citizens could be charged on the basis of use. The distribution pools and lead pipes functioned as 'meters', not unlike modern systems. There seem to have been ancient cheaters as well. Hartal found a pipeline that had been connected directly to the aqueduct, bypassing the metring system and providing someone with a free, and presumably illegal water supply![101]

Beyond these elegant neighbourhoods were the fertile fields and orchards, some belonging to the wealthy families who inhabited the villas, but many no doubt belonging to the small landholders who populated the many villages that formed the economic network of the district. These villages were where much of the population of 'greater Banias' lived, rather than in the city itself. This is no doubt the reason why large residential neighbourhoods of workers, craftsmen and peasants are lacking near the administrative and religious centre. It is significant that the visit of Jesus and his disciples to this area is described by the Gospel of Matthew as to the 'district of Caesarea Philippi' (16:13), and by the Gospel of Mark as specifically 'to the villages of Caesarea Philippi' (8:27).[102]

All in all, the prosperity of the region seems to be have been rather widely distributed among the citizens. As the larger economy of the empire deteriorated, this pocket of prosperity became a target for oppressive taxation. This situation is reflected in the *Jerusalem Talmud*,[103] which says that the emperor Diocletian so oppressed the inhabitants of Paneas that they threatened to leave the district.[104] This oppressive taxation fell particularly hard on the upper classes, leading, as noted above, to this interpretation of Numbers 11:5 in the *Midrash Rabbah*: 'The Lord bless thee with wealth and guard thee that thou not be compelled to take office in the province of Paneas and that no fine be imposed upon the district as a result of which they should say to you: "Give gold!"'[105] The result of this harsh policy was that Banias eventually fell victim to the general economic malaise of the last part of the third century.

THE NECROPOLIS

Ancient cities were typically surrounded by extensive cemeteries and the roads that led into them were lined with monumental tombs.[106] Several cemeteries exist along a line to the north and east of the city centre of Banias. Since burials did not take place inside Roman cities these cemeteries identify the northern boundaries of the city.[107] Over one hundred tombs may be seen here, cut into the rocks of the slopes above the red-rock cliff. In one case, Hartal found a funerary enclosure with seven burial shafts, constructed in Phoenician style. These had been used from the first through to the fourth centuries. All of these tombs had been robbed in antiquity.[108] The finest of the tombs seem to have been associated with the main road that entered Banias from the west. Elaborate burial caves have been discovered on lands controlled by the modern Israeli settlement, Snir, often during construction work associated with the life of the settlement.[109]

The most interesting discovery thus far in the ancient necropolis of Banias is a monumental burial complex within what now serves as a small zoo at Snir. Ma'oz, the excavator, describes it thus:

> Two successive rectangular courts, sunk deep in the rock, lead to a front porch, placed on the same axis. At the far corner of the porch floor, a narrow trench, originally blocked by a golal (rolling stone), descends into the first room. This large room is surrounded on all sides by loculi, and the floor is covered with ashlars that once blocked their entrances. From the bottom of a corner loculus a cone-hidden passage led to the lowermost, secluded room. The walls of this room are lined with arcosolia; in the centre of the room are a few decorated limestone sarcophagi. The burials and sarcophagi were all broken into in antiquity.[110]

No artifacts were found in the tomb that could assist in dating it. The excavator thought that the design and grandeur of the structure was highly reminiscent of first-century monumental tombs in Jerusalem such as the 'Tombs of the Kings'. An early date makes it tempting to associate this structure with the Herodian family, or at least with the aristocracy of Herodian Banias. But the style may also be dated to the Roman period, and thus definite conclusions must await further excavation in this part of the necropolis.

The only inscription found thus far in the Banias necropolis dates to the late Roman period (third/fourth centuries), but must be representative of the many that identified the deceased citizens of Banias. The sentiment is also typical of the unrequited sorrow so common on pagan epithets of the time:

> I am Markellinos
> whom Fate quickly took away along the road to Hades,
> lying under this stone.
> Ioulianos, son of Melas buried me,
> Unfortunate one,
> at the age of sixty years and twenty-five days.[111]

4 Religion in Roman Banias: Paganism

PAGAN BANIAS

Sometime at the beginning of the second century Heliodorus left his hometown of Banias to make a pilgrimage to the holy sites of Egypt. When he visited the solar cult at the Colossus of Memnon[1] he added a *graffito* to the numerous others incised on the leg of the great monument. 'I, Heliodorus, son of Zenon, of Caesarea Paneas,' he wrote, 'have visited here four times, remembering my brothers Zenon and Aianus.' Travelling on to Philae, to the temple of Isis, he scratched another message: 'I, Heliodorus, son of Zenon, of Caesarea Paneas, have come and performed an act of worship on behalf of my brothers Zenon and Aianus'.[2] Heliodorus was obviously a man of great piety, willing to go to great trouble to practise his religion. He lived in a time when paganism was seeking desperately to define itself in terms consistent with the social and philosophical realities of the vast multi-ethnic, multi-cultural Roman Empire. The names of his own family members illustrate the complexity of the situation in his own town of Banias. Alongside the very Greek name of his father and brother (Zenon), we find 'Aianus' – a Semitic name reminiscent of the Arabic 'Hayyan' ('the living one').[3] The religion of Heliodorus and his family straddled two worlds at the very least – the Hellenistic one, which had come to Banias by means of social and military conquest, and the old Semitic one, which had persisted through every change.

Even more instructive is the *graffito* left on the external temple wall at the Memnonion of Abydos in Egypt by another citizen of Banias, the priest Harpocras: 'I have slept here many times and I have seen dreams full of truth. I am Harpocras, citizen of Holy Paniados and priest, dear son of the priest Coprias. To Bes, the great god of prophetic oracles, the All Knowing!'[4]

Harpocras may have lived a century or more later than Heliodorus, but represents the same kind of popular paganism that dominated the culture of the city from which they came.[5] His choice of words is particularly helpful in throwing some light on his hometown, which he calls 'ζάθεος'. When applied to a city this title signifies a place 'rich in divinities' or 'inhabited by many gods'. That is it is a city possessing many sanctuaries and cults.[6] The reference brings to mind the row of sanctuaries at the foot of the red-rock cliff of Banias, and perhaps many others in the immediate area as well. Harpocras's designation asserts that Banias is not simply a pagan town; it is a pagan centre. This fact is also attested by the official name of the city abbreviated on its coins from the second century onward: 'ΚΑΙ CEB IEP ΚΑΙ ACYΛ T Π ΠΑΝΕΙW' ('Caesarea Sebaste, Holy City of Refuge, before the Panion'). Presumably, Harpocras served as priest at one of the Panian sanctuaries. His choice of words suggests that he is a man of letters – and a thorough Hellenist: the epitaph he chooses for his town (ζάθεος) and the word he uses in connection with his father (ἀρητήρ) both come directly from the opening lines of the *Iliad*.[7]

THE CULT OF PAN

Though pagan Banias boasted many temples and altars and worshipped a wide pantheon of deities, pride of place belonged to the god Pan. But this cult, along with the conception of the god himself, underwent significant development and change throughout the period of pagan supremacy in the city. The Hellenistic invaders had brought along a well-developed concept of the goat-god and his cult when they entered Palestine and Syria. We have suggested that, already in the days when the Ptolemaic kings of Egypt dominated the area, the spiritual force that inhabited the cave, the springs and the forests had been identified as Pan. But the cult of Pan was already ancient when it was introduced to this particular spot. Its origins were in Arcadia, from where it had spread to Athens, following the Battle of Marathon, then to northern Greece, and from there into Asia Minor and the East.[8] Despite its widespread popularity, the cult could best be described as belonging to 'folk religion'. It did not, in the words of Farnell, 'touch the higher life of the society or the higher religion of the state'. As for Pan, 'the rusticity of the wild Arcadian clung to him, his sacred haunt was the cave or the mountain-grove, and his associates the nymphs and other pasture-gods'.[9]

We have very little direct evidence of how the cult was practised in Banias in Roman times, but may safely assume that it had much in common with its Arcadian and Athenian antecedents. We know that on Mount Lykaios Pan was said to have presided, along with Zeus, over the great Arcadian games. Victories were at least partially dated by the name of his priest. We might therefore expect games in Banias as well. Pan-worship was apparently orgiastic in some aspects, bearing characteristics common to fertility rites. Thus, the herdsmen of Arcadia danced ritual dances in the spring, summoning the earth-goddess to awaken. For these rites they dressed in goatskins and worshiped the phallus as the symbol of replenishing life.[10] This rustic and lusty Pan found his place in an urban setting when he revealed himself to the Athenians as their divine helper in their crucial victory at Marathon. Thus, he became identified with wars and soldiering as well as nature and the powers of fertility. In gratitude for his services, Herodotus notes that the Athenians 'set up a temple to Pan under the Acropolis and … established in his honour yearly sacrifices and a torch race'. The cave of Pan on the Acropolis, mentioned by Pausanias, appears on coins minted in the Antonine period in Athens.[11] The cave was rediscovered in 1896–97 and is clearly visible today, complete with a rock-cut relief of Pan (Fig. 21).[12] Around it are niches cut in the cliff face as receptacles for votive offerings. A number of these offerings have been found and may be seen today in the National Museum at Athens. They typically depict Pan, the nymphs and other deities associated with Pan, including Zeus – and often the donor of the offering as well.[13] One of the niches contained the cult statue of Pan himself. All this finds a striking parallel at Banias.

The cult was exported to Rome as well, and it is to Roman writers, particularly Dionysius of Halicarnassus and Ovid, that we owe the most vivid pictures of the worship of Pan in its heyday. Dionysius claims that the cult existed at the site of Rome before the founding of the city, being practised by Greek settlers at a cave on the Palatine later called the Lupercal by the Romans.[14] The observance took place 'in the month of February, after the winter solstice'.[15] Calling the rites (anachronistically) the 'Lupercalia', he describes them as follows:

> The youths were going to celebrate in honour of Pan the Lupercalia, the Arcadian festival as instituted by Evander...the moment in the celebration when the youths living near the Palatine...after offering sacrifice...proceed from the Lupercal and run round the village naked, their loins girt with the skins of the victims just sacrificed. This ceremony signified a sort of traditional purification of the villagers, and is still performed even to this day.[16]

Ovid (43 BC–17/18 AD) provides a long passage on Pan (identified with Faunus, and tied in Roman thought to the founding of Rome) and the rites connected with his cult. He notes that

> The third morn after the Ides beholds the naked Luperci, and then, too, come the rites of two-horned Faunus...The Arcadians of old are said to have worshiped Pan...Evander brought with him across the sea his woodland deities; where now the city [Rome] stands, there was then naught but the city's site. Hence we worship the god, and the Flamen Dialis still performs in the olden way the rites brought hither by the Pelasgians [Arcadians]. You ask, Why then do the Luperci run? and why do they strip themselves and bear their bodies naked, for so it is their wont to run? The god himself loves to scamper, fleet of foot, about the high mountains, and he himself takes suddenly to flight. The god himself is nude and bids his ministers go nude.[17]

These young men were called 'creppi', an old form of the word *capri* ('he goats'). They ran a course around the city, striking everyone they met with strips made from the skins of the freshly sacrificed goats. They especially sought out women, who willingly held out their hands and allowed themselves to be whipped with the strips, believing that this would help ensure that they would have babies and that these would be delivered with ease. Held in February, these rites were essentially a ritual of purification to purge the community of the evils of barrenness and disease and ensure the fertility of the ground, the flocks and the women. They bear an amazing resemblance to the fertility rights of the ancient Phoenician/Canaanite population of Syria and provide further evidence as to why the transition from the worship of the ancient Ba'als of Canaan led quite comfortably to the worship of Pan.[18]

THE CULT AT BANIAS

Often, even on the votive plaques found near his cultic centres in Greece, Pan is a kind of bystander. He lurks somewhere to the side of the action, a quiet presence – playing his pipes and watching as the nymphs, Hermes, Zeus, or some other deity takes centre-stage. At Banias, however, the sanctuary is his; he is its *raison d'être*, and the other deities come here to join him. Also, it is important to remember that during its best-known period the cult as practised at Banias was essentially a Roman version of the Greek cult and seems to have been encouraged and supported by the imperial household itself. Thus, while the cult at Banias had its origins in folk religion, it was gradually transformed into an official religion of some social consequence. This development involved at least four stages. First, there were the simple beginnings, in which the Hellenistic mythology simply overlaid a traditional Semitic site, fitting comfortably into its role as a celebration of nature, fertility, purification and healing. This stage lasted until at least the end of the Herodian period. Next, during the second century, a Greco-Roman cult of some sophistication replaced the rustic Pan, introducing its own universalising, syncretistic theology. Then, in the waning days of paganism, the cult was revived spectacularly but briefly under the dynasties of Syrian origin that ruled the empire during the early third century. Finally, as paganism itself was deprived of its public place and its governmental support in the fourth and succeeding centuries, the cult went underground, along with many other aspects of the 'old religion', reappearing only in various disguises. This process continues to the present day.

This scenario, synthesised from a study of the inscriptions, coins, literary references and general historical context, is now confirmed in a rather remarkable way by the ceramic studies conducted at the cult site during recent excavations. For example, the excavators found many small fragments of cooking and table vessels dating from the first simple phase of development (the Hellenistic period: the third to the mid-first centuries BC). These they identified as debris left by informal worshippers who stopped by the rural shrine before any buildings stood there to make food offerings and ritualistically dine with the god.[19] The establishment of the Emperor Cult at Banias by Herod the Great, and the consequent development of the city of Caesarea Philippi, meant that the cult was of necessity urbanised. Some limited ornamentation seems to have been added near the cave during Herodian times (the so-called 'Court of Pan and the Nymphs'). The debris from this period contains many more lamp fragments (signs of an increase in their use as votive offerings), and has its origins from a wider area, including some imported ware. The presence of many Roman cooking vessels indicates that the ritual meals continued. All in all, however, the cult remained simple and rather uncomplicated.[20]

The cult received its first official recognition on record when King Agrippa II issued a coin featuring the likeness of Pan, already mentioned above (Fig. 15). The coin is thought to be dated 88 AD and bears on its obverse the facing busts of Titus and Domitian.[21] Pan is shown in full figure, nude, walking toward the left, playing his syrinx and holding the characteristic *lagobolon* ('rabbit thumper') over his shoulder. To the right is a tree trunk.[22] The image on the coin seems to be based on the relief cut in the rock above the cave of

Pan in Athens, providing a further indication of the connection between the cult of Pan at Banias and the ancient Greek traditions upon which it was based.[23] Meshorer has suggested that this coin, which flaunts the rabbinic rules in regard to pagan iconography and can only be interpreted from a rabbinic point of view as idolatrous, commemorates the gift of a cult statue of the god by the king himself.[24] We have no specific literary or inscriptional reference to the worship of Pan at the site previous to the issuance of this coin.[25] Josephus calls the place the Paneion but never mentions the cult. This coin may in fact depict the first cult statue of Pan to stand at the site, which was, as we shall see, eventually replaced by a quite different one.

With the passing of the Herodian dynasty and the imposition of direct Roman rule, Banias and its well-known pagan religious establishment underwent great growth, apparently at least partially under imperial patronage. The second century and the first quarter of the third century were to be the Golden Age of paganism in the city.[26] After the death of Agrippa II, perhaps during the reign of Trajan (98–117 AD), construction began near the cave of a temple dedicated to Zeus. The primary evidence for this is an inscription on a marble plaque that apparently came from the altar it mentions, and found in the ruins of the building that stood next to the so-called 'Court of Pan and the Nymphs'. Isaac's translation of the inscription reads: 'To Heliopolitan Zeus and to the god Pan who brings victory, for the salvation of our lord Trajan Caesar, with his entire house, Maronas, son of Publius Aristo has dedicated this holy altar'.[27] It is true that the dedicatory inscription on the altar of this edifice indicates that the benefactor was a private citizen, Maronas son of Publius Aristo. But the municipal and governmental implications of this donation can be seen in the fact that it was offered to the emperor, and that Pan was given the epitaph 'νεικηφόρωι' ('he who brings victory').

At the same time, pagan 'theology' was undergoing significant change and development. Stoic influences, and the process of syncretism, which sought to simplify and combine the identities of the myriad of deities worshiped throughout the empire, were gradually moving both the popular and official forms of religion in the direction of a sort of 'pagan monotheism'. This development was encouraged by the Emperor Marcus Aurelius (161–80 AD), who was himself a Stoic philosopher.[28] In fact, it was during his reign that pagan religious life in Banias apparently took a huge step forward. Pan, whose name means 'All', became a good candidate for development in such a universalising environment. The fact that the cave of Pan on the Athenian Acropolis began to appear on that city's coins during the reign of the Antonines suggests that the little goat-god was moving to the theological forefront in that city as well.[29]

The most striking evidence that the concept of Pan was being transformed during this period is the appearance of a new cult statue on the coins minted in Banias (Fig. 23). This image appeared first in 169 AD and continued until the mint closed in the third century. It appeared over and over in a variety of settings and was the most characteristic numismatic theme of the city.[30] The treatment of Pan here is not only totally different from the usual ugly little creature of classical Greek art, and a number of examples found elsewhere in Palestine,[31] but is greatly more 'civilised' than the image on the coin of Agrippa II mentioned earlier. The new statue is based on a classical work by Lysippos, made for Athens but widely copied in Hellenistic times.[32] Examples of this statue may be seen today in both the Louvre and the Vatican museums (Fig. 27).[33] By identifying this statue with Pan, the god is bestowed with the very essence of classical Greek beauty. He stands, his legs slightly crossed, leaning rather casually on the trunk of a tree, playing not a syrinx but a single reed flute, flared out at the end. He is nude, though there is an animal skin either draped around his neck and right shoulder or hanging on the tree beside him. He is no longer half-man, half-goat (though a goat may be seen listening to his music, somewhere in the background or at his feet – nothing more now than an 'attribute' or symbol of his identity). He brings to mind the young men who ran about naked during the Pan Festival each February. The Banias Pan thus abandons a long tradition of depicting Pan as an ugly, bestial creature.[34]

The memory of the dedication of this statue has survived in the *Historia Ecclesiastica* of Philostorgius, the fifth-century Arian Christian historian. 'The district of Paneas was formerly called Dan,' he says (a prevalent Byzantine theory). 'But in the course of time it came to be called Caesarea Philippi, and later still, when the heathen erected in it a statue of the god Pan, its name was changed to Paneas.'[35] Banias was known by a variety of names throughout its history, and sorting out a consistent chronology of the various name changes is a complex process. There is no question that the city was called Caesarea Paneas in the second and third centuries AD. Numerous citations – literary, numismatic and inscriptional – confirm this fact. Furthermore, several ancient writers, perhaps beginning with Porphyry (232 AD–*ca.* 300 AD) speak of 'the city now called Paneas', as though this is not its original name.[36] The earliest reference to the city as Paneas is in Ptolemy's *Geography*, a work dating very close to the time when the new statue of Pan was erected.[37] Pliny's statement that the 'Spring of Panias' gives Caesarea its 'second name' should be understood in the same way.[38] Elsewhere, he clearly distinguishes between the city, which he calls Caesarea, and the district, which he calls Panias.[39] Eventually the name was shortened from Caesarea Paneas to simply Paneas, and in fact it may be possible to date references at least roughly on the basis of which name is used. The combination 'Caesarea Paneas' occurs primarily in the second and third centuries. This is also the designation used on the Peutinger Map and the name Caesarea (or actually 'Little Caesarea' – to distinguish it from Caesarea Maritima) appears frequently in rabbinic references. These facts may be relevant in dating the sources of these documents.

Within the decade or two prior to the issuance of a series of coins featuring the key deities in the Banias Pantheon (Pan, Zeus and Tyche), two niches were cut into the red rock face near the large artificial niche east of the natural cave. These niches were designed to contain statues, and the dedicatory inscriptions for both have survived. Both were donated by the same individual, a certain Victor, son of Lysimachos.[40] Both expand the Pan circle by referring to specific deities connected to him in the tradition. The first inscription reads:

> For Pan and the Nymphs,
> Victor, son of Lysimachos, dedicated here a likeness in stone of Hermes,
> child of Maia,[41] son of Zeus,
> having made a vow, together with his children, Year 150.[42]

Hermes, identified here as the son of Maia and Zeus, often appears prominently in the votive plaques found in Pan caves in Greece, as do the nymphs. He is in fact Pan's father, according to some traditions, and, like Pan, is both a protector of shepherds and their flocks and a god of fertility. A second inscription, located beneath a niche directly over the artificial cave, says that this same Victor 'dedicated this goddess to the god Pan, lover of Echo' (Fig. 29).[43] Echo, of course, is closely associated with Pan in Greek mythology. This inscription may be considered contemporary with the dated inscription above. The niche must have contained a statue of Echo.[44]

In addition to these inscriptions, fragments of broken statues found in the debris of the various installations at the sanctuary point to an increasing patronage by the ruling classes of the city during the second century. These include renderings of Nemesis, Asclepios, Hermes, Artemis, Apollo and several others. Andrea Berlin, who has analysed the ceramic remains recovered from the sanctuary area, notes that precisely at the time when much labour and money was being expended to expand and enrich the cult, there is a surprising lack of the kind of ceramic material that indicates private worship. She attributes this to the fact that in the face of strong official sponsorship of the cult, the practice of private, small-scale devotion simply disappeared. The cult had been, as it were, 'captured' by the establishment and moved from the realm of popular adherence to state-sponsorship.[45]

This trend reached its climax during the time of the so-called 'Syrian Emperors' of the late second and early third centuries. We have already noted the appearance of many new coin types, which coincide with the visit of Septimius Severus, the founder of this dynasty, at the turn of the third century, and those which attest to the special nature of the year 220/21 AD. During this quarter century, several structures were built or rebuilt at the Pan sanctuary, most notably the circular colonnade that encircles the depiction of the cult statue of the god on several coins issued at this time (Fig. 25).[46] The cult statue is also shown in what appears to be a niche above an artificial cave, the latter clearly blocked with an iron grille. In some instances the artificial cave itself seems to contain a group of goats.[47]

The cult statue is seen in two other contexts on the coins of this period. In one, Pan stands between what appear to be two rough columns (tree trunks?).[48] In the other, he stands between two decorated objects (standards? flags? trees?) that are shown in some detail.[49] We have already noted the appearance of the female members of the family of Elagabalus (Julia Soaemus, Julia Maesa, Aquilia Severa and Annia Faustina) on coins dated 220 AD, and particularly on coins depicting Pan between the 'standards'.[50] In addition to the numismatic evidence, three inscriptions have survived from the same period that imply significant religious activity on the part of the local aristocracy, including the chief magistrate of the city and certain members of the town council.[51] We are led to conclude that in this year a great festival was held in honour of Pan, under imperial sponsorship (but with significant financial contributions by local leaders). Given the presence of Elagabalus's two wives on these coins, and Pan's connections with fertility, we have suggested that the festival had as its aim the conception of an heir to the imperial throne. The time may have been theologically ripe for such an event, particularly in view of a growing threat from Christianity, since Pan had become a cipher for the 'universal god' among pagan intellectuals. Ceramic evidence points to the conclusion that the imperial attention brought to the sanctuary at this time also caught the popular imagination, in stark contrast to the situation during the Antonine Period. Thousands of miniature saucer-lamps and lamp fragments were found at the site, dating from the third century (Fig. 5). Most of these were unused and seem to have been made locally, expressly for the shrine. This indicates, according to Berlin, that they were 'ceremonial rather than functional' and that most of the worshippers were from the immediate area of Banias. The nature and quantity of the offerings suggest a dramatic increase in the number of individual wor-shippers who came to the shrine and left a small lamp as a votive gift, and point to a sanctuary 'far more heavily visited at this time than at any other in its history'.[52]

THE PANIAN GAMES

As we have noted, in its Arcadian, Athenian and Roman forms the cult of Pan was connected with athletic competition, particularly foot-racing. Pan presided along with Zeus over the great Arcadian games on Mount Lykaios.[53] In Athens a torch race was held in his honour. The race began at an altar (perhaps the altar of Prometheus in the Academeia) and ended at the Pan grotto on the north face of the Acropolis. This event may have commemorated the run of Pheidippides (the original 'marathon'), during which he was confronted by Pan.[54] In Rome young men representing the god ran a circuit around the city, says Ovid, because 'the god himself loves to scamper, fleet of foot, about the high mountains, and he himself takes suddenly to flight'.[55] Since the rites connected with Pan took place in February, we may safely presume that this athletic competition took place at the same time.

Evidence of formal games at Banias exists from at least the second century. The 'Panian games' may have originated with the visit of Titus after the First Jewish Revolt, when thousands of Jewish captives were executed during the celebration of the birthday of Domitian.[56] However, that particular spectacle had its own purposes and was not strictly speaking a repeatable event. The presence of a shrine to Nemesis, who was particularly associated with the more violent kinds of contests, might suggest that such activities continued to be presented in Banias. However, the evidence for the nature of the Panian games of the second and third centuries suggests that they resembled the more traditional Greek games, emphasising prowess and skill rather than the blood and violence of the Roman arena. Nemesis's presence near the Pan sanctuary probably spoke more of her duties as the guardian of municipal bodies and her role as dispenser of justice and advocate of morality and decency than of the specific nature of the games. In any case, the available evidence seems most compatible with the conclusion that the Panian games (as distinguished from other more violent spectacles which may have taken place in the city) were primarily associated with a religious observance, as were most of the traditional 'games' of the Greco-Roman world.

Three inscriptions, all found far away from Banias, provide attestation to the games held there. The first comes from Aphrodisias in Caria and dates from the early second century.[57] In it are listed victories in a series of games by an athlete named M. Ailion Aurelion Menandros. These include events at Damascus, Berytus, Tyre, Caesarea Stratonis (Maritima), Neapolis, Scythopolis, Gaza and 'Caesarea Paniados'. Moretti, who dates the inscription 143 and 165 AD, thinks the games had been held in Banias since Herodian times and were connected with the emperor cult.[58] It is more likely, however, that they were held as a part of the renewed emphasis on the cult of Pan that occurred in the second century, beginning with Trajan and continuing under the Antonines. They were thus an extension of the somewhat rustic foot-races and other rites connected with the spring Pan festival that had been celebrated in Banias for generations. This conclusion is strengthened by evidence from other inscriptions. One of these was found at Didymas and honours a child athlete named Aurelius Philadelphos (who had begun his career at the age of four). He is described as a 'boxer' (or more precisely a 'shadow boxer' – a pantomime) who had won a contest at the 'Paneia in his own hometown'.[59] Here is not only evidence that games were indeed held in Banias, but also that they were held in honour of Pan. The epigrapher Robert provides additional evidence through his emendation of an inscription from Rhodes, which lists among the victories of a certain famous runner one that took place 'in his home town of Paneas'.[60]

THE CULT OF ZEUS

Zeus, the father of the gods, may have come to Banias on the coat-tails of the cult of his grandson or, by some accounts, foster brother, Pan,[61] but he was nevertheless a prominent and important part of the religious life of the city during the Roman period. Some recognition of the Hellenistic Zeus may have dated to Herodian times (the Augusteum at Caesarea Maritima had a cult statue of Olympian Zeus). But the earliest evidence at Banias itself suggests that Zeus, like Pan, began his career there in Eastern, Semitic, syncretistic manifestations. It was to the Heliopolitan Zeus that Quadratus the physician dedicated his statue of Asclepios at Banias in 63 AD.[62] This inscription, dating from the reign of Agrippa II, but dedicated to 'the salvation of our lords the emperors', may have been set up by a temporary resident of the city, a military man whose offering was intended for the temple of the imperial cult.[63] A half-century later, during the reign of Trajan, Maronas, son of Publius Aristo, along with his family, dedicated an altar 'To Heliopolitan Zeus and to the god Pan who brings victory'.[64] Since this inscription was found in the northeast corner of the building next to the 'court of Pan' (actually in the destruction layer of the 'court of Nemesis' east of the building), the excavator concluded that the building was itself a temple dedicated to Zeus. This is possible, if not yet proven. Once again, the connotations of the inscription are military; even the reference to Pan 'who brings victory' is consistent with the possibility that the dedicant was a part of the military contingent stationed in Banias at the time.

If the building was in fact dedicated to Zeus as well, its construction was most likely connected with the coming of Roman troops after the death of Agrippa II and the ascension of Trajan, and still represented Eastern popular religion (as did the cult of Pan during the same period). There are other indications that the cult of Zeus at Banias was initially of Semitic origins, or at least was not Olympian. We know that Zeus was often syncretised in the area with Ba'al Shamin, the Canaanite god.[65] Another altar found in a rubbish pit at the Sanctuary is in fact dedicated to Sehenus, that is Ba'al Shamin, for whom Herod the Great had erected a temple in the Hauran.[66] Isaac thinks that its dedicant, who has a Roman name (Ulpius Priscus), may have been a soldier from Siah, where that temple stood.[67] These early inscriptions, taken together, suggest that the earliest worship of Zeus in Banias took the form of *ad hoc* dedications, mostly by military or ex-military men, who brought along their devotion to Eastern deities syncretised with Zeus when they moved there.

The first clear evidence of a cult dedicated to the classical Greek Zeus in his Greco-Roman form appeared on the coins of the city during the Antonine period, at the same time as the dedication of the new statue of Pan.[68] From its beginnings under Marcus Aurelius to the time of Elagabalus, the city coinage of Banias featured Zeus prominently. The god is most often standing, nude, holding a sceptre in his right hand and a *patera* in his left (Fig. 22). On later coins he sometimes appears within a tetrastyle temple.[69] The coins suggest that the cult of Zeus was a major one in the religious life of the city during the second and third centuries, and that by this time an imposing temple dedicated to this god stood within the city. It is hardly coincidental that Zeus appears first on the coins of Marcus Aurelius, whose Stoic leanings brought Zeus to special religious prominence. The cult itself, or perhaps a new and impressive cult statue, may have appeared during this time, and is thus commemorated on the coins dated 169 AD.[70]

Zeus is several times depicted in a temple that is similar to the one shown on the coins of Philip the Tetrarch, however. The earliest depiction of the temple of Zeus is in 217 AD, on coins of Macrinus and Diadumenian.[71] It appears again on a coin of Elagabalus.[72] Among all the temples shown on coins of Banias, only this one is tetrastyle (with pediment and acroteria) and having an 'old-style' roof (a simple gable). It thus resembles the Augusteum on the coins of Philip very closely.[73] As we have suggested, this might indicate that the Augusteum was converted into a temple to Zeus sometime during the first century, first somewhat unofficially, in the time of Trajan, and later as a part of imperial policy, under the Antonines.[74] Alternatively, the absence of the Augusteum on the city coins of Banias may provide evidence that the Augusteum was not under the jurisdiction of the city of Banias. If Omrit is the site of the Augusteum, this becomes a plausible hypothesis.

ASSOCIATED DEITIES

A number of other deities in the 'Pan Circle' shared his sanctuary. The inscriptions mention the nymphs, demons of nature, who lived in springs, caves, mountains, forests and groves, and who often appear with Pan on bas-reliefs and paintings throughout the Greco-Roman world. Among these nymphs, one is specifically mentioned by name: Maia. She appears on a coin of Plautilla, minted in Banias, standing beside a tree, her left foot on an unidentified object.[75] She is also mentioned by name on one of the inscriptions of Victor, son of Lysimachos, as the mother of Hermes. Maia was a beautiful nymph, though very shy, spending all her time with her maidens in a remote cave. She was the daughter of Atlas, and was, according to the mythology, born from a tree (thus the iconography of the coin). Another coin of Plautilla from the Banias mint may represent Maia as well, this time in the guise of a Tyche, with a river god (the Banias spring) swimming at her feet.[76] Echo, another of the nymphs, is mentioned by name on two inscriptions, one of which, dated 221 AD, implies the dedication of a statue of her at the sanctuary. In the Hellenistic period a legend developed in a number of variants that depicts Pan as the unsuccessful lover of Echo.[77] In one version, refusing Pan, she was butchered by the shepherds at his command. The only thing surviving was her voice, the echo. Another myth says she was not killed, but paired with Pan, gave birth to a girl, the Iyx. Maia's son Hermes, sometimes identified as the father of Pan, and, like him, god of shepherds and protector of herds and pastures, also had a statue at the sanctuary, donated by Victor, son of Lysimachos. Though as yet not found in Banias, many *ex voto* plaques are known, originating at various sites throughout the Greek world, especially dating from the fifth to the third centuries BC, that feature all these characters together. They are usually depicted in a grotto or cave. There may be seen a group of three nymphs led by Hermes, with the river god (Acheloos) and Pan lurking somewhere at the periphery. Often the priests and the dedicants are also depicted. This traditional grouping had obviously taken hold at Banias, more than half a millennium after the classical Greek model.[78]

Nemesis might be thought of as another of the nymphs, though she was not traditionally included in their number. She does have ties with Zeus in classical mythology, having been commissioned by him to impose justice.[79] At Banias she was allotted her own court, a narrow passage leading to a niche in the cliffside. The dedicant, 'Valerios Hispanos, priest of the God Pan', left an inscription beside the niche, dated 178 AD. In order to display the statue of the goddess, he 'cut away the rock underneath' and installed an iron fence or grille.[80] The mortises designed to anchor the grill may still be seen near the niche, though the date is no longer readable. Nemesis's precise function in the pantheon of Banias is not clear. She is often identified with the emperor and also as a protector of cities, perhaps conflated with Tyche. Hornum, in his comprehensive work on the goddess, concludes that she had some role in the Roman period as 'a guardian of municipal bodies as well as individual'. Her most distinctive feature, however, was association with theatres, amphitheatres, and stadia, and especially with gladiatorial contests.[81] As we have seen, the Panian games seemed to take the form of their old Greek counterparts rather than featuring the violence characteristic of Roman public entertainment. Banias undoubtedly had other public events, including athletic contests, in its local theatre, and some of these may have involved gladiators and the execution of prisoners. Nemesis was sometimes connected to these activities because they represented the confirmation of order in the state by punishing those who had for some reason become its enemies.[82]

A statue of Marsyas found near Banias, now in the Louvre, most likely was originally displayed as a part of the Pan sanctuary.[83] The statue, which once was part of a larger group, is dated to the first or second century AD and is based on a third-century BC original. Marsyas was a flute-playing satyr who, having challenged Apollo to a musical contest, was defeated and punished for his insolence by being flayed alive and hanged on a pine tree. The 'woodland gods, and the fauns of the countryside wept, and his brother satyrs, Olympus his friend and pupil, still dear to him then, and the nymphs, and all who pastured their fleecy sheep and horned cattle on those mountains'. Their tears formed a stream that ran 'within sloping banks', becoming a river.[84] Nonnos of Panopolis, writing in the fifth century, recounts another myth claiming that the shepherd Marsyas's 'hairy skin', hanging on the tree, was filled with the wind and 'made his tune again'. Apollo, in pity, changed him into a stream, which itself continued this song, 'as if he were still playing on the reeds of his Phrygian pipe'.[85] The points of comparison with Pan are obvious and the appearance of Marsyas in the sanctuary of Banias among the sources of the River Jordan seems most appropriate, not only religiously but politically as well. A statue of Marsyas stood in the Forum at Rome and was frequently imitated by Roman colonies, and it came to be considered a symbol of autonomy.[86]

Many other Greco-Roman deities were represented at Banias by statues, fragments of which have been found in the excavations of the sanctuary. Some of these have associations with Pan in mythology. There is Artemis, who shared the woodlands with him;[87] Aphrodite, who sometimes associated with Pan in a kind of 'Beauty and the Beast' relationship and who, like Pan, is associated with sexuality and fertility;[88] Dionysus, who was often associated with Pan, inhabiting the same forests, caves, and fields along with the satyrs and Silenoi;[89] and Kybele, who was often depicted with Pan, and who shared many of his 'attributes' (pine trees, cones, syrinxes, lagobola etc.).[90] Other statue fragments were found of deities not directly associated with Pan, such as Athena, Apollo (or a Muse), Herakles, Orpheus and Asclepios (dedicatory inscription only).[91] These most likely were gifts from donors who had special relationships with these gods, and offered their images as votives at the Pan sanctuary. Almost all of these fragments may be dated to the second century AD.

CIVIC RELIGION: THE CULTS OF TYCHE AND THE EMPEROR

All the Greco-Roman cities of the region had cults dedicated to Tyche (Roman Fortuna), the goddess who represented the good fortune of the city and, in a sense, was symbolic of the city itself. The goddess may usually be identified by her turreted crown, which represents the walls of the city. She often holds a cornucopia, sheaf of grain, or some other symbol of abundance. Each city adopted its own distinctive Tyche, however, usually exhibiting aspects specifically associated with that city.[92] The Tyche of Banias first appeared in the late first century on a coin issued by Agrippa II at the same time as the one featuring the likeness of Pan.[93] Most likely the king had presented the city with a cult statue of the city goddess along with that of Pan, and the pair of coins commemorate the event. The goddess holds a rudder in her hand, typical of the image of Fortuna often found on Roman imperial coins, and is clad in military dress similar to that typically associated with the goddess Roma. The selection of this particular iconography may have been yet another way for Agrippa to show his kingdom's strong ties and loyalty to Rome. Though the image of Pan he selected apparently did not last, the image of Tyche did. It reappears on coins minted by Septimius Severus in 196 AD and often thereafter (Fig. 24).[94] Three coin types, all minted in 220 AD – a year with special significance in pagan Banias – picture the cult statue for the first time in a temple or some related structure.[95] The obverses of these coins depict Elagabalus, his mother Julia Soaemus, and his grandmother Julia Maesa.[96] The absence of a temple on coins minted prior to this time is probably explained by the fact that the statue stood in the open air, perhaps in the *agora*,[97] until it was covered by a rather simple distyle temple as part of the great celebration of 220 AD.

Two other female figures, both shown inside temples, are identified by Meshorer as Tyches. Of course it is possible for a city to have more than one Tyche, or even for other goddesses to function as or be assimilated with Tyche. However, it seems probable that in this case the female figures are in fact Maia, Nemesis, or one of the other nymphs honoured along with Pan in the sacred district of the city. The seated figure shown on coins of Elagabalus (dated 218 AD) and Julia Soaemus (dated 220 AD), with the personification of the Jordan beneath, may, for example, be Maia.[98] And the female figure wearing a chiton, standing face front, and holding what appears to be a sceptre (of Julia Soaemus; dated 220 AD), may be Nemesis.[99] That all three female figures appear on coins minted in the same year makes it likely that they represent three distinct cult statues in three distinct temples.

If the cult of Tyche was primarily a celebration of the city and its prosperity, the Imperial Cult at Banias emphasised the city's place in the larger Roman world. This cult had its impressive beginning with the erection of the 'very beautiful temple of white stone' by Herod the Great,[100] dedicated to Augustus, and providing a social, political and religious centre for Herod's northern territories that emphasised his loyalty to Rome. This temple and its cult were in a sense the seed from which the city of Banias sprung. It is the most prominent feature on the coins of Philip, the 'founder' of the city. Thus, from its earliest days as a Greco-Roman *polis*, Banias was the site not only of devotion to Pan but also the feasts, festivals, rituals and sacrifices directed to the genius of the emperor.[101] Tzaferis has suggested that when Agrippa II renamed the city 'Neronias' in honour of Nero, he may have expanded the imperial cult beyond Augustus himself, so that its focus was the imperial family as a whole, or at least the reigning emperor, whoever he might be. Just how long this arrangement continued is hard to determine. The visit of Vespasian to the city in 67 AD, during which he 'rendered thank offerings to God', may be a veiled reference to a visit to the Augusteum.[102] The beautiful bust of Hadrian's favourite, Antinous, found in Banias, may have been an offering to the temple of the imperial cult as well as the so-called 'statue of Christ' (actually of Hadrian).[103] The latter, according to Eusebius, Philostorgius and other early Christian writers, stood in the open air, in a prominent location 'near the fountain in the city among other statues'. If the Augusteum was located a considerable distance from the city centre, at Omrit, these statues are less likely to have been associated with that particular sanctuary, however.

It is indeed curious that the temple and its cult simply disappear from the record, even from its periphery. This may be due to the change in the city's fortunes, as it lost its status as a royal capital at the death of Agrippa II. But it is hard to see how the city fathers of the second and third centuries could simply ignore or close the Augusteum, unless they were directed to put it to new use by imperial command. One possibility, already suggested, is that the temple was re-dedicated to Zeus, and that the tetrastyle temple that appears on several coins in the early third century is in fact the old Augusteum in its new guise.[104] If the coin evidence is taken alone, we might conclude that the cult statue of Zeus was moved into the old temple in 217 AD, during the reign of Macrinus and Diadumenian. But it is simply not possible to settle the matter at this stage until further evidence becomes available.[105]

5 Jews and Christians in Pagan Banias

Roman paganism, despite enjoying official approval, a boom in the building and dedicating of new sanctuaries and statues, and a flourishing 'visitation' of the gods among the populace, did not have the city entirely to itself. A significant Jewish community existed in Banias from the beginning. Or perhaps, more accurately, the district of Banias was the home of several Jewish communities. We now know that Judaism was a complex phenomenon during the Hellenistic and Roman periods; the situation in the district of Banias furnishes a good illustration of this complexity. The same may be said of primitive Christianity, which appeared in Banias very early, and exhibited an amazing variety and creativity there as it developed within and alongside new expressions of Judaism.

HERODIAN JEWISH COMMUNITIES

According to Josephus, Aristobulus the Hasmonean not only conquered territory in northern Galilee, but also 'compelled the inhabitants, if they would continue in that country, to be circumcised, and to live according to the Jewish laws'.[1] He describes this territory, and the people in it, as 'Iturean'. These converts would certainly remain a factor in the history of Judaism in the area. With pagan roots, living far from the centre of Jewish culture in the Hellenistic period, and surrounded by a decidedly non-Jewish culture *milieu*, they might be expected either to exhibit the radical commitment sometimes characteristic of converts, or to be attracted to various kinds of heterodoxies. They were no doubt a matter of concern to the religious establishment in Jerusalem from the very beginning.

Another significant Jewish community existed in the Golan, not far from Banias and under its political jurisdiction.[2] This community, which had originated in Babylon, had been settled in Batanaea by Herod the Great for the purpose of maintaining order against the banditry of the Trachonites. He therefore built a large village called Bathyra. This town and its environs grew significantly as a great number of immigrants came 'from all those parts where the ancient Jewish laws were observed' and settled there, attracted by freedom from taxes. This community's task was primarily military – to keep the Trachonites under control and thereby make the area safe for Jews travelling from Babylonia to come to Jerusalem for the feasts. Herod, of course, had an additional motive, a less religious one, since the Romans had charged him with keeping general order in the area and the 'Babylonian Jews' could help him do that. The project was successful. The country, Josephus says, 'became full of people'[3] and remained generally loyal to both Rome and the house of Herod.

The leaders of this community developed very close ties with the Herodian family. Jacimus, son of the founder, trained a group of horsemen from there to serve as personal guards for the Herodian kings. His son Philip became a friend, confidant and general of the armies of Agrippa II. He was a man of significant power in his own right, taking the same pro-Roman position as did his royal masters Agrippa II and Berenice.[4] We have already described the conflict between Philip and Varus, Agrippa's viceroy at Banias.[5] Varus, a member of the old Iturean aristocracy, rallied the 'Syrians of Caesarea' (that is the non-Jewish population of Banias) with ideas of revolt against both Agrippa and the Romans. He contrived a plan to ally with the Trachonites in Batanaea and drive out the 'Babylonian Jews' as well. This plan was not successful, but he did manage to massacre the leadership of the Jewish communities in both Banias and Batanaea. The latter community fled to Gamla, where Philip was able to convince them to remain loyal to Agrippa and the Romans. Agrippa in the meantime got wind of Varus's plot 'to cut off the Jews of Caesarea [Banias] ... being many ten thousands' and replaced him with another governor, Equiculus Modius.[6] The impression we get is that the three Jewish communities of the district of Banias (the 'Itureans', the 'Babylonians' and the 'Caesareans') were all of significant size and influence.[7]

At least some Jews served in Agrippa's army. Jacimus, himself a Jew, was loyal to Agrippa's pro-Roman strategy and commanded a large army of 'Babylonian Jews'.[8] Many of the Jews in Agrippa's territories joined the revolt against Rome, of course. Gamla itself did so, once Philip and his 'Babylonians' were gone. Nevertheless, Josephus leaves the impression that the Jewish community in Banias, though concerned to follow the laws of purity (and thus be willing, for example, to pay exorbitant amounts for olive oil that was ritually pure), did not join in the revolt. They enjoyed the protection of Agrippa's viceroy Modius against the local pagan population, which ironically in this case was less loyal to Rome than were the Jews of Banias.[9] We have already noted the strong possibility that the latter not only inhabited an entire quarter of the city,[10] but that they also enjoyed some sort of self-government.[11] While these Jews surely must have been saddened to see the cruel destruction of thousands of their co-religionists in the games held after the war at Banias, there is no reason to believe that they themselves suffered greatly from the great defeat of the Jewish rebels. Like their king, Agrippa, they had been able to walk a very narrow tightrope of 'loyalty' to Rome, besieged on one side by rebellious fellow Jews and on the other by the potentially rebellious old Iturean pagan population. This pattern of collaboration with Roman interests continued into the next centuries as well, as we shall see.

APOCALYPTIC JUDAISM

The Jews who lived in the territories of Philip the Tetrarch and his successors inherited what was left of the old spirit of independence that had once expressed itself in the heterodoxy of the 'Northern Kingdom' of Israel. We should not imagine that the traditions of the 'Ten Lost Tribes' had totally disappeared from the scene.[12] It is true that the old altar at nearby Dan, with its golden calf, was in the hands of local pagans by Hellenistic times. And indeed the ancient cult there, far older than the Israelite state, had essentially disappeared by Roman times.[13] But the traditions of the sacredness of the area – the springs, the forests and especially mighty Mount Hermon – lived on.

Almost a century ago, Charles Clermont-Ganneau noticed the special place given to the region in the book of I Enoch, especially I Enoch 12–16 (a section dating from the third century BC).[14] For the author of this document, Mount Hermon is the 'Mountain of the Oath'. The area is quite familiar to him, as are the local legends concerning its sanctity. Here, then, is where he has the angels make their pact. The traditions underlying his treatment may have pagan origins, Clermont-Ganneau suggests, but have been appropriated into Jewish apocalypticism and later into apocalyptic Jewish Christianity (see below). There is thus an intermingling of Old Testament traditions and pagan legends regarding the mountain and various sites around the mountain. The author of I Enoch not only knows the legends, but also the geography of the mountain and its environs. In fact, he knows the area better than he does Mount Sinai or Mount Zion. This suggests that his community of faith was itself located nearby.

George Nickelsburg has expanded on this theme.[15] The author of I Enoch 13, he says, 'pinpoints with absolute specificity and precision the geographical location where Enoch's heavenly journey was supposed to have originated'. It is 'by the waters of Dan in the land of Dan, which is southwest of Hermon' (13:7). And the seer's proclamation to the angels takes place at the south end of the valley between the Lebanon and the Anti-Lebanon ranges, at Abel beth Maacah (13:9). Furthermore, the climactic descent of the rebel angels occurs on Mount Hermon itself. Nickelsburg says:

> Thus, the whole of this primordial drama unfolds in a narrowly circumscribed geographical region…Enoch, having been commissioned by the angels to intercede for them in God's presence, goes to Dan for the purpose of finding the presence of God. At the sacred place, he sits down by the waters – traditionally a place of revelation – and reads himself into a trance in which he is conveyed into the presence of God. If Mount Hermon is the ladder from the heavenly sanctuary [12:4; 15:3] to earth, the waters of Dan stand in polar relationship to the gates of heaven and, through them, to the sanctuary and the throne of God.[16]

He concludes 'that these chapters constitute a tradition of northern Galilean provenance which, in turn, reflects visionary activity in the area of Dan and Hermon'.[17] This theme is a persistent one that also appears in Jewish-Christian circles. The Testament of Levi (2–7) locates an ascent to the heavenly temple in the same area and even suggests that the patriarch of the priesthood at Jerusalem received his divine call in a vision that occurred near the site of one of the shrines in the Northern Kingdom.[18] Before turning to the Judaism of the rabbis, then, we must recognise the presence of other kinds of Judaism in the area, some of which, like this one, seem to have been absorbed by heterodox communities, including the Judeo-Christian sects discussed below.

BANIAS AND THE RABBIS

The city of Banias and region around it are often mentioned in rabbinic literature. We find here the home of some of the great rabbis who were formulating the Judaism that survived the destruction of the temple and the disappearance of the Jewish state: the Judaism of the Mishna and the *Talmud*. Though the references to Banias are frequent, the nature of these documents is such that their interpretation and evaluation are difficult. Clearly some of the stories involving Banias are legendary. Some surely originated many generations after the events they claim to describe. On the other hand, some late documents undoubtedly retain very early traditions that have historical significance. The difficulty in dating specific statements in rabbinic literature is well known. Even when a name may be placed chronologically, the possibility always exists that the story or statement or action attributed to a particular rabbi comes from a much later time. The stories about Rabbi Jose ben Kisma of Banias, for example, are most often found in the *Babylonian Talmud*, which was compiled centuries after his lifetime. We may nevertheless presume that at least some of these stories contain at least a substantial kernel of history. We must therefore proceed cautiously, and somewhat tentatively, aware of the slippery nature of the evidence, with no pretence of having placed the rabbinical materials into firm and precise chronological order. Taken as a whole, these materials give us some information about Banias from the second to fifth centuries. More precise dating is often impossible.

The reign of Hadrian (117–38 AD), so auspicious for the empire as a whole, was a tragic time for emerging rabbinical Judaism. The revolt of Bar Kochba once again rained devastation upon the Jews in Palestine, at least those in southern Palestine. This was the time of the Ten Martyrs, when many of the great teachers of the Torah lost their lives, and when the Holy City of Jerusalem was entirely paganised and declared off limits to the Jews. There is evidence, however, that the Jews of Banias followed the long tradition of their fathers in co-operating with the Romans and refused to join in the Second Revolt, just as they had refused to participate in the first.

Banias made a compatible home during this period for Rabbi Jose ben Kisma, one of the strongest rabbinical advocates of complicity with the Romans. He may indeed have moved to that city precisely because of its reputation for being at one time a centre for the study of the Torah and also pro-Roman.[19] The Bar Kochba Revolt, which destroyed so many Jewish communities further south, actually strengthened the Jewish community of Banias, as many refugees fled northward and settled in nearby upper Galilee, the Golan, and no doubt in Banias itself. In fact, Rabbi Jose ben Kisma was active there precisely during and immediately after the time of the revolt and, if the testimony of the Mishna is accurate, the city could actually be described as a 'place of the Torah', that is, the home of a strong Jewish community with an active group of Torah scholars.[20] This would be consistent with the picture of the Jewish community in Banias given by Josephus some fifty to seventy years earlier, in the affair involving John of Gischala.

On his deathbed, Rabbi Jose was visited by Rabbi Hanina ben Tardion, who was to become one of the Ten Martyrs. Rabbi Jose urged him to co-operate with the Romans. 'God handed the government to the Romans,' he said. 'They destroyed His house, burned His temple, slaughtered the pious, the best men of our people, and now I hear that you gather disciples and teach them from the book of the Torah you keep hidden in your bosom. Would it not be better for you to consider how all this will end?' Rabbi Hanina piously protested: 'God in heaven will have mercy!' Rabbi Jose retorted, 'I speak to you logically and you answer about the mercy of heaven. I should not be surprised if you are captured with the book of the Torah in your possession.' This is indeed what eventually happened, and was the cause of Rabbi Hanina's cruel martyrdom.[21]

Another rabbinical tradition suggests that this same rabbi maintained a school in Banias:

> The disciples of R. Jose b. Kisma asked him, 'When will the Messiah come?' – He answered, 'I fear lest ye demand a sign of me [that my answer is correct].' They assured him, 'We will demand no sign of you.' So he answered them, 'When this gate [of Paneas] falls down, is rebuilt, falls again, and is again rebuilt, and then falls a third time, before it can be rebuilt the son of David will come.' They said to him, 'Master, give us a sign.' He protested, 'Did you not assure me that ye would not demand a sign'. They replied, 'Even so, [we desire one].' He said to them, 'If so, let the waters of the grotto of Paneas turn into blood;' and they turned into blood.[22]

Despite his accommodation to the Romans, this reply may veil Rabbi Jose's private opinion that Rome would eventually have to give up Palestine to Persia (and in the process, the gate of Banias would 'fall down'). He instructed his disciples to bury him in a deep grave, since 'the time will come when there will not be a single palm tree in the land of Israel but a Persian horse will be tied to it'.[23] Remarkably, given the times and the general animosity between Jew and Roman, it is said that Roman officials attended his funeral and mourned at his grave.[24]

Other major figures among the rabbis had connections with the city. It is possible, though not certain, that Rabbi Yehudah bar Ilai, whose name appears in the Mishna many times, and is 'regarded as the main representative of his generation',[25] lived in Banias. According to the *Babylonian Talmud*: 'It happened that R. Eliezer [ben Hyrcanus of Lydda, a second-generation Tannaim *ca.* 90–130 AD] passed the Sabbath [of Tabernacles] in Upper Galilee in the Sukkah of R. Yehudah son of R. Ilai at Caesarea or, as some say in Caesarea [Philippi]'.[26] The guest was no less illustrious than the host. Rabbi Eliezer ben Hyrcanus was 'one of that generation's [the first after the Bar Kochba Revolt] most eminent sages'.[27]

Rabbi Abbahu, of the third generation of Tannaim (*ca.* 130–60 AD) was more certainly a citizen of Banias. In the *Midrash Rabbah*, in a context of traditions about demons, monsters and apparitions, is this story:

> R. Abbahu was once sitting and studying in a certain synagogue in Caesarea [Philippi]. He noticed one man pursuing another having in his hand a rod with which he wished to strike the other. He [Rabbi Abbahu] saw that a demon also followed after the same man having in his hand an iron rod. R. Abbahu went out and followed the pursuing man and said to him: 'Do not

strike him, lest he die!' Said the other: 'Master! Can he die by this?' He answered: 'There is a demon following behind you, and he has an iron rod in his hand. If you strike him with this and he strikes him with that he will die.'[28]

Traditions such as these remind us once again that after the Bar Kochba Revolt, the centre of the Jewish population, along with its scholars and religious leaders, moved into the Golan and northern Galilee, precisely those areas which had long been administratively centred at Banias. Jews were to play a significant role in the region for the next several centuries. Dan Urman's contention seems valid: that 'some of the important sages of Palestine who were involved in creating, editing and perhaps also writing parts of the Palestinian Halachah were born, studied and worked in the region. Therefore it is possible to assume that a sizeable part of the Palestinian Rabbinic sources were edited and written in the region.'[29] Here they benefited from the region's reputation for loyalty to Rome; the post-revolt rabbis accepted the new situation and flourished within it. Rabbi Judah the Patriarch, who initiated the recording of the Mishna, in contrast to the Jewish leadership before the revolt, enjoyed a good relationship with the Romans. He was said to be a friend of Antoninus Pius (138–61 AD), and perhaps also of his nephew Marcus Aurelius (161–80 AD). This positive relationship continued during the reigns of several succeeding emperors.[30]

It is the literary record of the Jewish community, discussed in Chapter 3, that provides a glimpse into the troubled times which followed. The conflicts and hardships that culminated with the reign of Diocletian (284–305 AD) are evident in the rabbinic sources. The economic situation in Banias, and indeed throughout the empire, had clearly darkened. However, the Jewish community in Banias probably suffered no more from the increasing burden of taxes during the waning days of the third century than did the area's Christians of various sects, or even the solid pagan majority,

BANIAS AS THE BOUNDARY OF ERETZ ISRAEL

The waters of Banias were of great interest to the rabbis, not only because they were the fountainhead of the Jordan, but also because they raised a number of interesting issues regarding ritual usage. Although the Jordan is created by the fusion of several tributaries, the rabbis regarded its source to be 'the cavern of Paneas'.[31] Since 'the chief supply of the Jordan comes from the cavern of Paneas', argues Rab Kahana, 'where a person says, "I will not drink waters from the cavern of Paneas," the water of the entire Jordan is forbidden to him'.[32] The water might not only be drunk, it was also suitable to be used for purification from the defilement caused by coming in contact with a corpse: 'The Well of Ahab and [the pool in] the Cave of Pamias [sic] are valid'.[33] These statements are remarkable given the fact that the cave itself was and had been from time immemorial a pagan cult site. The rabbinical literature consistently ignores these pagan associations. In its exegesis of Genesis 33:4, 'The fountains also of the deep...were stopped' (following the Flood of Noah) the Midrash Rabbah adds: 'But not all the fountains, the exceptions being the great well [of Biram], the gulf [of Gaddor], and the cavern spring of Paneas'[34] – as though the place were a special province of Yahweh and not the ancient home of the goat-god Pan. One would never know from reading the rabbinic literature that the cave and spring at Banias were literally covered with pagan temples and altars until at least the fourth century.

Among the rabbinical legends about Moses is one that involves Banias. As the story goes, Moses is negotiating with God, hoping to soften the prohibition against his setting foot in the Promised Land.

> Said Moses before him, 'Lord of the world, since a decree has been made that I shall not enter the land either as king or as commoner, let me enter it by the Cave of Caesarion below Paneas.' He said to him, 'But you shall not go over there' [Deuteronomy. 34:4]. He said to him, 'Lord of the world, since a decree has been issued that I shall not enter the land either as king or as commoner, not even by the cave of Caesarion below Panias then at least let my bones cross the Jordan.' He said to him, 'But you shall not go over this Jordan' (Deuteronomy 3:27).[35]

Moses's culminating argument seems to be that he will not have technically 'crossed' the Jordan if he enters the Promised Land by skirting the northern edge of the springs of Banias.

The *Jerusalem Talmud*, more ancient and more strongly connected with the land, evinces considerably more familiarity with the geographical setting of Banias than does the *Babylonian Talmud*. The former, for example, carefully distinguishes between the great coastal city of Caesarea Maritima and Kesariyon ('Little Caesarea').[36] As the northern limit of the land of Israel, Banias becomes a proverbial 'faraway place'. And so the proverbial description of a long voyage: 'So and so is going to Kesariyon'.[37] Furthermore, since Banias was located on the very border of Eretz Israel, the rabbis were at pains to determine just how the Torah's injunctions regarding the land were to be interpreted there. The border of the land as it was repopulated after the return from Babylonian exile runs through a place called 'Tarnegola Caesarion'. Anything lying below this Tarnegola is in Israel, anything lying above it is not. This 'Tarnegola' (the 'rooster-shaped') has not been definitely located, but it is reasonable to assume that the term refers to the high hill just behind and east of Banias where the ruins of the medieval castle of Subaybah now stand. J.T. Demai speaks on the issue of whether the tithes due the priests were to be paid from the fruits of the agriculture of Banias. In the section Zeraim ('seeds') Rabbi Jonah, in the name of Rabbi Simeon b. Zechariah, lists four kinds of produce 'which are forbidden in Paneas' – walnuts, rice, sesame seeds and cowpeas. Gameliel Zugga added to the list 'early ripening Damascene plums'. The situation was complicated by the fact that Banias stood precisely on the border. Thus, Rabbi Jonah adds, 'That which you have stated applies [in the area] from Tarnegola [which is above] but from Tarnegola Caesarion southward [the case is the same] as in Eretz Israel, [that is, all produce there is fully liable to tithing and sabbatical-year regulations]'.[38] In Yerushalmi Shebi'ith, the question of borders arises again. This time the issues include the kind of agricultural work that can be done during the sabbatical year, what must be done with produce from that year, and the geographical limits of such regulations. Once again, the northern border of Eretz Israel is placed at 'Tarnegola above Caesarion [Philippi]'.[39] At any rate, at least two things can be learned from this rabbinic exchange: the Jews of Banias engaged in agriculture, and living as they did at the very border of Eretz Israel, strict adherence to the demands of the Torah were for them quite complicated.

CONFUSING DAN AND BANIAS

The overall impression produced by the references to Banias in the rabbinical literature is that interest in and knowledge of the actual site eventually gives way to exegesis having no basis in either geography or history. This may have been the natural consequence of the shift of rabbinical scholarship away from Palestine and into Persia, where the *Babylonian Talmud*, for all practical purposes supplanting that of Jerusalem, concentrated far more on the words of the sages than on the temporal and spatial contexts of these words. This is probably the explanation for the growing confusion between Dan and Paneas, a confusion that was passed along to the Christian Fathers and lasted until modern times. The city of Banias, as we have seen, did not exist before Hellenistic times. By contrast, archaeological excavations at nearby Tel Dan have revealed a series of towns stretching far back before the time of the Israelites and Canaanites, and persisting until approximately the time of Constantine.[40] The distinction between these two places was clear to the author of the Jerusalem Targum Genesis 14:14: 'They pursued them to Dan of Caesarea', that is Dan, in the district of Caesarea;[41] and Numbers 24: 'at the snow mountain of Kisarion, i.e. Caesarea eastward of Dan'. This latter phrase describes precisely the geographical relationship of the two sites.

But the *Midrash Rabbah*, exegeting II Samuel 24:6, says: 'Thus it is written, Then they came to Gilead which is Geres [in Gilead]; And to the land of Tahtim – hodshi [*ib.*] – viz. Beth Yerah. And they came to Dan [*ib.*] which is Paneas.'[42] This false identification must have occurred because the author was so unfamiliar with the geography of northern Palestine that he did not know the distinction between Dan (which is literally within sight of the western outskirts of Banias, down in the Huleh valley) and Banias. The *Midrash Rabbah*'s subtle phrase 'Dan of Caesarea' is lost in the Pirke Rabbi Eliezer, which reads instead: 'They followed them to Dan, which is Paneas'.[43] And since the Hebrew Bible (Joshua 19:47) identifies Dan with Leshem, it seemed appropriate, according to the *Babylonian Talmud*, that 'R. Isaac said: "Leshem is Pamias [*sic*]"'.[44]

That these conclusions are drawn without reference to direct knowledge of the geography of northern Israel can be seen from the series of statements in the *Babylonian Talmud*:[45]

> So indeed it has been taught in a Baraitha: The Jordan issues from the cavern of Paneas, flows through the Lake of Sibkay, the Lake of Tiberias, and the Lake of Sodom, and proceeds to run into the Mediterranean Ocean. And the real Jordan is from Jericho and below. H. Hiyya b. Abba reported in the name of R. Johanan: Why is it called Yarden [Jordan]? Because it comes from Dan. Said R. Abba to R. Ashei: You learnt this from the name, we learn it from here: And they called Leshem Dan after the name of Dan their father. R. Isaac said: Leshem is Paneas.

Note the authorities cited: a Baraitha, etymology ('You learnt this from the name'), and a biblical text ('We learn it from here', that is from Joshua 19:47). It is difficult to believe that anyone with a direct knowledge of Israel could believe that the Jordan begins at Jericho or that it empties into the Mediterranean.

The Christian historian Eusebius (260–340 AD) knew that Dan was a village four milestones down the road from Banias in the direction of Tyre. He had visited the area himself and most likely had travelled down this very road.[46] Eucharius (ca. 440 AD) likewise says that 'Dan is a little village on that frontier of Judaea which looks towards the north, at the fourth milestone from Paneas as you go towards Tyre'.[47] When Jerome (early fifth century) depends on Eusebius, he also distinguishes between the two towns.[48] But elsewhere he contradicts himself, referring to 'Dan, which is also called Paneas'.[49] He also dabbles with etymologies connecting 'Dan' with the 'Jor-Dan', a favourite though impossible idea found in dozens of Jewish and Christian writers alike during the succeeding centuries.[50] Jerome had never visited the area himself, citing instead information he had received from the Jewish scholar from whom he learned Hebrew. This suggests that the confusion between Dan and Banias, and the generally garbled misconceptions about the geography of the region, were passed along from the rabbis to the Church fathers, primarily through Jerome himself.[51]

CHRISTIANS IN BANIAS

Once the dark days in the aftermath of the Bar Kochba Revolt were past, the Jews and the Romans once again came to accommodate one another. In contrast, the mortal struggle between paganism and Christianity gradually intensified. It was now the Christians' turn to suffer persecution, though intermittently. In this the Christians could expect no solace from the local rabbis, despite their common disdain for attempts that followed to shore up a waning paganism. From their point of view the nascent Church was already straying too far from its roots.

BANIAS AND THE BEGINNINGS OF CHRISTIANITY

The earliest Christians of Banias are entirely anonymous, if we discount the curious tradition that the first bishop of the city was Erastus of Corinth, an associate of Paul mentioned in the latter's epistle to the Romans.[52] Banias was located on the main road between Tyre and Damascus, both of which were centres of Christian activity very early – perhaps already in the decade following the public ministry of Jesus.[53] The intensively evangelistic new sect, spreading as it did along the major routes of travel, probably made its first converts among the Jewish population in Banias very shortly after Jesus's own visit to the 'region of Caesarea Philippi' (Matthew 16:13). Indeed, Jesus himself most likely made the first disciples in the area. It is noteworthy that a significant block of material from the Synoptic Gospels seems to have the region (not necessarily the city) of Caesarea Philippi, the territory Josephus calls 'the district of Paneas', as its backdrop.

The Synoptic materials in question include the account of Jesus's Admission of Messiahship, the Transfiguration, and the healing of the demon-possessed boy. All are found in each of the three Synoptic Gospels (Matthew, Mark and Luke) and thus would ordinarily be understood to have Mark as their source (if the commonly held theory of the priority of Mark is accepted). There is reason to believe that the geographical setting of the stories comes from even earlier sources, however. Mark derives the geographical references he sometimes supplies to his accounts from earlier sources, most likely themselves originating with the communities mentioned.[54] Their witness to the existence of these communities is therefore very strong. This is particularly true of materials sometimes identified as belonging to 'Ur-Markus', as the materials centred in Caesarea Philippi are.[55] Further, the account of these events in Matthew has, in addition to Mark, its own sources that seem to pre-date the second gospel.[56]

The interesting conclusion which may be drawn is that the cycle of Jesus-stories associated with the region of Caesarea Philippi is not only extremely early, but that it originated with equally early Christian (or more precisely, Jewish-Christian) communities in the region. This would place Christianity in the Banias district in its most primitive Jewish-Christian form, probably before the conversion of Paul, possibly the fruit of missions by Jesus's personal disciples. To these indigenous adherents of the new faith were most likely added disciples of Jesus displaced by the First Jewish Revolt, first from the lakeside towns where Jesus had conducted his most significant ministry, and then from Judaea itself.[57] To the already-vibrant theological turmoil of the area, through which the Jewish community was trying to come to terms with the destruction of the temple and cult of blood sacrifice, these disciples of Jesus proposed a solution quite different from that of the rabbis. Out of the ensuing struggle came a significant contribution to the literature of Christianity.[58]

THE ADMISSION OF MESSIAHSHIP

The Markan context for the 'Banias-Cycle' is a ministry by Jesus and his disciples extending from Bethsaida-Julias (Mark 8:22) to Caesarea Philippi, entirely within the territory of Herod Philip and between the two major cities in his tetrarchy.[59] Mark's account reads: 'Jesus and his disciples went on to the villages around Caesarea Philippi. On the way he asked them, "Who do people say I am?" They replied, "Some say John the Baptist; others say Elijah; and still others, one of the prophets." "But what about you?" he asked. "Who do you say I am?" Peter answered, "You are the Christ." Jesus warned them not to tell anyone about him' (Mark 8:27–30). Matthew uses the phrase 'the region of Caesarea Philippi' instead of 'the villages of Caesarea Philippi' (Matthew 16:13–16). Both phrases accurately describe the nature of the city's urban structure, noted above.[60] Matthew also adds the famous passage, 'I tell you that you are Peter, and on this rock I will build my church, and the gates of Hades will not overcome it. I will give you the keys of the kingdom of heaven. Whatever you bind on earth will be bound in heaven, and whatever you loose on earth will be loosed in heaven' (Matthew 16:18–19).[61]

THE TRANSFIGURATION ON MOUNT HERMON

Mount Hermon and Mount Tabor, several miles to the south, both appear in Christian tradition as the site of the Transfiguration. But the context in the Gospels clearly favours Mount Hermon. The two pericopes, the Admission of Messiahship and the Transfiguration, are tied firmly together by a common theme, namely Jesus's superiority over 'Moses and the Prophets'. The two events are clearly joined in the Synoptic tradition and there is no reason to think they occur in widely separate locations.[62] Mark, after an intervening prediction of and discussion about Jesus's death, continues: 'After six days Jesus took Peter, James and John with him and led them up a high mountain, where they were all alone. There he was transfigured before them [Mark 9:2].'[63]

Matthew's account of these events, which includes the commission to Peter, is particularly interesting. It exhibits ties with I Enoch 12–16 and the Testament of Levi 2–7, both of which depict the Hermon area as a place of revelation, a 'ladder to heaven' as it were. The holiness of the place was also recognised by the pagans of the area. Eusebius and Jerome testify to this, and Jerome notes the existence of a temple at the summit of Hermon 'where the Gentiles worship, from the region of Paneas and Libanus'.[64] Matthew 16:17–19 is widely held by New Testament critics to have come from a tradition earlier than the Gospel of Matthew itself.[65] The whole section (and not just vv. 17–19) seems to represent a single old tradition. Nickelsburg notes that

> the language and imagery in vv.18–19 can be read as a parabolising on the geographical environs of Caesarea Philippi, which are mentioned in v13. The polarity of heaven and earth corresponds to Mount Hermon. Both I Enoch and Testament of Levi see the mountain as a point of access to heaven, and for both authors, entrée to heaven is the prelude to a commissioning. The image of the rock calls to mind the rocky crags in the environs of the Paneion, and the reference to the gates of Hades finds a counterpart in the subterranean waters of the grotto.

He concludes that Matt. 16:13–19 reflects a pre-Marcan tradition.[66]

This analysis, which reveals the similarities between Matthew's sources on the one hand, and the Enoch-Levi tradition on the other, provides further evidence of a very early (pre-Markan, pre-70 AD) Christian community in the Banias area. It also suggests that this community had historical ties with the Jewish apocalyptic groups that circulated the Enoch-Levi tradition,[67] and that a significant point of contention between the Christians and their fellow Jews was the relative authority of Jesus versus 'Moses and the Prophets'. As we shall see, there is other evidence of such Jewish-Christian groups around Banias, groups which persisted long after the New Testament period, and which held the Gospel of Matthew in special regard.

THE HEALING OF THE DEMON-POSSESSED BOY

The third pericope in the 'Caesarea Philippi Cycle' is the account of Jesus's exorcism of a demon who had possessed a young boy in the area. Immediately after the Transfiguration, Jesus and his inner circle 'came down from the mountain'. And 'when they came to the other disciples' they were confronted with a boy who was 'possessed by a spirit that has robbed him of speech. Whenever it seizes him, it throws him to the ground. He foams at the mouth, grinds his teeth and becomes rigid.' When Jesus arrived the boy suddenly went into such a convulsion, falling to the ground and foaming at the mouth. After Jesus had exorcised the demon, 'they left that place and passed through Galilee', eventually arriving at Capernaum (Mark 9:14–30a). Matthew presents the same story, though somewhat less graphically (Matthew 17:14–23), as does Luke (Luke 9:37–45ff). The latter begins specifically, 'the next day, when they came down from the mountain...', though again he omits any specific geographical reference to Caesarea or Galilee.

If the other pericopes speak to the relationship between the Christians and their fellow Jews, this one seems to address the tensions between the Christians and the pagan majority among whom they lived. Although the modern diagnosis of the young man's condition would no doubt be epilepsy, it is significant that in ancient times Pan was among those deities believed to be capable of 'possessing' people ('panolepsy'). Iamblichus, the pagan apologist,[68] in his discussion of the various kinds of divine possession, notes that possession by the Mother Goddess 'has a vivific and replenishing power', because these are her distinctive powers. This fact illustrates the means by which one can tell which is the possessing god, since the symptoms of the possession will be 'according to the power of the Gods'. Though he then specifically mentions 'the inspirations of the Nymphs, or of Pan', he does not indicate precisely what possession by them does to the recipient. He does conclude, however, that by means of his maxim we are able to explain why some of the possessed 'leap and dwell in mountains...appear to be bound...' etc. Perhaps he means to connect these traits to Pan-possession. He insists that these phenomena are not caused by the seasons, or some medical problem, 'but each thing energises conformably to its nature; so that the spirits which are excited by the Gods, and which produce in men Bacchic inspiration, expel every other human and physical motion...'. Pan is described as 'blessed, leaper, running around, enthroned with the Horse, goat-limbed, filled with Bacchic frenzy, lover of divine frenzy, cave-dwelling', etc.[69] Examples of 'Pan possession' occur in Greek literature. Of Jason's bride in Medea (1167–77) Euripides says,

> There was a terrible sight to behold. For her colour changed, and with legs trembling she staggered back sidelong, and by falling on the chair barely escaped collapsing on the floor. And one old woman among the servants, thinking, I suppose, that a frenzy from Pan or one of the other gods had come upon her, raised a festal shout to the god, until she saw the white foam coming between her lips and her eyes starting out of their sockets and her skin all pale and bloodless. Then she raised a wail in answer to her former shout.[70]

A fourth-century Christian grave inscription to Athenodora, wife of Thaumasios, describes her as 'religious' ('φιλένθεος'), 'a term which in the Orphic hymns has the sense of one whom the god Pan had "inspired by divine frenzy"'.[71] Whether the young man's father had brought him to Caesarea Philippi hoping to implore Pan to free him from possession cannot be known, of course. But the possibility is intriguing.[72]

One additional Synoptic story became closely connected with Banias: the account of the woman cured of the issue of blood (Mark 5:25–34; Matthew 9:20–22; Luke

8:43–48). This connection is a part of the fascinating story of the so-called 'statue of Christ' at Banias, and likely had its beginnings much later than the first century, as we shall see.

BANIAS AND THE ANCIENT JEWISH-CHRISTIAN SECTS

Unfortunately, most of our information about Jewish followers of Jesus, particularly those communities that survived beyond the first century AD, comes to us through the exceedingly tendentious auspices of 'orthodox' historians, writing after the triumph of Byzantine Christianity. Thus very early communities, some perhaps with ties reaching back to Jesus and his Apostles, persisting in Palestine and Syria for centuries, are remembered and described only in terms of their 'heresies' (that is diversions from the form of gentile Christianity adopted by the court of Byzantium). Nevertheless, despite the difficulties in reconstructing the historical record, we can be sure that the district of Paneas was one of the centres of such movements, apparently from a very early period.

Our evidence comes from the writings of Epiphanius, Bishop of Salamis (*ca.* 315–403); specifically, from his catalogue of 'heresies' called *The Panarion*. Among the most famous of the Jewish-Christians were the Ebionites. This group Epiphanius traces directly back to the primitive followers of Jesus in Jerusalem, prior to the destruction of that city in 70 AD. These Christians, according to a well-known account in the *Ecclesiastical History of Eusebius of Caesarea* (*Maritima*) written in the mid-fourth century, fled from Jerusalem before its fall, guided by the prophetic warning of Jesus himself (Luke 21:20–21).[73] According to Eusebius, the community settled in Pella, a city of the Decapolis situated on the eastern bank of the Jordan.[74] From here, Epiphanius maintains, the community was diffused in several directions, becoming thus the 'mother church' of several types of Jewish Christianity found in his own day in a region stretching east of the Jordan from Damascus to the southern reaches of the Dead Sea.[75] Among these communities were the Ebionites, a Jewish-Christian sect founded, according to Epiphanius, by one Ebion, who 'preached in Asia and Rome, but the roots of those thorny weeds come mostly from Nabataea and Banias, Moabitis, and Cocabe in Bashanitis beyond Adrai – in Cyprus as well'.[76]

If, as seems to be the case, his use of the term 'Iturea' refers to the district of Banias rather than the Beka'a Valley, Epiphanius locates an additional Jewish-Christian sect in the Banias area, the Sampsaeans or Elkesaites. 'They are to be found, in the country called Peraea beyond the Salt, or, as it is called, the Dead Sea. They are [also] in Moabitis near the river Arnon, and on the other side in Ituraea and Nabatitis, as I have often said of them.'[77] Another name for this movement, he says, is the Ossaeans. 'I have been told that they originally came from Nabataea, Ituraea, Moabitis and Arielis.'[78]

The presence of these groups in and around Banias may also help explain the origins of the Gospel of Matthew, or at least of that aspect of the Gospel of Matthew that is not dependent on either Markan traditions or 'Q' – the so-called 'M' source. We have already noted a possible connection between the Gospel of Matthew and the Banias region. Jerome knew about a version of the Gospel of Matthew 'in Hebrew letters' and 'for the sake of those of the circumcision who believed'. This version, he says, could be found in the library at Caesarea (Maritima). 'From the Nazoraeans who use this book in Beroia, a city of Syria, I also received the opportunity to copy it.'[79] Some New Testament scholars have noticed that the canonical Gospel of Matthew has a 'northern Galilean/southern Syrian' point of view and have concluded that the community from which the gospel arose should be located 'somewhere along the border region between lower Galilee and Syria'.[80] Banias seems the most likely candidate, in terms of both location and theological *milieu*. An example of this 'northern Galilean/southern Syrian' perspective is found in Matthew 4:15. Building on the language of Isaiah 9:1, Matthew describes Jesus's use of the 'Way of the Sea' (the Damascus–Tyre road that passes through Banias) as a fulfilment of ancient prophecy. The effect of this use of Isaiah is to centre Jesus's ministry precisely in an area bordered on the south by Capernaum (with its sister communities Bethsaida and Chorazim) and the lake, and on the north by Tyre and Sidon – in short, the territories of Philip the Tetrarch.[81]

These very early Jewish-Christian groups possessed their own traditions about the ministry of Jesus that in turn became the basis for both their own literature and significant portions of the canonical gospels. Such works as the Gospel of the Nazoraeans and the so-called Gospel of the Ebionites show great similarities to the Gospel of Matthew, but do not seem to be directly dependent on the canonical form of the gospel. The explanation for this, as suggested by Klijn, is that these documents 'originated in an environment in which traditions used by the Gospel of Matthew were known but that such traditions had a different development'.[82] Thus, for example, the first Synoptic Gospel and the Gospel of the Nazoraeans represent two lines of development within a bilingual environment. 'We are at a border line between Aramaic and Greek speaking Christians.' These Jewish-Christian gospels were compiled at the close of the first century and beginning of the second century, and while using Synoptic material, 'provide evidence of the textual traditions known before the fixing of the canonical Gospels' text'.[83]

The host of issues surrounding the sources and origins of the Synoptic Gospels are far beyond the purview of our present discussion, but suffice it to say that the district of Banias (and perhaps the city itself) appears to have been a major centre in the development of Christianity – its structure, its theology and its literature. The Jewish form of the new faith persisted in the area, developing in its own distinct way a synthesis of ancient Jewish traditions and a belief in the messianic identity of the itinerant teacher from Galilee. It was a faith that was able to survive for more than four centuries, though its impact on the larger Christian community came primarily through its contribution to the Synoptic tradition.[84] We conclude then, that Christianity arrived in Banias during its earliest period, and that the Jewish-Christian community of the district of Banias left its imprint on the formative documents of the Church. Alongside this community, the rabbis of the Mishna, some of the most towering figures of the age, engaged in a different approach to the redefinition of Judaism. The extent and nature of the interaction between these two movements needs to be better understood, holding as they do the promise of important new insights into the development of both religions.[85]

Also awaiting further study is the connection between the Jewish-Christians of the Banias area and the development of both Syrian gentile Christianity and Manichaeism in Edessa, far to the east.[86] The Teaching of Addaeus the Apostle, in its surviving form a fifth-century document with earlier roots, was purportedly sent by one Addai (also called 'Thomas') to the king of Edessa in the mid-second century.[87] This document is somehow connected with the legends of Mani, the founder of Manichaeism, who is himself thought to have come from the Jewish-Christian sect of the Elkesaites. It has been suggested that Addai was sent east by the church at Antioch, since his successor was required to be ordained there. He may have been an Aramaic-speaking gentile. All this is of interest because the Teaching of Addaeus the Apostle contains the following statement:

> Those who are Hebrews, and knew only the Hebrew tongue in which they were born, behold today speak in all languages, that those who are far off, as those who are nigh, might hear and believe that He is the same, who confounded the tongues of the impious in this district, which lies before us; He it is who today teaches through us the faith of truth and verity, by humble and wretched men, who were from Galilee of Palestine. For I also, whom ye see, am from Paneas, from where the river Jordan goes forth. And I was chosen, with my companions, to be a preacher of this Gospel, by which, behold, the regions everywhere resound with the glorious name of the adorable Christ.

The presence of Jewish-Christian sects, including the Elkesaites, in the area of Banias; the curious reference to Banias as the home of those who 'knew only the Hebrew tongue in which they were born' but who now spread the 'faith of truth' to those who are far off; and the author's affirmation that he comes from Paneas, 'where the river Jordan goes forth' — these are thought-provoking to say the least, particularly in view of the apparent existence of an early Jewish-Christian community, somehow related to the Matthean traditions in the New Testament and centred in Banias.

6 Christ Versus Pan: Constantinian Banias

ASTYRIUS CHALLENGES PAN

Not long after the days of Diocletian, a renowned Roman senator named Astyrius of Caesarea Maritima visited Banias. A Christian, or at least a Christian sympathiser, Astyrius was a folk hero among the Christian communities during the days of the last persecutions before the reign of Constantine. Eusebius (*ca.* 260–*ca.* 340 AD) notes that 'many...stories are told about this man by acquaintances of his, who have survived my own time'. Among those stories, Eusebius continues, is 'the following miraculous incident':

> Near Caesarea Philippi, called Paneas by the Phoenicians, on the skirts of the mountain called Paneum, they point to springs believed to be the source of the Jordan. Into these they say that on a certain feast day a victim is thrown, and that by the demon's power it disappears from sight miraculously. This occurrence strikes the onlookers as a marvel to be talked of everywhere. One day Astyrius was there while this was going on, and when he saw that the business amazed the crowd he pitied their delusion, and looking up to heaven pleaded through Christ with God who is over all to refute the demon who was deluding the people and stop them from being deceived. When he had offered this prayer, it is said that the sacrifice instantly came to the surface of the water. Thus their miracle was gone, and nothing marvellous ever again happened at that spot.[1]

The story, somewhat reminiscent of the contest between Elijah and the prophets of Ba'al (I Kings 18), provides some important pieces of information, not the least of which is proof that a major pagan cult celebration was still to be seen in Banias only a generation before the time of Eusebius. Nevertheless, we could wish that Eusebius, who had visited the city and knew it well, had told us more than he chose to tell. He says the sacrificial victim (a goat?), thrown into the springs and pulled down by the power of the demon (Pan?), 'disappears from sight miraculously'. This occurs on 'a certain feast day' (during the annual festival of Pan?) Certainly this kind of ceremony was rooted in ancient Semitic traditions that pre-dated the cult of Pan. This is demonstrated by a story in Damascius of Damascus's *Life of Isodorus*. Damascius chronicles the travels of Isodorus of Gaza, a Neo-Platonic philosopher and near contemporary of Astyrius, as he makes a kind of pilgrimage to the (pagan) 'holy sites' of Palestine at the beginning of the fourth century. One of his stops was at a site on the Yarmuk River, not far from Banias, where he saw the performance of a rite with many similarities to the one that Eusebius describes in Banias. As at Banias, a victim was thrown into the water (though in this case the god's favour was shown if the victim floated, rather than if it sank into the water).[2]

The place of sacrifice mentioned in Eusebius's account was most likely the pool inside the cave, which Josephus describes as a 'yawning chasm' of 'immeasurable depth'. As we have already noted, no such chasm exists today, though it is possible that a pool once existed inside the cave, connected with the springs outside by some sort of conduit or covered channel. Christian apologists, in their attacks on paganism, often mentioned secret and forbidden recesses in the temples, where the pagan priests, by trickery and illusion, created 'miracles'. Such places were later to be exposed and destroyed by Constantine's soldiers and Christian mobs following the 'Triumph of the Church' during the second half of the fourth century. Eusebius accepts the phenomenon at Banias as truly miraculous, and not the result of deception. However, the point of his story, the triumph of Christ over the demon, is better served by this concession. In fact, access to the pool inside the cave may have been forbidden to all but the priests of Pan, so that even the historian Josephus had been forced to take their word for its depth. And who knows by what means the priests assisted Pan in drawing the sacrificial victim permanently into the 'bottomless' darkness?

The contest between Astyrius and Pan (or really, between Christ and Pan) becomes paradigmatic, a dramatic representation of the struggle that would grip the city for many generations. It was, in a sense, a contest eventually won primarily by the Christians active in the city who belonged to the party that enjoyed the favour of imperial policy. At the same time, it must be said that while Pan may no longer have been able to pull down the sacrificial victims into the deep, dark recesses of his cave sanctuary, he nevertheless continued to lurk in the shadows around his old home, even, as it might be argued, as he does to this day.

THE VICTORY OF 'ORTHODOXY'

Alongside the Jewish-Christian communities in Banias, communities of gentile Christians developed and grew there during the days of persecution in the second and third centuries. These communities at first exhibited the same diversity characteristic of Jewish-Christianity. But at least some, we may be sure, submitted themselves to a single monarchical bishop, as Ignatius of Antioch (*ca.* 110–17 AD), himself a Syrian, had so strongly urged. Such an arrangement protected the beleaguered movement from both Jewish-Christian and Gnostic 'heresies', on the one hand, and strengthened its defences against the horrible persecutions, on the other. Eusebius does not mention a Christian community in Banias in his tale of the contest between Astyrius and the pagans, but the appearance of the name 'Philokalos of Paneados' among those bishops who attended the famous Council of Nicea (325 AD) confirms the existence of such a community. The presence of a single

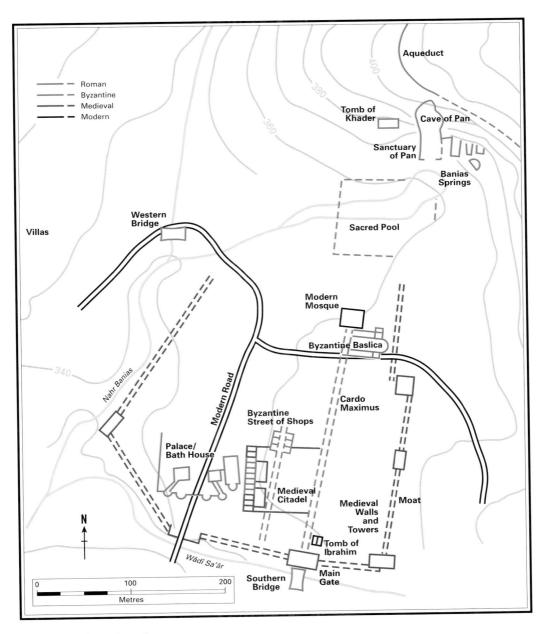

Aqueduct

Tomb of Khader

Cave of Pan

Sanctuary of Pan

Banias Springs

Villas

Western Bridge

Sacred Pool

Modern Mosque

Byzantine Baslica

Nahr Banias

Modern Road

Cardo Maximus

Byzantine Street of Shops

Palace/ Bath House

Medieval Citadel

Medieval Walls and Towers

Moat

N

Tomb of Ibrahim

Wâdî Sa'âr

Southern Bridge

Main Gate

0   100   200
Metres

1. Plan of the ancient city

2. Aerial View of the Site

The site of ancient Banias as seen from the fortress of Subaybah. 1. Modern Israeli settlement of Snir. 2. Site of ancient Dan. 3. The road to Tyre and the Mediterranean. 4. Unexcavated Roman villas. 5. The Roman and Byzantine necropolis. 6. The Cave of Pan. 7. Civic Centre. 8. Site of the Royal Palace. 9. The southern entrance gate. 10. Course of the Banias River. 11. Course of Wādī Saʻār. 12. Road to Damascus. 13. Tel ʻAzzaziyāt. 14. The Huleh.

3. Banias and the Foothills of Hermon

Northeast toward the foothills of Hermon. The foreground line of trees demarks the course of the Banias River. The Cave of Pan is behind the second row of trees at the base of the hills. Topping the central hill in the background is the medieval Fortress of Subaybah.

4. The Springs of Banias and the Cave of Pan

The great springs of Banias gush from the ground south of the Cave of Pan. To the right a large niche marks the site of a series of altars and temples. In Roman times a monumental entrance stood before the cave, and the waters of the springs were gathered into a 'sacred pool'. The worship of Pan continued here until at least the fourth Century AD.

5. Offering bowl from the Sanctuary
Locally made offering bowl from the Pan Sanctuary, one of hundreds left by worshippers between the second and fourth centuries.

6. *Opus reticulatum* wall above the Cave of Pan
Opus reticulatum wall on ridge above and 100 m southwest of the Cave of Pan. This style is characteristic of buildings built in Palestine by Herod the Great.

7. Coin of Antiochus III (223–187 BC) with Elephant

8. Zenodorus of Chalcis (30–20 BC) and Octavian (Augustus)

9. Portrait Coin of Herod Philip and the Augusteum, dated 1/2 BC

FORTVNAE AVGVSTAE

10. The Augusteum at Pompeii
Artist's reconstruction of the temple to Augustus
discovered at Pompeii, similar in size, date and
design to the Banias Augusteum.

11. Excavation of Temple at Omrit

First-century temple discovered approximately 2 km south of Banias along the road toward Bethsaida. The earliest phase of this building resembles the temple on the coins of Philip.

12. Portrait coin of Agrippa II as a youth, 41 AD

13. 'Neronias' coin of Agrippa II

14. Coin of Banias with ship (of Berenice?), 79/80 AD

15. Pan on coin of Agrippa II, 87/88 AD

16. Portrait coin (of Berenice?), 79/80 AD

17. Excavation of the palace of Agrippa II

Excavation of the Royal Palace-bathhouse complex of Banias. The view is to the west with the modern road leading southward into the Golan Heights crossing the top of the picture. In the foreground one of the round towers that fronted the massive complex is being uncovered.

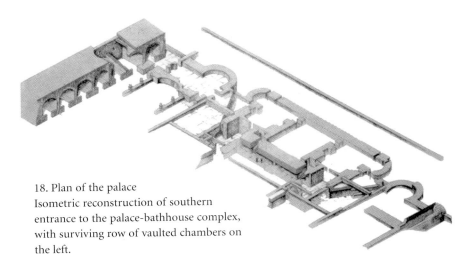

18. Plan of the palace
Isometric reconstruction of southern
entrance to the palace-bathhouse complex,
with surviving row of vaulted chambers on
the left.

19. Hypocaust system in remodelled palace
Excavation of the massive palace complex at Banias revealed evidence of remodeling
in the second and third centuries, transforming it into a public bathhouse. Here, one
of the rooms north of the formal palace basilica, originally adjoining an ornamental
pool, has been given a new floor and transformed into a hypocaust. Ceramic pillars
designed to support an upper floor stand here *in situ*. Water for the complex was
carried directly from the springs in ceramic pipes and stone channels.

Above

20. Pan Sanctuary

The Sanctuary of Pan following modern excavation. Earthquakes caused much of the front of the cave to collapse. Above the cave is the white-domed 'Tomb of Khader'. The ruins of the chapels to Pan, Zeus, and other gods to the right of the cave have been partially restored.

Below

21. Cave of Pan on Athenian Acropolis

The cave of Pan on the Acropolis in Athens, located in the centre of the photograph, was rediscovered in the nineteenth century. Yearly games and rituals were held in honour of the god that probably served as prototypes for similar exercises at Banias.

22. Banias Coin
of Zeus. Marcus
Aurelius, 169 AD

23. Banias Coin of Pan.
Caracalla, 196 AD

24. Banias Coin of Tyche and Julia Domna, dated 199 AD

25. Coin of Elagabal Commemorating 'Pan Festival'

26. Excavation of the Cardo Maximus

Ruins of the Cardo Maximus or 'Main Street' of ancient Banias. The column bases can be seen stretching toward the main southern gate of the city. During the Middle Ages the columns and paving stones were used to build a defensive wall (seen to the left of the column bases). Until its destruction in the 1960s, the main street of the modern village of Banias followed almost exactly the ancient course of the Cardo Maximus.

27. The 'Pan' of Lysippos
Copy of statue of
Lysippos in the Vatican
Museum. The cult
statue of Pan at Banias
was also based on this
work.

28. Philipos Antipatros inscription
Reused as the lintel of a doorway in a building near
the banks of the Banias River. Date c. 100–150 AD.

29. Inscription of Victor above Artificial Cave
Second-century inscription of Victor, son of Lysimachos,
priest of Pan, located in the Pan Sanctuary.

bishop also suggests that this community had heeded Ignatius's advice. In fact, in the increasingly centralising organisation of the church, Banias became one of the cities that fell under the jurisdiction of Ignatius's own successors, the Patriarchs of Antioch.[3]

CONSTANTINE'S ATTACK ON THE PAGAN TEMPLES

As the fourth century dawned, the Christian community in Banias found itself in a hostile environment – not only physically, but also intellectually. The resurgence of the cult of Pan reflected on the city's coins of 220 AD and beyond, the strong pro-pagan arguments represented by the Neo-Platonists Porphyry (233–*ca.*306) and his pupil Iamblichus (*ca.*250–*ca.*325), and the attempt to transform Pan into a sort of symbol for the universal Deity, may all be seen, at least partially, as responses to a growing Christian presence in Banias and elsewhere.

Then, suddenly, the Roman emperor Constantine declared himself the champion of the Christians and the tables were dramatically turned. Eusebius, in his *Life of Constantine*, describes how the power of the empire, so recently raging against the Christians, was now directed against the former persecutors. Constantine caused the doors to be stripped off the pagan temples and the roofs to be removed. Cult statues were dragged out of the sanctuaries and damaged or destroyed. The execution of this task required 'one or two only of his familiar circle', whom he sent out 'to every province'. They 'visited populous communities and nations, and city by city, country by country, they exposed the long-standing error, ordering the consecrated officials themselves to bring out their gods with much mockery and contempt from their dark recesses into daylight...'. Statues with gold or silver plating were stripped, and as for the bronze statues, 'these too were led captive, gods of stale legends dressed in hair cloth'.[4]

While Banias is not mentioned specifically as the site of such activity, other pagan sanctuaries in the immediate area are. For example, the temple of Aphrodite at Aphaca on part of the summit of Mount Libanos was destroyed.[5] Those delegates from Constantine's 'familiar circle' were particularly concerned to destroy cultic centres known for orgiastic worship. Pan, as we know, had a reputation for sexual misconduct. While we know only a little about how the worship of Pan was carried on at Banias, it is possible that the rites there involved sexual activity, or at least explicit sexual imagery.[6]

Thus, the cave of Pan may well have been one of those 'dark caves' described by Eusebius: '...every dark cave and every secret recess was readily accessible to the emperor's emissaries, and forbidden innermost sanctuaries of temples were trodden by soldiers feet...'. Carried away with his enthusiasm for this process, Eusebius seems oblivious to the irony of his words: some pagans, he says, when they 'observed the actual desolation of shrines and establishments everywhere...took refuge in the saving Word'.[7]

Of course there is always the chance that the pagan sanctuaries of Banias were overlooked. As Robin Lane Fox notes in his book *Pagans and Christians*, 'Nobody could hope to control every nook and cranny in the Mediterranean landscape'.[8] Given its location and prominence, however, Banias is likely to have been among those attacked. Archaeological evidence suggests that the sanctuary of Pan was not completely destroyed at this time, however. Rather, it gradually declined, in tandem with the general decline of the city itself, a century or more after the anti-pagan campaigns of Constantine.[9]

This means that the worship of Pan did not collapse under the onslaught. Far from it. Despite the widely quoted passage in Plutarch that claimed the death of 'the great god Pan' during the days of Tiberius Caesar,[10] worship of the goat-footed god continued to flourish – not only during the reign of Constantine, but for centuries thereafter. Iamblichus describes 'Pan-possession' in his day as if it were something very much within his readers' experience.[11] Elsewhere, we know that Pan-worship survived at the ancient cult sites. The cave of Pan at Phyle in Attica, for example, continued to attract pilgrims: two of them left inscriptions in its cave datable to the fourth century.[12] And subsequent events in Banias were to prove that his devotees, though subdued, had not abandoned the ancient faith, despite the pressure of Constantine's 'associates'.

EUSEBIUS VERSUS PORPHYRY

Paganism did not submit quietly to the new faith. Having failed to destroy it by force, the advocates of the old way now attempted to meet the Christians on the intellectual battlefield. In the regions near Banias they found an eloquent apologist in Iamblichus, a pupil of Porphyry and a leading Neo-Platonist. A native of nearby Chalcis (Anjar, in the Beka'a Valley, the one-time capital of the Iturean kingdom of Ptolemy and of Herod of Chalcis and Berenice), Iamblichus's works sought to provide a stronger intellectual base for the old religion, and earned him deification by his students, and the title 'theos'.[13]

The philosophical and theological lines of conflict, as opposed to the physical ones, can be illustrated by Eusebius's arguments in *Concerning Images*, a work in which he challenges Porphyry's defence of paganism, including the cult of the god Pan. Porphyry gives this explanation of the manner in which Pan was depicted by the ancients: 'They made Pan the symbol of the universe, and gave him his horns as symbols of sun and moon, and the fawn skin as emblem of the stars in heaven, or of the variety of the universe'.[14] Eusebius rejects this attempt to universalise the god out of hand. He calls to witness an oracle cited by Porphyry and accepted as authentic by him:

> To Pan, a god of kindred race,
> A mortal born my vows I pay;
> Whose hornéd brows and cloven feet
> And goat-like legs his lust betray.[15]

This oracle proves, Eusebius argues, that Pan is not a symbol of the universe at all, but only 'some such daemon as is described, who also gave forth the oracle: for of course it was not the universe, and the whole world, that gave the oracle which we have before us. The men therefore who fashioned the likeness of this daemon, and not that of the universe, imitated the figure before described.'

Nor will Eusebius accept Porphyry's contention that Pan is a 'good daemon', as claimed in the latter's lost work, *Of the Philosophy Derived from Oracles*. The oracle in question begins:

Lo! where the golden-hornéd Pan
In study Dionysos' train
Leaps o'er the mountains' wooded slopes!
His right hand holds a shepherd's staff,
His left a smooth shrill-breathing pipe,
That charms the gentle wood-nymph's soul.
But at the sound of that strange song
Each startled woodsman dropp'd his axe,
And all in frozen terror gaz'd
Upon the Daemon's frantic course.
Death's icy hand had seiz'd them all,
Had not the huntress Artemis
In anger stay'd his furious might,
To her address thy prayer for aid.[16]

But Pan cannot possibly be a 'good daemon' as Porphyry claims, says Eusebius, because in the very context of these verses nine woodsmen, so startled by the appearance of the god, were almost literally frightened to death when he appeared to them. 'Did then any good result to the beholders of this good daemon, or have they found him an evil daemon, and learned this by practical experience?' he derisively asks.[17]

The Christian scholar then drives home his argument with a reference to the famous story from Plutarch of the voice that called to some sailors 'during the time of Tiberius', telling them 'The Great God Pan is dead'.[18] 'It is important to observe the time at which he says that the death of the daemon took place,' Eusebius suggests. 'For it was the time of Tiberius, in which our Saviour, making His sojourn among men, is recorded to have been ridding human life from Daemons of every kind: so that there were some of them now kneeling before Him and beseeching Him not to deliver them over to the Tartarus that awaited them.'[19] Thus, Eusebius specifically identifies Pan as one of the demons overthrown by Jesus during his ministry.[20]

Despite the derisive, even sarcastic tone that Eusebius takes in this controversy, it is clear that he regards the worship of Pan, and of the pagan gods in general, a phenomenon still to be taken very seriously. If Jesus had brought the demonic world to its knees, this fact was not yet sufficiently recognised among the citizens of the empire. More than a century after Eusebius, the struggle between local Christians and the priests of Pan in the village of Pleuit in Egypt was still sufficiently intense to result in violence (by Christian monks) and consequent court action (by the priests of Pan).[21] Ironically, among certain heterodox Christians such as the Valentinian Gnostics Pan had even been identified with Jesus. The Jesus 'who passed through Mary' was, they claimed, possessed by a higher being, the Christ, who 'was also termed Pan'.[22] The struggle between Christ and Pan was certainly far from over in the city of Banias.[23]

THE 'STATUE OF CHRIST' AT BANIAS

To Eusebius we also owe the first literary reference to Banias's famous 'statue of Christ'. This work originally stood in some prominent spot in the city, and later was the precious possession of the local Christians, preserved in one of their churches. Because of it, the city became an important pilgrimage site. Having mentioned the city in connection with the visit of Astyrius, Eusebius remarks that he ought not to 'omit a story that deserves to be remembered by those who will follow us'. The story concerns that woman healed by Jesus of her persistent haemorrhage, mentioned in the Synoptic tradition,[24] a woman, Eusebius notes, who 'was stated to have come from here [Banias]'.

He continues:

> Her house was pointed out in the city, and a wonderful memorial of the benefit the Saviour conferred upon her was still there. On a tall stone base at the gates of her house stood a bronze statue of a woman, resting on one knee and resembling a suppliant with arms outstretched. Facing this was another of the same material, an upright figure of a man with a double cloak neatly draped over his shoulders and his hand stretched out to the woman. Near his feet on the stone slab grew an exotic plant, which climbed up on to the hem of the bronze cloak and served as a remedy for illnesses of every kind. This statue, which was said to resemble the features of Jesus, was still there in my own time, so that I saw it with my own eyes when I resided in the city.[25]

Note that Eusebius once 'resided' in Banias and presumably knew not only the statue, but also something of the town, its inhabitants and its Christian community. It is obvious, however, that while he admits the story 'deserves to be remembered', he nevertheless betrays a hint of scepticism in his accounting of it: she 'was stated' to have come from there; and the statue 'was said' to resemble the features of Jesus. It is particularly strange that Eusebius does not take the trouble to describe the features of the man depicted in the statue. Surely if he believed these were actually the features of Jesus he would have left some description, since he had seen them 'with his own eyes'.[26] We may, however, yet be able to find a record of those features, from a totally unexpected source – as we shall see.

It is worthwhile to review the whole biblical story, in order to see how the statue (or rather the grouping of statues) that Eusebius saw in Banias differs in important ways from the story as it is told in the New Testament:

> A woman was there [in Capernaum] who had been subject to bleeding for twelve years, but no one could heal her. She came up behind him and touched the edge of his cloak, and immediately her bleeding stopped. 'Who touched me?' Jesus asked. When they all denied it, Peter said, 'Master, the people are crowding and pressing against you'. But Jesus said, 'Someone touched me; I know that power has gone out from me'. Then the woman, seeing that she could not go unnoticed, came trembling and fell at his feet. In the presence of all the people, she told why she had touched him and how she had been instantly healed. Then he said to her, 'Daughter, your faith has healed you. Go in peace'.[27]

In the Synoptic story, Jesus has his back turned away from the woman when the healing occurs. It is true that she later falls at his feet, but not as a suppliant; the miracle had already been performed. Eusebius describes the woman in the grouping at Banias as 'resting on one knee and resembling a suppliant with arms outstretched'. Also, the 'power' which went out from Jesus's person via the hem of his garment has been transformed into 'an exotic plant, which climbed up on to the hem of the bronze cloak and served as a remedy for illnesses of every kind'. The language is not completely clear, but he seems to suggest that the plant is a living one, a vine growing on the statue's stone base or pedestal, which has climbed up and attached itself to the cloak of the male figure in the group.

Clearly, the statue that Eusebius saw at Banias did not draw its inspiration directly from the gospel account. In fact, though the statue was most likely of great antiquity when Eusebius saw it, his scepticism concerning its authenticity as an accurate depiction of Jesus was undoubtedly warranted. The reasons are several. First, it is inconceivable that a statue of Jesus, standing in a prominent place in the centre of a pagan city, could have survived the recurring persecutions of Christians during the second and third centuries. It would have been far too easy a target to overlook. We know, for example, that Diocletian ordered Maximinus, his governor in the East, to destroy all Christian buildings in 303 AD. But such a prominent statue would hardly have survived even that long.[28] Furthermore, the great Christian apologists of the second and third centuries (Origen, who had lived at nearby Tyre, Justin Martyr, who was from Palestine, and Clement of Alexandria) are all silent concerning the statue. Surely they would have used its existence as an argument for the authenticity of the Christian Gospel, and the power of Jesus, had they been able to do so. As for the woman, there is no hint in the gospels that she was connected with Banias in any way,[29] and no reason to consider her anything but a practising Jew, making the erection of a graven image by her extremely doubtful.

Later Christian historians, in embellishing the story, seem to sense these problems and begin to identify the woman as some wealthy gentile whose name was known from New Testament times (Berenice as Veronica; obviously representing some sort of conflation with Berenice, the Queen of Banias in the days of Agrippa II), or else to create a Greek name for her, based on the word used to describe her ailment in the Gospels ('Marinosa'). All these problems, when added to the disparities between the statue group described by Eusebius and the gospel account (in which the woman clearly touched Jesus from behind), must lead us to conclude that the sculptor was not attempting to portray the gospel story and therefore that the statue was not, in fact, a statue of Jesus.

The statue was most likely of great antiquity, nevertheless. Several possibilities have been suggested. The group described by Eusebius could quite plausibly have been a contemporary depiction of, say, Titus and Herod Agrippa II's half-sister Berenice, who were famous lovers prior to Titus's ascension to the imperial throne. This might explain the appearance of the name Berenice as that of the woman healed of haemorrhage in certain Byzantine church histories.[30] Alternately, the statues might have depicted some pagan myth such as that of the healing god Asclepios[31] and his daughter Panacea.[32] More likely, as we have already suggested, the figures represented the Emperor Hadrian accepting homage from a grateful province, depicted as a woman.

Whatever the intention of the sculptor, a period of time sufficiently long to allow a break in local memory and tradition would be necessary in order to allow for a new attribution. Just such a break is described in the account of the statue found in the *Ecclesiastical History* of the Arian historian Philostorgius, written between 425 and 433 AD.[33] The statue, he says, was originally 'placed near the fountain in the city among other statues, and presented a pleasant and agreeable sight to the passers-by'. However, because of the 'lapse of time', all memory of the statue's significance had been lost and 'it was even forgotten whose statue it was, and on what account it had been erected'. Not only this, but in the course of time the statue had become partially buried, so that even though 'the figure of our Saviour had long stood exposed in the open air…a great part of it was covered over by the earth which was perpetually carried down against the pediment [*sic*], especially during seasons of heavy rain'. An excavation followed and 'the part of the statue which had been covered up' was again brought to light.

Philostorgius had visited Banias and had apparently seen what was left of the statue approximately a century or so after the events he describes surrounding its 'rediscovery'. However, his account of these events cannot be regarded as entirely accurate. He claims, for example, that when uncovered and read, the inscription on the statue told the story of Jesus and the woman. And he fails altogether to mention the statue of the women kneeling before the male figure. Still, his information most likely came from the Christian community in Banias and seems quite plausible in general. Philostorgius was apparently told that the excavation of the statue was triggered by the discovery that 'a certain herb, which grew up at the foot of this statue' was 'a most effectual remedy against all diseases, and especially against consumption'. Unfortunately, so the tradition maintained, in the process of excavating the statue the plant itself was uprooted and 'thenceforth was never again seen either there or in any other place'.[34]

By the time Philostorgius visited Banias, the statue had undergone a whole series of adventures, as we shall see. In fact, nothing had survived but the head, which had been preserved and venerated in a local church. Eusebius, on the other hand, saw the statue intact while it still stood in a prominent public place, alongside the second statue, that of the woman supplicant. Both figures stood on 'a tall stone base' at the gates of a house that Eusebius was told had belonged to the woman. It is hardly possible that a private home would have stood in the city centre, near the spring of Pan, among the sanctuaries and public buildings.[35] It is possible that some building there was later identified by the Christians as the woman's house, merely because the statue seemed to be associated with it. If, as we suggest below, a bas-relief representation of the 'house' itself has survived from ancient times, its design as depicted is somewhat unusual for a private home. Eusebius saw the medicinal plant, so Philostorgius must be mistaken in thinking the plant disappeared when the statue's inscription was excavated. The plant, Eusebius explains, grew 'on the stone slab' and 'climbed up on to the hem of the bronze cloak' of the male figure, where it 'served as a remedy for illnesses of every kind'. All this Eusebius says he saw 'with my own eyes'.

We may conclude that the statue was an old one, 'rediscovered' sometime in the early fourth century. This date seems plausible, since the rediscovery of the statue must have occurred long enough before Eusebius's visit to allow the tradition to become firmly entrenched among the local Christians, but sometime after the official persecution of the local Christian community had ended. The statue had been attributed to Jesus partly because, taken together with that of the woman, it reminded the local Christians of the gospel story, and partly because of the inscription. While the inscription cannot have been as explicit as claimed by Philostorgius, it could well have contained words such as 'ΣΩΤΗΡ' ('Saviour') or 'ΚΥΡΙΟΣ' ('Lord') or 'ΕΥΕΡΓΕΤΗΣ' ('Benefactor') – titles used by pagans of rulers and gods, but also by the Christians of Jesus.[36] Eusebius makes no mention of a more explicit inscription, which he surely would have done, had one existed.

If the statue is not really a depiction of Jesus, then who was the subject the sculptor had in mind? We have already noted the interesting theory that the statue group represents Asclepios, the god of healing, and his daughter Panacea.[37] Adolf Harnack thinks that the presence of the healing plant favoured such identification.[38] Others, less convincingly, have suggested that the statue represented a Gnostic rendering of Veronica and Christ[39] or some Jewish celebrity such as Apollonius of Tyana (since a story exists of the latter healing a young woman, and since he was active in the Banias area).[40] Several political figures are possible subjects. The visits to Banias of Vespasian and his son Titus during the First Jewish Revolt might have been commemorated by the raising of a statue group. The woman might be a representation of the province, or, in the case of Titus, of his lover, Berenice. But most likely, as we have suggested, the victorious emperor depicted is Hadrian, the occasion the 'advent' of the emperor in the area, or perhaps the successful repression of the Bar Kochba Revolt, and the woman the province, in the manner of several coins issued at the time.[41] It is true that Eusebius describes the male figure as dressed in Greek style, but there are many examples of Roman generals and emperors depicted in this way – including Hadrian.

THE LATERAN SARCOPHAGUS

An ornate ancient sarcophagus formerly in the Lateran Museum in Rome, now in the Pio Christian Museum in the Vatican, may provide an important clue to the identity of the statue, and perhaps even allow us a glimpse of Banias itself in the early fourth century (Fig. 30). The sarcophagus, made of Greek marble and exhibiting excellent artistic skill, was found beneath the floor of the basilica of St Peter in Rome in 1591.[42] A fourth-century date is clear, not only on the grounds of artistic style, but also because the architecture of several buildings depicted on the sarcophagus; the style of the curtains in the entrance-ways is also consistent with this dating.[43] The sarcophagus belongs to the period during which the style of such objects moved from 'symbolic' themes to 'narrative' ones, and thus tended to depict topics in more realistic and less traditional ways.[44]

The front panel of the sarcophagus displays a series of biblical scenes, separated from each other by Corinthian columns. In the central scene Christ is shown in the manner of a triumphant youthful Apollo, with long curly hair – a convention with parallels in primitive Christian paintings in the catacombs.[45] The left side panel shows Jesus predicting Peter's denial. Between the two male figures is a statue of a cock mounted on a pedestal or column, toward which the figure of Jesus points. In the background can be seen a number of buildings.[46] Two scenes are depicted on the right panel. The first, on the left, is a rendering of Moses striking the rock. To the left of Moses a male supplicant, kneeling on one knee, left hand outstretched, looks up toward a tree growing on top of the rock. From the roots of the tree flows a fountain of water.[47]

But it is the right side of this panel, which catches our attention. A mature, laureate,[48] bearded man stands facing left, his left hand to his side, grasping the folds of his robe (Fig. 32). His right arm is extended, reaching out to touch the head of a female figure kneeling before him. Her mantle covers her head and her arms are outstretched in supplication. Her eyes are cast down.

The bas-relief is obviously meant to depict Jesus's healing of the woman with the issue of blood. But the treatment is very different from the usual conventions, not only in the way it organises the scene, but also in the way it depicts Jesus. Artistic representations of this healing are not uncommon, but they consistently follow the biblical text, that is they show Jesus with his back to the woman, while she touches his garment.[49] Furthermore, both figures are on the same scale, whereas the usual custom was to make Jesus much bigger than the woman. The woman, veiled and holding out her hand before the Saviour, without touching his robe, differs from all other depictions of this scene on sarcophagi. And a bearded Jesus in such a scene is almost unheard of during this period. The usual convention is to show Jesus without a beard, as he is shown on the front panel of the Lateran sarcophagus, except when he is depicted as the Resurrected Lord.[50]

All these anomalies were apparently first noticed in 1737 by the Italian scholar Bottari, in a work called *Sculture e Pitture Sagre*.[51] Bottari also noticed that, while the depiction did not fit the biblical account, it was an almost exact representation of the statue group at Banias, as described by an eyewitness, Eusebius of Caesarea. It is worth taking another look at Eusebius's account, to see the similarity:

> Her [the woman's] house was pointed out in the city, and a wonderful memorial of the benefit the Saviour conferred upon her was still there. On a tall stone base at the gates of her house stood a bronze statue of a woman, resting on one knee and resembling a suppliant with arms outstretched. Facing this was another of the same material, an upright figure of a man with a double cloak neatly draped over his shoulders and his hand stretched out to the woman.[52]

Bottari concludes that the reason the Lateran sarcophagus flaunted the artistic conventions was that, unlike the front panel (where the symbolic Apollo-image appears, surrounded by other conventional symbols), the right side panel (and probably the left one as well) depicted actual statues. Thus the model for the Healing of the Woman with the Issue of Blood, so different from the gospel account, but so much like that of Eusebius, must have been the very statue group pointed out to Eusebius on his visit to Banias. Furthermore, the artist must have based his work on the original statues, and not on Eusebius's account, since the latter said nothing about the beard or laureate head, both striking exceptions to conventional depictions of the Saviour.[53]

Some scholars who have argued that the statue was actually a contemporary rendering of Jesus, as Eusebius had been told, claim that Bottari's discovery shows that the figure on the Lateran sarcophagus is not a symbolic convention, but a 'portrait'.[54] And a 'portrait' it may be, though almost certainly not of Jesus, as we have shown. Rather, it is more likely a 'portrait' of the statue, as it could be seen in the early fourth century, standing, rediscovered after years of neglect and partial burial, by the spring near the centre of the city of Banias.[55]

Bottari also notices the clear similarity between the bearded laureate head of 'Jesus' – profile facing to the left, and the laureate head of Hadrian on certain coins (Fig. 31).[56] The similarity is in fact so striking as to suggest strongly that, if the sarcophagus indeed refers to Banias, the statue group must have originally commemorated Hadrian's subjugation of Judaea or the homage of the province of Syria, symbolised by the supplicant woman. Neither Vespasian nor his son Titus wore beards, making it much less likely that the statue group was inspired by the iconography of the well-known 'Judaea Capta' coins of the later first century.

The Bar Kochba Revolt was suppressed by 135 AD and the statue, along with others,[57] was probably erected in this gentile pagan city, where even the Jewish population remained loyal to the emperor, soon thereafter. Time and general neglect, however, particularly during the difficult third century, resulted in the partial burial of the imperial statue. When the citizens of Banias cleared away the debris of almost two centuries, the by-now substantial Christian community concluded that the statue, bearing some title by that time commonly attributed to the Lord Jesus, and associated with both a supplicant woman and a miraculous healing plant, must commemorate the healing recounted in the gospels.

A CONTEMPORARY DEPICTION OF THE
CONSTANTINIAN CHURCHES OF BANIAS?

A number of buildings appear in the background on both side panels of the Lateran sarcophagus. If the figures in the foreground represent actual statues, then it becomes possible that the buildings depicted are real, historical ones as well. Leclercq and Perate have suggested that the buildings behind the statue of the cock on the left panel of the sarcophagus are in fact the Church of the Holy Sepulchre and the Church of St Peter in Gallicantu ('the cock's crow') in Jerusalem.[58] There is evidence that such a bronze cock on a column stood in Byzantine Jerusalem.[59] The precedent for this kind of arrangement is the famous mosaic in the apse of the church of Saint Pudentiana in Rome (late fourth century), where a number of Constantinian ecclesiastical structures in Jerusalem are pictured in considerable detail.[60]

The 'Banias' panel pictures two planes, superimposed in such a way as to indicate distance between the upper row of buildings and the single building directly behind the kneeling woman. The upper level appears to feature two basilicas, each with an adjoining round tower or possibly depicting a baptistery. All three buildings exhibit considerable detail and the two basilicas differ in several ways, as do the round buildings adjoining them. These differences suggest that real models, rather than mere convention, determined the sculptor's renderings. The lower building (basilica?), with a stairway leading up to its curtained entrance, appears to be somewhat smaller than those above it. These buildings can hardly be merely decorative, Perate has noted, and since the buildings on the left panel seem to be real ones, those on the right are as well, representing in fact 'les édifices sacrés de Paneas'.[61]

The smaller building, situated directly behind the kneeling woman, may well represent the 'house' which Eusebius saw, now replaced or enlarged to become a church or memorial. The 'house' may have picked up its attribution from the statue. If, as the local Christian community thought, the statue and the house belonged together, and if the statue were to be understood as an *ex voto* erected by the woman, then, they would have concluded, the house must have belonged to the woman as well. Once the identification was made, the building would have been transformed in the community's mind into a holy site.

The two larger buildings on the sarcophagus panel perhaps depict the main ecclesiastical buildings in the town, represented as standing some distance from the woman's house. One of these would most likely be the cathedral under the charge of Bishop Philokalos of Paneas, who attended the Council of Nicea in 325 AD as the guest of Constantine.[62] The impression we get is of a vigorous and rather powerful 'orthodox' Christian community that boasted ownership of two or three impressive structures, one of which served no doubt as the centre for the community's worship, and another as an aspiring place of pilgrimage.

Excavations at Banias have revealed a large basilica that is almost certainly a very early Christian church (Figs 33, 34). The building was constructed directly over structures dating to the Herodian and Roman periods, and numerous architectural elements of these buildings have been incorporated into it. The fine grey granite columns which are widely scattered over the site today probably were incorporated into the church from an earlier Roman building, as were the well-made column bases found near the walls of the church. Particularly striking is the reuse of finely carved white limestone fragments in the walls and even in the foundation trenches. The building was very large but was itself mostly destroyed and its stones reused to build the towers and walls of the medieval fortress. A portion of the apse and the rooms and aisles of the northeast corner and the line of the north outside wall survive. This basilica was located directly in the centre of the city, its atrium opening directly on to the Cardo Maximus. This important location suggests that it was the seat of the bishops of Banias who attended the various ecumenical councils of the Church during the fourth and fifth centuries. It was likely the repository of the 'statue of Christ' as well.[63]

The church may be dated on the basis of ceramic evidence and general architectural style. It is possible, though not probable, that the church was built in the pre-Constantinian period. Eusebius records what Crowfoot called 'a perfect fever of church building' during the period of peace from the time of Gallienus to the middle years of Diocletian.[64] Eusebius says, 'No longer satisfied with the old buildings, they raised from the foundations in all the cities churches spacious in plan'.[65] Most of these early structures were destroyed during the 'Great Persecution', though some survived. The presence of a small, inscribed apse, the narrowness of the aisles, the colonnades, doors along the sides, and the use of stones from classical buildings all point to a fourth-century date at the latest.[66] Certainly a church stood in Banias at the time of the discovery of the 'statue of Christ', presumably prior to the reign of Julian. Sozomen (writing *ca.* 445 AD) says that the church was the depository of the statue in his day.[67] Both Sozomen[68] and Eusebius[69] recount the building of churches from the remains of recently destroyed pagan temples during Constantine's reign. The latter notes that in Heliopolis, Constantine destroyed the temple of Venus and ordered a Christian church to be built in its place. This might have been the occasion for the building of a church in Banias as well.

The memory of a church in Banias seems to be retained in a garbled fashion in a ninth- to tenth-century work entitled *The Life of Constantine*.[70] A stone commemorating the place where the woman was healed had been set up between Capernaum and the nearby 'Seven Wells' near the north shore of the Sea of Galilee, where the Monk Epiphanius (750–800 AD) saw it. *The Life of Constantine*, recounting the visit of the emperor's mother Helena to the Holy Land, says: 'When she found the stone bearing the sign of the cross, where he healed the woman with the issue of blood, she built a church at the spot'. This church is also later mentioned in two medieval manuscripts.[71] It is, however, in the words of Clemens Kopp, 'a church of the imagination'. These sources do indeed retain the memory of a very early church erected to commemorate the miracle, but they have moved the church, in error, from Paneas to the traditional site of the healing itself.[72] It is possible that the building is one of those depicted on the Lateran sarcophagus, perhaps the one which the locals believed was the woman's house, now transformed into a church. Sponsoring such a project would be an act of piety particularly appealing to the well-meaning, if somewhat credulous, queen mother.[73]

It should be noted that the traditions connecting Banias and the haemorrhaging woman were not entirely firm, even at the beginning of the fifth century. We have seen a hint of scepticism between the lines in Eusebius's account. Marcarius Magnes, a contemporary of Eusebius writing in about 400 AD, moves the woman, and perhaps also the statue, far to the northeast. He conflates the story of the haemorrhaging woman with that of Berenice, the sister of Herod Agrippa II, noting that the latter 'once was mistress of a famous place' but also making her 'the honoured ruler of the great city of Edessa'. He claims that the miracle is celebrated 'until our own time in Mesopotamia' and that 'the woman had that event represented in a living manner by means of a well-done image' – presumably located in Edessa as well, although he doesn't specifically say so.[74] Another contemporary, Asterius of Amaseia, writing at about the same time (*ca.* 380–90 AD), claims that the statue of Christ, though indeed once standing in Banias, had been destroyed by the emperor Maximian. Nevertheless, he pictures the fame of the statue as so extensive that it is hard to see how his contemporary Macarius could have misplaced it by several hundred miles.[75] And Eusebius had, after all, seen the statue in Banias; so had Philostorgius, a century later. Asterius has most likely been influenced and misled by the knowledge that Maximian did indeed destroy many Christian buildings under the command of Diocletian, in the year 303 AD. His credibility as an historical witness is weakened by the fact that he refers to Banias as 'a little village' at a time when archaeological evidences indicates it was in fact still a city of significant size.

7 Pan Versus Christ: Byzantine Banias

JULIAN THE APOSTATE AND THE 'STATUE OF CHRIST'

The 'rediscovery' of the 'statue of Christ' came during that half-century or so during which Constantine and his sons Constantine II (337–40 AD) and Constantius (337–61 AD) favoured and encouraged the Christians. Although, as we have seen, some action was taken against some pagan cult sites at this time, and particularly against some cult objects, there was no wholesale destruction of temples. Rather, according to Theodoret of Cyrrhus (writing *ca.* 449–50 AD), Constantine merely ordered that the temples be kept shut. His sons continued this policy.[1]

Matters took another unexpected and dramatic twist, however, when Constantine's brilliant but eccentric nephew Julian found himself on the imperial throne. Absolute power emboldened him to bring into the open his hitherto well-kept secret: he had repudiated the Christian faith of his family and returned to Hellenism – the worship of the old gods.

It is in the context of this turn of events that the story of the 'statue of Christ' at Banias advances to the next stage. The first witness is again Philostorgius (writing *ca.* 425–33 AD).[2] During Julian's reign, he says, the Christians placed the statue 'in the part of the church which was allotted to the deacons [that is the Sacristy or διακονικόν]'.[3] Byzantine churches had rooms on either side of the central apse, one of which was used by the priests and deacons to store offerings and other artifacts. A room has been excavated to the north of the apse in the great church at Banias which the excavator suggests may be the very room in question, constructed specifically to house the statue, and designed with multiple entrances to facilitate the visits of numerous pilgrims (Fig. 33).[4] Here, Philostorgius says, the Christians paid the statue 'due honour and respect, yet by no means adoring or worshipping it; and they showed their love for its great archetype by erecting it in that place with circumstances of honour, and by flocking thither in eager crowds to behold it'.

Then, however, disaster struck:

The Ἑλληνικοί [the Hellenists, that is the pagans] who inhabited Paneas were excited by an impious frenzy to pull down this statue from its pediment [sic], and to drag it through the midst of the streets with ropes fastened round its feet; afterwards they broke in pieces the rest of the body, while some persons, indignant at the whole proceeding, secretly obtained possession of the head, which had become detached from the neck as it was dragged along and they preserved it as far as was possible.

This remnant of the statue, Philostorgius asserts, he had seen for himself.[5]

The story cannot be accepted uncritically in every detail, but it does fit quite well with what is known about events in the Levant during Julian's short reign (361–63 AD). Fortunately another, independent, version of the story exists, written only a decade or two after that of Philostorgius. Sozomen, recounting the history of the Church during the years 323–425 AD, furnishes many additional details, as well as a wider context for the destruction of the statue.

Sozomen was born at Bethelia, a town not far from Gaza, and knew Palestine well.[6] He had at his disposal not only his own experience, but also no doubt the testimony of many local witnesses to the traditions of the area. Referring to the reign of Constantine, he notes that not all cult statues were destroyed; some, including the 'much extolled Pan' of Pausanias, were preserved for art's sake, being used to decorate public places such as streets, hippodromes and palaces. True, he continues, many cities 'without any command of the emperor, destroyed the adjacent temples and statues, and erected houses of prayer'.[7] Nevertheless, even in the decade beginning 380 AD, 'there were still pagans in many cities, who contended zealously in behalf of their temples; as, for instance, the inhabitants of Petraea and Areopolis, in Arabia; of Raphi and Gaza, in Palestine; of Hieropolis in Phoenicia; and of Apamea, on the river Axius, in Syria'.[8] A glance at a map will show that these cities describe a circle around Banias. Sozomen particularly notes that 'peasants of Lebanon' and 'men of Galilee' were employed by the city of Apamea in Syria 'in defence of their temples' when the local bishop Marcellus ordered their destruction.[9]

Banias, not only in the heartland of this pagan resistance, but itself a major cultic centre, was surely still overwhelmingly pagan in sentiment when Julian rose to the throne. The statue, already a prominent attraction for Christian pilgrims, must have been particularly odious to the local pagan establishment, as were the expensive ecclesiastical buildings, no doubt erected at public expense by the family of Constantine. And thus the stage was set for a confrontation, whose outcome, the Christian historian is sure, 'affords a sign of the power of Christ, and proof of the Divine wrath against the emperor'. Here is the story as Sozomen tells it:

> Having heard that at Caesarea Philippi, otherwise called Panease [Paneades], a city of Phoenicia, there was a celebrated statue of Christ, which had been erected by a woman whom the Lord had cured of a flow of blood. Julian commanded it to be taken down, and a statue of himself erected in its place; but a violent fire from heaven fell upon it, and broke off the parts contiguous to the breast; the head and neck were thrown prostrate, and it was transfixed to the ground with the face downwards at the point where the fracture of the bust was; and it has stood in that fashion from that day until now, full of the rust of the lightning.[10]

Philostorgius and Sozomen differ on a number of details. Did the mob tear the statue from a place of honour in the local basilica, where the Christians had already placed it, or was it only deposited there after it had been mutilated and rescued? The latter sequence seems more likely. It is curious that Philostorgius does not mention the statue of Julian, but having already located the statue of Christ in the church, prior to the anti-Christian riot, he can hardly find a logical way to incorporate that part of the story. Sozomen's account again makes more sense, and he does, after all, claim that the statue of Julian was still lying where it fell in his own day. Thus, fragments of both statues were still to be seen in the city a century after the riot.

Two contemporaries of Julian, one a friend and one an enemy, both personally acquainted with the emperor, provide corroboration for the feasibility of this story. Libanius (314–*ca.*392 AD) was, like Julian, a pagan. The emperor, he says,

> restored piety, as it were, from exile. Some temples he built, others he restored, while he furnished others with statues…If any city had temples still standing, he was delighted at the sight and thought them deserving of the greatest kindness, but if they had demolished all or the greater part of them, he called them polluted: he offered them a share in the benefits he dispensed, as being his subjects, but not without annoyance.[11]

Furthermore, '…many cities have set up his [portrait] in the temple of the gods and honour him as they do the gods, and before now people have offered up prayers to him also, asking some blessing, and they have not been disappointed. So obviously has he ascended to heaven and has partaken of the power of the divine by the will of the gods themselves.'[12]

Julian's practice of setting up statues of himself was particularly reprehensible to the Christian theologian Gregory of Nazianzos, who had also known the emperor when both were students in Athens. It is true that other emperors erected statues of themselves, he says, but Julian

> associates his own portraits with the figures of his demons, pretending that they were some other sort of customary representations. He exposes these figures to peoples and to cities, and above all to those in government of nations, so that he could not miss being in one way or another mischievous: for either by the honour paid to the sovereign that to idols was also insinuated, or else by the shunning of the latter the sovereign himself was insulted, the worship of the two being mixed up together.[13]

Sozomen's claim, then, that the 'statue of Christ' had been replaced in Banias with one of Julian seems to fit the contemporary situation well. Evidence also exists that Julian had a particular interest in the god Pan, which might partially account for his interest in Banias, the city of Pan. Gregory, complaining of Julian's refusal to use the word 'Christian' and using instead the term 'Nazarites' as a term of ridicule, ridicules the names of pagan gods in retaliation. Pan is a particular object of his derision: 'Venerable "Pan" himself, one god born out of many lovers, and receiving his disgrace for his name; for with them it is necessary either that the one and the most excellent Being should have sinned against many women, or else that he was the son of many fathers, and the most vile in his origin'.[14] Gregory is referring to the fable in which Pan is said to be the fruit of Penelope's amours with all her suitors. Pan's exalted name ('the all') suggests that this, 'the one and the most excellent Being', is either the child of monstrous adulteries, or else committed them himself. We have already suggested that the Pan of Banias was no longer the ancient rustic goat-god, but rather a late Roman syncretistic symbol of the 'All' – the essence of divinity. Julian's attempts to develop a pagan theology drew precisely on this kind of syncretistic 'monotheism'. Julian was himself a devotee of Pan, according to his friend Libanius: 'Who in worshipping the different gods at different times, Pan, Hermes, Hecate, Isis and the rest, has ever been so abstinent with the various foods?'[15]

A unique version of the story appears in an eighth- or ninth-century work called the *Parastaseis Syntomoi Chronikai*.[16] Earlier sources are easily recognisable in this account; indeed some are specifically mentioned.[17] There are, however, some intriguing new details of varying value. Julian himself is said to have visited the city of Banias, where he saw the statue and the miraculous healing plant that grew beside it. Discovering that these healings, including one of a person born blind, were being attributed to Jesus, he ordered the miraculous plant to be destroyed by fire. The emperor then replaced the statues (of Jesus and 'Veronica') with images of Zeus and Aphrodite[18] and erected a temple on the spot, bearing the following inscription:

TO THE DIVINE ALL-SEEING ZEUS.
PRESENTED AS A GIFT TO PANEAS
BY JULIAN[19]

Furthermore, the account continues, the bishop Martyrius, 'who strongly opposed the emperor, was burned near the temple, they say, as a sacrifice to the gods'.[20]

The movements of the emperor during his short reign are fully chronicled and seem to leave no room for a personal visit to Banias, so that assertion must be questioned. And, though the existence of pagan mobs capable of lynching the local Christian bishop and motivated enough to do so can well be imagined, that part of the story is nevertheless also suspect. That the martyred bishop's name should be 'Martyrius' is a suspicious coincidence. We find no further references to such a person. Julian certainly did not encourage the creation of additional Christian martyrs, though pagan mobs sometimes took matters into their own hands.[21] Perhaps the account has become confused with another story of the same period, recorded by Ammianus Marcellinus, concerning the martyrdom of the Arian bishop Georgius of Alexandria, after he had insulted the Temple of the Genius of that city.[22]

That Julian would have restored the Zeus temple in Banias is entirely plausible. The temple of Zeus that had existed in the city since at least the early second century may have suffered damage or destruction at the hands of Christians. Julian's reputation as a 'restorer of temples' was well known. In fact, the discovery of an inscription eight kilometres from Banias, near Kibbutz Ma'ayon Barukh, not only lends credence to this part of the story, but could even be a contemporary reference to the Julian incident in the city. The inscription, cut on a limestone column, may well have once stood in the city centre. It reads:

R[O]MANI ORBIS LIBERAT[ORI]
TEMPLORVM
[RE]STAVRATORI CVR
[IA]RVM ET REI PVBLICAE

RECREATORI BAR
BARORVM EXTINCTORI
D[OMINO] N[OSTRO] IOVLIANO
PERETRVO AVGVSTO
ALAMANNICO MAXIMO
[SAR]MATICO MAXIMO
PONTIFICI MAXIMO PA
[TRI] PATRIAE FOENICVM
[SOC]IVS OB IMPET[RATA]
[BENEFICIA][23]

It seems likely that this column was put up in April or May of 363 AD by the 'Koinon of Phoenicia' (FOENICUM [COE]TUS) after Julian, headquartered in Antioch, had taken his armies east to fight the Persians. Confident that he would return victorious, and wanting to court his favour, the pagan government of the province in which Banias lay, pronounces him not only 'Restorer of Temples' but also (in anticipation), 'Destroyer of Barbarians' (the Persians).[24] The confidence of the Koinon of Phoenicia was misplaced: Julian met his death in Persia at the age of 32, and his efforts to create a 'pagan church' died with him.

This inscription raises the possibility that the Koinon of Phoenicia was directly responsible for the erection of a statue of Julian in Banias, after the mobs there had pulled down and smashed the statue of Christ. But what can we make of Sozomen's account of the consequent destruction of Julian's statue? While the story is garbled, there seem to be reminiscences in it of real events. 'A violent fire from heaven fell upon [the statue],' Sozomen says, 'and broke off the parts contiguous to the breast; the head and neck were thrown prostrate, and it was transfixed to the ground with the face downwards at the point where the fracture of the bust was; and it has stood in that fashion from that day until now, full of the rust of the lightning.'[25] The precise description of the damage done, and the fact that the fallen statue was still to be seen in his own day, provide some credibility to Sozomen's account.

Taken at face value, these comments suggest that Julian's image was struck by lightning, a fate suffered by such blasphemers almost *pro forma*. But another event occurred in Banias, 'at the third hour, and partly at the ninth hour of the night', on 19 May 363 AD, which might well have toppled the statue and caused its damage by fire in a general conflagration. This was the famous earthquake that ripped up the Jordan Valley on that day, thwarting another of Julian's audacious projects, the rebuilding of the Jewish temple in Jerusalem. This earthquake, according to a letter attributed to Cyril of Jerusalem and preserved in a manuscript called *Harvard Syriac* 99, destroyed a third of the city of Banias.[26] Within weeks Julian himself was dead. Given the general destruction caused by the earthquake, no priority could be given to righting the prostrate image of the dead and divinely discredited prince. Once again the Christians had the upper hand and they would have been inclined to leave it lie – a silent witness to the fate of 'the Apostate'.

As for the 'statue of Christ', the ancient documents agree that the pagans tore it from its base and dragged it by its feet through the streets of the city, a fate also suffered by various pagan statues on various occasions at the instigation of Christian mobs.[27] Only the head could be rescued, by 'some persons, indignant at the whole proceeding', says Philostorgius, who 'secretly obtained possession of [it]'. He is undoubtedly referring to local Christians. Sozomen is more explicit. 'The Christians recovered the fragments,' he says, 'and deposited the statue in the church in which it is still preserved.' There it became once again an object of pilgrimage.[28]

The topographer Theodosius, writing between 518 and 530 AD,[29] claims that the statue was still there in his day, more than a century later. He says of Banias: 'The woman, whom the Lord Christ relieved from the issue of Blood, whose name was Marosa,[30] was from this place; and in the church there is an amber statue (*statua electrina*) of the Lord, made by Marosa'.[31] Perhaps the original bronze head had by that time been repaired and attached to a new body of more precious material. John Malalas (*ca.* 565 AD) mentions the statue, but it is not at all clear that his account is an eyewitness report. He notes that the statue was made of bronze mixed with 'a small quantity of gold and silver' and set up in the middle of the city, and that 'this statue remains in the city of Paneas to the present day, having been moved many years ago from the place where it stood in the middle of the city to a holy chapel'. Malalas says the story of the statue was in a book on the kings of Judaea found in Banias. But whether Malalas made this discovery himself in 'the house of a citizen of Paneas named Bassus, a Jewish convert to Christianity', which would indicate that he had visited the city,[32] or whether in fact it was Bassus who made the discovery in a library elsewhere and communicated the information to Malalas, is unfortunately unclear.

THE PERSISTENCE OF PAGANISM

Though the Christians may have won the 'battle of the statues' it would be a mistake to think that paganism had breathed its last.[33] Jovian (363–64 AD), who replaced Julian as emperor, did try to outlaw the old religion, but Valens, his successor in the Eastern empire (364–78 AD) made no attempt to do so. Theodoret says that while Valens, an Arian emperor, suppressed 'the champions of the Apostolic decrees', he

> allowed everyone else to worship any way they would and to honour their various objects of devotion...Accordingly during the whole period of his reign the altar fire was lit, libations and sacrifices were offered to idols, public feasts were celebrated in the Forum, and votaries initiated in the orgies of Dionysus ran about in goat-skins, mangling hounds in Bacchic frenzy, and generally behaving in such a way as to show the iniquity of their master.[34]

Theodosius I (378–95 AD) is often credited with the final victory over paganism, simply legislating it out of existence with his Edict of 391 AD.[35] When he found the sorts of evils tolerated by his predecessor, Theodoret assures us, Theodosius 'pulled them up by the roots, and consigned them to oblivion'.[36] But by the historian's own admission elsewhere, we know this statement is much exaggerated.[37] Paganism still continued to thrive in Phoenicia (the province to which Banias belonged) despite Herculean efforts by Christian activists such as John Chrysostom during the years 398–404 AD:

On receiving information that Phoenicia was still suffering from the madness of the demons' rites, John got together certain monks who were fired with divine zeal, armed them with imperial edicts [dated 399AD] and dispatched them against the idols' shrines. The money which was required to pay the craftsmen and their assistants who were engaged in the work of destruction was not taken by John from imperial resources, but he persuaded certain wealthy and faithful women to make liberal contributions, pointing out to them how great would be the blessing their generosity would win. Thus the remaining shrines of the demons were utterly destroyed.[38]

In fact, the 'remaining shrines of the demons' were not 'utterly destroyed'. When the next emperor, Arcadius (395–408 AD) was urged to destroy the temples in Gaza, he became angry and said, 'I know that that city is idolatrous, but it is well-disposed in the matter of the paying of taxes, contributing much money. If therefore we come suddenly upon them, and affright them, they will flee and we shall lose so much tribute.'[39] It is true that over time first the cult objects and then the sacred sanctuaries themselves were abused and ultimately destroyed. Even before Julian's ascendance, people had been using stones from the temples to build houses for themselves. Libanius remembered that 'you might have seen pillars carried by boat or by waggon for our plundered gods'.[40] Julian's own works of restoration remained for a while, if only as silent testimony against him. 'Of the temples, some have been pulled down,' Libanius laments, 'those which are half finished stand for a laughing stock to the Christian little ones.'[41] In 397 AD, Asterius, the *comes orientis*, was ordered by the emperor to repair roads, bridges and other public works with material taken from demolished temples.[42]

Some areas neighbouring Banias were accepting 'mainstream' Christianity in the early fifth century.[43] Nevertheless, it is clear that even the external practices of paganism, the public rites, lasted well into the sixth century in some important places. Bowersock has shown that in Edessa, for example, sacrifices were still being made at the temple of Zeus at the end of that century. 'The survival of such rites in the most important centre of the Syriac church tells its own story,' he notes.

> So late a date for the public celebration of Greek pagan cults is but one of many illustrations of the failure of imperial legislation against paganism to have much effect…By the end of the fifth century pagan festivals were still being celebrated with enthusiasm by a substantial part of the population of the city. These festivals included dancing, the telling of pagan stories, all-night vigils, and lascivious conduct.[44]

Other important Syrian towns such as Baalbek and Harran also remained resolutely pagan into the sixth century, and their ancient cultic practices continued.[45] All this happened despite increasing pressure from the government and the Church. In 580 AD, for example, there occurred a Great Persecution of pagans in the Beka'a Valley, not far from Banias, with a resulting reign of terror.[46]

Perhaps archaeological evidence will eventually help to clarify the religious situation in Banias during this period. But what evidence exists points to strong pagan persistence in the city. The conflict over the statues of Christ and Julian, and the evidence of pagan resistance throughout the region surrounding Banias, suggest that when Barachus of Paneas, the Christian bishop, journeyed from his home city to attend the Council of Constantinople in 381 AD, he hardly represented the citizenry of the city as a whole.[47]

The cult centre at the cave does seem to have been at least partially abandoned by the end of the fourth century.[48] In fact, however, the battle between Christianity and paganism continued for many centuries in Banias and in some respects the latter never really completely disappeared. Rather, with remarkable resilience, paganism merely adapted to each new religio-political situation that arose in the area, including the appearance of Islam. Pagan theological and cultic trajectories can be detected in communities such as the Nusārīyeh, the Ismā'līyeh, and the Druze, all of whom still live in the area, or at least did until very recent times. The first of these sects seems to have arisen among people moving directly from paganism to heretical forms of Islam, with no intermediate Christian phase at all.[49] And all three groups draw upon Gnostic and Neo-Platonic speculations in the tradition of Iamblichus and Porphyry, those second- and third-century Phoenician philosophers who had so long ago represented the intellectual alternative to emerging Christianity.

In 1930, a cult of 'Nebi Yehudah' still existed south of Banias, connected with a sacred tree. It celebrated spring and autumn pilgrim feasts, with offerings of the first fruits of the harvest and the first milk of the flock. These offerings were accepted by a hereditary priesthood, amid sacred dances held in the court of the sacred place. A few miles away certain graves and certain ancient oak trees were identified by the locals as belonging to 'the daughters of Jacob', most likely retaining the memory of the nymphs of the forest not unlike those mentioned in the red-rock bluff inscriptions near the cave of Pan at Banias.[50] William Thomson, in his popular nineteenth-century description of the Holy Land, notes that certain oaks in the area of Banias

> are believed to be inhabited by Jan and other spirits. Almost every village in these wadys and on those mountains [around Banias] has one or more of such thick oaks, which are sacred from the same superstition. Many of them in this region are believed to be inhabited by certain spirits, called Benat Ya'kob – daughters of Jacob – a strange and obscure notion, in regard to which I could never obtain an intelligible explanation. It seems to be a relic of ancient idolatry, which the stringent laws of Muhammad banished in form, but could not entirely eradicate from the minds of the multitude.[51]

One of the third-century coins issued in Banias depicts a woman emerging from a tree, identified by Meshorer as Maia, one of the nymphs and the mother of Pan.[52] Here may be the 'intelligible explanation' which Thomson was unable to find regarding the connection between the ancient oaks of the area and the 'daughters of Jacob' – a connection with direct ties to the ancient Pan cult.

Another characteristic shared by the indigenous religious communities of the area is their devotion to the cult of Khader. Above the cave of Pan itself, active worship continues to this day at the 'Shrine of Khader' (Figs 35, 36). The Christians identified this ancient building as the tomb of St George, and the Moslems and others understood it to be sacred to the mysterious Khader, the Ever Green or Ever Living One.[53] Khader certainly pre-dates both Christianity and Islam and seems to be none other than an incarnation of the old Ba'al, renamed Pan by the Greeks, whose name always persisted as the true designation of the place, regardless of what official name might be temporarily imposed.[54] Among the Nusārīyeh peasants, or 'uninitiated', Khader was the central divinity. He was, for them, 'Jesus,

Mohammed, and all the Prophets'.[55] Because his name was substituted for Christian or Moslem saints, shrines acquired his name in great numbers, including, most likely, the shrine at Banias.[56]

The origins of this 'tomb' are obscure and intriguing. Neither Khader, nor Elijah, as Christians and Jews often identified him, needed a real tomb, it must be remembered. One was by definition 'ever living' and the other had been taken directly into heaven without suffering death.[57] The building bearing Khader's name has undergone various alterations, some in recent times. M.V. Guérin, visiting the site in 1854, noted that the building still showed signs of having once been a Byzantine chapel.[58] The origins of this 'tomb' could very well parallel those of chapels found elsewhere: small, single-aisled churches erected in close proximity to pagan shrines for the purpose, as it were of 'keeping an eye on them'.[59] By the early sixth century, this practice had often superseded the older one of physically destroying the pagan shrines, or of commandeering them as churches.[60] In the late sixth century, a temple of Pan at Lycosura (in Arcadia), after having been exorcised by Church officials, was 'put under ecclesiastical surveillance' in just such a fashion.[61] At Banias, the Pan cult was practised at the cave and on the sacred platform stretching eastward along the base of the red cliff, where a series of chapels stood. Whatever remained of these installations during the period of Byzantine dominance, and whatever cultic practices still persisted among them, could be carefully watched, both literally and figuratively, by the chapel perched halfway up the steep incline just to the west of the cave, and almost literally looking down into it. It is unlikely that excavations will ever be possible at the site of the present shrine. It nevertheless seems reasonable to assign the foundation of the 'Tomb of St George' to the sixth century, or perhaps somewhat earlier.[62] Ironically, this chapel and its namesake (whether in the Jewish, Pagan, or Christian form) was eventually regarded by the locals as itself sacred to the original cave-spring divinity. As Bliss commented in 1912, surveying the religious situation in the area around Banias in his own day: 'As an organism, paganism indeed crumbled, but its soul continued to hover over the Holy Land'.[63]

The Christian community in Byzantine Banias struggled with internal, as well as external challenges. These were the centuries of constant theological controversy among Christians. The indigenous churches of the East more often than not found themselves at odds with the champions of emerging Byzantine orthodoxy. Local communities guarded their autonomy for cultural reasons as well as theological ones, and the increasingly centralised orthodox Church, ruled from Constantinople, mirroring the organisation of the empire itself, seemed to many Syrians foreign and oppressive. The bishops of Banias may have voted with the majority at the various ecumenical councils that recorded their names on participant lists, but Christianity as experienced by citizens of the city and its district no doubt exhibited considerable diversity.

For example, various Jewish-Christian sects still flourished in the area in the late fourth century, when Epiphanius, Bishop of Salamis, himself a native of Palestine, wrote his attack on heresies called the Panarion. A remnant of the Ossaeans, 'called Sampaeans at the present', he says, inhabited the same country where they originated, including Iturea, that is the region around Banias.[64] He speaks of the Ebionites in such a way as to indicate that they still flourished in his day in 'Nabataea and Banias, Moabitis, and Cocabe in Bashanitis'.[65] Recent surveys of the Golan have produced late-fourth-century carvings with Jewish and Christian symbols associated in such a way that they could not have been carved by different people at different times. These may well be attributed to the Ebionites.[66] Such groups also proved to be very persistent, and seem to have contributed a number of their theological ideas to later forms of Islamic 'heresies' – particularly the Ismā'īlis (Assassins), who at one time controlled Banias, as we shall see.[67]

THE FIFTH CENTURY: BYZANTINE GLORY AND URBAN DECLINE

Oddly, Jerome, whose erudite writings so dominated the Church at the turn of the fifth century, though he lived and worked for many years in Bethlehem, seems never to have bothered to visit Banias. Though he knew the city to be a living one, 'now called Paneas' he says, his knowledge of the place came from others. He quotes the Jewish scholar from whom he learned Hebrew to prove that 'Mount Hermon overhangs Paneas' – something he could surely have stated on his own authority, had he any personal knowledge of the place. As noted earlier, he also seems to be the source of the long-standing confusion among Christian writers between Caesarea Philippi and Dan. Forgetting the statement of Eusebius that he himself had quoted – which declared that the two sites were some distance apart – he took up instead the opinions of the Babylonian rabbis, whose statements show no personal knowledge of Banias either.[68] By the eleventh century even the Jewish community residing in Banias itself was calling the place 'Fort Dan'. The rabbis also seem to be his source for another mistaken theory: that the name 'Jordan' is derived from the names of two streams, whose confluence forms the river, called the 'Jor' and the 'Dan'. Countless later writers copied this assertion from Jerome, even though, as Edward Robinson pointed out, the name 'Jordan' is likely nothing more than the Greek form of the Hebrew 'Iarden'. As such it has no etymological relationship with the word 'Dan', which only appears hundreds of years after the first instances of the word 'Jordan'.[69]

It is equally curious that Jerome does not mention the story of the 'statue of Christ' in Banias. This may suggest that he was sceptical of the attribution, unlike his near-contemporary the Arian historian Philostorgius.[70] The latter, who had visited the city, says that 'the district of Paneas was formerly called Dan, from Dan the son of Jacob, who was the head of one of the twelve tribes, which was situated in those parts'.[71] This is a sort of intermediate stage in the development of the fallacious identification in which the district, as distinguished from the city itself, is called Dan. The real site of the city of Dan seems already to have dropped from the tradition, though less than a century had passed since Eusebius knew of its location.[72]

Philostorgius continues, 'But in the course of time it came to be called Caesarea Philippi, and later still, when the heathen erected in it a statue of the god Pan, its name was changed to Paneas'.[73] This assertion suggests that Philostorgius knew about one of the resurgences of the cult which had taken place from time to time in Banias, and that in his own day the worshippers of Pan were still advocating their cause. Even his explanation about the renaming of the town is not without foundation, as we have seen. We have already suggested that the appearance of the 'Universal Pan' on the coins of Marcus Aurelius in 169 AD may commemorate a re-dedication to the god, with the erection of a new cult statue, and, perhaps, an official re-christening of the city. Another 'Pan revival' apparently occurred in 220 AD, as both the coins and extant inscriptions show, furnishing another opportunity to 'rename' and re-dedicate the town to its ancient god. Philostorgius not only was aware of attempts to identify Pan as the universal god, but also took pains to refute the idea.[74]

THE COMING OF THE PILGRIMS

Gradually, during the fourth, fifth and sixth centuries, Palestine became the 'Holy Land' – and as such the destination of large numbers of pilgrims from the West. The indigenous Church continued to flourish, of course. The Bishop of Banias, named Olympios, was present at the Council of Chalcedon (451 AD). But it must be remembered that Syria became primarily Monophysite from the mid-fifth century on. Consequently, it is likely that even as the ancient Jewish-Christian communities began to disappear, a considerable number of citizens in Christian Banias were considered heterodox by the government in Byzantium.

Despite this, official orthodox attention to the Holy Land brought increasing immigration, with the building of many churches and monasteries, and, at least partially because of the large numbers of tourist-pilgrims, considerable prosperity. A final recension of the famous Peutinger Table, representing the Roman map of Palestine, may be dated roughly to the fourth or fifth century.[75] Pilgrims had access to such maps and other information to prepare them for their journeys to the holy places. Eucherius, the Bishop of Lyons (434–49 AD) says in his *Letter to Faustus* that he was inspired to write it by a traveller who had been to Jerusalem, and that he was able to supplement that account with material from his own library. Thus, he could describe the sources of the Jordan at Banias without having visited there himself.[76] But precisely because a body of literature developed describing the pilgrimages, and because the accounts, even those written by the travellers themselves, were often composites from several sources, it becomes increasingly difficult to find any new information about the city of Banias itself during this period.

An example of the kind of records that have survived is this passage from Theodosius, *De Situ Terrae Sanctae*, written during the time of Justinian. John Wilkinson suggests this analysis of sources:

> From Bethsaida it is fifty miles to Panias: [a group of civil itineraries of the fourth-to-sixth centuries][77] that is the place where the Jordan rises from the two places Ior and Dan. They run past Panias on either side, and below the city they join together. Hence the name 'Jordan'. [Theodosius, the compiler, who worked *ca.*518 AD]. That is the place from which came the woman whom my Lord Christ set free from an issue of blood [a religious itinerary, perhaps from fourth century, maybe near 500 AD], and this woman's name was Mariosa. In that place is also the electrum statue of my Lord which was made by this Mariosa. The beginning of Mount Lebanon is there [Theodosius, the compiler].[78]

Here we can see the beginnings of a fixed tradition based not on first-hand information, but traditional sources, several of which we have already discussed. As first-hand information became more and more scarce, geographical confusion among the pilgrims multiplied. The account of Antoninus Martyr (*ca.*560–570 AD) exhibits the extent to which this confusion had set in among the pilgrims by this time. Antoninus mistakenly identified Caesarea Palestina (on the Mediterranean coast) with Caesarea Philippi. Though he does go on from this bogus 'Caesarea Philippi' to visit the two fountains ('Jor' and 'Dan'), he does not seem to know that they are located near the real Caesarea Philippi, nor does he mention the city of Banias at all.[79]

Some pilgrims in the fifth and sixth centuries seem to have made Banias their last stop to the north, from where the travellers turned back south again.[80] If the statue of Christ was still there for them to see, they do not mention having seen it, though the reference to the woman with the issue of blood in Theodosius suggests that pilgrims still visited the site at least up until the time his sources were produced. More often they refer only to visiting the sources of the Jordan. Cyril of Scythopolis (*ca.*525–*ca.*559 AD) traces the last stages of the standard itinerary when he describes the pilgrimage made by St Sabas (439–532 AD) and his disciple Agapetus: 'Sabas and his companion went on their way, journeying a good distance across the country between the Sea of Tiberias and the Jordan and praying at Chrosia [Kursi], Heptapegus [Tabgha] and the other revered places there as far as Panias, where they turned back'.[81] John Malalas describes the statue at Banias and recounts its story in detail. He cites as his source a document that was either found by him 'in the city of Paneas in the house of a man called Bassus, a Jew who had become a Christian', or, as quoted by John of Damascus, found by Bassus, in some unstated location. Unfortunately, therefore, when he says that the statue 'remains in the city of Paneas to the present day, having been moved many years ago from the place where it stood in the middle of the city to a holy chapel' we cannot be sure that this was actually still true in his own day.[82] The Piacenza Pilgrim (*ca.*570 AD) obviously ended his pilgrimage near Banias and turned back south from there but he, like Antoninus Martyr, fails to mention the city itself: 'Going on from there [Capernaum] through various camps, villages, and cities, we came to two streams called Jor and Dan, which join together to form the single stream called Jordan, but this is really very small. It flows into the sea, passes right through and goes out at the far shore. On our way back…etc.'[83] This omission suggests that Banias had all but disappeared by this time.

THE DECLINE OF BYZANTINE SYRIA (SIXTH CENTURY)

Thus the region of Banias was the 'end of the pilgrims' trail' during the heyday of Byzantine pilgrimage. But what of the city itself? The pilgrims are strangely silent. After the fifth century, though the city and its statue are mentioned by various authors, none claims to have actually visited the place or seen its main attraction. What they have to say is clearly derived from earlier written sources or describes an earlier situation.[84]

We must remember that Banias stood at the very northernmost edge of the sacred geography of Christianity, just as it had for centuries represented the limits of Eretz Israel for the rabbis. The emerging archaeological record suggests that while at first it benefited from the general prosperity of the fourth century, signs of decline were already beginning to appear by the middle of the fifth century. Excavations in the city centre have produced one rather dramatic and poignant discovery that provides a glimpse into this period, and a hint of the decline. A street, some 3.5 metres wide, was found running parallel to the Cardo Maximus, and 25 metres east of the main street. Though the street undoubtedly was a part of the original Roman city grid, all the buildings found along it were Byzantine. Those on the western side of the street were, judging by their contents, mostly retail shops or workshops, showing that the once-magnificent public area of Banias had changed in character and use. These had fallen victim to a huge fire, and their floors, once a thick layer of ash had been removed, yielded large numbers of crushed storage jars, jugs, bowls, vessels of glass, tools (including a set of scales) and many coins (Figs 37, 38). All of these were dated to the fourth and fifth centuries. It is not clear whether the destruction was the result of one of the great earthquakes of the period, or some other local disaster. It is clear, however, that the buildings were left in ruins, and nothing was rebuilt where they had stood until medieval times. Surely, had the city fathers been able to do so, they would have cleared this disfiguring ruin from their city's centre.[85]

To some extent this pattern can be seen throughout the region. Despite the infusion of immigrants, tourists and government largess in the time of Constantine and his immediate successors, Byzantine Syrio-Palestine reached its zenith economically and culturally in the fifth century and almost immediately began to decline. While the population remained large, and certain local communities continue to thrive,[86] the central government, far away in Constantinople, had too many troubles of its own to continue to pour its resources into the Holy Land. Particularly throughout the old territories of Philip and Agrippa II, the sixth century was a time of great cultural change, economic downturn and even physical danger.[87] Hartal's extensive survey of the northern Golan revealed that the number of settlements increased to 51 during the early Roman period, reaching a peak of 69 during the late Roman period, but decreasing to 40 during the Byzantine period.[88] This pattern likely reflects declining security and a population more and more at the mercy of Bedouin raids. These settlements in the Golan were all virtually deserted by the end of the Byzantine period and the region was in the hands of nomadic tribes once more. Banias was swept along with all these currents. Excavations there reveal little or nothing from the latter part of the Byzantine period, not even coins or potsherds. The villas which surrounded the city seem to have been abandoned and the high-level aqueduct ceased to function. This does not mean that the city had entirely ceased to exist, but does indicate that it had fallen on very hard times.

The Byzantine emperor Justinian had appointed Arab tribes (the Ghassanids) to maintain order in the area. However, since they were not orthodox Christians but rather were Monophysites, they were eventually driven out, leaving a power vacuum and opening the way for the Persian and Moslem Arab invasions. Natural disasters played their part. The earthquake of 22 August 502 AD, which destroyed Akko, Tyre and Sidon, almost certainly struck Banias, though if Theodosius the topographer is to be believed it apparently did not destroy the statue or the church in which it stood.[89] Another earthquake occurred in the area on 9 July 551 AD, which may have spelled the end for the church and the statue.[90] Alternatively, the place of pilgrimage at Banias may simply have gradually become more and more inaccessible. As we have seen, there is no clear eyewitness account among those writers who mention the city during the sixth century.

References to Banias during this period become more and more rare. An inscription from the time of Tiberius II (578–82 AD), identifies the village of Chedaron (Hadar), northeast of Banias, as belonging to the city, and also mentions Phoenicia.[91] George of Cyprus's *Descriptio Orbis Romani*, which reflects the ecclesiastical organisation of the sixth century, and probably the political organisation as well, lists Banias as one of the πόλεις (cities) under the jurisdiction of the Tyre, which is called the μητρόπολις (metropolis) of the district of Phoenicia.[92] Nau notes a manuscript dating about 570 AD listing ὸ πανιάδος among the towns under the ecclesiastical jurisdiction of Tyre and, ultimately, the Patriarch of Antioch.[93] The Madeba Map, which pictures the situation in Palestine around 600 AD, might have provided information. Unfortunately, the section of the map that depicted Banias has not survived.[94] Thus the fortunes of the city itself become more and more obscure as the Byzantine era draws to a close. But something was clearly amiss.

FROM POLIS TO MADINA

While the excavation of Banias is not sufficiently advanced definitively to clarify the local situation, numerous other excavations and surveys in the area provide an increasingly clear context. Hugh Kennedy has shown that many of the changes in cities formerly associated with the coming of Islam were actually already occurring at the beginning of the sixth century, or even earlier, long before the armies from the Arabian Peninsula appeared on the scene.[95] The transformation of the Hellenistic *polis* into the Middle Eastern *madina* was not a question of one urban tradition overcoming another through conquest or cultural domination; the Arab conquerors had no urban tradition. Rather, it was a gradual return to the ancient Semitic patterns that pre-dated the coming of Alexander, whose programme of Hellenisation had persisted for almost a millennium, but never seems to have penetrated the inner soul of Syria.

The Roman model was, after all, 'an imperial model forced onto the land and the people; it was a model alien to the culture and not the outcome of a local development process rooted in history'.[96] Thus, we must look beyond the social unrest, destructive earthquakes and the natural decay that inevitably overtakes disused structures to understand the changes that occurred in cities like Banias during these centuries. Surviving Roman buildings were put to new purposes, and the programmatic Roman city plan gave way to the practical needs of the population. The streets narrowed; the large open public spaces filled with shops and houses, the monumental Roman civic structures were remodelled and put to new uses. The cumulative effect may seem chaotic and random, leading to the use of such phrases as 'urban decay'. In fact, at least some urban centres saw significant new construction during this period, but the urban model that drove this construction was different from the Roman one, and the architecture was, to borrow a word from Zeyadeh, 'vernacular'.[97]

Eventually,

> the broad, colonnaded streets were invaded and divided up by intrusive structures, both houses and shops, and became more like narrow winding lanes than the majestic thoroughfares of classical antiquity; and the extensive, open agora, scene for markets and meetings, was gone. The other main features of the ancient city, the monumental buildings, disappeared almost entirely, to be replaced by the mosque and the small urban hammam or bath-house.[98]

But the process began when the distant government of the empire stopped subsidising the cities of the East, as the early Roman Empire had done, and started to pull resources away instead, through heavy and oppressive taxation. The impressive marble porticoes, nymphaia and theatres gave way to crowded and dusty souks long before the Prophet's warriors appeared.[99] In Banias, excavations suggest that the magnificent Hellenistic-Roman buildings and infrastructure continued to stand, and to undergo the kind of transform-ation described above, but eventually simply were abandoned – to be used centuries later, during medieval times, as quarries and foundations.

For some cities, the trauma was terminal. Some, despite former glory, were unable to make the transition from *polis* to *madina* and withered into insignificance. Qinnasrin and Jerash, for example, were virtually uninhabited by the tenth century.[100]

Banias was probably headed for the same fate. Archaeological surveys indicate that during the late Roman period, a residential suburb of large dwellings stood in the area east of the spring, and another quarter of similar date, surrounded by a wall, has been discovered on the south side of Nahal Sa'âr, opposite the city centre. Thus, despite the paucity of literary references, we can conclude that the city reached its zenith, at least in terms of population and architectural splendour, in the late Roman and early Byzantine periods.[101] The descent from this high point was relatively rapid. The cumulative evidence suggests that Banias as a Greek *polis* was rapidly dying, even before the Persian invasions, precursors of the Islamic ones. Indeed, the city might have faded into total oblivion, had it had not been rescued by a massive influx of refugees fleeing Byzantine invasions in the north during the tenth century (see below). Excavations at the site tend to confirm this scenario as well, producing very limited ceramic and architectural evidence dating from the seventh to the tenth centuries.

THE PERSIAN INVASION (611–14 AD)

Since the days of the early Roman Empire, the Persians to the east had constituted a real and continuing threat to peace and stability. Between 611 and 614 AD, the worst nightmares of Christian Syria-Palestine came true.[102] With relentless success, the armies of Sassanian Persia, under Chosroes II, swept down on the helpless populace. The Jewish communities of the region, smarting from generations of mistreatment and humiliation by the Byzantine establishment, welcomed and assisted the invaders. Nor were the local Christians, many of whom followed their own native forms of the faith, inclined toward strong resistance. Sebeos, in his *History of Heraclius* (written *ca.* 670 AD), traces the progress of the Iranians southward and their conquest of Tarsus of Cilicia: 'Then the entire country of Palestine willingly submitted to the king of kings. The remnants of the Hebrew people especially rebelled from the Christians and taking in hand their native zeal wrought very damaging slaughters among the multitude of believers. Going [to the Iranians], [the Jews] united with them.'[103] The army pillaged Damascus and then headed south, eventually establishing itself at Caesarea Maritima.[104]

This invasion was characterised by atrocities committed against Christian clergy and a persistent policy of destroying Christian churches and holy sites. Even the Church of the Holy Sepulchre in Jerusalem was ruthlessly dismantled. A glance at the map suggests that Banias, lying directly in the path of the advancing Persians, could hardly have escaped catastrophe. As the last of the chain of Christian pilgrimage sites to the north in Palestine, and therefore the first of such sites encountered by the invaders, Banias, with its cathedral and 'statue of Christ' (if these were still standing) would have provided a tempting target. On the other hand, the presence of large Jewish populations in Galilee and the Golan may have tempered the ferocity of the invaders in those regions. In fact, more churches may have been destroyed by the Jews of the area, eager for revenge, than by the Sassanians themselves. Churches in the general vicinity of Tyre (as was Banias) were particularly vulnerable to this fate.[105]

In any case, the words of Rabbi Jose ben Kisma of Banias, spoken five centuries before, proved to be prophetic: 'The time will come when there will not be a single palm tree in the land of Israel but a Persian horse will be tied to it, and there will not be a single casket in the land that a Median horse will not feed from.'[106]

The invasion of Chosroes's army serves as a convenient marker for the end of Banias as a Hellenistic/Roman/Byzantine city and the beginning of a new era. The evidence for this is admittedly circumstantial, but it is nevertheless compelling. That is not to say that the city disappeared altogether. Rather, it entered a kind of 'dark age', the mists of which blur and obscure its history for almost four hundred years. Its churches and fine old Hellenistic urban infrastructure lay abandoned, the result of either wanton destruction or simple neglect. Whatever was left of communal life in the city after the invasion centred on agriculture and small industry. These modest activities were carried on in an atmosphere of danger and instability, due to the presence of marauding nomads on the one hand, and the absence of a strong central government on the other. It is true that the energetic Byzantine emperor Heraclius drove the Persians out of Syria-Palestine in 628–29 AD and even restored the 'true cross' to the city of Jerusalem on 14 September 629 AD. But of Banias the record is silent. The glory had departed.[107]

8 The Arab/Islamic Conquest

THE ARAB INVASION, CONQUEST AND OCCUPATION

Syria-Palestine's return to the Byzantine fold was short-lived. Inspired by the teachings of the Prophet Mohammed – and by the desire for booty – the Arabs attacked Palestine from the south. The Byzantine Emperor Heraclius, himself a Syrian, was in Emesa at the time. He quickly raised an army and placed it under the command of his brother Theodorus.[1] The Arab general Khalid led his troops from al-Iraq through the desert to meet this Byzantine challenge and won a bloody victory at Ajnādayn, between Ramleh and Beit Jibrin (Eleutheropolis), on Saturday, 30 July 634 AD. Central Palestine was suddenly in Arab control. A short time later the two armies met again, this time at Marj al-Suffār ('the meadow of birds'), a plain twenty miles south of Damascus and thus not far from Banias. After some initial success, the Byzantine army was routed and fled to safety behind the fortifications of Damascus.[2]

In the autumn of 635 AD, the great city itself surrendered to the desert warriors. The conquerors negotiated terms of capitulation with the Bishop of Damascus and with Mansur ibn-Sarjun, a high official in the finance department of the government and the grandfather of St John of Damascus. The terms were quite moderate and the cities of the area quickly agreed to them. The Moslem commander promised not to close the churches. How these events affected Banias we do not know. If the Christian structures there had already been badly damaged before or during the Persian invasion, the agreement was meaningless for the city – though the generous terms would have allowed the local Christians at least to begin plans for rebuilding. If the Persians had scattered the Christian population of the town, or even merely further reduced them to poverty, such an opportunity no longer existed in any case.

Heraclius was not ready to concede. He assembled another army, mostly Armenian and Arab mercenaries, again under the command of Theodorus. This time the army moved southward, not by way of Damascus, but by the Coele–Syria–Transjordan route.[3] For this reason Banias, which lay along the route, served as a staging area for the Byzantine

114

army of Heraclius just prior to the fateful Battle of the Yarmuk, which marked the end of Byzantine rule.[4] For at least the third time in its history, Banias hosted an army at war: the Seleucid troops under Antiochus the Great, the Romans under Vespasian and Titus, and now the army of Heraclius. These encampments had all been incursions into the normally quiet and cultivated life of this beautiful Greek town beside the cool waters of the springs of Hermon. But now an historical turning point had been reached. Henceforth the town would for centuries be known to history not for its temples or churches, nor for its idyllic setting, but as a military flashpoint, a border fortress never far removed from violence. It was not its beautiful forests and cool, flowing waters which ensured Banias's survival, but its strategic location.

Whatever was left of the old Banias eventually disappeared, as did so much of Greco-Roman Syria, from the time of the Battle of the Yarmuk on 20 August 636 AD, when the Byzantine army was decisively defeated, onward.[5] The pace of depopulation and decline quickened. Surveys of the nearby northern Golan, traditionally a part of 'greater Banias', reveal a sharp reduction in the number of occupied sites. Of 173 Byzantine sites, only 14 showed signs of occupation after the conquest. Deteriorating security and loss of traditional markets both played a central role in this situation. But, as we have noted, the city had most likely been drifting away from its Hellenistic past for many generations, becoming more and more Semitic and less and less Greco-Roman. This phenomenon was common in such places during the last centuries of Byzantine rule. As the central power grew weaker and weaker, the larger public buildings and installations of other kinds fell into disrepair and were often subdivided into small shops or residences. Streets narrowed and the disciplined Greco-Roman town plans were replaced by an oriental urban organisation of a different sort. To whatever extent inhabitants of the old town continued to live there, they most likely represented the least Hellenised element of the population. Like the citizens of Hims, who told the conquerors (according to al-Balādhurī), 'We like your rule and justice far better than the state of tyranny and oppression under which we have been living',[6] they probably did not view the change in overlords as disastrous. Despite an orthodox facade, Syria had been mostly Monophysite since the mid-fifth century. Its citizens felt little threat to their faith or their culture from the Arabs, who shared much of their own Semitic heritage and were less 'foreign' than the Greek-speaking Byzantines had been.[7] The Moslems allowed religious freedom, and even encouraged the heterodoxy that the Byzantine regime had suppressed. Far more threatening were the economic and social conditions, which had been spiralling rapidly downward for generations before the conquest.

In 639 AD, at al-Jabiyah, a place south of Damascus and not far from Banias, the Caliph 'Umar, successor to the Prophet, called a council to decide how to administer the new empire. Essentially, the Byzantine system of provincial government would be retained with little change, except for the introduction of 'a sort of religio-military aristocracy, keeping their blood pure and unmixed, living aloof and abstaining from holding or cultivating any landed property' – namely the Moslems of Arabia.[8] Syria was divided into four military districts (sing. *jund*), corresponding to the Byzantine provinces existing before the conquest: Dimashq, Hims, al-Urdunn (Jordan) and Filastin. Later records indicated that Banias belonged to the *jund* of Damascus. Even the Byzantine governmental structure was retained; local officials were allowed to keep their positions.[9]

We know that Banias under the Arabs became the chief town in the district of al-Djawlān (the Golan), on the northern border of which the town was located.[10] Archaeological surveys conducted in recent times show that the size of the town after the conquest was dramatically reduced – from about one thousand dunams during the late Roman and early Byzantine periods, down to a small area in the immediate vicinity of the spring.[11] Byzantine sherds and architectural remains, along with those of earlier periods, lie scattered on the surface over a wide area, whereas Islamic remains seem to be concentrated between the red-stone cliff on the north, the Banias River on the west, and the gorge of Wâdî Sa'âr on the south. Here the remains of a medieval fortress can be seen today, its vulnerable eastern wall protected by a deep moat, still clearly visible. Apparently the town known to both Christian and Moslem travellers after the conquest lay within these boundaries. Its *raison d'être* was now to serve as a fortress to guard the road from Damascus south into Palestine and west toward Tyre and the coast of Phoenicia.

All this is clear. What is not clear is precisely when this transformation from city to fortress took place, and what sort of place Banias was during the interim. While it is possible that the Persians damaged the city, it is highly unlikely that the Arab invaders destroyed the city and its churches. They simply did not follow such a destructive policy except in the case of some profoundly Hellenised towns that put up stiff resistance. We have no reason to think that Banias was among them. It is more likely that by this time there was little of consequence remaining to tempt any invader to make Banias the subject of looting and destruction.

CHRISTIANITY IN UMAYYAD BANIAS

The question of the fate of the 'statue of Christ' and the churches of Banias is a perplexing one. According to John Wilkinson,

> About half the ordinary churches [in Palestine] whose remains have been discovered were no longer occupied after the seventh century, but only one-fifth of the holy places cease to be mentioned by our pilgrims. This is consistent with what we know from other sources, that the Moslems converted the inhabitants of many Christian villages and cities to Islam, but that they permitted Christian pilgrims to continue visiting their holy places. Moslems indeed, with their special regard for the Hajj or pilgrimage, regarded it as natural that Christians should wish to come.[12]

Unfortunately, the few records we have of pilgrim visits to Banias give no clear indication of the state of the holy sites there after the conquest.

The Umayyads may have established a mint at Banias, as they did at numerous other cities throughout their domains that had produced coins for local use during pre-Byzantine Roman days, though this is doubtful.[13] The town seems to have had little significance by this time, and probably lay almost abandoned. The scarcity of Umayyad pottery, coins and architecture found during excavations, even within the fortress area, suggests little or no activity there during the period.

An investigation of surviving Christian sources from the late seventh and early eighth centuries might cast some light on this mysterious period in the city's history. Christianity certainly remained strong in Syria during Umayyad times; in addition to producing St John of Damascus, Syria provided five popes during the period: John V (685–86 AD), St Sergius (687–701 AD), Sisinnius (708 AD), Constantine (708–15 AD) and St Gregory III (731–41 AD).[14] Unfortunately, specific Christian references to Banias are scanty and ambiguous. We know that Sophronius, the Bishop of Jerusalem who surrendered that city to the Caliph 'Umar in 638 AD, was succeeded by a certain Athanasius, described by Nicephorus Callistus as 'the Bishop of Caesarea Philippi'.[15] Michael the Syrian lists a Monophysite bishop of Banias, John, as a participant in a synod held in 683–84 at Resh 'Aina.[16]

Mu'āwiyah (661–80 AD), founder of the Umayyad dynasty, with its capital in nearby Damascus, was very open and tolerant toward Christianity – the religion of his wife. Most Syrians, including the Christians, were fiercely loyal to him.[17] But another caliph, 'Umar II (717–20 AD), persecuted Christians, providing another potential occasion when the churches of Banias, and its famous statue (if it still stood), might have been harmed. But we have no specific evidence that ties either of these conflicting Umayyad policies to events in Banias.

We do have a record of a visit to the area by a bishop from the west, Bishop Arculf, sometime in the early to mid-seventh century. Arculf related his experiences to Adomnan, the Abbot of Iona (679–704 AD), years after they occurred. Unfortunately, the abbot seems to have supplemented Arculf's dim memories with details based on research in the monastery library. The sections of the account below in italics are apparently copied from the *Letter to Faustus* by Eucherius, Bishop of Lyons (434–49 AD), who in turn had identified his sources as both a traveller's account and his own library. This means that we can hardly accept Adomnan's reconstruction as an accurate reflection of conditions in Banias during the seventh century:

> Our friend Arculf went as far as that part of the district of *Phoenicia*, where one can see the Jordan *issuing from the foot of Libanus* from two neighbouring *springs. One is called Jor and the other Dan, and, when they join they get the composite name 'Jordan.'* But one should realise that the actual source of the Jordan *is not at Panias, but in the region of Trachonities, at a distance of 120 stades from Caesarea Philippi.* Panias is a district which takes its name from Mount Panius. This spring in Trachonitis is called Phiala. It is always full of water, and feeds the Jordan *through underground channels*, which come to the surface at Panius as two separate springs which, as we have said, are commonly called Jor and Dan. *Flowing down from there*, they join to form a single stream...etc.[18]

There is little here to enlighten us. The account mostly reflects Adomnan's library research and almost nothing is directly attributable to Arculf himself. And reference to the city of Banias is entirely missing.

St John of Damascus's (b.*ca.*675 AD, d. before 754 AD) reference to Banias and its statue serve to confuse matters further. John would appear to be a significant witness. He came from aristocratic Damascene circles, close to the caliphate itself. His grandfather, Mansur ibn-Sarjun, a high official in the finance department of the government, helped turn Damascus over to the Arab-Moslems.[19] As a boy, he was a friend of the caliph-to-be Yazīd.[20] Early in Hishām's caliphate, however (*ca.*724 AD), John retired to the monastery of St Saba, southeast of Jerusalem.[21] Shortly thereafter (*ca.*725 AD) he recounted the story of the statue. Having lived so close to Banias for so long, John's assertion that the statue was 'still kept in Paneas' in early Umayyad times should be decisive. But close analysis shows that he is entirely dependent on the work of John Malalas.[22] His account of the statue is in the context of his vigorous defence of the use of images as instruments of worship in the Christian community during the iconoclastic controversy of the day, precipitated by Emperor Leo the Isaurian.[23] As strange as it seems, he gives no indication that he had ever visited Banias (only some thirty miles from his hometown of Damascus), or that he had ever seen the statue himself.[24]

Another work from the same period, the *Parastaseis Syntomoi Chronikai*, discussed at length above, provides many interesting details concerning the story of the statue, but makes no claim that the statue was still in existence at the time of writing. In fact, reliance on earlier literary references is freely admitted by the anonymous author of this document. References to the statue in other works of the period such as the letter of Germanus, Patriarch of Constantinople, to Thomas of Claudiopolis, and the *Life of Saint Stephen the Younger*, likewise prove to be based on secondary sources.[25]

The next witness, the pilgrim Willibald, did visit Banias, and at almost the same time as John of Damascus was writing his account, namely 724–26 AD.[26] There is some confusion in the passage which has come down to us, written down many years after the visit (*ca.*780 AD) by a nun named Hugeburc. It does, however, contain one potentially helpful piece of information:

> After their prayers there [Chorazim] they went on and came to a place where there flow from the ground two springs, the Jor and the Dan, and then, further down from the mountain join to form one stream, the Jordan. There between the two springs they stayed a night, and shepherds gave us sour milk to drink. They breed remarkable cattle there, long in the back, short in the leg, and with huge horns. They are all the same colour, purple. In that place there are deep swamps, so when summer comes, and the sun is very hot and scorches the land, these cattle move to the swamps, and submerge their whole body, with only their head sticking out. Moving on from there they came to Caesarea, which had a church and a great many Christians. They rested there for a time, and then went on again to the monastery of St. John the Baptist…[27]

Do we have testimony here that the church, if not the statue, was still extant *ca.*725 AD? Certainly the reference to the 'purple cattle' (water buffalo), which still could been seen in the Huleh swamps until relatively recently, provides a note of authenticity. But certain difficulties in the text also suggest caution. First, the fabled place 'between the two fountains' of Jor and Dan, often itself identified as Caesarea Philippi, obviously refers in this account to Dan, for the pilgrims move on from there to Caesarea. Second, a serious break occurs in the narrative just after this reference, the next sites mentioned being in the far south of Palestine, with no reference at all to an intervening journey through Transjordan. These facts suggest imprecision in the account, to say the least. Clemens

Kopp notes the use of the perfect tense in the crucial sentence: 'Caesarea, where there was [*fuit*] a church and a multitude of Christians'. Willibald chooses this tense, Kopp suggests, 'not because he depicts his visit as something in the past, but because the church was no longer there'.[28] He thinks that the church and its congregation 'disappeared, along with the statue, under some early Islamic oppression'.[29] Actually, the last firm reference to the statue by an eyewitness is in the fifth century; the numerous references after that time are all derivative. Unfortunately, there is insufficient evidence to reveal the final fate of Banias's famous statue. If by some chance it survived the various catastrophes of the sixth and seventh centuries, it would certainly have been destroyed by iconoclastic Christians in the eighth century.

The church may have survived longer than the statue. Unfortunately the large basilica discovered during the excavation of the city, if it is the church in question, was so damaged by medieval intrusions that it is not possible to determine when it was first destroyed or went out of use.[30] A ninth- or tenth-century document entitled the *Life of Constantine* may provide circumstantial evidence that a church was still in existence at Banias in Abbasid times.[31] It seems that a stone commemorating the healing of the haemorrhaging woman stood between Capernaum and the Seven Wells, on the shores of the Sea of Galilee, where it was seen by the Monk Epiphanius (750–800 AD).[32] Helena, the mother of Constantine, came across this memorial, according to this *Life of Constantine*. And, 'finding a stone with the sign of the Cross at which Christ healed the woman with the issue of blood, she erected a church in the name of his venerable and life-giving "Holy Cross"'.[33] This church is subsequently mentioned in at least two eleventh-century manuscripts.

No such church existed on the shores of the Sea of Galilee. Thus this is certainly, in Kopp's words, a 'church of the imagination'.[34] But this does not mean that it was an imaginary church. Rather, most likely, 'It was known that very early a church had been erected in memory of this miracle, and so it now was moved, in error, from Paneas to this place'.[35] The question, of course, is whether the church at Banias, certainly known at the time of the writing of the *Life of Constantine*, was still in existence in the ninth or tenth century. If so, the writer of the *Life*, using and confusing the story from Epiphanius, may have added a reference to the church in order to attribute it, as the document does with almost every church standing in the Holy Land at that time, to the largess of the emperor's mother Helena.[36]

One additional piece of evidence exists: a statement in the writings of Eutychius, Bishop of Alexandria from 933–40 AD that 'the church at Banyas in the Huleh bears witness [to] the woman with the issue of blood'.[37] The latest possible date for this statement is 944 AD. Kopp may be correct, however, in asserting that Eutychius used a source even earlier than Willibald and thus does not provide independent evidence of the existence of church or statue.[38] In any case, it is very doubtful that a Christian Banias existed any longer by the mid-tenth century.

The cumulative evidence remains ambiguous. The statue was certainly not seen by eyewitnesses during the seventh to the ninth centuries, and references to it, such as those in John of Damascus, Germanicus, the *Parastaseis Syntomoi Chronikai*, the *Chronographia* of Theophanes the Confessor (d. 818 AD),[39] or the *Artemii Passio* ('The Ordeal of Artemius')[40] can all be shown to be dependent on earlier, literary sources. Still, a church and the remnants of a Christian community may have continued to exist in Banias throughout the period. No document proves the contrary. The answer to the question of the fate of the church and the Christian community during these centuries probably lies within the answer to a larger question, namely the fate of the city itself.

BANIAS IN ABBASID TIMES (750–868 AD)

Al-Wadin b. 'Ata al-Dimashkī (d. 764 or 766 AD) perhaps one of the Umayyad era's three greatest scholars, is said to have come from the town of Banias, though he lived and died in or near Damascus and was a part of the scholarly community there. He seems to have been a supporter of the Abbasids, rather than the Umayyads. If he did come from Banias, he provides at least a trace of evidence for the presence of Moslems in the town during the Umayyad period.[41]

Lacking further literary evidence, we can only look to an analysis of the general political and social situation in southern Lebanon, northern Palestine and the Hauran, together with archaeological evidence, to help us penetrate the darkness that fell over Banias during the two centuries that followed the fall of the Umayyad Empire. The collapse of that empire, larger at its zenith than Rome's had ever been, and the rise of a new political centre for Islam at Baghdad, far to the east, constituted an historical water-shed of monumental proportions. Alexander's conquests had initiated a millennium of Hellenism in Egypt and Syria. These great civilisations became part and parcel of the 'West' – tied by language and culture more closely to Greeks, Italians and Spaniards than to the Persians in the East. Christian Byzantium, moving the centre of power eastward, held Syria even closer to its breast than Rome had done. But now the ties to the West, looking to the sea, had been broken. The Arab conquest turned the face of Syria around, toward the eastern desert. Then, the Abbasid revolution of 750 AD definitively rearranged the centres of political and cultural gravity. Constantinople, the 'new Rome', became in some ways no more than a buffer between the new worlds of Charlemagne (768–810 AD) in the West and Hārum al-Rashīd (786–813 AD) in the East. Syria became a frontier – a western frontier. Damascus found itself far to the west of the centre of power (and Banias was no more than a backwater of Damascus). The ancient world was at an end; the medieval world had begun.

Byzantium, Islam's major rival in Umayyad times, was of much less consequence to the Abbasids in far-off Baghdad. Syria, chafing and disgruntled over its loss of empire, dissolved into chaos and rebellion. The era began ominously, with a disastrous earthquake in 749 AD. Uprisings against the distant Baghdad government arose almost immediately after 750 AD, spreading across the Hauran. Besides this, throughout the rest of the eighth century struggles between rival tribes, the Qays and the Yamanites, centred in the Hauran and

Damascus, made life hard for the area's inhabitants. The ninth century was no better; revolts jolted Palestine (840/41 AD) and Damascus (844/45 AD).

Still significantly Christian, the remnants of the population of Banias must also have suffered from the gradual pressure and discrimination against Christians instituted by the Abbasids. In 759–60 AD, Christians in the mountains of Lebanon revolted against the new regime and the Abbasid governor uprooted many Christian villages and dispersed the inhabitants.[42] Could Banias have been among them? Strong anti-Christian legislation by the Abbasids reached a peak after 850 AD and successfully began to undermine the old faith, gradually transforming Syria, one of the earliest centres of Christianity, into an Islamic society – not simply in terms of political power, but also as an expression of the hearts and minds of the people. Whatever remained of Christian Banias was doomed.

The decline of Abbasid power in the area, and the rise of Egyptian-based dynasties such as the Tulunid (868–905 AD), and the Ilkhshidid (935–69 AD), renewing a tie between Syria and Egypt broken over a thousand years before in the battle of Panium, were to determine the course of the succeeding chapters in the history of Banias. Meanwhile, Christian pilgrimage came to a virtual end. There are no detailed accounts of pilgrimage anywhere in the area dating from the tenth or eleventh centuries.[43]

Thus, the next literary reference to the city, not surprisingly, comes from a Moslem writer. It reveals a town emerging from the dark mists of the seventh, eighth and ninth centuries almost totally transformed. The author is al-Ya'qūbī, writing at the end of the ninth century.[44] Banias, he says, is the capital of al-Golan, in the *jund* of Damascus. Its inhabitants are Qays, mostly belonging to the Banu Murra (a northern tribe), though some Yamani families also live there. Alongside its traditional name the town has also become known as a madīnat al-askat ('city of the tribes').[45] This probably indicates that Banias has become the market centre for what had now reverted to an almost exclusively nomadic culture. Precisely when this transformation from Christian *polis* to Moslem *madina* had occurred is, as we have seen, extremely difficult to pinpoint.[46] It was in any case more a process than an event. We should probably envision this early Islamic Banias as no more than a village and a meeting place for Bedouin tribes, who lived in tents and followed their flocks. It is only in this sense that the town served as 'capital of the Golan'. The whole area was in a period of severe decline. One can picture stone huts among and alongside the still essentially intact Roman/Byzantine monumental buildings and the ancient cardo; this corresponds well with the archaeological evidence. The once magnificent chapels and courtyards of the sanctuary of Pan had long since fallen into ruin. At some point during the ninth century, inhabitants of the town gathered up the pagan sculpture fragments that lay scattered about the Pan sanctuary terrace and deposited them within the ruins of the 'Tripartite Building'. There Zvi Ma'oz found them in the early 1990s.[47]

Kamal Salibi's description of Syria as a whole seems to fit the local situation in Banias quite specifically:

> The triumph of tribalism by the early tenth century ushered in a new period in the history of Syria. The Hellenistic and Roman past and the urban prosperity that went with it were by now forgotten; even the silver age of the Umayyads was barely remembered. The efforts of the

Abbasids to maintain even a minimum of organisation in the country had ended in failure. Hims, Damascus and the few other cities which had continued to flourish in the Seventh and Eighth centuries, had by now been reduced to drab and undistinguished provincial market towns serving small and impoverished neighbourhoods.

If Damascus could be described as a 'drab and undistinguished provincial market town' serving a 'small and impoverished neighborhood' – how much more could Banias.[48]

A TOWN REBORN: AL-NABÛLUSI AND THE SUFIS

A renaissance was soon to dawn for the old town, triggered by larger events which once again thrust Syria into the centre-stage in the Islamic world. Between Fatimid Egypt, where a Shi'ite Ismā'il sect now controlled the government, and the weakened Abbasid Empire in Baghdad, lay several small states strong enough to maintain independence of a sort, but constantly vulnerable to incursions by the Byzantines. When the Byzantine usurper Nicephorus Phocas (963–69 AD) fell upon such frontier cities as Tarsus of Cilicia (taken by the Christians in 965 AD), the Moslem inhabitants fled south in terror. Nicephorus and his successor John Zimisces pushed further and further toward Palestine, driving a multitude of refugees before them.[49]

For reasons not entirely obvious, the destination of choice for a considerable segment of this multitude was the quiet little 'City of the Tribes' – Banias. We owe this important information to the erudite Arab geographer, al-Muqaddasī (946 AD–*ca.* 1000 AD). Writing some two decades after the initial displacement, al-Muqaddasī states that Banias was a major destination for these refugees, and that the influx was continuing at the time he wrote *Ahsan al-Taqāsim fi Ma'rifat al-Aqālim* ('The Best Divisions for Knowledge of the Regions') in 985 AD: 'Thither have gone most of the people of the frontiers since Tarsus was taken; it was thus enlarged, and continues to grow every day'.[50] Apparently the newcomers soon outnumbered the earlier inhabitants of the town.[51]

If the refugees had been looking for peace and quiet along the cool banks of the river of Banias, they were not to find it. In fact, Banias was to become a centre for much of the unrest that followed. The Fatimids, Shi'ite Moslems, were considered by both the old and new inhabitants of the Banias region to be heretics. Nearby Damascus, which dominated the area, was in constant turmoil for the entire twenty years in question, racked by internecine struggle. The Bedouin Qarāmita, an extreme Shi'ite sect, took the city in 968 AD.[52] The Fatimids were back in control briefly in 970 AD, but lost the city almost immediately to the Qarāmita again. In the meantime, among the refugees arriving in Banias were many Sufi ascetics who were fanatical Sunnis. These holy men brought their ideas along with them, and began to combine them creatively with various local legends and theological/philosophical concepts. In the relative safety and isolation of the mountain forests around Banias, they developed a thriving ascetic community. Stories began to circulate about their miraculous powers, such as the ability to heal and to walk on water, presumably the water of the Banias springs, reminiscent of both pagan and

Christian traditions also connected with the place.[53] These Sunnite Sufis had a particular affection for Khader, the Moslem 'saint', sometimes called the 'Green Man', who inhabited the forests and mountains. Khader was the 'ever living one' who had connections with the Jewish Elijah and the Christian St George in popular religion. It is probably during this period that the old shrine of St George, built, as we have suggested, during Byzantine times, became the 'Tomb of Khader' instead. If this chapel had been originally built above the cave of Pan to counteract the power of that 'demon', there is a profound irony in the fact that the shrine itself was now dedicated to Khader, who seems here to be a thinly veiled reincarnation of the old goat-god himself. Khader is honoured at this spot to this day by the only remaining indigenous population of the region, the Druze (see below).

In addition to providing a haven for the mystical activities of the Sufis, Banias became a centre for political and theological agitation. An anti-Fatimid campaign emerged under the leadership of Abû Bakr al-Ramli, or Muhammad b. Ahmad al-Nabûlusi. Originally from Nablus, as his name implies, al-Nabûlusi had operated out of Ramla for a time. Forced to leave there, he found a sympathetic following in Banias and there established the most important Sunnite educational centre of the time.[54] Students flocked from far away to study *hadith* (Moslem tradition) under him and other notable scholars who gathered there. Many of these students were from Iraq and, returning from Banias, carried with them an anti-Fatimid version of history that became the official line in Abbasid Baghdad. Al-Nabûlusi was uncompromising in his opposition to the Shi'ite Fatimids. He urged armed resistance. He repudiated those who collaborated or made any sort of compromise with the Fatimid authorities. He proclaimed that *jihad* (holy war) against the Fatimids must take priority even over the struggle against the Byzantine Christians.[55]

In 975 AD, the Abbasids took Damascus, only to find John Zimisces menacing the city and demanding tribute immediately thereafter. The new Fatimid caliph, al-'Azîz (975–96 AD) was determined to expand his control into Syria, push back both the Abbasids and the Byzantines and stamp out the opposition that was emanating from Banias.

Al-Nabûlusi was arrested in the same year and taken away in a wooden cage to Cairo, along with 300 of his followers. These were all beheaded, except al-Nabûlusi. He remained defiant to the end, proclaiming 'If I had ten arrows, I would shoot one of them at the Christians, while the other nine would be for the Banu 'Ubayd [Fatimids]'. Up to the moment of his death he poured scorn and abuse on his captors. He was flayed and his skin stuffed with straw, then crucified, becoming thus a famous martyr for the Sunni cause.[56] His school of *hadith* at Banias continued to thrive, surviving until the beginning of the eleventh century under the leadership of such scholars as Abû Ishaq (Ibrâhim b. Hatim), al-Balluti (another refugee from Tarsus) and a number of others.[57] This was true in spite of the fact that al-'Azîz was able to establish control and a modicum of stability for the area in 982/83 AD with victories over the Qarāmita. To do so, however, he called upon Turkish mercenary soldiers, and thereby introduced a new player into the already complicated political and military scene in Syria. And even so, Syria remained only nominally under his control for a considerable period thereafter, allowing the anti-Fatimid activities in Banias to continue.[58]

In the writings of Muqaddasī we have the first detailed description of Banias for many centuries. A native of Jerusalem, Muqaddasī asserts that his great book on geography depends not on literary sources, but rather on his own experiences and observations.[59] He locates the city in what he calls the 'Third Belt' of Syria, namely the valleys of the Ghawr, 'wherein are villages and streams, palm trees, cultivated fields, and indigo'. Banias is the northernmost of the major towns in the belt: 'Wayla, Tabūk, Sughar, Arihā, Baysān, Tiberias, and Bāniyas'.[60] The city is near the border of the Huleh, at the foot of Mount Hermon,[61] in the district of Damascus,[62] two days journey from the capital.[63] The road from Damascus to Banias continues to Kadas, or to Jubb Yusaf (Joseph's Pit, near Safed), either destination being about two post stages away.[64] The town is, he says, 'more comfortable and more prosperous than Damascus'.[65] Muqaddasī notes that the river Jordan 'rises from above Baniyas, and descending, forms a lake over against Kadas [namely the Huleh]'.[66] It is at least possible that the geographer, due to his intimate knowledge of the area, is thus able to distinguish between the sources of the Jordan that lie west of the city, and the Banias spring itself. The latter is 'an extremely cold river, emerging from under the Mountain of Snow [Hermon]', which 'gushes forth in the middle of the city'.[67] Despite its value in irrigating crops and its beauty, however, the water in this river, Muqaddasī claims, is unsuitable for drinking – acting, unfortunately, 'aperiently'.[68] Excepting this single drawback, the city is 'bounteous to its inhabitants, lying amidst splendid country districts', he concludes.[69] The rising economic importance of Banias lay in its abundant water and nearby fertile fields where its river irrigates cotton and rice fields, earning for the town the impressive title: the Granary of Damascus.[70]

AL-HĀKIM, THE MILLENNIUM AND THE DRUZE

Al-'Azîz was succeeded by one of the most unusual characters of the early Middle Ages, the so-called 'mad caliph' al-Hākim (996–1021 AD).[71] It was during his reign that Banias reached its millennial year (997 AD), though almost certainly no inhabitant of the city at that time had the least idea that such a significant anniversary had been attained. The ancient citizens of the town, pagan and Christian alike, had been scattered by the winds of history and had disappeared. Al-Hākim's mistreatment of Christians within his realm and his destruction of Christian shrines, including the Church of the Holy Sepulchre in Jerusalem (1010 AD), helped to ensure a virtually complete isolation between the Fatimid Empire and the Christian West and provided a *casus belli* for the Crusaders. Serious revolts broke out against his bizarre and autocratic rule in Palestine in 1012–13 AD. But at least one sect accepted al-Hākim's claims of divinity. For them he became none other than the Messiah – and remains so to this day. This sect found its most fertile soil precisely in the foothills of Mount Hermon, so near Banias that the Druze have been a part of the history of the town for almost a thousand years. Of all the indigenous cultures that had lived in the Banias district during its first thousand years, only they remain today.

A Persian named Muhammad ibn-Ismā'īl al-Darazi gave the sect its central theological premise – that al-Hākim was an incarnation of the deity in human form – and its name: the Druze. The Druze era may be said to begin in 1017 AD, when al-Hākim was proclaimed to be divine.[72] Al-Darazi took the new faith to Wâdî al-Taym, at the foot of Mount Hermon, where it was embraced by many of the mountain people, characterised for ages by a series of stubborn heterodoxies.[73] Their beliefs exhibited Neo-Platonist influences,[74] and an elaborate eschatology. Frederick Bliss suggests that it was 'the survival of the spirit of paganism around the roots of Mount Hermon' which helped explain the ready acceptance by the inhabitants of 'the strange doctrines of the Druses'.[75] Al-Darazi's successor, Hamzah, denied that al-Hākim had died, though non-Druze accepted the theory that his strange disappearance on 13 February 1042 was the result of assassination, and announced that he would one day return in triumph.

In the beginning, the movement was aggressively evangelistic, even resorting to forced conversions. But the next leader, Baha' al-Dîn, gathered the holy writings, pronounced the teachings of the sect to be secret, and closed the community to new converts in the year 1042 AD. From that day to the present, neither conversion nor apostasy has been permitted.[76] The teachings are kept strictly secret, known fully only by the *uggal* (initiated) within the community. On Thursday evenings and special feast days, ceremonies are held to this day by the Druze in the Tomb of St George or Khader and at the tomb of the Sheikh Ibrâhim, within the boundaries of modern Banias – the only ancient religious rites at the site that have survived to the present time. Whatever traditions are maintained from ancient times, perhaps reaching back to the sylvan Pan, or even to the Ba'als of the mountains, are kept as closely guarded secrets by the black-costumed, white-turbaned *uggal*.

The Druze of the eleventh century were apparently not technically citizens of Banias but did play their part in the general disorder and unrest in the district. The next Fatimid caliph, al-Zahîr (1021–35 AD), was faced with constant civil unrest and rebellion in Palestine. The populace suffered from this terribly, as well as from the terrors of unrestrained robber bands and constant violence. Syria, and indeed the Middle East in general, was descending into its own dark age. Centuries of anarchy, pillage, death and destruction were to follow. Banias was at least able to contribute something of cultural value during the eleventh century, producing two prominent scholars of *hadith*: Abû 'Ali Jamil ben Yusf ben Ismā'īl al-Mardan, who studied *hadith* in Damascus in 1064 AD and died in 1091 AD, and Samdun ben Husayn, who died in Banias in 1098 AD.[77] And in 1107/8 AD, Malik b. Ahmad al-Baniyasi, a noted collector of *hadith,* was born in the city.[78]

FORT DAN, AND THE JEWS OF ELEVENTH-CENTURY BANIAS

Sometime during the century following al-Ya'qūbī's description of Banias as a *madinat al-asbat*, another significant change took place. Surrounded by violence, and well-placed on the Fatimid frontier, the city had to defend itself. It drew within defensive walls, not only as a part of the Fatimid defence system, but for bare survival. In the process of describing a gigantic natural disaster, the earthquake of 5 December 1033 AD, a Jewish eyewitness coincidentally reveals the nature of this shift at Banias from *madina* to fortress. The man, probably named Solomon ben Yehudah, records a mighty shaking of the earth in vivid terms. 'Those that travelled on the high roads relate the mighty acts of the living God,' he says. 'They say, "We have seen the mountains shake, leap like stags, their stones broken into pieces, the hillocks swaying to and fro, and the trees bending down."' Aftershocks continued for several days. 'The event,' he continues, 'took place on Thursday, Tebet 12th, suddenly before sunset, alike in Ramlah, in the whole of Filastin, from fortified city to open village, in all the fortresses of Egypt [i.e. the Fatimid territory] from the sea to Fort Dan.'[79]

The terminology reverts to that of the *Babylonian Talmud*, which, as we have seen, regularly identified Dan with Banias. At least within the Jewish community, the place was called not simply Dan, but Fort Dan, revealing both the nature of the city and its identity as one of the 'fortresses of Egypt'. Banias was to continue to function primarily as a fort for the next four centuries.[80] Another earthquake struck the hapless city on 18 March 1069. This time, according to Sibt Ibn al-Gawzi, the town was destroyed,[81] though apparently immediately rebuilt by its surviving inhabitants.

There is considerable evidence for a thriving Jewish community in Banias during the eleventh century. The Fatimid rulers were on the whole tolerant of Judaism and during their period of power Jews experienced something of a 'golden age' in the Near East.[82] It is likely that Jews accompanied the Moslem refugees from Cilicia after 965 AD, sharing the same terror of Byzantine oppression, though al-Muqaddasī had no particular reason to mention them. Once a community was established, it was gradually augmented by Jews from other areas under Fatimid control, particularly Egypt itself, though at least one of the religious communities in the town appears to have been under the religious jurisdiction of Damascus.[83] 'Baniasites' (the Jews of Banias) appear frequently in letters and documents of the period preserved in the Cairo Geniza. The community was large enough to support two liturgical forms, one based on the Palestinian traditions and another on those of Babylonian Jewry, perhaps an indication of emigration from the East as well.[84] The reference to 'Fort Dan' by the Jewish writer above reveals the influence of the *Babylonian Talmud*, which, unlike the *Jerusalem Talmud*, identifies Banias as the site of ancient Dan. A number of names of members of this community have been preserved – such as Ghaliya, 'the daughter of Ashlimun, al-Baniyasiya'.[85]

Evidence concerning one of the synagogues of Banias comes from a letter in the Cairo Geniza dated 8 May 1041 AD. The letter was written from Ramlah by Joseph ben Kulayb to Rabbi Nathan ben Abraham. It reports that the rabbi's followers in Ramlah have been approached by 'the son of the haver who is in Baniyas' asking for the title rosh ha-seder, and claiming that Nathan ben Abraham had visited Banias himself.[86] Another document in the Geniza, a power of attorney, dated 11 July 1056 AD, originated in the *medinat dan ha-qeruya pamis* (the city of Dan, called Pamis). The nomenclature corresponds to that of the *Babylonian Talmud*. In this document, Husayn ben Hillel, also known as Qitos, empowers Joseph ben Mahfuz to receive as his agent 'one and three fourth dinars' from a cheesemaker named Jacob ben al-Jabban. Seven signatures of Baniasites are appended for validation, among them 'Boaz ben David the Cantor'.[87]

The community was to survive in Banias for a few more decades, though tales of the fearful massacres perpetrated by the Crusaders, who after 1099 AD began to establish themselves through out Palestine from Judaea to nearby Galilee, boded ill for the future. A letter from ca. 1100 AD, also found in the Cairo Geniza, is particularly interesting in this regard. Its author, Eleazer ha-Levi ben Joseph (of Damascus?) writes to 'Eli ha-Kohen the 'haver ha-me'ulle ben Abraham' (the father of Tobiah) in Banias. Eleazer speaks of a man named Jacob, who, along with his brother, has escaped from captivity 'in the hands of the Ashkenaz', that is the Crusaders. The letter mentions the acquisition of some object, apparently for a Banias synagogue.[88] Another letter in the Geniza, dated 28 May 1112 AD, was authored by Tobiah ha-Kohen ben 'Eli. Though a Baniasite, Tobiah writes the letter to his father, 'Eli ha-Kohen the haver, from Egypt, where he has recently emigrated. Along with the names of several Jewish inhabitants of Banias, he mentions the two Jewish communities 'living in the fortress of Dan'.[89] A small basilica has been uncovered during modern excavations of the city centre (Fig. 39). The building was constructed from fragments of old Roman/Byzantine buildings in the late eleventh century, perhaps after the second of the two great earthquakes of that century. It stands directly above the large internal basilica of the ancient palace and in fact takes the shape of that chamber, though its dimensions are much smaller. Beside it, to the east, is the row of ancient Roman vaulted rooms that had been incorporated into the medieval fortress. This building has a north–south orientation and was obviously used at one point as a mosque. However, the fact that the *mihrab* (niche signifying the direction of Mecca) in the apse is a later addition has led to the theory that the building was originally meant to be a synagogue – perhaps one of the two mentioned in the Geniza documents.

The emigration of Tobiah and his family from Banias to Egypt probably signals a larger emigration of Baniasites in the second decade of the twelfth century. The anti-Semitic record of the Crusaders, combined with ominous troop movements in the area in 1111 AD,[90] was enough to drive many, perhaps most, Jews from Banias to safer regions under Fatimid control.

But there was no escaping the chaos of the times. The long reign of the Fatimid Caliph al-Mustansir (1036–94 AD) was marked by continuing unrest, famine and general misery, both in Syria and Egypt. Fatimid weakness prompted the successful invasion of Palestine by the Seljuk Turks, who dominated the area from 1070 AD until the end of the century. Atsiz, the Turkoman, seized Jerusalem in 1071 AD and Damascus in 1076 AD, striking a deal with Intisar, the Fatimid governor 'whereby Atsiz left Baniyas and Jaffa to Intisar in exchange for the surrender of Damascus'.[91] Shortly thereafter, however, Damascus was given up by Atsiz to Tutush, the brother of the Seljuk king Malik-shāh, becoming in this way the capital of the new Seljuk principality of Syria and Palestine. Thus did the Fatimids lose Syria, including the fortress at Banias.[92]

9 Banias and the Crusades

O nce a traveller (or an invader) from the West reaches Banias, firmly planted above the Huleh, secure on its shelf among the foothills of Hermon, and deeply rooted on the northern bank of the precipitous Wâdî Sa'âr,[1] no natural barrier to Damascus remains except the steep incline up and over the mountain itself. By the time the Crusaders had established themselves in the Holy Land, it was clear both to them and to their Saracen enemies that the one who held the fortress of Banias thereby posed a serious threat to the security of the other. The modern, abandoned Syrian trenches, mortar and gun emplacements which now dot the countryside around the site, looking ominously down upon the Israeli *kibbutzim* in the Huleh, furnish a remarkable analogy. Everything here is designed to guard the road to Damascus. When the Israeli tanks mounted the steep slope from the valley in 1967, across the border and up into the Syrian village that rested on the ancient site, their concerns were not unlike those of the eleventh-century Crusaders.

It is not yet clear when the first fortress at Banias was built, nor by whom. This puzzle awaits an archaeological solution. During the Roman and Byzantine periods whatever walls the surrounded Banias may have served to symbolise the status of the city rather than to provide adequate defence.[2] But, as we have seen, by the early eleventh century the place had become as much a fort as a town. Strong fortifications certainly existed then, though the excavations have thus far not revealed them. Tzaferis suggests that the Crusaders planned and constructed fortifications that completed the transformation of the city into a massive citadel complex. The fortress walls probably stood more or less where the ruins of the surviving, mostly Ayyûbid and Mamlûk structures, may be seen today. The builders made maximum use of the natural topography. On the south, the Wâdî Sa'âr provided a steep declivity upon which the walls could perch. To the west and north, use could be made of the banks and torrent of the river Banias, pouring from the springs of Pan. The weakest link was on the east, where access to the spot was relatively level and direct. This problem was solved by the construction of a large moat, into which some of the waters of the river were diverted. The fortifications of the first version of 'Fort Dan' were constructed with the most convenient materials at hand – the monumental and magnificent ruins of the Hellenistic-Roman city. Indeed, the later towers, still standing today, are full of columns, column bases, entablatures and beautifully cut stones no doubt originally crafted by the artisans of Herod Agrippa II and his Roman successors.[3]

The first Crusaders to see Fort Dan with their own eyes seem to have been Bohemond, the Prince of Antioch, and Baldwin, the Count of Edessa and erstwhile King of Jerusalem. These two Christian noblemen journeyed to Jerusalem soon after the Holy City had been wrested from Fatimid hands by the armies of Baldwin's brother Godfrey amid frightful and merciless slaughter. Their journey south took the form of a pilgrimage. Their motives in selecting a return route north, however, seemed less pious. Leaving Jerusalem on 1 January 1100 AD, they did not take the coastal route, but rather went up the Jordan valley, through Tiberias on the Lake of Galilee. They were accompanied by the historian Fulcher of Chartres (1058–1127 AD), who notes that this particular route 'pleased our princes' and that, from Tiberias, 'we passed through Caesarea Philippi which is called Paneas in the Syrian tongue'. This place, he explains, is 'situated at the foot of Mount Lebanon at a place where two springs emerge and give rise to the River Jordan'.[4] We must at least suspect that the two warriors were taking an opportunity to reconnoitre the area, and particularly to see first-hand the manner in which the gateway to Damascus was being defended.

Fulcher, in the company of military commanders, had an advantage not shared by the ordinary pilgrims of the day. Saewulf, for example, travelling in 1102–03 AD, describes Banias in some detail, but makes use of literary sources and does not claim to have visited the place himself.[5] Abbot Daniel, whose pilgrimage occurred in 1106–07 AD, throws light on the reason such visits were impossible. After confusing Caesarea Philippi with Caesarea Maritima, he admits, 'I could not reach Mount Lebanon on foot myself for fear of the pagans, but the Christians who lived there and were our guides told us of it in detail and would not let us go to the mountain because of the many pagans there'.[6] Even Fulcher allowed himself to be persuaded by reading Jerome's *Commentary of Amos* (8:14) that the Old Testament city of Dan 'was within the limits of the land of Judaea where Paneas is now located'.[7] The country around Banias remained so dangerous that it was still more prudent for Christians to depend on literary sources than to explore the area first hand.

Hostile armies were often on the move nearby. Hugh of Saint-Omer, the Prince of Galilee under the Crusader King Baldwin, pursued an aggressive policy against Moslems in the area. In 1105 AD he constructed a fortress called Toron (now Tibnin) on the old road from Tyre through Banias to Damascus.[8] The Crusaders' nemesis in the area was Toghtekin, the Atabeg of the King of Damascus, Duqaq. During 1112–13 AD, when the Franks attacked Tyre, its citizens sent an urgent call to Toghtekin to rescue them. The *atabeg* advanced to Banias, which he used as his base of operations, giving instructions through the governor of the city, one Seif ed-Daula Mes'oud. Toghtekin called for help from the Turks. In 1113 AD, the Turkish army, in the words of Fulcher of Chartres, 'left the territory of Antioch to their right, traversed Syria not far from Apamea, left Damascus to their left, and crossed between Tyre and Caesarea Philippi, which is called Paneas, into the regions of Phoenicia'. Their objective: to attack Crusader King Baldwin.[9]

A KARAITE MESSIAH IN BANIAS

In the fall of 1102 AD, a Norman of noble descent, a Roman Catholic priest and scholar from Oppido in southern Italy, converted to Judaism. His Christian name was Johannes; as a son of the 'Covenant of the God of Israel' he took the name 'Obadyah. The reasons for this highly unusual conversion are probably complex. He was certainly influenced by the conversion to Judaism of Andreas, Archbishop of Bari.[10] Perhaps he was also motivated by a sense of empathy toward the Jews, as he saw the vicious persecutions perpetrated upon them in the early days of the Crusades.[11] Bits and pieces of documents written by him have turned up among medieval Geniza fragments. A badly damaged manuscript has survived which records his movements between 1113 and 1121 AD. Jewish communities in the cities of Aleppo, Damascus and Banias provided him support for his journeys. On his way to Tyre, in the autumn of 1121 AD, he visited Banias.[12]

There occurred a curious meeting and debate between the converted Norman and a messianic pretender or 'forerunner' of the Karaite sect of the Jews named Solomon Hakkohen.[13] Solomon is an equally shadowy figure. He seems to have been an inhabitant of Jerusalem prior to the Crusaders' conquest of the city in 1099 AD. His presence in Banias suggests the existence of a Karaite community there. We have already seen evidence that the mainline Jewish community of Banias began to leave the city between 1100 AD and 1112 AD, the year in which Tobiah, the former Baniasite, wrote a letter to his father from his new home in Egypt. This letter, however, implies that Jewish communities of both the Babylonian and Palestinian types still resided in the 'fortress of Dan'. Perhaps the Karaite disciples of Solomon were moving into the city as these older communities gradually moved out.[14]

At any rate, 'Obadyah, if the surviving manuscript is to be believed, got the best of the pretender in the debate and then moved on toward Tyre, never to be heard of again. Whoever remained in Banias after this event, Jewish or not, was about to be caught up in one of the most tumultuous of all times in the ancient city.

BANIAS: CITY OF THE ASSASSINS

In the spring of 1124 AD Banias became once more the campground for troops of the Atabeg of Damascus, Toghtekin. Toghtekin encamped his soldiers by the cool waters of the city while he prepared his response to a siege that the Crusaders had laid against the city of Tyre. He hesitated, waiting for the Fatimid navy to join in the rescue. Though this help was, as it turned out, not forthcoming, the Crusaders were nevertheless alarmed by his presence. They sent an army of their own in the direction of Banias, led by Pons of Tripoli and William of Bures. Toghtekin decided not to fight and withdrew to Damascus, leaving Tyre to its fate.

In 1125 AD, the Crusaders began to menace Damascus itself, invading the Hauran and coming within 25 miles of the city.[15] Toghtekin, realising that Banias must remain in

Moslem hands if Damascus were to be safe from the Crusaders, made a fateful decision. He struck a deal with a dreaded and mysterious sect of the Ismā'īlis. The sect already had a considerable presence in Toghtekin's capital. It was well-known for the fanatical loyalty of its adherents, its habit of killing any leader who stood in its way, and its willingness to commit murder for a fee. The Ismā'īli people generated much terror and were believed by many to have supernatural powers. Among the rumours concerning them was the belief that Ismā'īli operatives killed while under the influence of hashish, hence the nickname *hasishiyya* ('Assassins'). Ismā'īli theology was complex and esoteric. Along with Moslem, Jewish and Christian influences, there were similarities to ancient Gnostic systems such as those associated with the Samaritan Simon Magus, various related 'Ophite' and 'Barbelo-Gnostic' ideas, and Mandaeanism.[16]

The leader ('*dai*') of the Syrian branch of the Assassins was a Persian named Bahrām. He had come to Damascus, gathered a large group of followers and converts, and gained the confidence of Toghtekin's vizier, al-Mazdaghani. The vizier convinced Toghtekin that turning the city over to Bahrām could save Banias. Surely a city controlled and populated by the Assassins would be daunting enough to ward off any aggressive Frankish designs upon it. And so, leaving enough of his followers in Damascus to ensure continued influence there, Bahrām took control of the old Fatimid 'fortress of Dan' in November of 1125 AD.[17]

In describing this development, the Moslem historian al-Qalânisî does not disguise his partisan disgust. Bahrām established himself in Banias, he says, with 'his rabble of varlets, half-wits, peasants, low fellows and vile scum'.[18] Then, al-Qalânisî continues, he 'set about fortifying it and rebuilding what of it was in ruins or out of repair'.[19] The latter comment is interesting in that it implies the existence of ruins in the city, many perhaps belonging to structures dating from Byzantine and Roman times. As for those parts of the city 'out of repair', it is quite possible that they were in fact parts of the Fatimid fortifications that Bahrām restored to usefulness.

Bahrām now began to assert himself in the neighbourhood. His followers alternatively propagandised and terrorised the people of the district. Nothing is recorded about the fate of those citizens of Banias who were living in the town when the Assassins arrived. It is unlikely that any Christian, Jew or even Moslem who resisted conversion would have been allowed to stay. Some may have even lost their lives. For all practical purposes, the city was entirely repopulated and the civic structure and life dating from the city's rebirth in the late tenth century disappeared (though the rural villages in its district no doubt continued much as they had during all the turbulent period preceding). It is remarkable that the old mint of Banias was reactivated by the Assassins, an indication of the high degree of favour shown them by the government of Damascus. A bronze coin dated 541 H (1126/7 AD) and clearly inscribed 'minted at Banias' has been identified in the collection of the University of Tübingen in Germany.[20] Two additional examples of this very rare coin have been found in the excavations at Banias.[21]

Apparently Bahrām and his followers were able to capture and control a number of towns in the surrounding area. Encouraged by these successes, they set out to take control of the Wâdî al-Taym, an area on the western slope of Mount Hermon to the north of Banias.

This valley was inhabited by Druze, Nusayris and Bedouin tribes, and seemed a fertile field for converts. But Bahrām had miscalculated. His followers were confronted and defeated in battle by the local population. He himself was killed in the conflict. His head and hands were cut off and sent to Cairo. Despite this setback, the Assassins were able to keep control of Banias. Another Persian, Ismā'īl al-'Ajami, succeeded Bahrām as chief *dai* of the sect in Syria. The new leader stayed in the city and continued Bahrām's policies there.[22]

On 12 February 1128 AD, a second, far more grievous disaster struck the Assassins. Toghtekin, their benefactor, died. His son, Taj al-Mulk Bûrî, immediately began to plan to free himself from the special relationship with the unpredictable and dangerous sect. In September, at a reception in the Rose Pavilion in Damascus, Bûrî had al-Mazdaghani murdered while he sat in council. The pro-Assassin vizier's head was displayed to the populace and a massacre ensued. Ismā'īlis were hunted down in the streets of Damascus and killed by the thousands. The fury of the mob was fuelled by the rumour that the vizier had actually been plotting, along with the Assassins, to betray the city of Damascus into the hands of the Franks, in exchange for an agreement to turn Tyre over to the sect.[23]

At Banias, Ismā'īl al-'Ajami was understandably distraught. He immediately sent a delegation to King Baldwin with an offer that could not have pleased the Crusader monarch more. In exchange for his rescue, and the removal of his followers to some safe place in Frankish territory, he would hand over the city of Banias. The opportunity to take control of such a strategic location bloodlessly was welcome indeed. The deal was struck and the exchange began immediately. Ismā'īl al-'Ajami kept his part of the bargain, as did the Franks. But soon after his resettlement, the Assassin leader became sick and died of that disease which in those days so often proved fatal – dysentery. Meanwhile, Crusader troops began to gather at Banias, first only enough to secure the city, then, in November of 1129 AD, a great host – the entire army of Jerusalem, augmented by many others recently recruited in Europe. Al-Qalânisî numbers this assembly at 60,000 men.[24]

With Banias firmly in hand, and a massive army eager for battle, Baldwin was ready for a victory which would almost match the glory of the restoration of Jerusalem – the conquest of Damascus. But a combination of misfortunes – including a breach of discipline among the newcomers and a terrible rainstorm, dashed his hopes. The city could not be taken. The Crusader host made a downhearted but orderly retreat back to Banias and from there disbanded.

FIRST CRUSADER OCCUPATION OF BANIAS (1129–32 AD)

Despite the disappointing outcome of the attempt on Damascus, the Crusaders were now in control of Banias, from which they could mount additional attacks whenever they chose to do so. Baldwin moved to consolidate Christian hegemony over the city. Following the usual feudal system adopted in Crusader territory, Banias was designated as capital of an hereditary *seigneurie* and given to a respected nobleman named Renier de Brus. Brus, an Englishman by heritage, appears in various documents as Brusco, de Bruso, Bruns,

Brusch, Bruis etc.[25] His family, originally from the village of Brus in Normandy, became a distinguished part of the English aristocracy during the twelfth century.[26] Renier may have been one of those younger brothers who, not eligible to inherit either wealth or title at home, set out on the Crusades to find both for themselves.

During the brief period of Crusader-occupation of Banias, both the Latins and the Saracens experienced significant changes in leadership. Bohemond II of Antioch died in 1130 AD. In August 1131 AD, Baldwin of Jerusalem also died and was buried some weeks later in the Church of the Holy Sepulchre. The first generation of Crusaders thus came to an end. Meanwhile, Bûrî of Damascus fell victim to the vengeance of the Assassins, being stabbed by two of them in May of 1131 AD and dying a lingering death a year later.

A manuscript in the library of Leiden, attributed to the Moslem historian Ibn Cheddad, and entitled *Description of Damascus* (*ca.*1280 AD), claims that the Franks built a castle on the high hill just a few hundred yards north and east of the city during this period of occupation.[27] Thus, according to this account, began the long and eventful history of Subaybah or, as it is now called, Nimrod's Castle. This assertion has been accepted by numerous writers since,[28] but has recently come into serious question. Benvenisti notes, 'It is significant that no Frankish chronicler or even contemporary Moslem mentioned the construction of such a great castle, or its whereabouts, until the end of the 13th Century'.[29] We may be confident that the 'citadel of Banias' that begins to appear in accounts of the battles fought throughout the middle decades of the twelfth century is in fact an installation inside the city walls, recently excavated, and not the fortress of Subaybah. We will return to this issue later.

Bûrî of Damascus was succeeded in 1132 AD by his son Shams al Mulûk Ismâ'îl. Ismâ'îl wasted no time in moving against Banias, deeply concerned about the vulnerability of Damascus as long as the city remained in hostile hands.[30] Renier de Brus provided a perfect opportunity by leaving the city minimally defended and taking many of his knights off to Jaffa to assist the new ruler of the Kingdom of Jerusalem, Fulk. Fulk was Baldwin's son-in-law and had only arrived in the Holy Land from France in 1129 AD. Brus left a garrison made up of knights and mercenaries to guard the city.

In December 1132 AD, Shams al Mulûk Ismâ'îl suddenly appeared before the walls of Banias. King Fulk, no doubt feeling a special sense of responsibility, and loathe to lose the city, tried to intervene. But before he could act, Ismâ'îl's soldiers tunnelled beneath the outer walls and caused them to collapse. The defenders then fled to the citadel inside the city, which had its own set of defences. This same scenario was to be played out more than once during the next several years, though sometimes the roles of defender and attacker were reversed. On this occasion the badly outnumbered Franks, after holding out for a while, were forced to surrender. A sack of the city followed, accompanied by the taking of many prisoners. Ismâ'îl's troops returned to Damascus in triumph, driving the survivors before them and brandishing the heads of Frankish soldiers on the points of their lances. A Moslem garrison remained to guard Banias. The Franks, says Ibn al-Qalânisî, 'were greatly astonished that Banyas should have been taken with such ease…in spite of the strength of its fortifications'.[31]

An additional humiliation had occurred. Among the captives taken away to Damascus was (in the words of William of Tyre) none other than 'the wife of the noble and valiant Renier'.[32] We shall hear of this woman again.

This short Crusader occupation had been tenuous at best. That it survived for some three years speaks more to the confused state of Moslem politics than to the strength of its defenders. Crusader Banias had never been more than a Frankish island outpost surrounded by a sea of enemies. The situation may be illustrated by the fact that, despite the Crusader presence in the Holy Land, no pilgrim of the period leaves an account of a visit to Banias-Caesarea Philippi.[33] Fetellus, for example, whose work may be dated to the time of this first occupation, obviously depends on hearsay for his description, though he does supply an interesting theory regarding the name of the city. He explains the Crusader name, Belinas, as deriving from the word Belina, 'on account of the beauty of its site'.[34] An anonymous *Work of Geography*, compiled during this period (*ca.* 1128–37 AD) and reconstructed from later documents by John Wilkinson, seems more dependent on Jerome than on first-hand accounts. The author presents a very confused picture of Palestinian geography, claiming, for example, that the River Jordan begins south of the Sea of Galilee (at the confluence of the Yarmuk). 'At the foot of Libanus, not far from Paneas, are the Jor and the Dan. Those are the two sources from which, under Gilboa, the Jordan is formed.' 'Not far from Paneas,' says this account, 'the Jor makes itself into a lake [the Huleh].' The river Dan, 'goes beneath the city of Kedar', by the 'plain of thorns', and then joins the Jor 'under Gilboa'. Then comes the etymology, a variation of that of Fetellus: 'Twenty-four miles from Damascus to the south, at the foot of Libanus, is Paneas, a noble city, which is called Belynas Abilina, from the "ableness" of the places to be inhabited'.[35]

The Crusader citizens of Banias were to spend almost two years in captivity in Damascus. Fortunately for them, the government at Damascus was itself on increasingly shaky ground, and in October of 1134 AD officials in the city actually proposed a truce with the Crusaders. The latter agreed, probably with great relief, but did insist as a condition that the Baniasites be released, including the wife of Renier de Brus.[36] At this point William of Tyre records the sad fate of this woman, in terms so delicate that it is difficult to answer the inevitable questions that arise in the reader's mind.

> The wife of the valiant Renier de Brus was returned to her distinguished husband after an absence of two years, and he graciously restored her to her position as his wife. Later, however, he discovered that her conduct while with the enemy had not been altogether discreet. She had not satisfactorily preserved the sanctity of the marriage couch as a noble matron should. Accordingly, he cast her off. She did not deny her guilt, but entered a convent of holy women at Jerusalem, took the vows of perpetual chastity, and became a nun.[37]

What is hidden between the lines in this story? Did the Lady of Banias, whose name William does not utter, have a consensual affair with someone in Damascus? Sexual adventures were certainly not unknown among the Crusader nobility of both genders. Was this affair with one of her colleagues in captivity, or with a Moslem? Was the affair really consensual, given the circumstances, or did she succumb to threats of violence against her? William's choice of words seems strangely muted for the times. She had 'not been altogether discreet'.

Nevertheless, she admits to 'guilt' and thus, given the standards of the day, was held responsible for what happened. At the same time, her 'punishment' was, again considering the times, rather mild; though from a modern standpoint it may not seem so. She simply took vows of perpetual chastity and disappeared into a convent. It is also worthy of note that Renier did not divorce her, and did not marry again while she was alive. Apparently she did not live long in the convent, and following her death, Renier married a niece of William de Bury named Agnes. There is undoubtedly a tragic story worthy of Hollywood here, but it is not possible to reconstruct it from what has been passed along to us.[38]

THE CRUSADERS REGAIN BANIAS

The new Moslem governor of Banias was Ibrâhim ibn Turghut, appointed by Shams al Mulûk Ismā'īl. He set out to repair the damage done to the city during the siege, and in the very year when the wife of Renier de Brus and her fellow prisoners were released, he caused an inscription mentioning this work to be raised in the city. The inscription, found in 1898 incorporated into the wall of a house near the site of the citadel, mentions the reconstruction, and lists grandiose titles for Ibrâhim ibn Turghut: 'pride of the realm, glory of the amirs, beauty of the intimate associates [of the prince], elect, strength of the Commander of the Faithful' etc.[39]

The rise of a formidable new personality, 'Imâd al-Dîn Zengî, Atabeg of Mosul (1127–46 AD),[40] precipitated a curious chapter in the history of Banias, during which Jerusalem and Damascus actually joined hands against a mutual foe. Zengî had designs on Damascus. Ibrâhim ibn Turghut, who seems to have enjoyed a certain amount of independence and was able to maintain and command his own army, rebelled against his overlord, Mu'in al-Dîn Unur, Emir of Damascus, in 1137 AD and declared loyalty to Zengî. Unur was in a very precarious position, caught between the powerful Zengî and the traitorous Turghut.[41] Unur, now an old man, was a Mamlûk, one of that rising class of soldiers who had been kidnapped, mostly from Christian areas, and raised as Moslems, and who would presumably be loyal to their captors, who often treated them like sons. Zengî had already driven him out of Homs, where he had been governor. He had then proceeded to Damascus, where he took power as a champion of the Burids (the family of Toghtekin, Bûrî and Ismā'īl), whose heir was but a boy.

Zengî's troops hovered over Damascus, ready to take the city. Unur made a desperate and controversial decision – he called for help from the Franks. He sent Prince Usama (to whom we will return later) as an envoy to Fulk, now King of Jerusalem (1131–44 AD). Usama carried the following offer: if the Franks would unite with him to drive Zengî away from Damascus and Zengî's ally Ibrâhim ibn Turghut out of Banias, he would put control of Banias in Crusader hands once again. Furthermore, he would provide the Franks with tribute of 20,000 besants a month.[42] Unur, through Usama, had made such an offer before. But this time it could not be refused. Crusaders and Saracens united against a common foe – how inconceivable such an arrangement would have been to those pioneer Crusaders, whose religious fervour had called for the total destruction of Islam. And how could the Damascenes, implacable enemies of the 'polytheists' who had invaded their ancestral lands, agree to this alliance, and particularly to handing over the crucial fortress of Banias? William, Archbishop of Tyre, explained the motivations of the Damascenes: They preferred, he says, that Banias 'should be restored to the Christians, whose favour they enjoyed, rather than see it held by an enemy whom they greatly feared and distrusted'.[43] Theological considerations had obviously been replaced by practical considerations in the complex world of the Middle East.

Fulk brought his army into Galilee in the spring of 1140 AD. His troops joined those of Unur east of Lake Huleh, very near Banias. Zengî, intimidated by this show of force, withdrew from the area even before the two forces met. He was, says William, of 'no mind to come into conflict with two armies at the same time on hostile soil'.[44] Thus, without having to fight at all, the alliance had rescued the city of Damascus. Unur then honoured his part of the agreement. The entire combined force moved toward Banias.

In the meantime, Ibrâhim ibn Turghut, off on a raid toward Tyre, had been killed by the soldiers of Raymond of Antioch, and control of the city had passed to his heir.[45] The survivors of Ibrâhim's fatal raid returned to Banias and raised a defending force from among the tribes of the Wâdî al-Taym, presumably mostly Druze, and the surrounding area.[46]

THE SIEGE BEGINS

The two armies were deployed in such a way as to cut the town off on all sides. The Franks moved into the open fields on the west, now lying within the modern Israeli Kibbutz Snir. Unur's men positioned themselves east of the city at a place that William of Tyre calls 'Cohagar' – 'between the city and the woods'.[47] This is undoubtedly the strip of ground between the northern edge of Wâdî Sa'âr and the southern slopes of the hill of Subaybah, along which ran the road to Damascus, all of which is on higher ground than the city itself. Natural impediments blocked access and escape to the north and south of the fortress. The citizens of Banias were trapped.

The besiegers began to harass the town in the usual manner of the day. William describes the scene:

> From the hurling engines called petraries they threw huge stones of great weight, which shook the walls and demolished the buildings within the city itself. Showers of arrows and darts also rained like hail upon the harassed townspeople, so that it was impossible to find any place of security within the walls. Even the defenders, though protected by wall and ramparts, as they hurled stones or drew their bows scarcely ventured to look upon the assailants without.

While William admits that this situation, in which Christian and Moslem armies co-operated against a common enemy, provided a 'strange and novel sight', he nevertheless seems to approve. He expresses admiration for the skills and courage of the Damascene soldiers and the integrity of their commander Unur. At the same time he also admires the defenders of Banias, who, 'wearied to the point of exhaustion by the ceaseless attacks and by the burden of vigils and excessive toil, still kept up a vigorous resistance. As far as their strength permitted, they made every effort to defend their wives and children and, above all, their liberty.'[48]

The defenders were also buoyed by rumours that Zengî, encamped at Baalbek, planned to send a Turkoman force to drive away the besieging armies.[49] The resistance of the inhabitants of Banias was so persistent that the besiegers realised something dramatic must be done to break their spirit. In such cases, the most effective tactic was to bring a tall wooden tower up next to the walls, from which stones and arrows could be rained down upon the hapless defenders. But despite the proximity of the fabled oak forests of Banias, the local trees were not the type that could supply the gigantic timbers necessary for constructing such a tower. Unur once again stepped forward. He had, he said, just the sort of timbers needed – in Damascus: 'tall beams of great size which long ago had been set aside especially for such a purpose'. He sent some of his men back over Mount Hermon to his capital, ordering them to bring the timbers back with all haste.[50]

In the meantime, to further exacerbate the desperation of the defenders, fresh troops arrived under the command of the Crusader Prince of Antioch and the Count of Tripoli. They eagerly joined the fray. The Christians were further encouraged by a high-level ecclesiastical delegation that appeared to urge them on. The delegation was led by Alberic of Beauvais, Bishop of Ostia, who was in Palestine on a mission representing the Pope, accompanied by William, the Patriarch of Jerusalem, and Fulcher, Archbishop of Tyre. William notes that the 'sanction of apostolic authority' spurred the Christian soldiers on. The entire Crusader establishment was concentrated before the walls of Banias.

Zengî's promise of help for the defenders did not materialise. But the siege tower did. Unur's men returned from Damascus with the massive beams that, says William of Tyre, 'were quickly dressed by the carpenters and workmen and put together solidly with iron nails'. He continues his account:

> Soon an engine of great height towered aloft, from whose top the entire city could be surveyed. From this vantage point, arrows and missiles of every sort could be sent, while great stones hurled by hand would also help to keep the defenders back. As soon as the engine was ready, the ground between it and the walls was leveled off, and the machine was attached to the ramparts. There, as it looked down upon the whole city, it seemed as if a tower had been suddenly erected in the very midst of the place.[51]

The tower was obviously erected along the eastern wall of the city, the one nearest the road to Damascus, and the most vulnerable spot in the city's defences. We do not know whether the large moat that can still be seen along the ruined eastern wall existed at that time. Most likely it did. This would mean that William's statement that the ground between the siege tower and the wall 'was leveled off' should be taken to mean that the moat was filled in, so that the machine could be rolled up close to the wall.

A delightful near-contemporary depiction of this event has survived (Fig. 42). A late thirteenth-century illuminated manuscript of the *Chronicle of the Crusades* features a colourful rendering of the 'siege of Caesarea Philippi'.[52] It depicts the tower resting against the walls of Banias, next to one of the ramparts. Carried on four large wooden wheels, the tower consists of a turreted platform, held aloft by strong timbers, reached by a ladder from behind. A soldier, clad in his coat of metal scales, sword in one hand and triangular shield in the other, does battle with a defender, eye-to-eye at the top of the city wall. He and his companion wear bowl-shaped helmets. Their feet, hands, ears and chins are covered with mail. Another soldier, with a large shield but apparently no weapon, climbs up the ladder. Foot soldiers surround the base of the tower, waiting with anxious eyes to enter the battle. Behind the tower the knights, mounted on magnificent horses and waving colourful flags, watch the action through the visors in their *casques des Croisades*, heavy iron helmets almost completely covering their heads. The defenders are variously dressed: two sport *baidas* (egg-shaped helmets), one is bareheaded; they protect themselves with heart-shaped shields decorated with ribbons; they have long hair and beards, and a look of gravity mixed with terror.

And indeed the tower did produce terror within the city. The brave defenders, says William of Tyre,

> were driven to the last extremity, for it was impossible to devise any remedy against the downpour of stones and missiles which fell without intermission from the moveable tower. Moreover, there was no safe place within the city for the sick and wounded, or where those who, still strong and vigorous, were sacrificing themselves in defence of the others might withdraw to rest after their labors.

The numbers of dead, wounded and exhausted grew by the hour. The end was obviously near.

Perhaps at this point Unur's conscience began to prick him, as he saw his co-religionists in such dire straits. At any rate, he secretly sent a delegation into the city to formulate an agreement of surrender that would spare them from the massacre likely to begin at any moment. Reluctantly, the inhabitants agreed to put down their arms, in exchange for safe passage out of the city. The governor of the city, however, drove a hard bargain – remarkable for one with so little bargaining leverage remaining. He insisted that he be given some compensation for surrendering Banias, for 'it seemed shameful and disgraceful that a noble lord, the former ruler of a great city, should be driven from his hereditary possessions and compelled to beg'.[53] This audacious man's name is not recorded. He is apparently the heir of the recently deceased Ibrâhim ibn Turghut, and thus had only been in possession of the city for a matter of weeks. Nevertheless, Unur agreed to a very generous settlement. The former Lord of Banias was to receive payment of an annual revenue, payable from the proceeds of the baths and the orchards of the town. The reference to baths is particularly interesting in view of the impressive ruins of the baths dating from Roman and Byzantine to medieval times, discovered in the modern excavations at the site – quite possibly the very ones mentioned by William in his account of the settlement.[54]

The citizens of the city were given a choice: they could leave the city with their families and possessions, with assurance of safe passage, or they could stay and continue to run their estates, whether in the city or the countryside, provided they promised fealty to the new Crusader government of the city. That the latter option was provided may hint at the presence of Christians, perhaps of some Eastern rite, among the citizens of Banias. That such an enlightened and moderate settlement was accepted by the Crusaders is something of a wonder, given the usual harshness with which vanquished enemies were treated. Unur, says William, had placed the proposal before 'the king, the patriarch, the prince, and the count' in a 'friendly way'. They accepted, he says, 'out of respect for the wisdom and sincere fidelity of the man'.[55] Saladin was not the first Moslem prince to gain the respect of his erstwhile enemies through righteous behaviour, sincere respect and flawless integrity. Usama, who considered Unur his patron, confirms this respect from the Moslem side in his famous *Memoirs*, composing in Unur's honour these verses:

O Mu'in-al-Dîn, how numerous are thy necklaces of bounty
On my neck, irremovable as the rings around the pigeon's throat!
Thy benevolence has made me indeed thy voluntary bondsman,
For to the noble, benevolence is his fetters.
So much so that I have now begun to trace my genealogy to thy friendship.[56]

USAMA'S MEMOIRS

The siege of Banias, which had lasted almost a month (20 May to 12 June 1140 AD), was over. A period of peace and co-operation began between the Moslems of Damascus and the Kingdom of Jerusalem, due in no small part to the personality and moral authority of Muin al-Dîn Unur. Renier de Brus returned to his *seigneurie*, once again the *de facto* Lord of Banias. Fulcher, Archbishop of Tyre, exercised his right as Metropolitan over the church at Banias, and selected an archdeacon from Acre, named Adam, as bishop of the city. The armies, Crusader and Damascene, dispersed, and life took on some measure of civility in Banias.[57]

We are provided a remarkably personal insight into this short period of peace through the survival of a single manuscript of the *Memoirs* of Usama ibn Munqidh (1095–1188 AD). Born to nobility in northern Syria, he moved in the highest circles. He enjoyed intimate friendship with all the major Moslem leaders of the time, beginning with Unur and continuing with Nûr ed-Dîn, and ultimately with Saladin himself. He was well acquainted with the Crusader nobility as well, having served as an envoy to Frankish Jerusalem more than once, and dealing with Franks often during the time of truce. He was a sophisticated man, an intellectual and a poet, as well as a warrior and sportsman. Philip Hitti calls his life 'an epitome of Arab civilisation as it flourished during the early crusading period on Syrian soil. He was a flower of Arab-Syrian chivalry which found its full bloom later in his patron and friend, the great Saladin.'[58]

Though he seems to have genuinely liked some of the Franks he knew, he never let an opportunity pass in his *Memoirs* to illustrate his opinion that they were at heart semi-civilised bumpkins, the proper subjects of ridicule: 'When one comes to recount cases regarding the Franks, he cannot but glorify Allah (exalted is he!) and sanctify him, for he sees them as animals possessing the virtues of courage and fighting, but nothing else; just as animals have only the virtues of strength and carrying loads'.[59] Writing during extreme old age (around ninety), he remembers clearly examples of Frankish foolishness. He recounts with amusement the story of an old deacon who, at the time of the siege of Banias, was put in charge of the great tent erected in the Crusader camp by William the Patriarch to serve as a church. The floor of the tent was covered with grass and bulrushes taken from the banks of the streams of Banias. Unfortunately, this floor became the home, says Usama, of a 'pest of fleas'. Thus, he continues, 'it occurred to that deacon to burn the bulrushes and grass in order to burn thereby the fleas. So he started the fire in the bulrushes and grass, which were all dried up by this time, and the fire sent flames that caught the tent and left it in ashes. This man acted with his reason absent.'[60] It is not hard to imagine the Moslem troops from Damascus, watching the smoke from this fire from their camp on the other side of the river, and laughing up their sleeves at the foolish barbarians.

Soon after the truce went into effect, Usama had occasion to test the integrity of the Franks' resolve to keep their word. Renier de Brus, in violation of the spirit of the accord, confiscated a number of sheep that belonged to the Moslems from the forest of Banias. This happened during lambing time, and many of the newborn lambs died. Usama, residing in Damascus at the time, brought a complaint against Renier directly to King Fulk. The king appointed a commission of six or seven knights to settle the matter. After private deliberation they came back to Fulk with their decision: 'We have passed judgment to the effect that the lord of Baniyas should be fined the amount of the damage he wrought among their sheep'. So the king ordered Renier to pay the fine. Renier then negotiated directly with Usama to set an amount. 'He pleaded with me, urged and implored me until I finally accepted from him four hundred dinars,' Usama reports, somewhat amazed at the power which the knights could exercise over a lord in such circumstances. At any rate, the event seemed to indicate good faith on the Crusader side – at least for the time being.[61]

THE SECOND CRUSADE

But matters soon took a turn for the worse. King Fulk was killed in a hunting accident in 1143 AD. His wife, Queen Melisende, took control in the name of his 13-year-old son Baldwin. Zengî then besieged and took control of the Crusader state of Edessa in 1144 AD. Alarm began to spread in Christian circles, both in the East and in Europe. Zengî was murdered in 1146 AD and succeeded by his son Nūr ed-Dîn. Nūr ed-Dîn was only 29 years old, but already a seasoned and wise leader. He was to become the major opponent of the Crusaders for many years to come. Foolishly, a group of powerful demagogues in Jerusalem overruled the judgment of the queen and her young son, and invaded the Hauran, part of Unur's territory. Unur turned to Nūr ed-Dîn, son of his old opponent Zengî, and proposed an alliance.

Meanwhile, alarmed at the fall of Edessa, the Pope called for another Crusade, to be led by the German Emperor Conrad III and Louis VII of France. These arrived in the Holy Land, accompanied by many other nobles and adventurers. On 24 June 1148 AD a great council was held in Acre between the Westerners and the local leadership, both temporal and ecclesiastical. Among the participants was Adam, Bishop of Banias. Together they organised the largest Frankish army ever seen in Palestine, representing, says William of Tyre, 'the entire military strength of the realm, both cavalry and infantry, natives and pilgrims alike'.[62]

But the strategy adopted by the leaders of this great host was incredibly foolish. The army was to be used to attack the only Moslem leader in the area who had tried to live in harmony with the Franks, Unur of Damascus. Already driven toward Nūr ed-Dîn by earlier Frankish perfidy, such a strategy was sure to finish the process. A stronger alliance with a man who had shown a willingness to co-operate against a common enemy might have resulted in dispensing with Nūr ed-Dîn. Instead, the Crusaders were playing into his hands.

The great army moved first to Tiberias and then to Banias, arriving in mid-July 1148 AD. Adam no doubt became an important liaison in a meeting held in Banias 'with persons well acquainted with the situation of Damascus and the adjacent country'. The years of peace had provided plenty of opportunity for locals to know Damascus well. And so, from there, the Crusaders climbed the skirts of Mount Hermon and descended into the plain of Damascus to meet their old friend, Mu'in al-Dîn Unur, in battle. It was a battle in which, according to al-Qalânisî, Unur, 'performed prodigious feats...showing unparalleled valour, tenacity and indefatigable prowess in his onslaught on the enemy'. He also called for help from Nūr ed-Dîn, who began to move toward Damascus. He was not needed. In less than five days the mighty Frankish host was fleeing back toward the mountain in disarray. Thousands were killed during the retreat and the stench of dead bodies was so strong, al-Qalânisî says, 'that the birds almost fell out of the sky'.[63]

THE RISE OF NŪR ED-DÎN (1146–74 AD)

The local Franks seemed to have learned their lesson as far as Unur was concerned, and in May 1149 AD, they made a new truce with him, to last two years, based on a mutual fear of Nūr ed-Dîn. The old man died in August of the same year and was succeeded by Mujir ed-Dîn Abaq, the grandson of Toghtekin, in whose name he had ruled all these years. The new ruler showed himself to be true to his word. When a group of Turkomans attacked Banias, probably at the instigation of Nūr ed-Dîn, and were defeated by troops from the city, led by its governor, Mujir punished the Turkomans for breaking the truce. This occurred in December of 1151 AD.[64]

But Mujir had none of his predecessor's skills or virtues. Under him, Damascus fell almost to the status of a Crusader protectorate and was forced to pay a yearly tribute.[65] In 1153 AD, Nūr ed-Dîn proposed an alliance with Mujir to take Banias, but the two could not agree on the project and nothing came of it. Nūr ed-Dîn bided his time and then, in April 1154 AD, he rather easily wrested real control of Damascus from Mujir, but without actually displacing him. Shortly thereafter (in May) he besieged Banias, hoping by this stratagem to pull Frankish troops away from their own siege of Askelon. A weakly defended Banias would have been easy prey. But both the siege and the stratagem failed, due to internal disputes among the troops.[66] At this point he removed the unpopular Mujir as governor of Damascus. Distracted by other problems, he then agreed to renew the truce with the Franks for another two-year term, beginning in 1156 AD, and to continue paying the tribute each year. But the situation in Banias was precarious, to say the least. Nūr ed-Dîn was again simply biding his time.

THE TRUCE DISINTEGRATES

A series of big earthquakes ravaged Syria from the autumn of 1156 AD to August of 1157 AD. The resulting chaos, death and destruction furnished an opportunity for Nūr ed-Dîn to threaten a number of Frankish strongholds, including Banias.[67] Baldwin III (1144–62 AD) made matters worse by committing a flagrant offence against the truce agreement himself. This occurred in February of 1157. Large numbers of Turkomans (itinerant, tent-dwelling Turkish tribes of Iranian origin) had come into the region to take advantage of the excellent pastures in the 'Forest of Banias'.[68] They received solemn assurances of safe conduct, under the terms of the truce. But Baldwin, needing money, could not resist temptation when he saw the huge flocks of sheep and herds of horses. He confiscated them, in complete disregard of his promise, and thus gave an additional *causus belli* to Nūr ed-Dîn.

During the period of relative cordiality between the Crusaders and the Moslems, Renier de Brus had passed from the scene and Humphrey of Toron had inherited the *seigneurie* of Banias.[69] With the disintegration of the truce, the vulnerable city became a millstone around his neck. He was, as William of Tyre says, 'weary of the continual responsibility and expense which devolved upon him in the care of the city of Banias'.[70] With Baldwin's consent he made an agreement with the Brothers of the Hospital. In exchange for their assistance in financing and defending the city, he would give them control of half of it, along with half of its the territories and villages. The Brothers were an order of military monks headquartered in Jerusalem who had vowed personal poverty, chastity and obedience and to fight against the 'heathen'. Consequently, they were especially hated by the Moslems.

The situation in Banias was so precarious, says William, that 'no one could approach or leave the city without danger unless in a strong company or by following secret ways'.[71] A vanguard of the Brothers entered the city and took charge of their designated area. They began to gather supplies, arms and troops, 'desiring to put the place in a good state of defence'. A very large convoy of camels and pack animals, carrying supplies and guarded by knights, proceeded north toward the city, prepared to fight their way through if necessary. The Moslems, led by Nosret ed-Dîn, the brother of Nūr ed-Dîn, carefully monitored their progress. They waited until the convoy was quite near the city and then fell upon it in a furious ambush. The battle seems to have taken place before the walls of the city itself, for Abû Chama notes that the troops stationed in the city came out to join the fight.[72] The result was disaster. The entire caravan was captured, many Brothers were killed and all the supplies were taken. The Brothers had had enough.

They withdrew from Banias, and from their agreement with Humphrey, and left the city to its fate.

Nūr ed-Dîn made his move. It was mid-May 1157 AD. Nūr ed-Dîn surrounded Banias with his cavalry and his siege machines. The city, still staggering from the Hospitallers' disaster, was hemmed in on every side. Nūr ed-Dîn's strategy followed that of the successful Moslem siege of the city in 1132 AD. His sappers began to dig tunnels, reinforced by wooden pillars, beneath the walls. The wood was then set on fire, the pillars collapsed, and along with them, large sections of the walls. Then, on Tuesday, 21 May 1157 AD, at the fourth hour, the Moslems 'rushed in, slaughtering the defenders and pillaging the fort'. At least this is the version of the story reported by the Moslem historian Ibn al-Qalânisî.[73]

William of Tyre gives the Crusader version. The citizens of Banias, he says, had great confidence in the fortifications of their city, and despite the fact that Nūr ed-Dîn's machines and hurling engines were pelting them with 'a steady, incessant shower of arrows which gave the besieged no respite', they were holding fast. He particularly praises the constable Humphrey and his son, who showed themselves 'ready to fight zealously for their hereditary possessions and by their example encouraged others to resist. Without doubt the citizens, exhausted by their heroic efforts, would have given way before the superior strength of their foes.'[74] Then, William says, the citizens of Banias made a serious mistake. They opened the city gate and tried to take the offensive, attacking the besiegers outside. When this attempt failed, they panicked and rushed back through the open gate. The press was so great that the gate could not be shut and the Turks entered the city with them, 'intermingling with the townspeople'.

At this point Humphrey and the townspeople fled into the city's citadel. William simply locates this facility 'in one part of Banias'. Excavations of the city have uncovered the ancient citadel, discovering that it incorporated and was built upon a massive Roman structure now thought to be the palace of Agrippa II. Unlike the internal citadel in Jerusalem, which abutted the outer wall of the city, and is to this day still called 'the citadel', the citadel of Banias sat in the centre of the town, its walls forming a second line of defence on all four sides.[75] The retreat was accomplished at great risk and with much loss of life. Humphrey and the Franks in the citadel were in dire straits. Al-Qalânisî says they 'dreaded the end of their resistance, and urgently entreated our Lord Nūr ed-Dîn to have pity on them. They offered to hand over the citadel and all its contents in exchange for their lives.' Nūr ed-Dîn refused to negotiate. In the meantime, the city itself was wholly at the mercy of the Moslem troops. It was at this point, according to William, when the outer walls were undermined and caused to collapse. Fires were set, houses were destroyed and unrestrained pillage ensued.[76]

Nūr ed-Dîn finished the work of destruction, placed troops along the roads into Banias ready to ambush anyone seeking to bring in supplies, and called for reinforcements. But what seemed a sure victory slipped from his hands. A formidable rescue force led by King Baldwin suddenly appeared, and the practical Nūr ed-Dîn decided, in al-Qalânisî's words that 'the only prudent thing to do was to retire and allow him to reach the defenders and bring them help'. Once again, his strong desire to take control of Banias had been thwarted.

Al-Qalânisî says that when Baldwin saw that the walls and buildings of the city were destroyed, 'he saw no hope of making the place habitable'. William, on the other hand, says that the king 'promised that he would remain until the fallen places had been raised, the breaches mended, and the city, its walls repaired, restored to its former state'. Thus,

> from the neighbouring cities and the whole region, he summoned masons and all who had some experience in the art of building. The walls and towers were thoroughly repaired and the ramparts renewed. Within the circuit of the walls, the houses of the inhabitants were rebuilt and the public buildings restored to their original condition, for Nūr ed-Dîn, during his occupancy of the city, had taken great care to destroy them completely.[77]

Unless the historians of this event have completely exaggerated the situation, Banias was rebuilt with such haste that aesthetic considerations were out of the question. Defence was everything. The city was purely and simply a military installation.

After the rebuilding of Banias, Baldwin led his army south. On the way, it was ambushed at the River Jordan and destroyed. William, ever the ethicist, attributes this disaster to the judgment of God, levelled on Baldwin because he had flagrantly violated his oath in the matter of the Turkoman flocks and herds: 'The Lord rendered to us the fruits of our evil doing; and we, who in scorn of the laws of humanity had wrongfully oppressed the innocent and those who relied on our good faith, were ourselves overwhelmed with confusion in like measure'.[78]

The beleaguered citizens of Banias, to their great dismay, saw the army of Nūr ed-Dîn immediately resume the siege. The blockade was again set up. The siege machines were put back in place. The huge stone missiles began once again to pummel the town, shaking the new towers and weakening the new walls. Arrows and darts poured down upon the hapless inhabitants. The entire population retreated to the citadel once again.

And once again, rescue came at the last moment, this time, from the Prince of Antioch and the Count of Tripoli. They arrived at the royal camps, near Chastel Neuf, at the place called Noire Garde (Ain Belatha?), from where Banias could actually be seen.[79] Nūr ed-Dîn, although he had made considerable progress in once again knocking down the city's defences, decided to pull back once again.[80]

THE FALL OF BANIAS (16 OCTOBER 1164)

For seven years Crusader Banias enjoyed relative peace as Nūr ed-Dîn remained distracted with other matters. The fall of the city came with surprising speed and ease and seemed almost anticlimactic, given the decades of struggle that preceded it. Nūr ed-Dîn used a ruse. First, he threatened Antioch. Amalric, who had succeeded his brother Baldwin III as King of Jerusalem, headed north to meet the challenge. Then, pulling back, Nūr ed-Dîn encouraged a rumour that his next objective was Tiberias. Most of the local Frankish troops gathered there. Humphrey, Lord of Banias, and John, the city's bishop, were in Egypt with the army of the King of Jerusalem. Banias was left under the command of a knight named Walter de Quesnoy. The city lay essentially helpless. Nūr ed-Dîn appeared suddenly before the walls in mid-October 1164. What few troops were there first fought bravely, but resistance crumbled so quickly that some suspected treachery. William of Tyre even recounts a rumour that Walter, in collusion with a priest named Roger, accepted a bribe to surrender.[81] On 18 November 1164, Nūr ed-Dîn's dream was finally realised. Banias was in his hands. Despite several attempts to do so, the Crusaders never held the city again.[82]

The account of Nūr ed-Dîn's victory at Banias took a prominent place in Moslem lore, particularly the *bon mots* of the leader himself regarding the events that took place at the time. To his brother, Nosret ed-Dîn, who lost an eye during the battle, he was remembered to say, 'If you could see the reward which awaits you in the other world, you would wish to lose the other eye as well'.[83] Following the battle, it was said that Nūr ed-Dîn saw the son of Unur, who had delivered Banias to the Franks in 1148, standing behind him. He turned to him and said, 'This victory is a cause for joy for everyone, but for you the joy must be ten times as strong'. 'Why should that be?' asked the man. 'Because today God has cooled the skin of your father as he passes through the fires of hell.'[84] According to Ibn al-Athîr, as he left Banias and passed through the thick forests, Nūr ed-Dîn lost his famous ring, which had a ruby so large it was called *el djebel* ('the mountain'). When he discovered his loss, Nūr ed-Dîn sent some of his men back to search for the ring among the thickets of Banias – a veritable 'needle in a haystack'. Miraculously, they found it and returned it to him. This ring, says the Arab historian, is 'the mountain' referred to in a poem about the expedition written by the Syrian poet Ibn Mouir.[85]

Though they occupied it for more than two decades (1140–64 AD), the Crusaders left little imprint on Banias. In addition to Adam, the first Latin bishop of Banias, the names of three other Crusader bishops have survived, John, Peter and Natale. Bishop John was in office when the city fell. We will have occasion to mention him later. The others are known only from medallions, upon which have been recorded their likenesses and the following inscriptions: '+Fr[ater] Petrus, Dei gra[ti]a Paneade[nsis] ep[iscopu]s]' and, 'S[igillum] D[omini] Natalis Ep[iscopu]s Pan[e]ad[ensis]'.[86]

The beautiful architecture found at many Crusader sites is missing at Banias. Almost no Crusader coins have been found in the excavations there.[87] Apparently the series of sieges, each bringing its share of devastation, and the hurried nature of most of the buildings erected during the Crusader occupation, simply did not allow for a quality of life much beyond mere subsistence and survival. A single stone found at the site may provide a poignant reminder of the Crusader presence. A large limestone block, containing an important inscription by a later Ayyûbid governor of Banias (see below), when turned on its side, reveals a credibly carved *fleur de lis*, a trademark of the Crusaders.[88] The stone had obviously once been a part of some building, perhaps a church, which, despite the stress of daily life, the citizens of Banias had taken the trouble to touch with a certain beauty. The same stone, turned on its back, reveals the egg-and-dart motif found on buildings from the glory days of Roman paganism. It thus encapsulates the story of an old, old town in its progression from one culture to another.

10 Ayyûbids, Mamlûks and Turks

BANIAS UNDER SALADIN

Al-Malik al-Nâsir Salah al-Dîn Yusuf ibn Ayyub (1138–93), known in the West as Saladin, was not yet thirty years old when he accompanied his uncle to Egypt in the service of Nūr ed-Dîn. By 1169 he was the vizier of al-'Ādid, the Fatimid Caliph in Cairo. Intensely religious, this young Kurd longed to wrest control of Egypt from the Shi'ite Fatimids and restore it to his own Sunni brand of Islam. His opportunity came as al-'Ādid lay helpless on his deathbed. Saladin boldly ordered that the Friday prayers no longer be said in the name of the Fatimid caliph but rather in the name of the Abbasid caliph in Baghdad.[1] With incredible ease, in one fell swoop, the Fatimid era came to an end.

After Nūr ed-Dîn's death in May 1174, Banias took centre-stage once again when the Crusaders, led by King Amaury, attempted to take advantage of the situation. Within weeks Amaury marched on Banias and laid siege.[2] The governor of Damascus, still loyal to the family of Nūr ed-Dîn, came out to meet him and struck a deal. Amaury would withdraw in exchange for a large sum of money, the release of all Frankish prisoners and an alliance against the rising power of Saladin.[3] But Amaury himself died shortly thereafter (on 11 July 1174), and the situation remained very unstable.

Meanwhile, before the end of the year, Saladin had pushed aside the young heir of his former master and made himself sole ruler of an empire that included both Egypt and Syria. The young prince was now positioned to proceed with his religious and political passion – the expulsion of the hated Franks from their strongholds in the Holy Land.[4] He declared all-out *jihad* on the intruders. Control of the area around Banias was, as so often before, central to the struggle. In 1177, King Baldwin IV, 'the Leper', (1174–85) besieged the town. But again the Frankish king accepted tribute from the local Moslem authorities to withdraw.

Both sides understood how crucial was a strong fortified line between upper Galilee and the Huleh on the Crusader side, and Damascus on the Moslem side. Having lost Banias, the Crusaders determined to erect strong forts along this frontier to protect themselves. Humphrey of Toron (formerly the governor of Banias) had built a castle on the hill of

Hunîn on the road from Banias to Toron. The King of Jerusalem built another – designed to control Jacob's Ford on the upper Jordan between the Sea of Galilee and Lake Huleh.[5]

In 1179, Saladin left Damascus to take personal command in the area, making his camp at Banias and stretching a defence line across the Huleh through Tel ed-Khadhi (Tel Dan) and beyond, in order to threaten Toron. He stayed for several months, using Banias as a base for forays against the enemy. The local governor assisted him. On 15 June 1179, for example, al-Maqrizî, the Arab historian of the period, notes that 'the Sultan rode forth at the head of his troops, accompanied by Samsan al-Dîn Ajuk, the governor of Banias'.[6] In the same year, Humphrey of Toron was killed during the fighting. Moslem rivals of Saladin attempted to use Banias as bait to draw the Crusaders into plots against his sultanate. In the year 1182, for example, 'Imâd ed-Dîn and Izz ed-Dîn offered to give the city back to the Crusaders if they would join in an alliance with them against Saladin, but nothing came of the matter.[7]

An uneasy stability was thus established on the Damascene frontier, while Saladin and the Franks remained in almost constant warfare elsewhere. The famous Moslem traveller Ibn Jubair paid a visit to Banias in 1185 and provides an interesting record of the town during this period when events were moving rapidly toward the climactic confrontation between the Crusaders and Saladin.

> This city is a frontier fortress of the Muslims. It is small, but has a castle, round which, under the wall, flows a stream. This stream flows out from the town by one of the gates, and turns a mill…The town has broad arable lands in the adjacent plain. Commanding the town is the fortress, still belonging to the Franks, called Hunîn, which lies 3 leagues distant from Baniyas. The lands in the plain belong half to the Franks and half to the Moslems; and there is here the boundary called Hadd al Mukasimah – the 'Boundary of Dividing.' The Moslems and Franks apportion the crops equally between them, and their cattle mingle freely without fear of any being stolen.[8]

The picture is a curious one: Crusader troops looking down on the upper Huleh from the west (Hunîn), and Moslems doing the same from the east (Banias), while the hardy common folk, Christian and Moslem, tended to their farms and herds in the same valley. Despite the stalemate dangers remained, however. A certain large tree marked the boundary of safety, and those straying to the wrong side of it were likely to find themselves taken prisoner.[9]

As fighting intensified towards the south, Banias remained in a state of readiness. Husam al-Dîn was the governor of the district,[10] and Saladin's son al-Afdal served as 'commander of the camp', a situation similar to that existing when Saladin himself had been in the area. In each case command of the permanent fortifications was different from that of the mobile forces evidently encamped on the outskirts of the town.[11]

Christian itineraries of the 1180s are obviously written with little or no first-hand information of the area, and understandably so. Jacques de Vitry's *The History of Jerusalem* (1180) confuses the site with Caesarea Maritima, and calls it the 'capital of the Philistines'.[12] Johannes Phocas makes the same mistake (1185).[13] An anonymous pilgrim ('V.2'), writing sometime before 1187, lists four suffragans under the bishop of Tyre: 'The bishops of Acre, Sidon, Beyrout, and him of Bleinas, which is Caesarea Philippi' – reflecting the old Byzantine ecclesiastical arrangement that had reappeared during the short period of

Crusader occupation of the town.[14] At the same time, a Frankish nobleman named Josecelin de Courtney 'was granted six casales for four knights' service, and in addition Toron, Neufchâtel, and Banias, the fiefs formerly held by Humphrey of Toron, which he should hold for the same service which Humphrey had given'.[15] But these arrangements represented nothing but wishful thinking. Obviously, neither Frankish bishop nor Frankish governor was in *de facto* control of Banias at the time. The actual Lord of Banias, Toron and Hunîn was the Moslem Husâm al-Dîn Bishârah.[16]

Saladin was very sick during the first part of 1186, but recovered in time to press on toward the fateful encounter at the remains of an ancient volcano called the Horns of Hattim. He ordered al-Afdal to send an envoy to Count Raymond of Tiberias, requesting safe passage through his territories for a reconnaissance force. The count, bound by a treaty with Saladin, was forced to comply. The Moslem forces set out from Banias. The results were disastrous for the Knights Templar, whose fighting force was essentially destroyed in the encounter with these troops.[17] Saladin was now ready for a decisive confrontation. He marched from Kerak to Tiberias and laid siege to the town. After six days Tiberias fell. The huge Crusader army, coming to the rescue, was cut off from drinking water, and on a scorching 4 July 1187, high above the Sea of Galilee, next to the Horns of Hattim, the flower of the Crusader leadership was struck down and its army cut to pieces. There followed quickly one Crusader defeat after another, eventually climaxing with the loss of the holy city of Jerusalem on 2 October 1187.

The Crusaders were left with only Tripoli, Antioch and Tyre (and some smaller places). Because Tyre lies so close, Banias continued to have strategic importance. Saladin visited there again on 11 April 1189[18] and used the place from time to time as a prison for important Christian prisoners. In August of the same year he sent the Christian governor of Tyre to be incarcerated at Banias,[19] as well as Renaud, the Lord of Sidon.[20] However, the third Crusade, source of much of the romantic mythology that raised both Richard the Lionheart (1118–92) and Saladin himself to the status of legend, had little effect on life at Banias.

THE SUCCESSORS OF SALADIN

The next century was characterised by political chaos and a loss of high ideals on both sides. In Europe, the passion to restore the holy places had cooled and only Louis, King of France, seemed to retain the religious ardour which had provided these Western incursions with their *raison d'être* and generated their high-sounding appellation: the Crusades. For their part, Saladin's successors shared little of his religious fervour and impulse to *jihad*. Both sides were torn by internal dissensions motivated largely by greed, factionalism and the will to power. Ironically, though genuine religious commitment was on the wane, the religious tolerance that had characterised the Fatimid period (with the exception of the reign of al-Hākim) did not reappear. Saladin, in his efforts to eliminate the Shi'ite 'heresy' in Egypt, and then to make *jihad* on the Crusaders, had introduced a level of religious intolerance that did not disappear at his death. Persecution of Jews and Christians continued to be common in the period.[21]

When Saladin died in Damascus on 4 March 1193, at the age of 55, Banias and its surrounding territory continued to be a place of some importance, functioning at times as a quasi-independent state. Powerful and important governors ruled its territory. 'Prince of Banias' was a title of considerable significance.

During the succession struggle among the quarrelling sons of Saladin, and after the subsequent victory over them all by his younger brother, al-'Adil, the name Fakhr al-Dîn Iyas Jahârkas[22] begins to figure prominently. A *mamlûk* (slave) of Saladin, Jahârkas attracted little attention during his master's lifetime. But he was a central figure in the battle for succession, and, eventually, in the history of Ayyûbid Banias.

Saladin's empire was divided among his heirs. Damascus went to his son al-Afdal. But al-Afdal's vizier persuaded him to dismiss all the *salâhîs* (*mamlûks* of Saladin) and appoint men of his own choosing. Thus a number of emirs, including Jahârkas, called by Maqrizî 'great men of the state',[23] were banished and fled to Al-'Azîz, another of Saladin's sons, who ruled Egypt. Jahârkas rose to great prominence in Cairo, being appointed in 1193 by al-'Azîz as his ustadar (master of the household). During the next year Jahârkas served as envoy for al-'Azîz in negotiations designed to bring peace between the brothers.[24] al-'Adil, brother of Saladin and uncle of the feuding brothers, sided with al-Afdal. At one point Jahârkas found himself under siege by both al-'Adil and al-Afdal in Bilbis.[25] He was a diligent fundraiser for his sultan as well.[26] He reached the zenith of his power in 1196 when al-'Azîz, having been persuaded not to demolish the pyramids, left Alexandria for a time, leaving Jahârkas and one other official in charge. During that time Jahârkas built a grand *qaysariyah*, a sort of 'shopping centre' in Cairo (with its own mosque) that was widely admired.[27]

Al-'Azîz died in November of 1198 at the age of 27. He left a nine-year-old heir, al-Mansur. Jahârkas tried, at considerable personal risk, to keep al-Afdal from wresting Egypt away from the boy. When his efforts proved to be unsuccessful, he fled to Jerusalem, along with a number of other *salâhî* emirs.[28] There, he decided to throw his lot with al-'Adil, apparently hoping the latter would allow al-Mansur to remain on the throne. But on 4 August 1200, al-'Adil deposed the boy and declared himself sultan.[29] The *salâhî* emirs were indignant, but were persuaded through a ruse to accept the situation and declare loyalty to al-'Adil.[30] In the meantime, Jahârkas had besieged and taken the fortress of Banias from the Emir Husâm al-Dîn Bishârah, who had long been governor of the place.[31]

FAKHR AL-DÎN JAHÂRKAS, LORD OF BANIAS

Having cast his lot with al-'Adil, the winner of the struggle to succeed Saladin, Jahârkas now reaped the benefits. In 1201, the year of al-'Adil's accession, he was appointed as *muqta'* of Bilad al-Shaqif – a territory including the forts of Beaufort, Tyron, Toron, Chastel-Neuf etc. – most of southern Lebanon.[32] Taking possession of Banias and ousting Emir Husâm al-Dîn Bishârah, its governor, required a siege and combat.[33] Once secured, the town served as his capital, from where he controlled Tibnin, Hunîn, the Huleh and all the dependencies of these places.[34] He was obviously a man of great importance in the Ayyûbid sphere of influence.

Disaster struck Jahârkas's principality shortly after he had acquired it. A terrible earthquake ravaged the area, badly damaging Banias, as well as Baalbek, Tibnin, Tyre, Hunîn, Safed, Tiberias, Beth Shean, Nablus and many other places.[35] A beautiful inscription stone, known earlier, lost, then rediscovered during modern excavations at the site, attributes the building of a '*burj*' (fortress tower) to Jahârkas (Fig. 41). The inscription is dated AH 597 (1204 AD).[36] This undoubtedly represents one of the projects carried out by him in order to repair the damage done to the city by this earthquake.

Soon after the construction of Jahârkas's tower at Banias, the Sultan al-'Adil and the Franks agreed upon another truce (1204/5), and the armies of both were dispersed.[37] Jahârkas continued to enjoy considerable power and prestige, serving, for example, as agent of reconciliation between Sultan al-'Adil and his vizier in 1209/10.[38] He died soon after this effort, on 28 December 1211.[39] Although he had resided in his *iqta* (grant of land given by the Sultan to important emirs as a reward for service), presumably at Banias, he was buried in Damascus, evidence of his importance within the Ayyûbid ruling class. Humphreys describes him as 'perhaps the most powerful and important of the *salâhî* amirs in the decade after Saladin's death'.[40] Banias, as his base of operations, may thus safely be described as 'powerful and important' as well.

During this period Christian travellers were barred from visiting the city, but Banias did have a Jewish visitor during the days of Jahârkas. Samuel ben Samson visited the city in 1210, identifying it as ancient Dan, as had Jewish (and Christian) scholars and travellers for centuries. After visiting Ba'ram, he says 'we journeyed to Dan, where we saw the cave called Pameas [*sic*], from which the Jordan issues. Beyond this city is the sepulchre of Iddo the Prophet.'[41] Jewish travellers of the period were particularly interested in the tombs of famous rabbis or persons named in the Hebrew scriptures. Perhaps this Iddo is 'the Seer' mentioned in II Chronicles 9:29 and 12:15 – the author of a lost book detailing events in the northern Kingdom of Israel.[42] Samuel places the tomb 'beyond the city' – a phrase sufficiently ambiguous to make a more precise location impossible. It is interesting, at any rate, to find Banias on the itinerary of Jewish pilgrims at a time when it was totally inaccessible to Christians from the West.[43]

Jahârkas left a minor son as heir. His Mamlûk Salim al-Dîn Khutluba served as *atabeg* to the boy and thus was *de facto* lord of the principality of Banias. Though some Arab historians imply that the territory was almost immediately given to al-'Azîz 'Uthmân, the son of al-'Adil, brother of Saladin, it seems likely that Atabeg Khutluba exercised some sort of control over Banias until 1218/19.[44] Maqrizî is likely simply summarising a decade of developments when he says (under 'The Year 608H'): 'The power of the Salâhî party collapsed with the fall of the Emir Qaraja, the Emir ('Izz-al-Dîn) Usama, and the Emir (Fakhr al-Dîn) Jahârkas; and all their fortresses passed to al-'Adil and his son al-Mu'azzan'.[45] At any rate, in March of 1219 Khutluba was forced not only to give up Jahârkas's fortresses (including Banias) but also to dismantle them.[46]

In 1217 the Crusaders made another attempt on Banias, pushing up from Tell al-Fars to a position only three miles east of the city.[47] They pillaged the area for three days, and then returned to the Acre Plain. The action, says Maqrizî, 'inflicted on the Muslims great distress'. In fact, it convinced al-Mu'azzam that a strongly fortified Banias was a dangerous temptation to the Franks and would be the source of great trouble should it fall into their hands. Consequently, he decided to destroy its fortifications as a matter of strategy. He applied this same strategy over a large area, purposely dismantling the defences of not only Banias, but of Tiberias, Safed, Hunîn, Tibnin and other nearby places as well.[48] He even sent his brother al-'Azîz 'Uthmân, now styled 'Lord of Banias', to destroy the fortifications of Jerusalem, where 'Uthmân had previously served as governor (February 1219).[49] As for Banias, its territory was wrested from Salim al-Dîn Khutluba, *atabeg* of Jahârkas's young son, and placed under the direct control of the ruling family, ensuring a level of support less likely to come from Jahârkas's successors, with their family history of loyalty to a different branch of the Ayyûbid family tree.

AL-'AZÎZ 'UTHMÂN, LORD OF BANIAS

In the midst of these developments al-'Adil died (31 August 1218) and was succeeded by his son al-Kamil. Al-Kamil's brother al-Mu'azzam continued to rule as Prince of Damascus. 'Uthmân became Prince of Banias in 1219. Though clearly third in the brotherly hierarchy, his star began to rise. By 1223, he was referring to himself by the title 'Sultan'. By 1227, 'Uthmân, undoubtedly helped by his brother in Damascus, had built at least the first stages of the great fortress that stands to this day above the site of Banias – al Subaybah (Fig. 43). Al-Mu'azzam's motives for participating in this project no doubt lay in his concern to protect Damascus from the Crusaders, and particularly from the designs of King Frederick of Germany. Al-Mu'azzam died shortly thereafter, and 'Uthmân found himself in a very favourable position.

Though technically a vassal, he considered himself to be head of a quasi-independent state centred at Banias, which was called by the contemporary Moslem geographer Yāqūt, 'capital of the Province of al-Jaulan'.[50] Though menaced by the Crusaders, the city remained inaccessible and something of a mystery to Christian writers of the day.[51] 'Uthmân began to rebuild the capital of his principality and to leave his stamp upon it in ways still clearly visible to those who visit the site today. Several extant inscriptions, including one on the surviving city gate and others affixed to the walls of Qal'at es-Subeiba on the high ridge northeast of the city, attribute massive building projects to 'Uthmân.[52] These inscriptions are dated 1227 and 1230. The one that adorns the southern (main) gate of the Banias fortress has survived essentially intact (Fig. 40). It elaborately glorifies 'Uthmân, calling him 'Our Lord the Sultan, who carries on Holy War, who protects the frontiers, who is always on campaign, the wise, the just, pillar of the world and of the faith, El-Malik el-'Azîz 'Uthmân (may God glorify his victories)'. The inscription takes note of his father, al-'Adil, but makes no mention of either of his brothers. Clearly, 'Uthmân was comfortable in his position and confident in this public display of self-promotion.

By building the fortress of Subaybah (now called Qalat Nimrud) 'Uthmân changed the nature of Banias itself. The fortress towers above the city on the top of the ridge that rises from the red-rock cliff, site of the Pan sanctuary and the springs that flow below it. The rise is relatively gentle, moving east and slightly north from the city to the summit. But on the north, east and south, once the summit is reached, the ridge drops precipitously into the surrounding valleys. The origins of the great castle, much of which survives, were formerly attributed to the Crusaders. More recent consensus regards it as essentially an Ayyûbid foundation. Thus, references before the thirteenth century to the 'fortress of Banias' must be taken as referring to a structure within the walls of the city and not to Subaybah.[53] A careful reading of the literary sources shows them to be consistent with this conclusion, and indeed recent excavations within the medieval fortress have revealed just such a structure – one which utilises Roman remains in a manner observed elsewhere in the area at sites like Baalbek.[54]

Situated so as to command the road to Damascus and to give strong protection to the city, Subaybah allowed Banias to become a *madina* again after several centuries of service as an essentially military outpost. Excavations have shown that areas within the walls of the city, previously set apart for military use, were in the thirteenth century gradually filled with domestic structures. By moving the main defence system high above the town 'Uthmân was able to create for himself a true capital – a city (albeit a rather modest one) and not simply a fort.

'Uthmân continued to figure prominently in the affairs of the ruling clique which surrounded his brother, Sultan al-Kamil. When the latter sent a robe to honour the ascension of his nephew, the son and successor of al-Mu'azzam of Damascus, 'Uthmân, Prince of Banias, did the same.[55] He remained staunchly loyal to his brother al-Kamil in Cairo and supported his policies. When al-Mu'azzam died in 1227/28 and Emperor Frederick II of Germany appeared on the scene a year later, 'Uthmân consented to his brother's policy of appeasement toward the latest, and strangest, of all the 'soldiers of the cross'. In Damascus, the successors of al-Mu'azzam and the populace at large were outraged. 'Uthmân was by his brother's side when the latter rode off to Damascus (during March and April of 1229) to put down this rebellion.[56] Nevertheless, when the occasion called for it, 'Uthmân did not shrink from confronting the Franks with armed force. In the year previous to the internecine struggle in Damascus, he had attacked and killed some Franks near Tyre, and even tried to gain control of Tyre itself.[57] He was, after all, according to the inscription on the Banias city gate, he 'who carries on Holy War' and 'who protects the frontiers'.

Al-'Azîz 'Uthmân died in 1233. He had placed his personal stamp on Banias in a measure probably only exceeded by Agrippa II more than a millennium before.[58] He left a rejuvenated city with a powerful fortress to protect it, and a prosperous principality firmly established between the two centres of Saladin's Ayyûbid empire: Cairo and Damascus. 'Uthmân's son and heir, al-Zahîr Ghazi, died in the same year as his father, so the principality passed to another son, al-Sa'id Hasan.[59] Al-Sa'id left an inscription at Subaybah, dated 1239/40, above a delicately carved public fountain. The fountain and its inscription are well preserved and may be seen today. His relationship with Banias was a long one, extending from 1233 to 1258 (though with significant interruptions, as we shall see).

AYYŪBID TWILIGHT

When al-Kamil died in 1238 the same squabbling and internecine warfare that had plagued the Ayyûbid dynasty at the deaths of Saladin (1193) and al-'Adil (1218) broke out again. Furthermore, the Ayyûbid princes had introduced two ominous new players into their struggles against each other. The first of these were the Khwarazmian Tatars – Mongol tribes whose atrocities were well known, but who could be used in alliances of convenience, as one Ayyûbid prince might play them off against another. The second were the increasingly influential Mamlûks (mostly Kipchalk Turks) – slave boys raised in the princes' households and trained to be (at least theoretically) more loyal than their own kinsmen. The most outstanding (and ruthless) of these rose to occupy more and more of the seats of *de facto* power, beginning with the reign of al-Kamil's son al-Sālih in 1240.

Al-Sālih invited the Khwarazmians to invade Syria in 1244. They swept down upon the country with merciless violence and cruelty, ravaging the country around Damascus so that 'the populations fled in panic before them'.[60] Banias can hardly have escaped their fury as they passed through the area on the way to Jerusalem, there to engage in an orgy of killing, 'exterminating the men, and leading away captive the women and children'. In addition, they 'destroyed the structures of the Church of the Resurrection, and ransacked the graves of the Christians and burned their bones'.

The Moslem population of Damascus allied themselves with the Frankish army near Gaza to try to stop the onslaught, but the Tatars, in alliance with the Ayyûbid forces of Egypt, slaughtered both indiscriminately.[61] Al-Sālih's Mamlûk Rukn al-Dîn Baybars, who would one day rule his master's kingdom, was prominent in all these events. The Khwarazmians proved very difficult to control and no doubt caused great terror in Banias and other districts near Damascus that were probably pillaged by them. In the midst of this turmoil, al-Sa'id, the governor of Banias (and son of 'Uthmân) was removed from power by the lieutenants of the sultan. On 25 April 1247, these took possession of the fortress Subaybah.[62] This action was apparently an attempt to place Banias under leadership more suitable to the Sultan of Egypt's purposes, since Damascus was under much pressure, and besides could not be trusted.[63]

But the political situation was unstable to say the least. In 1249, al-Sālih died and after a short regency by his widow Shajar al-Durr, he was succeeded by his son al-Mu'azzam Turanshah. Turanshah was killed by the Mamlûks on 1 May 1250, after only 71 days as sultan. Thus ended the Ayyûbid dynasty of Egypt. 'Uthmân's son, al-Sa'id, however, we shall hear from again.

BANIAS AND THE CRUSADE OF SAINT LOUIS OF FRANCE

While Egypt fell under Mamlûk rule, a great-grandson of Saladin, al-Nâsir Yusuf ben al-'Azîz Muhammad, maintained Ayyûbid control over a doomed Syria for the next few years, as the Mongols were inexorably progressing in their march of horror toward the west. Banias fell under the control of Damascus during this period of turmoil and uncertainty. Louis IX, the saintly king of France, had met with initial success and then disaster in attempting to conquer Egypt in 1249–50. By 1253 he was still in the Holy Land, operating in the narrow strip along the coast controlled by the Crusaders, and still aching for a fight with the Moslems. While camped near Tyre, he hit upon the idea of attacking Banias, perhaps sensing both its strategic importance in maintaining the coastal toehold, and its vulnerability.

Louis's counsellors were wary, and quite concerned for his safety. After all, he had already been captured once by the enemy, in Egypt, and was lucky to be alive. He was of more value in keeping morale high and hope alive than as a field commander. So it was decided that, while the attack on Banias was a good idea, the king himself should not carry it out. Instead, the operation would be led by the Comte d'Eu, Philippe de Montfort, Gilles le Brun, the king's chamberlain Pierre, the Masters of the Temple and of the Hospital, and Jean of Joinville. Joinville's inclusion was fortunate from an historical point of view. He was to become Louis's biographer, and as such included in that work a vivid eyewitness account of the events that took place at Banias. Though in some ways the whole affair was hardly more than a minor skirmish, Joinville's account, growing out of his personal involvement, is so detailed that it is possible to identify many of the places in and around the city which he mentions and thus is a significant document in the history of Banias.

The Franks left Tyre at nightfall and arrived just before daybreak 'at a plain outside the city' (that is the upper Huleh Valley near the site of ancient Dan).[64] The battle plan called for the king's troops (of which Joinville was a part) to 'take their stand between the castle [Subaybah] and the city'. The 'barons of the land' (local Franks) would enter the city by the left (that is the north), the Hospitallers by the right (that is the south), and the Templars would 'ride straight on along the road by which we had come, to effect an entry that way' (that is from the west).[65] The troops with Joinville were evidently to be placed so as to prevent the townspeople from escaping up the hill to Subaybah. It is strange that no troops were assigned to the most vulnerable of all the city's defences, the eastern wall, the only one where the terrain allowed easy access.

As was often the case in Crusader battles, discipline quickly broke down, and many of the soldiers apparently rode directly into the city. Joinville was alarmed, particularly when he saw that things were going very badly for those already inside the city walls. 'Gentlemen,' he said to his fellow officers, 'unless you go where we have been ordered to go, between the city and the castle, the Saracens will kill all those who have already entered Banyas.'[66] A look at the terrain showed that this was easier said than done. The ground rose so steeply that horses could hardly keep their footing, and the defenders had constructed three double lines of dry walls that had to be crossed. Furthermore, the spot they need to take (a 'low hill') was 'crowded with mounted Turks'. Nevertheless, with great difficulty, Joinville and at least some of the designated troops headed up the hill, but on foot, leading their horses. To their great relief the mounted Turks abandoned their position and headed up toward Subaybah.

Anyone standing in the centre of the site of ancient Banias today can see quite clearly the spot Joinville describes. From it, he says, 'a rocky precipice went down sheer into the city'. This can only be the top of the bluff above the red-rock cliff that contains the cave of Pan and from which the springs pour forth – the ancient Paneion.[67] Once the Moslem inhabitants of Banias saw the small group of Crusaders high above them, looking down from the cliff, they 'gave up the fight, and abandoned the city to our people without offering any resistance'.[68]

Believing Joinville to be in danger, some troops headed up the slope to assist him, particularly some Germans under Comte d'Eu's command. But when they saw the Turks fleeing up the hill toward Subaybah they foolishly headed off after them. Joinville shouted out after them, upbraiding them for exceeding their orders, but to no avail. The Turks saw their opportunity. They dismounted, and climbed up on the many boulders strewn along the incline, 'great rocks as big as chests'. It is not difficult today to find the place; the boulders are still there (Fig. 44). The Germans realised their mistake and tried to turn their horses around, but descent was treacherous indeed. The Turks, 'aiming at them great blows from the tops of the rocks with their maces', were able to grab the horses' bridles and create general havoc.[69]

Seeing what was happening to the Germans, the troops around Joinville thought to retreat, but he berated them. They in turn complained that his bravery came from the fact that he was on horseback now and they were not. So he dismounted and vowed to stay with them. (Throughout the account, Joinville depicts himself in the most favourable light, of course – cool-headed and right-thinking.) When one of the knights who had rushed up the hill was struck in the throat by a quarrel and killed, Joinville would not even consent to help the man's uncle remove the body. 'You went up there without my orders, and if you've met with misfortune, you deserved it. Carry him down to the rubbish-heap yourself, for I'll not stir from here till I'm sent for.'[70]

At this point Jean de Valenciennes and Olivier de Termes arrive, bent on rescuing Joinville from his perilous situation. Olivier points out the problem: 'If we went down by the way we have come up we could not do so without great loss, since the slope was too steep and slippery, and the Saracens would come down on us from above [that is, from Subaybah]'. But he also has a solution:

We'll go right along this slope, as if we were making for Damascus. [This route is easily identifiable today, as one stands on the modern road through the site, facing the red-rock cliff.] The Saracens you see up there will think we're intending to attack them in the rear. As soon as we're down on the plains we'll set spurs to our horses and go round the city. [This would necessitate a southern route, then a turn to the west. At some point Joinville's party would have to cross Wâdî Sa'âr, no little task.] We shall be across the stream before they can catch up with us [that is the River Banias – again, a formidable task, since the river runs through a deep declivity]. And in addition we shall do them great harm, for we'll set fire to the threshed corn lying over there in those fields. [The grain fields still cultivated today by the inhabitants of the Israeli Kibbutz Snir.]

The stratagem worked. The Franks burned the fields by means of 'those hollow canes such as are used for making flutes'. These they stuffed with live coals and 'thrust them in amongst the threshed corn'.

The battle had no lasting effect, despite the fact that at one point the Saracens seem to have temporarily abandoned the town. Joinville, who had been somewhat out of sorts at the behaviour of his colleagues during the entire engagement, suffered one final indignity. When he and his companions arrived back at the Crusader camp they found that their comrades 'had all put off their armour; for no one there had given a thought to us'.[71]

CRUSADERS, MONGOLS AND MAMLÛKS

Al-Sa'id Hasan, the son of al-'Azîz 'Uthmân, son of al-'Adil, the last Ayyûbid to rule Banias, was deposed and imprisoned by the Mamlûk rulers who usurped the Ayyûbid throne. When the Mongol hordes swept down on Syria in 1259, taking control of Aleppo, Damascus and Banias-Subaybah, Hulegu, the Mongol leader, freed al-Sa'id. He was promised the restored governorship of his little fiefdom in return for alliance with the invaders.[72] Thus he fought alongside the Mongols in the fateful Battle of Ain Jaloot (the spring of Goliath), which took place between Afula and Beisan (ancient Beth Shean) on 3 September 1260. But the Mamlûk army, led by Qutuz, Sultan of Egypt, was able to stop the Mongol advance, and the hapless al-Sa'id was captured and executed for his collaboration with the invaders.[73] With his death, Ayyûbid rule in Banias permanently ended.

Under Mamlûk administration, Banias benefited from a relatively quiet period, particularly when compared to the disturbances of Crusader times, except for a second Mongol incursion in December of 1260 (also repulsed) and another in 1289. The town served as the 'chief town' or administrative centre ('wilâyah') of the southernmost of the five divisions of the Mamlaka of Damascus.[74] As such, it controlled a large number of villages in the Golan and the Huleh Valley.[75] During this period the Golan enjoyed something of a revival; surveys have found signs of occupation at more than 130 sites. Banias itself seems to have decreased in size, however. It is described by Arab geographers of the time as a bulayda or balda saghira, a town that became smaller after the transition from Ayyûbid to Mamlûk rule.[76] The town and the fortress of Subaybah were placed under different governors, though the latter was 'attached' to the former, an arrangement dating from the time of Saladin.[77] The relatively high rank of its governor shows that the fortress continued to have considerable importance as late as the fifteenth century. This was no doubt due to its position as a key fortress along the Mamlûkan communication road between Cairo and Damascus. Traces of this road are still visible between Subaybah and the next fortress along the way, Nebi Hazuri.[78]

The Mongols had left considerable devastation in their wake. But Sultan Baybars Bunduqdari (1260–77), who had killed his predecessor Qutuz almost immediately after the latter's victory over the Mongols at Ain Jaloot, 'took an interest in the reconstruction of these forts and the completion of the destroyed buildings, because those were the strongholds of Islam. All these were repaired during his time; their fosses were cleared out, the fosses of their walls were broadened, the equipment was transported to them, and he sent Mamlûks and soldiers to them.'[79] In the case of Subaybah, this policy is evident in recent archaeological discoveries by Moshe Hartal, including large and beautifully rendered inscriptions bearing Baybars' name.[80] Ibn 'Abd al-Zahîr (1223–92), a confidant of Baybars, provides this interesting confirmation of the extent to which the sultan valued the place:

> Among his Mamlûks, he [Baybars] brought up the amir Badr al-Dîn Bîlîk al-Khizndâr, and when he tested his piety and fidelity he did not find in him anything but goodness and good council. He made him an amir and gave him a higher command in the army. The amir Badr al-Dîn carried on the administration of the army to the satisfaction of the sultan and made good distribution of the fiefs, thereby gaining the hearts of the people. The sultan married him to the daughter of al-Malik al-Rahim, the fulter of Mosul. The marriage contract was performed at Gaza in the month of Shawwal of the year 659 A.H., and the sultan attended the ceremony with the dowry. When the sultan reached Syria in this year, he gave him the sole possession of the fort of Subaybah with Banias and its dependencies, and gave him fiefs with the command of more than 50 horsemen in Syria, and entrusted these to his deputies.[81]

The remaining Crusaders were still a factor in the area. In 1262, according to Ibn 'Abd al-Zahîr, they complained that Banias was being used as a base for Moslem raids into Crusader territories.[82] The antagonism continued, and two years later the Franks, assisted by the citizens of Tyre, made a raid on Banias which resulted in the death of one of Baybars' subjects, thus breaking a truce then in force.[83] Some years later (in 1275), Baybars stationed a company of his troops in Banias as a part of a new policy to disperse the army into 'the various regions in an attempt to keep down costs and prices' – and no doubt to discourage further hostile action on the part of the Crusaders.[84] Banias is mentioned in a treaty between the Latin Kingdom and Baybars' successor Qalawun (1283), apparently now as a part of the province of Safad: 'Baniyas and its districts; the stronghold of al-Subaybah and its districts, and its accompanying lakes and districts…'.[85] Banias, and indeed Syria as a whole, were at this time firmly under the control of the Sultan of Egypt.

As we have seen, by the thirteenth century Banias was *terra incognita* to the Christian world. Popes like Gregory X continued to appoint Latin 'Bishops of Banias' but such gestures were only symbolic.[86] Back in Europe Roger Bacon, in his *Opus Maius* (*ca.* 1268), wrote at length about the sources of the Jordan and mentioned Banias. But his information obviously came from the ancient sources (Jerome, Pliny, Isidore, Hegesippus, Josephus etc.) and not from anyone who had visited the place in his own time.[87] The pilgrim Burchard of Mount Zion (1280) described the Holy Land, as he says, 'according to the best of my observation when I saw it with my eyes, and walked over it with my feet…but it is true that I only went a little way beyond Jordan, and did not pass through the land of the two tribes and the half-tribe'.[88]

In 1291 the last Frankish stronghold, Acre, fell to the Moslems, effectively ringing down the curtain on the Crusader states of Palestine. The Mamlûk sultan, al-Ashraf Khalil (1290–93), combined the governorships of Banias and Subaybah and gave them to Emir Badr d. Baktas al-Marsuri.[89] The latter was soon assigned to a new post in Bhasna, however. In 1298, al-Nâsir Muhammad began his second reign as sultan (1298–1308) and his partisans awarded the governorship of Subaybah to a certain Shams al-Dîn Qara Sunqur, who had spent over a year in prison under the previous regime. Qara Sunqur was unhappy with his new assignment, however, complaining that Subaybah was 'an unhealthy place'. He was therefore sent to become the governor of Hamah instead.[90] The unhealthiness probably stemmed from the proximity of the Huleh, which was to be for many succeeding centuries a malarial swamp and a source of misery for the town's inhabitants.

The area remained fertile and in many ways attractive, however. The author of the *Marasid* (1300) refers to Banias as a village 'in the country of lemons and citrons'.[91] Shams-al-Dîn al-Dimashkî (d. 1326/27), also writing in 1300, provides a valuable, if historically garbled, account of Banias, which contains the intriguing fact that many ancient structures still existed in the town at that time.

> 'Banias belongs to the Damascus Province,' he says. 'Its fortress is called As Subaybah. It is a very ancient and well-fortified town, and there is plenty of sage-plant here. The soil and climate are good, and water is abundant. There are many remains of the Greeks here. It was built, it is said, by Balnias [Pliny] the Sage, or, it is said, by Abuna Nawwas; the meaning of Abuna being 'master,' 'teacher.' He also was a Greek.[92]

Abû l Fida (1273–1321) provides another contemporary reference, calling Banias 'a small town, possessing many shrubs of the [bitter] sage-plant called Harnd and the like, also streams of water...As Subaybah is the name of its castle, which is very strong.'[93]

Having rid themselves of the Crusaders, the Mamlûks gained a great victory over yet another Mongol incursion in the battle of Shaqhab (20–22 April 1303). The battle took place at Ghabaghib, on the main road twenty-five miles south of Damascus (and thus not far from Banias). The Mongols, who had actually occupied Damascus prior to the battle, were finally pushed out of the area. The Mamlûks were now free from threats coming from either the East or the West. The local non-Moslems seem to have been treated badly during the first half of the fourteenth century, and though lists of Greek bishops of Banias exist for the period, they remained only titular.[94] European visitors were almost totally excluded from the area. In 1321, Marino Sanuto, the Venetian noble, produced a gazetteer and map of Palestine which is reliable in some respects, but Banias is placed much too far west, and is not on the Jordan nor connected with Mount Hermon. Even Damascus is misplaced, appearing west of Hermon.[95] Clearly, available information about the area was quite scanty. Ludolf van Suchens (1350) depended for information on 'the Soldan's couriers, and from exceeding trustworthy people of the country' who described the area to him. 'Not far from Dan, toward the north,' they told him, 'is the once fair city of Balynas, now called Caesarea Philippi, pleasantly situated at the foot of Mount Lebanon, but scantily peopled.'[96] Edward Robinson, speaking of Banias, says, 'since the time of the Crusades, I find no account of its having been visited by an Frank traveller, until Seetzen took it in his way from Damascus to Tiberias in AD 1806'.[97]

THE BURGI MAMLŪKS (1382–1517)

The year 1382 marks a division in the long reign of the Mamlûk sultans. Prior to that year the slave-kings had been of Turkish extraction; after it came a period of some 135 years during which the rulers were of Circassian ethnicity: collectively these were known as the Burgi Mamlûks. The era was characterised by the dominance of a strong leader, followed by chaos at his death, followed by the emergence of another strong leader who would restore order to the empire. The fortress Subaybah continued to be an important link in the chain of defence maintained by the sultans.[98] Arab historians of the period, such as Ibn al-Furat (1334–1405), seem to have had rather limited knowledge of the rich history of Banias previous to the Crusader period. He cites 'the unique and learned Qadi 'Izz al-Dîn Muhammad b. 'Ali b. Ibrâhim Ibn Shaddad al-Halabi, the leading Imam', who admits that he had 'not come across anything about the beginnings of Baniyas except for what I have read in an elegant history written by one of the banu Munqidh, 'Abd al-Rahman b. Muhammad'. This later work traces the struggle between the Moslems and the Crusaders in some detail (and with some inaccuracies, such as the attribution of the building of Subaybah to the Crusaders).[99] But it reveals nothing further about the history of the city. The names Banias and Subaybah became interchangeable, so that the fifteenth-century author of the *Kitāb Zubdat Kashf al-Mamalik* could say, 'As for the city of al-Subayba, known also as Banias, it has a strong fortress'.[100] Such confusion was understandable, as Ellenblum notes, since 'the magnificent fort at al-Subayba was a living reality [in the author's day], and outshone in the size and splendour of its walls the partially ruined town at the bottom of the slope'.[101]

The citadel of Banias continued to be used as a prison for important figures who had fallen out of favour. Around 1458, for example, we read of the incarceration of Ganibak al-Frangi by the governor of Damascus, who 'sent him in chains to the citadel of Banias'.[102] Westerners continued to observe the site only from a considerable distance. Felix Fabri (*ca.* 1480–83) gives a confused account of the area of the sources of the 'Jor' and 'Dan', obviously depending primarily on earlier accounts. 'In describing the Jordan,' he admits, 'I must needs make mention of places which I have not seen with my eyes, because our pilgrimage did indeed reach as far as the Jordan, but not to its beginning'.[103] The anonymous monk who recorded the 'Pilgrimage of Sir Richard Guylford' (which occurred in 1506) did not claim to have visited 'Belinas' himself, but he does record some rather standard information about the place, obtained perhaps from 'certayne freres of Moute Syon' who provided information to travellers about places they could not visit.[104]

BANIAS ENTERS THE OTTOMAN EMPIRE

As the sixteenth century began, Sultan Salim I (1512–20) incorporated the Arab world into the empire of the Ottoman Turks. Syria became an Ottoman province and Palestine disappeared into that vast empire which three quarters of a century earlier, with the fall of Constantinople, had obliterated the last vestiges of Christian Byzantium. Thus were the final ruins of Near Eastern Hellenica, fashioned by Alexander almost two millennia before and bound together by the power and the concept of 'Rome', buried beneath a Turkish-Islamic flood. Banias became a '*baj* station' (a site for the collection of customs duties from merchants transporting goods) – one of less than a dozen cities in the area that made up one of the four '*safqas*' of the province of Damascus. The population in the area continued its long decline, dropping rather dramatically over the next several generations.[105] To make matters worse, the Mamlûk governor of the province of Damascus, al-Ghazali, allowed to remain in power by the Ottomans, attempted to rebel against them and brought down the full ire of the conquerors upon his province. Banias and its neighbours were drifting into disrepute and obscurity. The government in Damascus was hopelessly unstable. In its initial 184 years Ottoman Damascus had had 135 different governors, only 33 of whom held office for as long as two years.[106]

By mid-century, Banias's isolation from the Christian West was so complete that Petrus Bellonius, visiting Baalbek in 1548, thought he was in Caesarea Philippi[107] and a certain Spanish Franciscan, travelling in 1553–55, reported that he had seen Caesarea Philippi on the shores of the Sea of Galilee near Chorazim.[108] Maps produced on the area, such as that in *The Atlas of Ortelius* (*ca.* 1591) or that of Ioanne Cotorico (1598) were actually inferior to that of Marino Sanuto, produced more than two centuries earlier.[109]

Banias (still mis-associated with Dan) was understood in Jewish circles during this period to possess significant burial sites for important biblical and rabbinical characters. A certain Jacob, son of Naftali ha-Khohen de Gazolo, purportedly produced a work entitled *Jichus Ha-Tsadikim* or 'Sepulchres of the Just' around 1537.[110] In it he describes two revered tombs at Banias (spelled 'Bagias'), one identified as the resting place of Iddo the Prophet and the other of Schebuel, son of Gershom, son of Moses. Both of these tombs lay under large trees: the first an immense pistachio tree which 'looked like a lion', and the second a large acacia tree. Revered tombs lying at the base of large trees are common in the area, even up to today. In fact, a similar tomb (dedicated to 'Sultan Ibrâhim') may still be seen at the site of Banias, where it is actively honoured by the local Druze. Such sites tend to persist across confessional lines, simply being identified with some honoured individual in each of the local religious communities.

The author of II Chronicles cites certain visions of Iddo the Seer concerning Jeroboam, founding ruler of the northern kingdom after the death of Solomon (II Chron. 9:29).[111] Shebuel was one of the grandsons of Moses, chief among the sons of Gershom (I Chron. 23:15–16; 25:4; 26:24). The Talmudists identified Shebuel with Jonathan, son of Gershom, whose family served as priests for the tribe of Dan, officiating at the cult centre of the graven image of Micah (Judges 17–18).[112] Thus these two tomb shrines were both associated with the history of the northern tribes and specifically with the traditional territories of 'Dan'/Banias. The 'Sepulchers of the Just' is a work full of inaccuracies, however, and seems to have plagiarised earlier accounts such as that of Rabbi, the Messenger of the Yeshiva of Acre (*ca.* 1258–70).[113] *Qivrei Avoth* (*Tombs of the Ancestors*), which Prawer dates to between 1120 and 1187, is the earliest extant example of this kind of Jewish-pilgrimage literature, and is even more likely to be an original source.[114]

The *Jichus Ha-Tsadikim* also notes that two fourteenth-century Persian rabbis, Rab Papa and Rab Asche, are buried along with their children 'in a cave' near the tombs of Gershom and Iddo.[115] The textual history of this work is complicated and invites caution in using it as a source for information about Banias in the fifteenth and sixteenth centuries. The most that can be said is that strong traditions existed in Jewish circles during those centuries identifying Banias as a place of significant burial sites. These traditions may have been literary, but given the evidence that there were Jews among the inhabitants of Banias in the early Ottoman period, it is possible that they were maintained by the locals as well.[116]

11 European 'Rediscovery'

EUROPE LOOKS EASTWARD

While Banias and the nearby castle Subaybah quietly served their role within the larger policies of Ayyûbid, Mamlûk and Ottoman conquerors and politicians, Europe was undergoing profound changes. These changes were to constitute the foundation of a new and 'modern' world. The medieval Islamic East, the true heir to the intellectual, artistic and cultural achievements of Byzantium (and thus of Greece and Rome) had had its moment of glory. Europe had nothing to compare with the magnificent urban achievements of cities like Baghdad and Cairo, with their universities, monumental architecture and sophisticated, if brutal, political and military institutions. But a sleeping Europe began to reawaken. The rediscovery of the classical world and the rise of science and technology, coupled with the prosperity born of exploration and aggressive trade and the appearance of the nation-state, were creating an entirely new world.

By the fifteenth century it was the Middle East that was falling asleep, languishing in the grip of a far-flung but ill-governed Ottoman Empire. Having begun in glory, this empire was now gradually sucking the life out of its own subjects. The new European powers – particularly England and France and the Italian city-states, began to look toward the East – first for trade and eventually for empire. European ships sailed into the ports of the Levant, including those lining the coasts of Palestine and Lebanon. Cities such as Tyre, Sidon and Beirut, which had served as the cultural and economic lifeline for Banias for more than two millennia, greeted these new Crusaders. The local Arab population, never comfortable under Ottoman despotism, began to look to the West for assistance, oblivious to the possibility that one imperialism might simply be exchanged for another.

FAKHR AL-DÎN II THE DRUZE

Among the first of the Arab leaders who looked to the West was an unlikely little man, son of Emir Qorgmas of the Arab tribe of Beni Ma'n, named Fakhr al-Dîn (Fig. 47). The Beni Ma'n were adherents to the Druze religion, which for half a millennium had been a dominant force in the mountains and valleys of Lebanon and southern Syria. Fakhr al-Dîn was born in 1572. He was a tiny man (according to a proverb of the time, 'Should an egg drop from that man's pocket to the ground, it won't break'),[1] but a very clever leader. After becoming the Emir of Shuf in Lebanon, he began an aggressive programme of expansion, taking every advantage of his good relationships with the enemies of the Turks, both Arab and European. By the turn of the century he controlled the whole coast from the Dog River to Mount Carmel. He also expanded his rule toward the interior – gaining control of Safed, Nazareth, Tiberius and Banias. A number of old Crusader castles fell under his control, allowing him to dominate the strategic roads. He renovated these castles and invested them with troops loyal to his cause.[2]

Fakhr al-Dîn captured Subaybah, which should have proven impregnable, by means of a clever ruse. The story was recorded by the early-seventeenth-century English traveller George Sandys, who visited the area, though apparently not Banias itself, in 1610. Despite the fact that Subaybah 'standeth on a hill by itself, and is indeed by nature invincible', Sandys tells us, Fakhr al-Dîn was able to capture it without the loss of a drop of blood. Pitching his tents 'in peaceable manner' not far from the walls of the fortress, he invited the local sheikh to visit him. Expressing an interest in seeing the inside of the fortress, he convinced the sheikh to give him a tour. Only twenty or thirty of his men accompanied him, so the sheikh saw nothing amiss. But Fakhr al-Dîn's men had hidden weapons, and besides, the rest of his troops, in groups of two or three, were quietly and unobtrusively ascending the slopes up to the fortress while the tour was in progress. Suddenly Fakhr al-Dîn's men appeared on all sides of the hapless sheikh and the Druze leader simply announced that he was now in command. The mighty fortress had fallen into his hands without bloodshed.[3]

Fakhr al-Dîn was, at least theoretically, a vassal of the Ottomans. They became increasingly distressed about his activities. He was not only operating independently – he was also busy cultivating European friends, particularly the Medici family in Italy. In 1612–13, he was finally forced into exile and went to Florence, entrusting his domains to his brother Yunus and his son Ali. As he left, Fakhr al-Dîn stocked the fortresses of Banias and Beaufort (Qal'at al-Shaqif) with ammunition and supplies, telling the commanders not to surrender even if surrender were demanded to redeem his life.[4] Ali was made Emir of Banias, indicating something of the continuing importance of this place. While in Europe, Fakhr al-Dîn developed ties with the Pope and the Franciscans. He is even thought by some to have converted to Roman Catholicism, albeit secretly. He invited Cosimo II de Medici to send envoys back to see his emirate and thus came to pass a most unlikely scenario: Florentine diplomats touring the muddy streets of Banias (along with Beaufort and Toron).[5]

Having somehow convinced the Ottomans once again of his loyalty, he was allowed to return to the East, but soon took up his old independent ways. He was accused of opening up the port of Sidon to European ships, and of trying to unite his country to drive out the Turks. Confronted by a large Ottoman army in June 1632, he was taken to Damascus a prisoner, and executed there on 14 March 1635. Despite his sad end, Fakhr al-Dîn personified the transition that characterised his times. The Italian diplomats who walked through the streets of the village of Banias on their way up the slopes of Subaybah were merely the precursors of a host of Europeans who would one day follow.

OBSCURITY

With the elimination of the threat posed by Fahkr al-Dîn, Banias's descent into obscurity accelerated. The famous European travellers of the time either simply ignored the town, since the main routes East and West no longer passed through it, or they relied on their libraries and the accounts of the ancients to take the place of personal observation.[6] When John Milton referred to the 'doubled founted stream' at Banias in *Paradise Lost*,[7] it was the world of mythology and not of seventeenth-century Syria that he had in mind.

THE EIGHTEENTH CENTURY

Between the Battle of Vienna (1683) and the appearance of Napoleon in the East (1799), the Ottoman Empire fell into deeper and deeper decline. As for the town of Banias, it wasted away in a manner unparalleled in its long existence. Even casual literary references become exceedingly rare.[8] Jesuit missionaries seem to have had some contact with the village and one, Pere Nacchi, supplied what might be an eyewitness account of a visit there. Describing the 'Mountain of the Sheikh' (Jabal al-Shaykh, the Arabic name for Mount Hermon) in a missionary report he says, 'It is ten leagues in length from South-West to North-East, and reaches nearly as far as Caesarea Philippi (now Banias). Which city, so famous heretofore, is at present no more but a village, preserving nothing of its ancient grandeur except the castle, which commands a few half ruined houses.'[9] Nacchi describes Dan as well, and while he does not confuse Banias and Dan, he does identify the springs at Dan as both the 'Jor' and the 'Dan' so often spoken of by European authors throughout the centuries.[10] It is particularly interesting that, according to Nacchi, local tradition at this time located the pericope of Peter's confession in the gospels at Dan rather than at Banias. The fact that he places the sources of the Jordan at Dan exclusively, and makes no mention at all of the springs at Banias, casts some doubt on whether he actually personally visited the village. More certain are the visits of three Russian travellers. Two monks named Makarii and Sil'vestr visited Banias between 1704 and 97, and Vasilii Grigor'evich-Barskii sometime between 1723 and 1747.[11] Since their reports appeared only in Russian, however, they made no contribution to European knowledge of the site.

Otherwise, eighteenth-century travellers took alternative routes between the coast and Damascus, missing Banias altogether.[12]

Subaybah, the 'fortress of Banias', played a part in one last military confrontation before falling into final ruin. The districts of Rasheya and Hasbeya to the north and west of Banias (known together as Wâdî 'l-Taym) were by now under amirs who controlled the Banias area as well. One of these, Amir Ismā'īl, the Shihab governor of Hasbeya, reconstructed the fortress of Banias. In 1760–61, 'Uthmân Pasha al Kurji, the Ottoman Governor of Damascus, alarmed at this development, attacked Ismā'īl (who was at least theoretically under the jurisdiction of Damascus) and destroyed the fortress once again, leaving it the ruin described by the first European 'discoverers' half a century later. This he did in order to 'safeguard lines of communication'.[13]

Despite this precaution, the area nevertheless fell into almost total anarchy and became the haunt of marauding robbers and thieves. These carried on their activities with almost complete freedom of movement. This description of the situation, written many years later, characterises the area in the late eighteenth century:

> Nominally under the dominion of Turkey, the Sultan appoints his governors, who extort tributes from the people, without giving them protection. Not a single road is made or repaired. No wagon or carriage is seen in all this country. Hostile tribes hew each other to pieces; and the sons of Ishmael come from the Desert and carry off the annual harvests, drive away the flocks, and, if resisted, fiendlike seek revenge in destroying their last hope of subsistence by cutting down their fig and olive-trees and covering up their wells. No arm of Justice shields the innocent.[14]

BANIAS 'REDISCOVERED': SEETZEN AND BURCKHARDT

When Ulrich Jasper Seetzen arrived in Banias on Monday 27 January 1806, the locals were of two minds regarding the purpose of his visit. Seetzen (b. 1767) was a German, but held an appointment as 'Collegian-Assessor' of the Emperor of Russia. Consequently, the local Christians were convinced that he was a Russian agent, sent to spy out the land. Surely then, they reasoned, the Tsar is poised to invade the Holy Land and drive out the hated Turk. The Moslems, on the other hand, reckoned he was merely there to find treasure and make off with it.[15] Seetzen's own motives, incomprehensible to the villagers, rested in his intellectual curiosity and love of adventure. 'I have in vain consulted the geographical books of the Arabs to discover some light on the modern state of this country,' he explains. Having found nothing in the libraries of Damascus, 'we must conclude that modern travellers have not judged these districts sufficiently worthy of their attention, to prosecute their researches there'.[16] Seetzen had been warned not to go into the regions of Arabia Petraea, Transjordan, the Hauran, the Huleh and Banias. He discounted the talk of danger, claiming it came from people who had never been in these regions themselves and who were alarmed by mere hearsay. The reports of danger, he says, are 'perhaps false, or at least exaggerated'.[17] Thus did curiosity win out over caution (the danger was real enough),[18] and he set out from Damascus on 19 January 1806, to explore districts of Rasheya and

Hasbeya – 'they being the least known of all Syria'. In doing so, he marked his place in history as the first modern European to 'rediscover' ancient Banias.[19]

Making his way from Hasbeya, he entered Banias, a 'little hamlet of about twenty miserable huts'. In his report he describes the walls of the old fortress, the grotto with its cave and fountain, the inscriptions along the red-rock cliff ('dedicated to Pan and the Nymphs'), the great ruined castle on the mountain overlooking the city and the general environs. The latter, he said, 'are very pleasing, especially for a lover of chace, as there are panthers, bears, a prodigious quantity of wild boars, foxes, jackalls, antelopes, bucks, wolves, hyaenas, hares etc'.[20] Three days after his arrival, on 29 January, he moved on.[21]

Almost five years later, in October 1810, the famous Swiss explorer John Lewis Burckhardt (1784–1817) visited Banias. Unfortunately, he was short of cash. 'My money being almost expended,' he explains, 'I had no time to lose in gratifying my curiosity in the environs of Banias.'[22] He described the setting of the town, the cave and spring, the niches and inscriptions along the cliff, and the 'mosque dedicated to Neby Khuder, called by the Christians Mar Georgius'. His description of the village and the remaining ruins is rather cursory, and not always accurate. This may partly be the result of a faulty compass, as his editor suggests, or a combination of his haste and the rain and cloudy weather which plagued his visit.[23] One evening was spent under the large tree before the *Menzel* (see below) 'conversing till very late' with the locals about 'the researches which Mr. Seetzen made here four years ago'. Then he hurried away, concerned that his funds were almost gone.

THE NINETEENTH-CENTURY VILLAGE

Between the time of Seetzen and Burckhardt, when a visit to Banias was a rare and dangerous adventure, and the late nineteenth century, when Lawrence Oliphant could say that Banias was 'on the beaten track of the tourist and traveler',[24] the physical appearance of the village seems to have changed very little. The massive earthquake that struck the area on New Year's Day 1837, may have ravaged the poorly constructed houses of the village. The quake seems to have caused rock falls within the cave of Pan, covering the floor and entrance with the huge boulders that remained there until they were removed during the recent archaeological excavations.[25] The poorly constructed houses seen by Europeans after this event had no doubt been simply thrown together in an effort to provide warmth and safety for the villagers as soon as possible.

Almost all European explorers mentioned the ancient bridge (the Jisr ed-Daulah)[26] that spanned the Wâdî Sa'âr to the south of the village (Fig. 40). This bridge led the traveller inside the ruins of the fortress, through a large stone gate with an Arabic inscription above it. This gate had been the principal entry into the fortress in medieval times. A mosque was incorporated into the gate on one side and a customs office on the other. This structure has survived relatively intact, though the bridge has not. This gate, or rather its predecessor, was also, presumably, the principal entry into the Roman-Byzantine city centre from the south, leading directly to the Cardo Maximus. In fact, the medieval gatehouse is obviously

30. The Lateran Sarcophagus
Fourth-century Christian sarcophagus discovered in 1591 in Rome. The standing figure at the right may represent the famous 'statue of Christ' in Banias, and the buildings behind actual ecclesiastical structures in the city.

31. Coin of Hadrian with kneeling woman (Judea)

32. 'Christ' and the kneeling woman

33. Aerial View of the Byzantine Cathedral during excavations

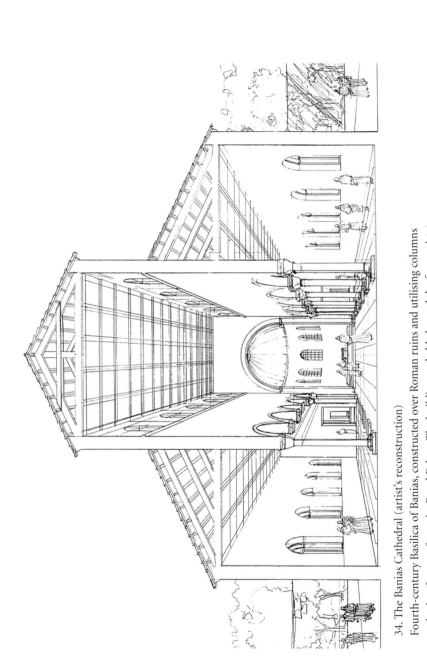

34. The Banias Cathedral (artist's reconstruction)

Fourth-century Basilica of Banias, constructed over Roman ruins and utilising columns and other features from the Royal Palace. The building probably housed the famous 'statue of Christ' – a major pilgrimage site during the fourth and fifth centuries. Eventually its ruins were incorporated into the medieval Islamic fortifications of the town.

35. and 36. The Shrine of
Khader (nineteenth century,
above, modern, *left*)
The Shrine of Khader looks
down on the cave and
excavations at the Sanctuary
of Pan. Khader, the
mysterious 'Ever-Living' or
'Green One' is still honoured
here today by the local Druze.
The shrine dates to at least
Byzantine times and probably
extends the ancient worship of
the Spirit of the cave and
springs originating in earlier
cults.

37. The 'Street of Burnt Shops' as discovered (*above*); 38. Artifacts from the excavation (*below*) Debris from a Byzantine street in Banias that suffered destruction by fire in the late fourth or early fifth century. Excavators were able to restore dozens of pots and jugs (a few of which are shown *below*), along with many other artifacts.

39. The 'Synagogue'

This small eleventh-century basilica is oriented north–south and thus cannot be a church. Constructed from bits and pieces of Roman and Byzantine buildings, it seems to have originally served as a synagogue for the medieval Jewish community in Banias, and later as a mosque. It stands directly over the huge basilica (throne room?) of the first-century palace.

40. The Southern Entrance Gate of Banias Ninetenth-century inhabitants of Banias cross the ancient bridge over Wâdî Sa'âr that led to the Roman Cardo Maximus. This bridge survived until relatively recent times. Columns that once lined the Cardo have been incorporated into the gate, which bears an inscription of al-'Azîz 'Uthmân dated 1227 AD. The gate contained a mosque on one side and a customs office on the other, and served as the main entrance into the city from the south.

41. Jahârkas's inscription
Inscription, dated 1204–5 AD, found during the modern excavation of the city. It commemorates Fakhr al-Dîn Iyâs Jahârkas, a Mamlûk of Saladin who became governor of the area around Banias in 1201 and made the town his capitol. The stone is reused, probably originally belonging to a building from Roman times.

42. Medieval depiction of the Crusader siege of Banias
Late-thirteenth-century illuminated manuscript of the *Chronicle of the Crusades*
depicting Crusaders besieging Muslim defenders at the walls of Banias.

43. The Fortress of Subaybah

The great castle of Subaybah (also called 'Nimrod's Fortress') dominating the hill northeast of Banias is now thought to have been founded in the thirteenth century. Subaybah was used until relatively modern times, and is remarkably well preserved.

44. Massive stones between Banias and Subaybah

'Great rocks as big as chests' on the incline from Banias to Subaybah. In 1252, it was from these stones the Turks 'aimed great blows with their maces', according to Jean of Joinville, preventing the Crusaders from taking control of Banias. The fortress of Subaybah looms above the scene on the right.

45. The Western Roman Bridge
Late-nineteenth-century depiction of the ancient bridge across the Banias River by which the city was approached from the west. Buildings in the background include the Sheikh's residence.

Above
46. Basket dwellings on rooftops of nineteenth-century Banias

Right
47. Fakhr al-Dîn II the Druze (1572–1635)
Based on a contemporary engraving.

Above

48. View of the nineteenth-century village

On the right is the present archaeological site where the Cardo Maximus and Royal Palace are being excavated. The village was destroyed, except for religious structures, in the late 1960s. The nineteenth-century photograph on the left shows the village as it was seen and described by many European travellers.

Right

49. Similar view today

50. The Sheikh's House
Field sketch of the house of 'Ismā'īl, the nineteenth-century Sheikh of Banias. The house surmounts one of the surviving medieval defensive towers that is, in turn, constructed from remains of the Roman city.

51. Funeral of the Bishop of Banias
The 1902 funeral of Butrus Jurajeery, the nineteenth-century Greek
Uniate 'Bishop of Paneas or Caesarea Philippi'. Patriarch of Antioch at
the time of his death, his body, brilliantly bedecked, is paraded
through the streets of Beirut.

constructed out of Roman-Byzantine bits and pieces, at least some of which probably had once belonged to the colonnades along the Cardo. Numerous columns, their bases and capitals removed, can still be seen, laid on their sides and incorporated into the construction. Several large sarcophagi, decorated with wreaths and other symbols, have been used in a similar manner. The bridge, with its single slightly-pointed arch and impressive gateway, spanned the deep ravine. Beneath it waters rushed over the dark grey boulders and through thickets of flowering vines and bushes, providing a picturesque sight. It was often drawn and photographed during the nineteenth century, and survived intact until the Arab–Israeli conflicts of modern times. Along the sides of Wâdî Sa'âr sheep grazed and women descended a steep path down the slope to fill their large clay jars with water. Below the gatehouse a water mill could be heard turning, powered by water conveyed from the springs at the cave by means of a covered channel that had no doubt once distributed water to the public fountains of Roman Banias. Other channels, some ancient and some modern, diverted water to turn other mills on the west side of the village or to irrigate village gardens. Van de Velde, during a visit in 1852, found that 'the water from the rich fountain of the rock of Pan runs in all directions through the village, so that one cannot even walk through its streets with dry feet'.[27] Lord Kitchener, describing the village in 1875, remarked that, 'little streams seem to be running in every direction, cooling the air, and making this one of the most lively spots in Palestine'.[28]

Another bridge with ancient foundations spanned the Banias River itself, near where the spring waters, which flow first to the west, turn south toward the Huleh (Fig. 45). Here De Saulcy noticed the ancient walls that channelled and controlled the flow of water from the spring and the two bridges[29] that spanned them, allowing access to the city from the west. He found both the walls and the bridges in a poor state, and forded the river rather than use them. Other travellers, particularly those who were either arriving from the west or continuing their journey in that direction, seem to have entered or left the city by this route, which no doubt also followed the Roman road leading towards Tyre and the Mediterranean. In 1898, Cunningham Giekie found this western road, once a major thoroughfare, to be in deplorable condition. He hoped 'that of old the road was better than it is now, for such a chaos of stones, large and small, rolled or thrown into a narrow path between banks, or piled into loose walls, needs to be seen to be believed. The very horses seemed at a loss where to put down their feet'.[30]

In 1843, W.M. Thomson found that the village of Banias lay almost entirely within the northeastern corner of the medieval walls which were still 'very thick and solid,…and strengthened by eight castles or towers' (Figs 48, 49).[31] The western area inside the walls was 'overgrown with luxuriant briars and thorns, which cover up, and quite conceal, two or three flouring mills'.[32] Estimates of the population of the town varied widely among nineteenth-century visitors. Seetzen counted twenty huts, Burckhardt one hundred and fifty. Thompson, Robinson and Wilson agreed that the number was fifty or sixty. Buckingham estimated the population at five hundred, as did Freese, fifty years later. Wortabet counted only one hundred and fifty. Newbold estimated one hundred and forty families. Most visitors agreed, however, that while it rested in a beautiful environment, one which led more than one visitor to burst into poetic ecstasy, Banias had little beyond its history to commend it. Some travellers, no doubt carried away with the poetic aspects of the site and its beautiful environs, found the place charming. De Saulcy notes that 'in every direction, magnificent trees incline over the houses, and convey the aspect of a European village'. In addition to the great oaks, the village was dotted with mulberry trees, grown more for their fruit than for the production of silkworms.[33] One of these trees has survived to the present day, standing just north of the mosque, where it furnishes shade for visitors picnicking in the park that has replaced the village. Kean, observing the old women sitting in the doors of their 'cottages', pronounced the scene to be 'peaceful' and 'rustic'. 'The place,' he says, 'might be described as a garden dotted with trees and cottages, rather than as a village.'[34] Even Lord Kitchener thought the village, surrounded as it was and shut in with all kinds of trees, looked 'remarkably green and lovely'.[35] Those who examined these 'cottages' at closer hand tended to be less complimentary. Words like 'miserable', 'mean', 'wretched hovels', 'devoid of comfort', 'dirty' and 'squalid' occur with regularity in the reports of visitors. Mark Twain (Samuel Clemens) visited Banias in 1867. He thrust his poison pen at the hapless little town with characteristic ferocity in *Innocents Abroad* – calling it a 'little execrable village' with a 'sleepy, stupid, rural look about it'.[36] Shortly after the turn of the century, Libbey and Hoskins delivered the *coup de grâce*: 'The town of Banias,' they said, 'is about as dismal a contrast to the natural beauties of the scene as anything could be. It is a mass of wretched and foul-smelling ruins, covered everywhere with nettles, weeds and filth. It is the very ideal of dilapidation and desolation.'[37]

The houses of the village were mostly one storey high, built of stones robbed from the ancient ruins stacked up without mortar. Their flat roofs consisted of timbers, brushwood and hardened mud. They were crowded together within the northeastern part of the medieval fort, with only a few standing outside the walls. Recent excavations show that the village lay directly over the centre of the Roman city, and within the precincts of the medieval citadel so often mentioned in Crusader-period records. The rough path that served as the village 'main street' followed almost exactly the course of the ancient Roman Cardo Maximus.[38]

Travellers often noted that near the street, among the houses, a series of ancient arches could be seen. Clogged with garbage and debris and almost completely buried, these arches formed the foundation for a rough stone garden wall. Condor and Kitchener thought they might be the remains of a Roman aqueduct designed to carry water through the town. Twain was horrified to observe his travelling companions, whom he derisively called 'the pilgrims', hacking and chipping off chunks of the arches to carry away as souvenirs. These arches were rediscovered amid the ruins of the Syrian village while the site was being cleared for excavation in the mid-1980s (Fig. 18). When completely exposed, they were found to be the tops of the vaulted ceilings of a series of large and impressive rooms, that had once been a part of the huge royal palace of Herodian Banias. In the Middle Ages they had been incorporated into the city's citadel and had evidently served as barracks for soldiers. Stone huts and garden plots of the Syrian village had been constructed directly on top of these rooms and in some cases they had been utilised as underground refuse pits.[39]

THE NINETEENTH-CENTURY BANIASITES

The inhabitants of the village were described in a variety of ways. Frequently the verdict was not a positive one. In 1851, De Saulcy found them to be 'mild and inoffensive' and in 1863, Tristram called them 'a harmless lot, without either carrying arms, nor inflicting on others the necessity for carrying them. Law and order reign.' There was even a village policeman.[40] Giekie describes the 'mothers and daughters of Caesarea Philippi' who came to his party for medical treatment during their visit in 1898 as 'very fine-looking, and all were clean, and very modestly dressed'.[41] These judgments are in sharp contrast to the majority view, however. In 1849, Finn notes that 'the people of this place bear a bad character'; and in 1859, Emily Beaufort found them 'disagreeable and troublesome to strangers'. Libbey and Hoskins (1905) described them as of 'low type' and having 'a deservedly evil reputation'. In their earliest contacts with Europeans, the citizens of Banias were sometimes hostile, believing the visitors were after treasures buried in the ruins. Buckingham, for example, was never even allowed inside the town since he was, they believed, a 'Muggrebin [North African Arab] magician, come to raise treasures'.[42]

Eventually, however, the Baniasites began to see these visitors as valuable sources of income. Telling them of the great dangers around them, the villagers suggested that they be hired as 'guards' to ensure safety. Finn accepted the offer in 1849, but in 1852 Porter rejected it.

> As we sat in our tent in the still evening an armed retainer of the sheikh was announced on business. Being introduced, he said the country was in a state of rebellion, the Arabs were close to the village, and robbers infested the neighbourhood: his master, therefore, would not be answerable for the safety of our persons or property unless we engaged a watch for the night. I replied that our persons we were prepared and able to protect, and that, as our property was within the village, and as the sheikh, according to his own admission, had power to protect it by placing guards, I would hold him responsible for anything that might be stolen; but I would neither employ nor pay a guard. We got no reply, and nothing was stolen.[43]

Emily Beaufort complains of 'several alarms of robbers' during her three-night stay in the olive grove near the village – the usual site where visitors were allowed to set up their tents. Though to some extent the dangers were real, these 'alarms' were no doubt a bit of theatre on the part of the villagers. The olive-grove campground was also a financial boon for Banias, since, as Beaufort further complains, the price for permission to camp there was exorbitant.[44] Eventually, the locals made the best of their growing popularity as a tourist attraction. In 1880, Henry Coleman notes that 'Travelers here are numerous and greedy of the best accommodations. Every party has its dragomans and its needs, and the chaffering that goes on between them and the natives for milk and provender and other necessaries keeps all Banias in an uproar.'[45]

Many mid-nineteenth-century visitors who did not wish to accept the sheikh's hospitality in the village '*Medhaafe*' (see below) used this grove as a camping site. It lay on the other side of the river from the village itself. In 1857, Prime's party, for example, stayed on the banks quite close to the spectacular waterfall that still draws busloads of tourists today. By the 1880s, however, visitors were camping among the oaks north of the village, this being 'the only camping-place of travelers' according to J.W. McGarvey.[46] The area directly north of the cluster of houses, situated between the dwellings and the cave, was used by the villagers as shelter for their flocks. Benjamin Bausman (in 1857) watched the activity there from his nearby camp, as the day ended in Banias. 'Most of the people seem to live from their flocks,' he says. 'In the evening the village flocks were gathered into "sheep-folds" in the rear of the town. These consisted simply of enclosures, some of wood, and others of stone…Quite a busy scene ensured, when a goodly number of the villagers milked their respective goats.'[47] This was, of course, the very spot where so many centuries before the ancients had gathered to offer sacrifices to the little goat-god of the forests.

John Macgregor (1825–92), famous for his daring canoe trips in exotic lands, spent the night in Banias prior to heading down the Jordan in his trusty craft the *Rob Roy*. Caught by the rain, he put his horse in Pan's cave and made himself at home in a little stone shanty built up against the red-rock cliff. The shepherd who used the shanty had left a fire going, and there was no door on the structure. Macgregor 'greeted the venerable proprietor when he returned, telling him the one cardinal fact that I was an Englishman'. Presumably, this revelation alleviated any concern on the part of the surprised shepherd. Left alone, Macgregor fell into a 'fit of melancholy meditation, deploring our degenerate days that leave such a noble stronghold [Subaybah] in the hands of the feeble Turk – his, too, for the last seven hundred years'.[48] From such sentiments grew the imperialism of the nineteenth-century European powers.

In 1873, Edwin Hodder described the 'business district' of the village: 'One shop seemed to monopolise all the trade of the town', he says, 'and was filled with a multitude of dirty things, rough tobacco for Narghillis, in damp rotten sacks; figs, dried, and lying in heaps on the filthy floor, where a couple of hens were taking their ease'.[49]

By the late nineteenth century, some unfortunate citizens of Banias were resorting to begging from the ever-increasing numbers of tourists. Coleman (travelling in 1880) describes one such incident: A 'venerable grandfather, old and blind, sitting with a crust in his hand, but no teeth to eat it with, is mumbling out Bassiz, as he has done for three score years and ten…Five of the children are standing round, flea-haunted, lice-haunted, vice-haunted, with hands outstretched ready when they should catch my wearied eye to whisper gently backsheesh howadji.'[50] This rather patronising account should be put in some perspective, however, as should those accounts of townspeople 'loafing in the shadow of the walls'. Or Twain's disdainful (and racist) characterisation of people as 'infested with vermin, and the dirt had caked on them till it amounted to bark'. They 'reminded me much of Indians', he says.

In fact, most of the inhabitants of nineteenth-century Banias were sick. Twain noted that the children all had sore eyes, and that the people crowded around a physician in his group, who distributed medicine to them. Indeed, much of the 'begging' was a desperate appeal for medicine. A more sympathetic picture of the situation is provided by Tristram, who says, 'The inhabitants of Banias look wretched, pallid, and yellow, and the very infant at the breast has ague stamped on its face. Many of the women have fine features, but are haggard and worn from the effects of the deadly miasma which rises in autumn from the marshes of the Hulah.'[51] Knowledgeable travellers like James Finn (the British Consul from Jerusalem) were well aware of the danger of malaria, originating in the nearby swamps of Lake Huleh. During his visit in 1849, the sheikh of the village came out to him 'begging some quinine medicine'. Finn gave him eight of his remaining twelve pills, but became so alarmed that he pulled up stakes immediately. 'On the adjacent plain there must needs be fever and ague,' he says, 'in fact, so unwilling was I on account of malaria to remain longer at Banias, that we resumed traveling by night.'[52]

Other less dangerous but significant discomforts plagued the villagers. There were, of course, the ever-present hoards of fleas, thieves of sleep and potential carriers of disease. In the summer, the village suffered infestations of snakes and scorpions as well. Through-out the second half of the nineteenth century, visitors to Banias mention the picturesque way in which the citizens coped with this unpleasant situation. The flat mud roof of almost every house in the village was topped by graceful 'baskets' or 'tents' shaped like beehives – wickerwork cages of leafy oleander boughs with woven cane floors (Fig. 46). Such structures were not uncommon throughout Palestine and Syria. They provided protection from the sun during the day, and cool breezes during the humid nights. But the Baniasites had extended the concept, making these lithe and delicate accommodations vermin-proof as well by thrusting them up into the air three to six feet above the rooftops. Resting thus on a fragile system of scaffolding, they could be entered by climbing up a pole and opening a trap door in the floor, and thus be out of the reach of all the creeping things of the night.

THE SHEIKH

During the early years of the nineteenth century, Mohammed Ali of Egypt dominated Palestine. Direct Turkish rule was re-established in 1840, and in the wake of the Crimean War, European (particularly British and French) influence and power became more evident. These changes seemed to have little effect on the civic structure or daily life of Banias, except for the increasing number of European visitors who found their way to the city once the area became relatively peaceful. The higher country surrounding Banias was a separate district (the Ardh el Banias) within the Mukata of Hasbeya and the Pashalik of Damascus.[53] Thus the Emir of Hasbeya ruled Banias through a local sheikh of his own choice, most probably usually a relative.[54]

During the early years of the century the Emir of Hasbeya was a man named Sa'ad ad-Dîn. Several European travellers mention him. For much of the second half of the century, the Sheikh of Banias, answering to the emir, was an interesting character named Ismā'īl, who is often mentioned in the accounts of travellers. From them we learn that he was about forty years of age in 1851, 'middle aged' in 1855, and an old man in 1880. De Saulcy, who enjoyed an hour's conversation with him in 1851 ('while taking our coffee and smoking our chibouks'), describes him as 'perfectly polite'. 'He is far superior in intelligence and good breeding to any one I have met with up to this moment in Syria. He has the most ardent curiosity respecting France, and inundates me with questions, which I answer readily, and with much satisfaction.'[55] The author, Bayard Taylor, writing in 1852 found the sheikh equally curious about the United States, 'talking with me a long time about America'. Taylor found that the sheikh and his villagers 'exhibit a very sensible curiosity, desiring to know the extent of our country, the number of inhabitants, the amount of taxation, the price of grain, and other solid information'.[56] Mark Twain, on the other hand, used the old sheikh as a foil for his acid tongue, describing him as 'a poor old mummy that looked as if he would be more at home in the poor-house than in the Chief Magistracy of this tribe of hopeless, shirtless savages'. Twain was somewhat more generous in his evaluation of the sheikh's daughter, however, who 'was only thirteen or fourteen years old, and had a very sweet face and a pretty one. She was the only Syrian female we have seen yet who was not so sinfully ugly that she couldn't smile after ten o'clock Saturday night without breaking the Sabbath.'

THE SHEIKH'S RESIDENCE AND THE MEDHAAFE

The Sheikh of Banias resided in an imposing structure built on top of one of the towers of the medieval fortress (Fig. 50). This edifice survives to this day, one of the few buildings that escaped the general destruction of the town by the Israelis following the Six Day War. The house was perched high above the mostly one-storey houses in the town. In contrast to their haphazard construction, this building is built of rather large stones and bits of ancient masonry either still *in situ* or robbed from the ancient ruins. In fact, one can trace the history of Banias in the stratigraphy of this masonry, from a Roman foundation and Roman architectural fragments visible in the exposed core of the structure on the north, through to the Crusader/Ayyûbid walls and Mamlûk/Ottoman additions. The moat that helped protect the relatively weak western approach to the city lies along the eastern side of the structure.

Gregory M. Wortabet, an anglicised Syrian who had been converted by missionaries and became the pastor of the Protestant church in Hasbeya, was a houseguest of the sheikh in 1855. Because his brother, a physician, had helped the sheikh during a severe illness, he was assigned the 'best room in the house'. This was a dubious honour, since the place was infested with fleas, and the night was a miserable one. He was led to change an old proverb to read, 'The Queen of fleas holds court, not at Tiberias, but at Banias'. Seeing a host of men and their horses in the courtyard below, he was amazed to hear that they were all guests for the night and that indeed the house was full of guests every night. He learned that the house had been in the possession of the sheikh's family since the time of his great-grandmother. This woman had apparently been presented with it sometime during the late eighteenth century, along with 'a great amount of land', by one of the governors of Damascus. The gift was in consequence of her great hospitality to the governor on some occasion. Her family thus became the hereditary aristocracy of the town, receiving an annual levy on the lands and crops of the village in a manner not unlike the feudal system of medieval Europe. She in turn bequeathed the property to her family on the condition that they would 'keep an open house for every stranger'. Thus, 'now all who pass through Banias come and take up their abode in the house of the sheikh, who provides for them and their horses'.[57]

Such an arrangement was not unusual in Syria. Burckhardt, who is the first recorded recipient of this hospitality at Banias, says that '*Menzels*' or '*Medhaafes*' like this one were found in 'almost every village through which there is a frequented route'. It was the duty of the local sheikh not only to provide housing and stable space, but also to send along dinner for his guests. De Saulcy was also a guest there. In 1873, Edwin Hodder found the house, though 'thoroughly Oriental', to be nevertheless 'scrupulously clean'.

One has only to read the humourous account of Laurence Oliphant's stay at the house (in 1880) to see why many European visitors decided to camp by the stream, outside the village, instead of accepting this hospitality.

> We were kindly received by the old sheikh Ismaîl, but unfortunately his hospitality was not limited to ourselves. First arrived a handsome Druze sheikh, apparently a great friend of our host's, for they embraced with great demonstration of affection, and kissed each other on both cheeks. Then came a soldier, or rather a subordinate officer, who had been at Plevna, and who showed us with pride two bullet-holes in his leg. Then arrived three visitors of distinction from a distant village; and when night came we found, to our dismay, that they were all beginning to say their prayers and make their beds on the opposite side of the room we had fondly hoped had been placed exclusively at our disposal. Their idea of going to bed consisted on simply stretching themselves on the floor, throwing off their outside garments, and getting under a quilt; and they watched with some interest our more elaborate arrangements. As for sleep, it proved out of the question: each one of the five either snored, or moaned, or puffed, or talked in his sleep; and these noises, diversified with the incessant barking of dogs and a slight sprinkling of fleas, kept me awake, and indeed to some extent occupied, until the first streak of dawn warranted me in waking my companion and rousing the household generally.[58]

Even those who chose to set up their own camp away from the village did not always escape the vermin, however. In 1857, Benjamin Bausman's party discovered this unfortunate fact. 'By some means or other a vast army of fleas got possession of our tent,' he complains, 'to our almost insufferable annoyance. I can still see my comrades, half-unclad, diligent in their pursuit.'[59]

The *menzel* at Banias was still in operation in 1905 when such an arrangement had become very rare in western Palestine. Travellers could still have a meal and a cover for the night in relative safety, and without cost. The facility continued to be administered by Sheikh Ismā'īl's heirs.[60]

In front of the sheikh's house was a paved courtyard or square, shaded by a huge terebinth (oak tree) said to be 13 feet eight inches in circumference, and whose branches cast a shadow 75 paces in circumference.[61] At the foot of this magnificent tree stood a raised platform, encircled to the height of three feet by fluted and chiselled marble blocks, remnants of former glory.[62] Here was the public lounge, or as Bayard Taylor described it 'the town-hall of Banias, where the Shekh dispenses justice and at the same time the resort of all the idlers of the place'.[63] This square was surrounded on the south by houses, and on its east side stood the sheikh's house. Among the houses next to the square De Saulcy and his party stayed in a barn that served them as 'drawing-room, dining-room, and bedroom'.[64] Taylor, who enjoyed a good smoke, waxes eloquent about his experience under the big oak. 'We were given seats of honour near the Shekh,' he says, among the villagers, dressed in the shirt and trousers of the northern peasantry, complete with Bedouin *kaffiyehs* and *agal* (the black ring on the traditional Bedouin headdress).

> The day [10 May 1852] has been, and still is, excessively hot. The atmosphere is sweltering, and all around us, over the thick patches of mallow and wild mustard, the bees are humming with a continuous sultry sound. The Shekh, with a number of lazy villagers, is still seated under the terebinth, in a tent of shade. I can hear the rush of the fountains of Banias – the holy springs of Hermon, whence Jordan is born. But what is this? The odour of the velvety weed of Shiraz meets my nostrils; a dark-eyed son of Pan places the narghileh [hadah] at my feet; and, bubbling more sweetly than the streams of Jordan, the incense most dear to the god dims the crystal censer, and floats from my lips in rhythmic ejaculations. I, too, am in Arcadia![65]

The temptation to break into rapturous poetry full of classical references to Pan and the other gods proved irresistible to more than one nineteenth-century visitor to the site. George William Curtis, reflecting with romantic nostalgia on the disappearance of the ancient gods and the scattered ruins and inscriptions that remained, breaks into verse:

> Do ye leave your rivers flowing
> All alone, O Naiades,
> While your drenched locks dry slow in
> This cold, feeble sun and breeze?
>
> From the gloaming of the oak wood
> O ye Dryads, could ye flee?
> At the rushing thunder stroke would
> No sob tremble through the tree?
>
> Have ye left the mountain places
> Oreads wild, for other tryst,
> Shall we see no sudden faces
> Strike a glory through the mist?[66]

RELIGION IN NINETEENTH-CENTURY BANIAS

European or American visitors to nineteenth-century Banias often comment on the religious situation there but again their reports tend to be inconsistent with each other. This may be because the visits were usually quite brief, and the travellers were dependent on sometimes-questionable local reports or their own superficial observations. Seetzen thought the town was entirely Moslem; Burckhardt noted some Christian inhabitants. Buckingham thought that, though the citizens were Moslems and Metawalis, there was no place of worship of any kind. But of course he never actually visited the village itself, and seems even to have overlooked the shrine at the Tomb of Khader.[67] Poussou, visiting in the year of the earthquake, 1837 could find only 'Ausairies' (descendants of the Ismā'īlis or Assassins), goat-herders who, he says, 'do not worship the God of Heaven, but rather the most shameful things of this earth'.[68] A mosque for Banias's Moslems, complete with minaret, is attested in the mid-nineteenth century.[69] Newbold, visiting in mid-century, made a more careful assessment of the situation and found the town to be quite diverse religiously, and its district even more so. In the surrounding area he found Moslem *fellahs* (peasants), Druze, Greek and Roman Catholic Christians, and a few Nosairis[70] and Metawalis. In Banias itself he found the population to be chiefly Moslem, Metawali and Greek Christian, along with a few Druze and Nosairis.[71]

In addition to the active cult at the Tomb of Khader, above the cave and thus outside the nineteenth-century village, the Moslems of the village venerated the tomb of 'Sultan Ibrâhim',[72] which stood alongside the main road that entered Banias from the south. This tomb was located just inside the gate and would have been the first structure observed as one crossed the Wâdî Sa'âr bridge and entered through the medieval gate. A rather elaborate structure today maintained by the local Druze, it seems earlier to have been a relatively simple tomb located beneath a large terebinth. Devotees covered the branches of the tree with strips of cloth intended as votive offerings. While Ibrâhim himself seems to have lived in Ottoman times, this form of veneration had a long history in the area and may be connected with very ancient beliefs about the 'genies' in certain old trees.[73] Certainly the other active cult, at the Tomb of Khader, had ancient connections. Such sites and practices led Bliss to conclude, in 1912, that the vestiges of paganism were 'neither faint nor innate' in the region.[74]

THE 'BISHOP OF BANIAS'

One day in 1880, in the town of Zahleh, the local Melchite[75] priest, Butrus Jurajeery (Géraïgiry), had an altercation with a local Protestant bookshop employee named Mr Dale. Fisticuffs followed. Mr Dale complained to Rustem Pasha, the governor-general of Lebanon, who proceeded to throw both combatants out of the country. Jurajeery, now more convinced than ever of the danger of Protestant intrusions, went to France to raise money for the establishment of Roman Catholic schools to combat this growing danger. Then he hit upon a new plan – to revive the ancient bishopric of Banias. After all, Christian bishops are attested in Banias from the period of the great Church councils of the fourth and fifth centuries to at least the coming of the Arabs in the seventh century.[76] During the Crusades, Latin bishops were appointed at Banias, but of course once the town fell permanently into Moslem hands this office no longer served a realistic purpose.[77] Now, Jurajeery was convinced, the need had arisen once more. He went directly to the Pope with his idea: 'Why was it that the most ancient of all bishoprics, the very spot where the famous "rock verse" [Matthew 16:18] was uttered by Christ to Peter, should lie in ruins and forgetfulness? and here was a second Peter ['Butrus' means Peter] who would undertake to restore its ancient glory!'[78]

The Pope agreed, and on 22 February 1886, Jurajeery was named Bishop Butrus (Peter) of Banias. However, there were apparently few Christians actually living in Banias by this time, and he was unable to purchase property there. So he made the town of Jedaideh the seat of the bishopric and built a fine church in that town.[79] And thus, in 1897, Cuinet lists the non-Moslem religious authorities in the Vilayet of Syria as 'the Greek orthodox bishop of Emesa [Homs] and Amath [Hamah], the Syrian Jacobite bishop of Hamah, and the Greek Uniate Bishop of Paneas or Caesarea Philippi'.[80] In 1898, Butrus was given the title 'Patriarch of Antioch and all the East' (despite opposition by the Papal Nuncio, the Jesuits, and the Turkish government) and at the time of his death was revered and much-lamented. At his funeral, which took place in Beyrout in 1902, his body, seated, dressed in magnificent robes, covered with gold and jewels, was placed on a throne, pontifical staff in hand, carried through the streets in a gilded carriage and then placed on view in a vault under the cathedral pavement (Fig. 51). An eyewitness commented, 'I could hardly realize that the patriarch was dead; he sat there so naturally with his long gray beard resting upon his golden vestments, and his large, calm features seemed still to be animated by the vital power of his dauntless spirit'.[81]

Epilogue: The Twentieth Century

BANIAS AND THE BORDER

Having chosen to ally itself with the losing side in World War I, the decrepit and ineffectual Ottoman Empire collapsed and its territories were partitioned among the winners of that conflict, primarily the French and the British. In 1918 British troops drove the Turks from Palestine and themselves withdrew to a line a few miles north of Tel Hazor, not far from Banias, to await determination of borders. At the Paris Peace Conference of 1919–20 the British and French began the process of dividing the spoils, and at San Remo (April, 1920) created two 'mandates' – a British Mandate over Palestine and a French Mandate over Syria. As for Banias, history was yet again repeating itself. The little town lay in the crucial border area between the spheres of the two European powers; on which side of the new border would it lie? The negotiations were intense, and carried out with little concern about the ancient territorial system created by the Turks – itself based, at least in part, on even older systems.[1]

France was concerned to have a route between Quneitra (and thus Damascus) and Tyre that would lie entirely in territory under its own control. Britain, on the other hand, wanted the whole Jordan water system to lie within its own mandate. The road ran directly through Banias, but the Jordan springs lay north of the road. A difficult dilemma indeed. In December 1920 a decision was made. The border would be defined in such a way that the French would control the Quneitra–Tyre road, ensuring France a transportation link to the Mediterranean. This decision created a number of problems for villages that lay along the road since some of them (Banias included) had territories that lay on both sides of the proposed border. In order to try to accommodate these villages, the surveyors adapted the line here and there, in order to keep the villages and their territories on one side of the line or the other. One Bedouin sheikh in the northern Golan, technically in British territory, wanted to be in Syria instead. The British agreed, provided that they be given control of the entire Jordan River system in return. Thus, the Golan went to France and the Sea of Galilee to Great Britain. The British compromised on the matter of the springs at Banias, which, as we have seen, lay on the north side of the Damascus–Tyre road. They agreed to have the border set 750 metres south of the springs, but wrote into the agreement a clause reserving the right to 'correct' the border and put Banias within their Palestine Mandate at some further date.[2]

During these negotiations Zionist leaders in Europe, intent on re-establishing a Jewish state in Palestine, had their own ideas about borders, ideas that placed Banias within that proposed state. Chaim Weizman told the British prime minister, David Lloyd George, that 'The whole economic future of Palestine is dependent upon its water supply for irrigation and for electric power, and the water supply must mainly be derived from the slopes of Mount Hermon, from the headwaters of the Jordan' and the streams originating in the southern Lebanon. The western and southern slopes of Mount Hermon (and thus, Banias) were 'essential' to the new state, he said. Taking into consideration the water system and the trade routes of the area, the Zionist publication *Palestine* declared in 1919: 'Baneas, the old Dan, must, by reason of its immense military importance, be included with Palestine'.[3] A half-century was to pass, however, before the springs of Banias came under the control of a Jewish state.

The French Mandate ended in 1946, after a long period of bad blood between the European power and the Syrian population, and an independent state of Syria appeared, its borders determined by the earlier agreements between Britain and France. The government of the new state was very unstable for a long time after its establishment, and became strongly anti-Western in sentiment and policy. Meanwhile, the State of Israel was born in 1948 and the stage set for the modern version of an ancient border conflict.

Syria claimed that France's signature on the border agreement was invalid, but the British would not discuss the situation. A 'demilitarized zone' was created at three disputed points along the border, one of which was the territory around Banias, with Syria withdrawing troops, but continuing to lay claim to the territory within that zone. Thus, from the beginning of the Syrian state to the Six Day War, there was no settled border. In 1951 Israel began work on a channel that would drain the swamps of the Huleh and carry the waters to the Negev Desert. Arab villages in the path of this development were bulldozed and the inhabitants scattered. By the spring of 1951 the Israelis had occupied the two southern 'demilitarized zones' and Syria had taken possession of the Banias area. During the 1950s and 1960s the Syrians established a series of fortifications and artillery positions within this zone and the area's economy and culture were dominated by the presence of the military. Banias once again saw an influx of soldiers. A swimming facility on the Banias River just south of the village still carries the name 'Syrian Officers' Pool'. The fields around the town were crisscrossed with trenches, machine-gun nests and watchtowers, many of which may still be seen today. Agricultural lands became minefields. Taking advantage of its position high above the Huleh and the valley of southern Lebanon, the Syrians used the little town as a base for attacks on Israeli positions, such as those near Dan.[4] Banias became a 'secondary training facility' for Syrian units planning to move into the Jordan Valley.[5] Consequently, the town became a target for Israeli bomb attacks.[6]

SEEDS OF WAR

The two new states rattled their sabres at each other across the ancient border throughout the decades after the departure of the British and French. This became the bloodiest of all the borders that lay between Israelis and Arabs.[7] Both states depended on the melted snows of Hermon to enliven the arid lands whose fertility was so necessary to survival.[8] Banias entered the maelstrom again, not only because it lay on a disputed border, but because its dirty little streets and paths were washed with the precious water that gushed up beneath the cave of Pan.[9] Israel announced that it would begin to pump water from the Banias into the National Water Carrier. In 1964 the Arab League launched a counter-plan to divert the waters of Banias, along with those of the Hasbani and the Yarmuk, into Syrian territory.[10] A canal would be constructed from Banias to the Yarmuk, a distance of 70 kilometres, carrying the waters completely away from the new State of Israel.[11] The Israelis felt gravely threatened by this plan, which would cut their supply of water by one-third, and increase the salinity of the Sea of Galilee – effectively destroying Israel's water system.[12] They warned the Arabs that this would not be tolerated. The construction of the canal began on 17 March 1965. Israeli guns immediately destroyed the earth-moving machines brought in by the Syrians, forcing them to move south to a location near the Benot Ya'aqov Bridge.[13] Between 1965 and 1967 the Israelis carried out a number of armed attacks by land and air at the work sites for the project – the prelude to war.[14]

War clouds thickened. In Syria, a coup brought the Alawites into power, and the new regime immediately allied with the Soviet Union. The British announced that they were abandoning all commitments 'east of Suez'. There were repeated incidents along the 'demilitarized zone', and Banias was often involved in these hostilities.

THE SIX DAY WAR, 1967

On Friday, 9 June 1967, war returned to Banias.[15] On the same hills and fields where the Egyptian general Scopas had led his troops against the elephants of King Antiochus, Israel and Syria met in battle (see map on page 5). Tanks played the part of elephants this time. Syrian tanks were operating in the area when the Israelis attacked with their own armoured corps and infantry. Setting out from Kfar Szold, they headed for the Syrian positions on Tel 'Azzaziyāt and Tel Fahr – the same hills where the ancient 'Battle of Paneion' likely took place.[16] Fierce fighting ensued, and the ancient battlefield was once again strewn with the debris of battle and the blood of young soldiers. One of the three Israeli armoured forces roared into Banias on that day and took possession of the village. Unlike their ancient antecedents, however, these modern armies were able to take to the skies. Helicopters from the Israeli Golani brigade landed on Mount Hermon.

On that fateful Friday, and the next day, Saturday, the remaining residents of the villages in the path of war, the Sunnis of Jubath and the Alamites of Za'ura, 'Ayn Fit and Banias, fled to the Druze village of Majdal Shams, a few miles up the ancient road that led from Banias to Damascus. There they waited for seven weeks, hoping to return. But this was not to be. Fearful and hopeless, the villagers made their way across the mountain and disappeared into Syria.[17] A few months later, bulldozers demolished the village itself, leaving only the religious buildings – the mosque, the church the tombs of Khader and of Sheikh Ibrâhim – and the old *Menzel* where so many nineteenth-century guests had spent the night chasing fleas. Within days, Israeli volunteers settled along the banks of the Banias River, a short distance from the ancient site. This settlement, now called 'Senir' (one of the biblical names for Mount Hermon),[18] was the first permanent outpost of the new inhabitants of the area.[19]

Banias, after two thousand years, was no more.

Notes on the Text

ABBREVIATIONS

AE	*L'Année Épigraphique*
Ant.	*Antiquities*
BAR	*Biblical Archaeology Review*
BMC	*A catalogue of Greek coins in the British Museum*
BT	*Babylonian Talmud*
CMH	*The Cambridge Medieval History*
EI	*The Encyclopaedia of Islam. New Edition*
EJ	*Encyclopaedia Judaica*
DACL	*Dictionnaire d'Archéologie Chrétienne et de Liturgie*
ESI	*Excavations and Surveys in Israel*
Geog.	*The Geography of Strabo* (H.L. Jones)
HE	*Ecclesiastical History*
IEJ	*Israel Exploration Journal*
INJ	*Israel Numismatic Journal*
JT	*Jerusalem Talmud*
Jos.	*Josephus*
LCL	*Loeb Classical Library*
OGIS	*Orientis Graeci Inscriptiones Selectae* (Dittenberger)
PEQ	*Palestine Exploration Quarterly*
PE	*The Preparation for the Gospel (Evangelicae Praeparationis)*
PG	*Patrologia Graeca*
PL	*Patrologia Latina*
PPTS	*The Library of the Palestine Pilgrims' Text Society*
RHCHO	*Recueils des Historiens des Croisades. Historiens Orientaux*
RPC	*Roman Provincial Coins*
SEG	*Supplementum Epigraphicum Graecum*
TLI	*Talmud of the Land of Israel*
War	*The Jewish War*

CHAPTER 1

1   II Kings 15:29. See Anson Rainey's letter to the editor, *Biblical Archaeology Review* 24:5 (1998), p.16. The use of this passage by the author of the Gospel of Matthew, in connection with the ministry of Jesus, will be discussed below.

2   II Kings 15:29.

3   II Kings 15:28.

4   Biran, 1974, pp.168–82; 1980, pp.26–51; 1981, pp.142–51.

5   I Enoch 12–16, which dates from the third century BC, shows that in Jewish apocalyptic thought the region also continued to have a special revelatory significance. See Nickelsburg, 1981, pp.583–84, 586, Testament of Levi 2–7; discussion of Matthew 16:1–19 below.

6   Dussaud, 1936, pp.283, 295 ('A l'époque séleucide Alijan s'est mué en Pan, lui aussi dieu des sources...'); Baramki, 1961, p.57. When the ancient Hebrew scriptures described the northern reaches of the Land of Promise, they measured the territory up 'unto *Baal-gad* in the valley of Lebanon under mount Hermon'. They spoke as well of *Baal-Hermon*. Some have suggested that one or both of these lords may have had an altar at the springs of Banias, thus giving the place its most ancient name. Josh. 11:17; see Josh. 12:7; 13:5; comp. Judges 3:3; I Chron. 5:23; Neubauer, 1868, p.237; Robinson, 1857, p.410. It is unlikely, however, that these names refer directly to Banias. It has likewise been suggested that the much later name that the Crusaders used, Belinas, retains such a memory – the survival of the ancient Phoenician *Bal Yaar* (Balinas), e.g. Merrill, 1889, p.155. The Crusader historian, William of Tyre, says that 'Belinas' is no more than a Crusader corruption of the name 'Paneas'. Babcock and Krey 2, 1946, p.309.

7   'Pan must represent some earlier Semitic deity, but his identity is not known', Walbank, 1957, p.523. For the persistence of the old Semitic gods, even among Greek settlers, see Avi-Yonah, 1959, pp.1–12. And for the 'repackaging' of the old gods by means of Greek iconography see Hill, 1908. The absence of ceramic evidence at the cave from pre-Hellenistic times does not by itself obviate the existence of a simple Ba'al cult there (cf. Berlin, 1999, p.43, n.5). The *absence* of a Ba'al cult at a huge spring, however, would require an explanation.

8   See Picard, 1935, pp.11–24; Dussaud, 1936, pp.283, 295.

9   Eusebius, *PE* 2.1.b.

10   Guérin, 1880, p.314 f; Milne, 1898, p.133.

11   'The coinage of Phoenicia reflects an almost complete Hellenization of the native deities along with (in the Roman Age) the reassertion of old religious elements which it is clear, had never been suppressed' (Cook, 1930, pp.155–56).

12   'And first, while they were yet in the city, the generals sent as a herald to Sparta Phidippides, an Athenian, and one, moreover, that was a runner of long distances and made that his calling. This man, as he said himself and told the Athenians, when he was in the Parthenian hills above Tegea, met with Pan; who, calling to Phidippides by name, bade him say to the Athenians, "Why is it that ye take no thought for me, that am your friend, and ere now have oft been serviceable to you, and will be so again?" This story the Athenians believed to be true, and when their state won to prosperity they founded a temple of Pan beneath the acropolis, and for that message sought the gods' favour with yearly sacrifices and torch-races.' Herodotus, *The Histories* 6.105 (Godley 3, 1928, p.259); see also Pausanias, *Description of Greece*, 1.28.4 Borgeaud, 1988. The latter work deals with the cult of Pan during the fourth and fifth centuries BC, providing an important historical background.

13   The interest in Pan continued, and was even intensified, in the Roman period. See Imhoof-Blumer and Gardner, 1964, pp.128–29, pl. Z, iii–vii, for a depiction of the cave of Pan, located to the left of the stairway leading up to the Propylaea on the Acropolis. Pan sits to the left of the cave. The coins, however, are all from the Antonine period. Dionysius of Halicarnassus, *The Roman Antiquties*, 1.32.3, claims that the Arcadians also established a Panium in archaic Rome.

14   Farnell, 1977, p.431: 'nothing more than a generative daimon who watches over the herds, ithyphallic, half-goat, half-man'. For a list of classical references to Pan cultic centres see Farnell, 1977, pp.464–68.

15   Plato, *Phaedrus* 279b–c.

16   Evelyn-White (trans.) 1959, pp.443–44.

17   Strabo, *Geog.* 17.1.10. It has been suggested that the Banias cult was set up to compete with Dan, nearby, which was still active in the third and fourth centuries BC. The reason for such competition, however, is unclear. It seems more likely that these two cult sites were complementary rather than competitive. See Ma'oz, 1993b, p.137.

18   Berlin, 1997, p.14; 1999, pp.30–31. We should be careful, however, not to push this evidence too far. It certainly attests to the introduction of new ceramic forms, and perhaps new cultic

practices, at the site. But it does not foreclose the possibility of earlier, very simple, cultic activity that may have left no artifacts behind. Furthermore, in this early transitional period, since we have no literary or inscriptional evidence, we cannot be sure whether the dedicatory vessels indicated a Hellenised Pan cult as such, or merely new, and more Hellenistic, ways of addressing the old deity of the site. At nearby Dan, the old deity was similarly Hellenised, but remained nameless, at least in the famous Greek 'Zoilus' inscription found there, which simply mentions 'the god who dwells at Dan'. This inscription proves that the cult at Dan and the one at Banias were contemporary and not successive, though the cult at the Paneion appears to have been much more modest, at least until the introduction of Roman influence. See Biran, 1981, pp.142–51; Berlin, 1997, p.27.

19 Ma'oz, 1993a, p.5; Friedland, 1997, p.25.

20 Polybius, *The Histories* 16.18.2 (Paton 1926).

21 See Holleaux, 1942, pp.321–36; Landau, 1966, pp.54–70.

22 Tzaferis, 1992.

23 Even in an urban context, like that at Athens, Pan caves were left in a natural state.

24 Bar-Kochva, 1976, p.151.

25 Polybius, *The Histories* 16.18.2–6.

26 Polybius finds considerable fault with Zeno's record. Bar-Kochva suggests, however, that in 'judging Zeno's account by Polybius' standards, his main fault was in failing to make clear that the river separated the battlefield into two arenas, and that the battle was fought simultaneously in both'. Thus, the mistakes of Zeno came from not knowing the topography, and Polybius, not knowing it either, attributed this lack of clarity to carelessness. Bar-Kochva, 1976, p.154.

27 Jerome (*ca.* 400 AD), *Commentary on Daniel* 11:15–16, catches the essence of the account, and its importance, with his summary of the battle: 'Proposing to retake Judaea and the many cities of Syria, Antiochus joined battle with Scopas, Ptolemy's general, near the sources of the Jordan near where the city now called Paneas was founded, and he put him to flight…' (Migne, *PL* 25.563; Archer, 1958, p.126).

28 Polybius, *The Histories* 28.1.2–3 of events occurring in 170–69 BC: 'At this time Antiochus was in possession of Coele Syria in Phoenicia. For ever since the father of this King Antiochus had defeated Ptolemy's generals in the battle at the Panium, all the above districts yielded obedience to the Kings of Syria' (Paton 6, 1937, p.3).

29 Hitti, 1965, p.54.

30 This type begins to appear in the second and third centuries BC, but probably existed earlier. Dar, 1993, p.18.

31 Probable references to Itureans ('Jetur') in the Hebrew Scriptures may be found in Gen. 25:15 and I Chron. 1:31; 5:19. 'After Macras one comes to the Massyas Plain [Beka'a Valley], which contains also some mountainous parts, among which is Chalcis, the acropolis, as it were, of the Massyas. The beginning of this plain is the Laodiceia near Libanus. Now all the mountainous parts are held by Itureans and Arabians, all of whom are robbers, but the people in the plains are farmers; and when the latter are harassed by the robbers at different times they require different kinds of help. These robbers use strongholds as bases of operations…' Strabo, *Geog.* 16.2.18 (H.L. Jones, 7, 1954, p.263).

32 Sullivan, 1990, pp.70–72, 206–8.

33 Schürer 1, 1972, p.564. For the extent of the Iturean hegemony see Grainger, 1991, p.150.

34 Though his forebears, including his father Mennaeus, probably already had political control, and may have ruled during the conflicts between the Hasmoneans Aristobulus I and Alexander Jannaeus.

35 Strabo, *Geog.* 16.2.18. This place is usually identified with modern Anjar, overlooking the Beka'a Valley in Lebanon. Ma'oz, forthcoming, suggests that it was nothing more than an

isolated sheikh's villa or palace not associated with a town at all. He also questions whether the principality over which Ptolemy and his successors ruled was in fact 'Iturean'.

36   Schürer 1, 1972, p.217.

37   Josephus quotes Strabo, who follows Timagenes, *Ant.* 13.318–19. This is usually understood to mean that the conversion was forced, but it may in fact have been a gradual assimilation into Judaism, as suggested by Kasher, 1988, pp.83–85.

38   The citizens of Damascus became so alarmed by this development (Chalcis dominated the road from Damascus to the coast) that they called on the Nabatean ruler Aretas III to rule over them. Coins were minted in Damascus with his portrait that proclaimed him to be a 'lover of the Greeks'.

39   This according to Kasher, 1990, p.159, based upon *Jos., Ant.* 13.94; *War* 1.105.

40   Dar, 1993, p.7.

41   Dar, 1993, p.7. For a general survey of Iturean cult sites in the Hellenistic and Roman periods see Dar, 1993.

42   Thus Grainger, 1991, p.152.

43   Dar, 1993, p.20.

44   This story is a strange one. Ptolemy sent his son Philippion to Askelon to get Mattathias Antigonus and his sisters. Philippion, however, kidnapped and married one of the sisters, Alexandra. Ptolemy then killed his son and married Alexandra himself, making her Queen of Chalcis. Perhaps he had ambitions of combining the dynasties and, with Persian help, maintaining a kingdom powerful enough to remain independent from the Romans. See *Jos., Ant.* 14.126; *War* 1.185–86, and Horvitz, 1996, pp.38–39.

45   *Jos., Ant.* 14.38–40. See Grainger, 1991, p.160.

46   Kasher, 1990, p.180.

47   His first series of coins did not have any identifying inscriptions. However, shortly after the settlement with Pompey, he minted a second series (dated 61 BC and 59 BC) bearing his name and titles. Wayne Moore, 'Coins of the Iturean Dynasts of Chalcis sub Libano', 1990 (unpublished). The coins of Ptolemy are an interesting contrast to those of the Hasmoneans. The latter family, though highly Hellenised themselves, used no human portraits on their coins and used Hebrew inscriptions, in archaic script, alongside the Greek ones. A third series of coins seems to have been minted in around 42 BC, at the time when Ptolemy helped to finance an expedition of Mattathias Antigonus against the rising threat of Herod. These show an eagle flying, along with images of Zeus, Athena, the Dioscuri and Artemis.

48   Millar, 1993, pp.17–18.

49   Millar, 1993, p.35.

50   *RPC* 1: no 4768.

51   *Jos., Ant.* 14.88–95; *War* 1.361–63; Schürer I, 1972, p.565; Sullivan, 1990, p.207.

52   *Jos., Ant.* 15.344.

53   *RPC* 1: no 4771.

54   *RPC* 1: no 4776.

55   *RPC* 1: nos 4774–75. The obverse of this type bears the head of Octavian and either 'BΠΣ' or 'ZΠ', probably referring to the Seleucid era, and thus 31/30 BC and 27/26 BC.

56   Strabo, *Geog.* 16.2.20. He describes these robbers as 'Arabians and Itureans'.

57   *Jos., War* 1.399–400; *Ant.* 15.343–48. Zenodorus was deposed by the Roman legate Varro.

58   *Jos., Ant.* 15.342–53: 'There was a certain Zenodorus who had leased the domain of Lysanias, but not being satisfied with the revenues, he increased his income by using robber bands in Trachonitis'. The people there, 'had neither city nor field of their own but only underground shelters and caves…'.

59   See Urman, 1985, pp.104–5.

60   Strabo, *Geog.* 16.2.20 (Jones, *LCL*, 7, 1957, p.263).

61   As we have seen, Zenodorus's territories had originally been much larger. See Jones, 1931, p.266.

62   It is interesting to note that nothing is said of Iturea proper or its chief city, Chalcis. Apparently these were no longer under Zenodorus's control. If not, then an intriguing question arises: where was Zenodorus's capital – somewhere in the territories of Banias or the Huleh?

63   *Jos., Ant.* 15.359–60. Cf. Dio Cassius *Roman History* 54.9.3. Jones suggests that 'this region was apparently all that was left to Zenodorus when he died…' – the original kingdom having been much larger. Jones, 1931, p.266.

64   Cf. Neubauer, 1868, pp.24, 27ff; Schürer I, 1972, p.566.

65   See Millar, 1993, p.37.

66   *Jos., Ant.* 15.359.

67   *Jos., Ant.* 15.360–61.

68   *Jos., Ant.* 15.363. Such a project would presumably required special permission, not only from the emperor, but from the senate as well. This was at least the case in Asia Minor. Price, 1984, pp.66–67.

69   *Jos., Ant.* 15.364.

70   *Jos., War* 1.404–6. The context is a list of Herod's building projects. This passage is immediately preceded by a description of the Temple of Augustus in Sebaste.

71   Thompson, 1846, p.189. 'Probably the ruins of Herod's temple and other ancient buildings have entirely choked up the entrance of the cave; and if the vast mass of rocks and rubbish, through which the water now bursts out, were removed, we should find the "cavern abrupt, and prodigiously deep, and full of still water." And probably it might be found arched over, in order to form the floor of the temple. Perhaps upon this arch are heaped together the broken rocks that now cover the bottom of the cave. This supposition seems necessary, in order to explain the various accounts of ancient historians.' The issues connected with locating the Augusteum itself before the cave are discussed below.

72   See Ma'oz, 1990, p.59: 'A deep natural cavity containing boulders, some of which are set into a travertine fill, is located south of the perpendicular wall, near its juncture with the niched wall. In the Roman period a subterranean vault, part of which has collapsed, was built between the boulders.' See also Ma'oz, 1993b, p.140.

73   Ma'oz, 1994–99, pp.97–99.

74   Josephus may not have known about the channel itself (cf. his ignorance of the man-made tunnel through which the Siloam 'spring' was conducted to the surface) but he did know that there was a pool of water inside the cave. S. Gibson has published a cave spring at Sataf where the water was gathered into a channel and collected into a pool below. He thinks the installation is Roman and may serve as a parallel to Banias. Gibson et al., 1991, illus. p.32, description pp.41–42, 49.

75   Perhaps 'light coloured polished local limestone' (Fischer and Stein, 1994, p.85). Archaeological evidence does allow for the possibility that marble may have been used for 'wall revetments.' Fischer and Stein, 1994, p.80, n.8. Roller, 1998, pp.190–92, takes Josephus literally, despite the lack of archaeological evidence, claiming that Herod would not have skimped on a Temple of Augustus by using something less than marble. But we have the evidence of Sebaste and Caesarea Maritima to the contrary.

76   Meshorer 2, 1982, p.88, thinks Agrippa II gave a Pan statue, depicted on one of his coins (see below), to a local temple, though as yet there is no evidence for the existence of such a temple during the first century AD. The existing niches, inscriptions and coins related to the Pan cult mostly date from the third century and seem to represent a renewal and restructuring of the cult in response to Christianity and in line with the 'reformed paganism' of that time. A semi-circular colonnade and cult grotto associated with Pan appear first on the coins of Diadumenian (217 AD). Other than the name of the place, evidence for Pan-worship there

before the third century is very limited. Pan playing the flute appears on coins from the time of Marcus Aurelius, when the mint was first reopened, and is part of the first issue of the new mint. This new Pan statue may represent a significant break with the Canaanite roots of the cult. See discussion below.

77 Suetonius, *Div. Aug.* 52 ('he would not accept one [a temple] even in a province save jointly in his own name and that of Rome'). See Schürer 2, 1972, pp.34–35.

78 *Jos., Ant.* 15.339; *War* 1.414.

79 Friedland, 1997, Cat. 1.

80 *Jos., Ant.* 15.328–29.

81 For the policy of vassals to encourage the emperor cult, see Suetonius, *Div. Aug.* 59–60.

82 Urman, 1985, pp.117, 119–20.

83 Urman, 1985, pp.104–5.

84 The earliest designation of the temple complex at Banias was probably 'Caesarea at the Paneion', changed to 'Caesarea Philippi' at the time of the 'founding' of the city by Herod's son Philip. See below.

85 *Jos., Ant.* 15.339.

86 See Kahn, 1996 for general description.

87 *Jos., Ant.* 15.298.

88 Barag, 1993, pp.4–8; Crowfoot, Kenyon and Sukenik, 1942; Reisner, Fisher and Lyon, 1924; Hamilton, 1936, pp.46–47.

89 Parrot, 1955, p.83. See Fig. 28. Cf. Watzinger 2, 1935, p.50. See also Barag, 1993, pp.3–18.

90 Particularly useful parallels are the temples to Augustus Fortuna in Pompeii and to Roman and Augustus in Pula (Croatia), both of which were constructed at approximately the same time as the temple near the Paneion, and seem to have been very similar to Herod's Augusteum.

91 Notably the temple to the Jewish god in Jerusalem, and the temple at Siah in Trachonitis, dedicated to Ba'al Shamin. Wilson 4, 1884: p.248; Le Bas-Waddington III, no 2364=*OGIS* 415. These two temples, however, represent a different policy on Herod's part, namely identity with and support for the native religious sensitivities. They rise out of very different motivations than do the temples to Augustus.

92 Meshorer 2, 1982, pp.244–46, pls 7–8.

93 Designs depicted in the pediment vary: the first in the series has an object which may be a floral design (a lily?) or, more likely, an eagle; most have a dot, often used to symbolise decoration too complex to be shown on a small coin, and examples exist with a branch, a 'V', and an 'L'. On some examples the pediment is surrounded with an extra border, a sort of triangle inside a triangle. On some issues the lines of the roof of the building extend upward, forming a 'V'. On one coin, Meshorer 2, 1982, pl 7:2, some sort of rectangular object stands at the same apex. In general, it appears that this particular coin is the most detailed of the series and, as the first, may be the most accurate representation of the actual temple. It also depicts an iron grille guarding the steps up into the temple, a common feature of such buildings, and apparently also present in the temple at Pompeii (Fig. 10).

94 Though it must be admitted that similar tetrastyle temples are common in the period, e.g., a remarkably similar temple appears on a coin of Sidon dated 9/8 BC (*BMC* 164). Sidon is very close to Banias. Might there be some connection between the minting of this coin and the construction of the Augusteum at Banias?

95 Meshorer 2, 1982, pls 7:3, 4a, 5, 5a etc.

96 An exception is the shield-like object appearing between the columns on a coin whose obverse depicts Augustus and Livia together, which is most likely a cult object of some sort. See Meshorer 2, 1982, pls 7:6.

97 In Nicolaus's *The Life of Augustus*, apparently written during the period Herod was building his three temples to the emperor, the author reports that 'Men gave him this name [Augustus]

in view of his claim to honour; and, scattered over islands and continents, through city and tribe, they revere him by building temples and by sacrificing to him, thus requiting him for his great virtue and acts of kindness toward themselves' (Hall, 1923, p.3).

98 See pp.29ff.

99 Dittenberger, *OGIS* 532. This oath was 'sworn in country districts at the *Sebastos* and at Neapolis in the *Sebasteon*, at the altar of the *Sebastos*' (Millar and Segal, 1984, p.55).

100 Ma'oz, 1991, p.59; 1994–99, p.91.

101 Dionysius of Halicarnassas *The Roman Antiquities* 1.32.3 (Cary 1, 1937, p.105).

102 Dionysius of Halicarnassas *The Roman Antiquities* 1.79.8 (Cary 1, 1937, p.267).

103 Agrippa II apparently even provided a statue of Pan for the cult (see below).

104 Ma'oz, 1994–99, p.91; Friedland, 1997, p.27. Dating is based on a lamp fragment, the *opus quadratum*, and the style of the niches, which resemble those from a similar period at Jericho.

105 These difficulties can be illustrated by the discussion of this building in Roller, 1998, pp.191–92. Maintaining that tetrastyle temples were of necessity small and 'merely chapels' he doubts whether the temple depicted on the coins of Philip is historically accurate, since 'Herod would not have skimped on a Temple of Augustus'. But then, faced with the cramped situation in front of the cave, he suggests that 'the limited space at the grotto, and the need to incorporate the temple into an existing area, may have meant this structure, however elaborate, was more modest in size than Herod's other temples' and finally concedes that the site may have actually been elsewhere (pp.160–61). In fact, tetrastyle temples could be quite large, provided that the columns were also large. The temple of Sul Minerva at Bath in England is an interesting example. Another is the temple of Hercules in Amman (ancient Philadelphia). The latter, built in the mid-second century, was tetrastyle, but the columns are 10 metres long and 'consist of five to six drums weighing an average of 7 tons each, so the foundation must be restored to a condition in which it can hold columns of 35 to 40 tons each' (Russell, 1991, p.3). This temple could hardly be described as 'merely a chapel'! Furthermore, tetrastyle temples to Augustus were built in other parts of the empire, e.g. at Pompeii, Pola, and numerous other places.

106 In Sebaste, where a long-standing sanctuary to Kore was located, the Augusteum was established alongside, but not in the place of the older cult.

107 *Jos., War* 1.404.

108 'If the imperial cult was an attempt by the city to find a position for the ruler, it is perfectly fitting that the physical expression of this position would be within the civic space rather than in some separate area outside the city.' Price, 1984, pp.144–45.

109 Overman, Olive and Nelson, 2003, pp.46–47.

110 See Netzer, 1977.

111 Quoted by Urman, 1985, p.135.

112 Netzer's report was published in *Hadashot Archeologiot*.

CHAPTER 2

1 *Jos., Ant.* 17.319; *War* 2.95; cf. Luke 3:1.

2 Philip's control of the area was more successful in the territories of Banias and Trachonitis than in the mountains to the north and west (which perhaps were not his responsibility), where the Iturean population continued to cause trouble. The famous Quirinius inscription recounts a battle between them and the Roman troops in 6 AD. 'Full scale military operations were therefore still going on in southern Syria in the early years AD, some seventy years after the formation of the province [of Syria]' (Millar, 1993, p.35).

3 Kokkinos, 1998, p.236, thinks that Cleopatra was actually of Syro-Phoenician stock, and this may have had something to do with Philip's selection to rule over the Iturean territory.

Though evidence is lacking for this thesis, it is intriguing to imagine that Philip may have shared an ethnicity with many of his subjects – contributing to his longevity and popularity.

4   *Jos., Ant.* 18.136–37. Kokkinos, 1998, p.237, questions Josephus's accuracy on this point, since Philip would have been around 40 years old at the time of the marriage. He thinks Philip was married instead to Salome's mother Herodias who had divorced her first husband ('Herod') and who then married Antipas after Philip's death. It is somewhat problematic that Josephus could have been so confused on this matter, given his close association with the Herodian family only one generation removed from Philip. Kasher thinks that Herodias had an affair with Antipas 'while still married to his brother' – Philip the Tetrarch (Kasher, 1988, p.178), joining those who believe that one of the sons of Herod the Great was a phantom. Here is Josephus's statement: '…Herodias was married to Herod, the son of Herod the Great by Mariamme, daughter of Simon the high priest. They had a daughter Salome, after whose birth Herodias, taking it into her head to flout the way of our fathers, married Herod, her husband's brother by the same father, who was tetrarch of Galilee; to do this she parted from a living husband. Her daughter Salome was married to Philip, Herod's son and tetrarch of Trachonitis. When he died childless, Aristobulus, the son of Agrippa's brother Herod, married her.' *Jos., Ant.* 16.137 (Feldman, *LCL* 8, 1981, p.93).

5   The scope of this diversity can be seen in the first epigraphical record of Philip, other than his coins, a Nabatean inscription from a temple at Siah, on the western slopes of the Hauran. Found by Butler in 1909, the inscription is cut on a pedestal shaped like an altar with a capital of lions' heads and wreaths. It reads:

'In the year 33 [or possibly read 23] of our lord Philippos;
there was made by Witr son of Budar (?) and Kaisu son of
Sudai and Hann'el son of Masak'el and Nuna (?) son of Garm,
this altar of the statue of Galis the son of Banat (?).
'An'am son of Asb (was) the sculptor. Peace!'

Offord, 1919, p.83; Littmann, 1914, no 101; photo Littmann, III. 12, p.78; drawing, p.78.

6   Meshorer, 1984–85, p.40. This dating system survived for several centuries, long after the memories of the Herodian Dynasty were dimmed.

7   *Jos., War* 2.167–69.

8   Rosenberger 1, 1972, p.25 (Nero as 'founder').

9   Rosenberger 1, 1972, p.1.

10   Rosenberger 2, 1975, p.78 (Antoninus Pius, 138–61 AD, as 'founder'); p.8, (Septimius Severus, 193–211 AD and Caracalla, 198–217 AD, as 'founders').

11   *Jos., War* 2.167–69.

12   Meshorer 2, 1982, pp.244–45, nos 1–6a.

13   *Jos., Ant.* 18.26–28.

14   Meshorer 2, 1982, p.49.

15   Meshorer, 1982, Vol. 2, pl. 8:11; Suppl. 3:1; and pl. 8:12. See p.278 for dating of the coin.

16   Several scholars have recently attempted to identify this series with the founding of Bethsaida rather than Banias. See Gitler, 1990, pp.101ff. The suggestion is from Sh. Qedar. See Kindler, 1989; Gitler, 1990, pp.101–2; Kuhn and Arav, 1995, pp.77–106. This seems highly unlikely given the very bad relationship between Livia and Tiberius during the precise time when the coin series was issued. In fact, the type depicting Livia, calling her 'ΙΟΥΛΙΑ ϹΕΒΑϹΤΗ', should perhaps be dated according to the imperial era rather than Philip's, making its minting date fall more than a decade earlier, when her relationship to the emperor was still a positive one. If so, this particular coin is not connected with the celebration of the founding of Caesarea Philippi at all. Kokkinos, 1998, p.238, thinks that Bethsaida was founded at the same time as Caesarea Philippi, 'by early 2 BCE at the latest'. This conclusion is based on the identification of 'Julia' as the wicked daughter of Augustus, who was in fact banished in that year. After her

disgrace, the town quickly 'revert[ed] to what it was called originally – thus known to the Gospels unanimously as 'Bethsaida' (Kokkinos, 1998, p.238).

17 Hamilton, 1936, p.47.

18 Hamilton, 1936, p.47.

19 Kasher, 1990, p.220. This mixture of cultures proved volatile later, and finally resulted in violence in the early days of the Jewish Revolt. Herod established two colonies to police the area east of Banias, one in Trachonitis (el Lejah) (*Jos., Ant.* 16.285), and the other in Bathyra in Batanaea (*Jos., Ant.* 17.24–17.5). The latter consisted of Babylonian Jews and, Philip, the grandson of the founder, became Agrippa II's general (*Jos., Ant.* 17.31). See Gracey, 1986, pp.311–23.

20 For evidence of buildings around the Augusteum at Sebaste that seem to have been connected to the imperial cult see Parrot, 1955, p.83 and Fig. 28. Barag, however, thinks these structures formed a part of the royal palace (Barag, 1993).

21 Harper, 1928, pp.13ff.

22 *Jos., Ant.* 18.37–38.

23 Mark 8:27.

24 See below.

25 Whigham, and Jay, 1975, Epigram 54. The epigram is 'doubtless based on some statue of Pan ('in this town'), Note 54.

26 Robert, 1948, p.11. Compare a much later inscription (359–60 AD) by a governor of Achaia, Ampelius, on the Island of Aegina, in a private sanctuary to the Muses. Under a statue of Pan: 'no longer do I delight in gamboling across the hills with my wax-bound pipes, nor in caves, nor under the dense foliage of trees; I no longer love Echo, nor do I take pleasure in the goatherds. Yearning for the magnificent works of a man of justice, Ampelius, I come leaping, delighted in a place where the Muses, enchanted by the plane trees and bubbling brooks, have made their abode.' Chuvin, 1990, p.5.

27 Kasher apparently believes that the city existed even before Herod's reign. During Cleopatra's day, he says, 'the expressly Iturean areas were concentrated in the northern Golan Heights around the city of Paneas'. Kasher, 1988, p.144.

28 Rufinus, (345–411 AD), calls the Hellenistic Jewish scholar Aristobulus, one of the translators of the Septuagint (whose writings date *ca.*176–70 BC) 'Aristobulus of Paneas'. However, this designation, which would certainly prove the existence of the city in the Hellenistic period, 'clearly results from Rufinus' misunderstanding of the textual tradition' (Holladay, 1995, pp.75, 118, 202).

29 Millar, 1993, p.355, noting the prominence of gladiatorial combats and wild-beast hunts, 'some of the relatively few Roman imports into the popular culture of the Greek East'.

30 *Jos., War* 2.167–69; 9.1.

31 *Jos., Ant.* 18.26–28.

32 *Contra* Kindler, 1971, pp.161–63. See photos pl. 32B, 32C. Kindler is correct in identifying the portrait on the coin shown in pl. 32A as Philip. The coin features the temple on the reverse. A. Reifenberg, who first published the coin (Reifenberg, 1950–51, p.176, pl. 32:2) did not identify the portrait as belonging to Philip, and wondered why it bore Philip's name.

33 *Jos., War* 3.509–15.

34 This designation is interesting. Trachonitis lies east of the Panion-Huleh region and represents a very different cultural *milieu* than that of the much more Hellenised areas near the Jordan and around the Sea of Galilee. A Nabatean inscription mentioning the 'Lord Philippos' was found at Siah, on the western slopes of the Hauran. Offord, 1919, p.83; Littmann, 1914, p.78.

35 Urman, 1985, p.49: 'The capacity of Birket Ram is about 3 million cubic metres, while the flow of the Banias reaches about one hundred eighty million cubic metres annually and therefore, if Birket Ram were really the source of the Banias River, it would be empty after a week'.

36 *Jos., Ant.* 18.6.

37 Kokkinos dates his death as occurring 'around September CE 33'. Kokkinos, 1998, p.237.

38 *Jos., Ant.* 18.106–8.

39 So Kokkinos, who further suggests that the monument may have been built in imitation of Augustus's Mausoleum at Rome. Kokkinos, 1998, p.238, and note 121.

40 See Meshorer, 1990–91.

41 Burnett, 1987, pp.25–28; Schwartz, 1990, p.73.

42 Agrippa's daughter, probably born in the same year, was named Drusilla as well. Kokkinos thinks the name commemorates Agrippa's son Drusus, who may have died at this time. Kokkinos, 1998, p.277. But the name may simply be an extension of Agrippa's obeisance to the Roman imperial house.

43 Meshorer, 1990–91, pl. 26:1.

44 Meshorer, 1990–91, pl. 26:2. The coin is dated LB (year two=38 AD).

45 Meshorer, 1991, pl. 26:3. This coin is highly reminiscent of the one minted by Philip to honour Tiberius's mother, discussed above.

46 Meshorer, 1991, pl. 26:4.

47 *Jos., Ant.* 18.252; *War* I2.181–83.

48 Meshorer 2, 1982, pl. 9:2, 3, 4, 7; Meshorer, 1991, pp.5–8.

49 This conclusion is based upon the fact that an example of the third coin in this series (depicting Agrippa himself) was found in Banias, making it likely, given the rarity of all the coins in this series, and the tendency of such issues not to stray far from their place of origins, that it came from the Banias mint. The coin was published by Meyshan, 1963, pp.66–67, pl.IV:15, but dated incorrectly as AD 44/45 (p.66).

50 *Jos., Ant.* 17.237; 19.274–19.275; *War* 2.181; 2.215–7; Dio Cassius, *Roman History* 59.8.2.

51 The precise city from which his various coin issues came remains an open question. See Meshorer 2, 1982, pp.55–57.

52 *Jos., Ant.* 19.131.

53 *Jos., Ant.* 19.350–51. Had he lived, he might have found himself in serious trouble with Claudius, however, who was much displeased with his strengthening of the defences of Jerusalem without Roman authorisation (*Ant.* 19.326).

54 Acts 12:1–10; 19–23.

55 *Jos., Ant.* 19.362 (Feldman, *LCL* 9, 1981, p.387). Portraits of the teen-aged Agrippa II may be seen on several coins minted by his father: Meshorer, 1991, pl. 28:2 (minted in 38 AD); pl. 26:8 (minted in AD 40/41); pl. 28:13 (minted in AD 42/43).

56 *Jos., War* 2.223; *Ant.* 20.104. The sons of Berenice were named Bernicianus and Hyrcanus.

57 Meshorer, 1990–91, pl. 32:1–3. See also *RPC* 1, pp.699–70, nos 4842–44.

58 The extensive kingdom of Agrippa I, Banias included, had been attached to the province of Syria. Tacitus, *The Annals* 12.23.

59 *Jos., Ant.* 20.138; *War* 2.247: 'When he had completed the twelfth year of his reign, he granted to Agrippa the tetrarchy of Philip together with Batanaea, adding thereto Trachonitis and Lysanias's former tetrarchy of Abila; but he deprived him of Chalcis, after he had ruled it for four years.'

60 Meshorer, 1990–91, pl. 31:4.

61 Meshorer, 1990–91, pl. 31:5. See also *RPC* 1, pp.669–70 and nos 4845–46.

62 *Jos., Ant.*, 19.357; *War* 2.253.

63 *Jos., Ant.*, 20.139.

64 *Jos., Ant.*, 20.159.

65 *Jos., War*, 3.514.

66 This conclusion is drawn by Kasher, based on the fact that Jews could not have been regular citizens of a pagan *polis*, but rather, would have been recognised as permanent residents, protected by the Tetrarch, and allowed the privilege of keeping ancestral laws. Thus they

formed a group, the 'Jews of Caesarea' distinguished from the pagan population, the 'Syrians of Caesarea'. Kasher, 1990, p.279–80; cf. *Jos., Life*, 52–53,59,61,74.

67   *Jos., Life*, 52–53; 61; cf. *War* 2.481–83.

68   E.g. *Jos., War* 2.310–14, 333.

69   See Tzaferis, 1992, p.8. It remains a curious fact that the temple is dropped from Banias's numismatic iconography, unless it appears re-dedicated once again as the temple of Zeus on the coins of the second and third centuries. If the temple recently excavated at Omrit is the Augusteum, it was certainly rebuilt and enlarged, possibly in the second century, though whether it no longer served the imperial cult cannot yet be determined. Overman, Olive, and Nelson, 2003, p.46. If it was in fact reconsecrated to Nero in 61 AD it may have been transformed, or disappeared, along with the name Neronias, as a result of the *damnatio memoriae* imposed on Nero following his death.

70   *Jos., Ant.* 20.211–12 (Feldman, *LCL* 20, 1981, p.113). This is probably the time of the famous inscription found in Beirut (ancient Berytus) naming 'Queen Berenice daughter of the great King Agrippa and King Agrippa her brother' as the donors of 'marbles and columns' in a building 'which their ancestor Herod had made'. See below.

71   De Beausobre noted this centuries ago (1727) in his *Dissertation sur la Statue du Panéade*, suggesting that Agrippa set up a number of statues to decorate the area 'near the fountain' (i.e., the spring beneath the Cave of Pan).

72   Acts 25–26. Earlier, says the author of Acts, Paul had appeared before the governor Felix and his wife, Agrippa's sister Drusilla (Acts 24). In view of the scandalous nature of that marriage, one can imagine what Paul must have said to the couple regarding 'righteousness, self-control and the judgment to come' (v. 25).

73   *Jos., Ant.* 20:211: 'At this time King Agrippa enlarged Caesarea Philippi, and renamed it Neronias in honour of Nero'. This was during the time when Albinus was the procurator of Judaea. Kokkinos, 1998, p.323.

74   Kokkinos (1998, p.323) suggests this was 'almost certainly as a response to Nero's celebration of the first shaving of his beard, followed by the institution of the "Neronia"'. See Suetonius, *Nero* 12.3–4.

75   Juvenal, *Satire* 6: 156–60 (Ramsey, *LCL*, 1950, p.95). This was probably written during the reign of Hadrian and shows the wide-ranging and long lasting fame of both Agrippa and Berenice among Rome's elite. The reference to bare feet is probably based on Josephus's account of how Berenice once offered sacrifice in Jerusalem with bare feet and shaved head (*Jos., War* 2.313–14).

76   Polemon was interested in the union 'chiefly on account of her riches' – an interest sufficiently powerful to cause him to agree to be circumcised (*Jos., Ant.* 20.146).

77   It is interesting to note that Josephus says this appointment was made jointly by Agrippa and Berenice (*Life* 49). This statement provides further confirmation that Berenice held a position of power and influence within the little kingdom, as well as in the wider Roman world.

78   *Jos., Life*, 52–53.

79   And here we must make allowance for Josephus's tendency to inflate numbers.

80   *Jos., Life* 46–48; *Ant.* 17.23f, 31.

81   See Kasher, 1990, p.279.

82   *Jos., Life*, 52–53.

83   Not to be confused with the better known Ecbatana in Persia, this is the name of a fort in Batanaea established by Herod the Great and manned by Jews from Babylonia transferred there for that purpose.

84   *Jos., Life*, 54–58.

85   *Jos., Life*, 61; cf. *War* 2.483.

86   Kasher, 1990, p.279.

87   *Jos., Life*, 74ff.

88   Kasher, 1990, p.28. The word is 'συγκεκλεισμένους'.

89   *Jos., Life*, 74ff.

90   *Jos., Life*, 74–76.

91   Kasher, 1990, p.28.

92   Meshorer, 1990–91, pp.113–14.

93   In this same year (66/67 AD), Agrippa II visited Egypt to congratulate Tiberius Julius Alexander on his appointment as Prefect of Egypt (*Jos., War* 2.309).

94   See Meshorer, Vol. 2, p.74 regarding the complex issues involved in dating these coins, due to his use of multiple eras.

95   Meshorer, 1984–85, pl. 7:C; 1982, pl. 11:5.

96   Meshorer, 1984–85, pl. 7:D; 1982, pl. 11:6; cf. Philip's similar coin above.

97   Meshorer 2, 1982, p.74; pl. 11:4–4a.

98   Meshorer, 1964–65, p.39; pl. 7.B; and 1982, Vol. 2, pp.73–74, 250: 1–3, pl. 11:1–3. The later date seems now to be the favoured one. See Stein, 1984–85, pp.9–11.

99   On the expense of hosting a Roman army, and the potential for financial disaster accompanying such a visit in a provincial city see Garnsey, 1988, pp.247–48, 252–53.

100   *Jos., War* 3.443–44.

101   Evidence for a temple and cult of Zeus is found on the coins of all the second- and early-third-century emperors minted in Banias. See Meshorer, 1984–85, pp.41–42.

102   Kasher, 1990, p.304. For identification of Pan with the Jewish deity, see Hengel 1, 1974, p.164.

103   For this theory see Sullivan, 1953, pp.69–70. Sullivan notes that 'the persons supporting Vespasian were closely connected by ties of blood, marriage or intimate friendship'. He even suggests that 'the prime conspirator was the beautiful Jewish princess Berenice'. The key to Vespasian's success was Egypt, and Egypt's governor was Tiberius Julius Alexander, a close friend of the Herodian family whose brother Marcus had once been Berenice's husband (p.67). Thus, though the sources do not explicitly say so, Berenice may well have been the main go-between in the negotiations between Vespasian and Alexander that enabled Vespasian to take the throne. See *Jos., War*, 4.616–20; 5.44–46; Tacitus, *The Histories*, 2:74. 'The second element in the Flavian party was what may be called an Oriental group, led by that powerful prefect of Egypt, the apostate Jew Ti. Julius Alexander. It owed its influence in no small measure to Julia Berenice, the sister of Agrippa II, who had for a short time been Alexander's sister-in-law (Crook, 1951, p.163).

104   Tacitus, *The Histories* 2.2 (Moore, *LCL*, 1925, p.163). Tacitus doubts this, however; 'the young man's heart was not insensible to Berenice, but his feelings towards her proved no obstacle to action'.

105   *Jos., War* 7.23–24.

106   *Jos., War* 7.37–38. These activities would seem to require a large amphitheatre, but thus far excavators have not found this facility.

107   Kasher, 1990, p.305.

108   Schürer 1, 1977, p.477.

109   Pliny, *Hist. Nat.* 5.15.71. Tacitus, probably writing after Agrippa's death (c. 105–08 AD), does not mention the city, but obviously knows the place. See *The Histories* 5.6.

110   His kingdom, which was bestowed upon him by Claudius, was extended by Nero, and still more by Vespasian (Photius, *Biblioteca*;. Freese (trans.) 1920:1, p.29). See also Alon, 1980:1, pp.76, 150–51. Josephus (*War* 3.57–58) describes the kingdom thus: '... beginning at Mount Libanus and the sources of the Jordan, (it) extends in breath (from north to south) to the lake of Tiberias, and in length (from east to west) from a village called Arpha (unidentified, but to the east of Trachonitis) to Julias (Bethsaida-Julias on the Sea of Galilee)...' Kokkinos, 1998, p.331, describes it as including 'the districts of Abilene (extending over the Anti-Lebanon), the

Hermon, Panias, Ulatha (perhaps separated from Panias), Gaulanitis, Batanaea, Trachonitis, and northern Auranitis'. To this might be added, at the time of its greatest extent, parts of northern Galilee (including the city of Tiberias) and, perhaps, even Sepphoris.

111 Agrippa minted a coin in this year in the city of Tiberias that seems to commemorate the Roman victory over the Jews. Dated ET IE ('Year 15'=75 AD). It pictures a palm branch and prominently features the words 'the Victory of Augustus'. See Qedar, 1989, pp.33–36; Meshorer, 1990–91, p.110, pl. 29:A. This may have been an attempt to create good feelings on Berenice's behalf as she came to Rome.

112 Dio, *Roman History* 65.15.3–5 (Cary, *LCL* 8, 1925, p.291). Her powerful position in Rome may be seen in Suetonius, *Titus* 7:7; and Quintilian, *The Orator's Education* 4.1.19.

113 'Titus after becoming ruler committed no act of murder or of amatory passion, but showed himself upright, though plotted against, and self-controlled, though Berenice came to Rome again.' Dio, *Roman History* 66.18.1 (Cary, *LCL* 8, 1925, p.297).

114 Suetonius, *Titus* 7:2.

115 Meshorer 2, 1982, pl. 13:18, 20.

116 Maltiel-Gerstenfeld, 1980, pp.25–26.

117 So Kokkinos, 1998, p.330; Jordan, 1974, p.222.

118 'It can by no means be taken that Berenice's second dismissal was intended as final. Possibly only Titus' death dealt the last crushing blow to her ambitions. Of her own death nothing is recorded; she must have been a bitterly disappointed woman' (Crook, 1951, p.172). Some might say that the silence of the record, given her proactive approach to life, is evidence that she did not live long after her return to Banias. If she were alive, surely we would have heard something from her. But we have no evidence beyond the silence itself. Nor do we know what happened to Berenice's two sons who should have had some claim on the throne in Chalcis, which had been bestowed on the young Agrippa II. Their ultimate fate, and whether or not they were given consideration as potential heirs to the throne of their uncle Agrippa II, remain mysteries.

119 So Meshorer 2, 1982, pp.82–83. He further suggests that these coins, which bear Latin inscriptions, may have been minted at a new place, not in Banias.

120 Meshorer, 1984–85, p.39; 2 1982, p.256, pl. 15:39,41. Meshorer dates these coins to 88 AD. The immensely complicated question of the dating of Agrippa II's coins, and of the various eras used on his coins, very much complicates the dating of these two issues. Alla Kushnir-Stein has suggested that the relevant era in this case is 49 AD, and thus the date of issue 75/76 AD (private correspondence). If so, these coins may commemorate a donation made at that time, or even an earlier donation made at the time when Agrippa was beautifying the city soon after his arrival there several decades before (*War* 3.514; *Ant.* 20.211–12). Along the walls of the approach to the cave of Pan, excavated by Ma'oz, are found a number of niches for statues. Since these appear to be dated to the first century, they may have been designed to hold these and other similar works given to the city by various benefactors. See Ma'oz, 1993b.

121 Meshorer, 1984–85, pl. 7:F.

122 See Wycherley, 1978, Fig. 50, p.173, Travlos, 1971, Fig. 386–87, p.296.

123 Meshorer 2, 1982, p.88.

124 *Mishna Aboda Zarah* 3.1: 'All images are forbidden since they are worshiped once a year. So R. Meir. But the Sages say, Only that is forbidden as bears in its hand a staff or a bird or a sphere. Rabban Simeon B. Gamaliel says, That which bears aught in its hand' (Danby, 1933, p.440).

125 Meshorer 2, 1982, pl. 7:G.

126 Meshorer 2, 1982, p.89.

127 Meshorer, 1984–85, p.39.

128 A famous inscription was found in Beirut stating that Berenice and Agrippa had decorated a building of their ancestor Herod with marble. Lauffray, 1944–45, pp.55–56, believes this is

referring to the huge civic basilica (100 m long) that stood next to the Forum in Beirut. The inscription was found lying next to this structure. A drawing of this inscription may be seen in Roller, 1998, p.249.

129 Millar, 1993, p.91.
130 Freese, 1920, p.29.
131 This complicated issue cannot be discussed in detail here. Complete discussions of the state of the question, with the evidence for the trustworthiness of Photius' account, can be found in Schwartz, 1992, pp.243ff.; and Kokkinos, 1996, pp.338–39 and especially, pp.396ff.
132 Meshorer 2, 1982, p.90. If coins dated 'Year 35' are based on the era beginning in 61 AD they should be dated *ca*.96 AD. However, Alla Kushnir-Stein has suggested these may actually be based on an earlier era, and thus date to the early 80s (private correspondence).
133 See Seyrig, 1965, pp.31–34.
134 Especially important is a lead weight from Tiberias which apparently proves that he ruled there for over 43 years (with an era in that city which began in 55/56), and thus until at least 98 AD. See Qedar, 1986–87, pp.29–33. Unfortunately this weight is now missing, and cannot be rechecked to confirm the late date.
135 See Schwartz, 1992, pp.243–82.
136 Tacitus, *The Annals* 12.23. Cf. *Jos., Ant.* 16.28.
137 Only Nabataea remained, and it would also be absorbed some six year later in 106 AD.
138 Millar, 1993, p.64.

CHAPTER 3

1   Solinus, *Collectanea Rerum Memorabilium* 35:1 (Mommsen, 1864, p.161; Stern [trans.] 1980:2, p.419). Solinus is likely only quoting Pliny, however.
2   Porphyry, *Adversus Christianos*, as quoted by Jerome.
3   These coins are conveniently catalogued in Meshorer, 1984–85, pp.37–58. Some additional types have come to light since this article was written.
4   Most of these have been collected by Benjamin Isaac and will be published in the forthcoming excavation report edited by Zvi Ma'oz.
5   Seven of the nine stylistically dateable sculptures that were found by Ma'oz at the Pan Sanctuary come from the second century AD, and thus 'the stylistic evidence corresponds to the epigraphic evidence in revealing a peak in sculptural dedication during this period' (Friedland, 1997, p.70).
6   Isaac, in Ma'oz, forthcoming, nos 4 and 13.
7   Ma'oz, 1994–99, pp.92–93.
8   Isaac, in Ma'oz, forthcoming, no 8.
9   We have already noted Josephus's ambiguous reference to Vespasian's act of worship at Banias during his military campaign in the area, in which he 'gave thanks to God' (see above).
10 Isaac, in Ma'oz, forthcoming. See also Borgeaud, 1988, pp.89–96.
11 Seyrig, 1965, pp.32–33.
12 Isaac, in Ma'oz, forthcoming, no 7a. Isaac is able to identify the cohort as the Thracian, despite the fact that only the initial 'T' remains on the inscription.
13 Isaac, in Ma'oz, forthcoming. See also Russell, 'A Roman Military Diploma…', 1995, pp.118–20 for the later activities of the *Cohors I Miliaria Thracum*.
14 Overman, Olive, and Nelson, 2003, pp.46–47.
15 See Tzaferis's excavation report (forthcoming). Interesting parallels, including the conversion of large halls into baths in the second century palace at Gortyn, are surveyed in Burrell, 1996 (see especially p.237).

16 Birley, 1997, pp.230–34; Holum, 1997.

17 Russell, 'A Roman Military Diploma… ', 1995, pp.76–77.

18 Ridder, 1906, pp.39–40, pls 15–17. The bust appeared on the art market in Germany in 1983 and was re-published by Meyer, 1991, pp.99–100, Pls. 88:4–5, 89. It probably dates between the years 130 and 138 AD and may have been carved in Antioch. Friedland, 1997, pp.243–44.

19 Philostorgius *HE* 7.3, as epitomised by Photius (Walford, 1855, p.475).

20 Eusebius, *HE* 7.18 (Williamson, 1965, pp.301–2). He simply locates the statue 'in the city…at the gates of her house'.

21 The coin may be seen in Hettger, 1988, p.14; Meshorer, 1989, p.22. This excessively rare coin is in the collection of the National Museum of Naples. See discussion and analysis in Toynbee, 1934, pp.119–21. Toynbee suggests that the coin commemorates the founding of Aelia Capitolina (p.121, note 1) and specifically represents 'the actual visit of the Emperor to the province and the ceremonies connected therewith'. What is represented on the coin, therefore, is 'Judaea's reception, as the Emperor's gift and as a result of his personal visit, of the Roman colony of Aelia Capitolina and the creation thereby of a new centre of urban life and of all the amenities of Graeco-Roman civilisation which the founding of a colony implied' (p.120). For several examples of other types of coins with the same theme, see Toynbee, 1934, pl. V: 1–5; pl. XVI: 16–21; pl. XVII: 1–14.

22 On the other hand, some cities in the area appeared to have commemorated the advent of Hadrian with coin issues produced locally, but which, not issuing from the imperial mint, used more subtle themes. This seems to be the case with Tiberias and Aelia Capitolina, and possibly also in Gaba and Askelon.

23 Waddington, 1870, no 1891, no 1892.

24 Waddington, 1870, no 1892. Isaac suggests the word 'ἀνέθηκε' may have been used in the sense of 'suppliant' (in Ma'oz, forthcoming). Friedland suggests that one of the statue fragments found by Ma'oz, a torso, may have come from this very shrine. Friedland, 1997, p.66, Cat. 11.

25 This object is identified by Meshorer as a tree trunk, but on clear examples of the coin it is obviously an altar, possibly with flames leaping up on it.

26 Meshorer, 1984–85, nos 5, 5a, 8, 10, 10a, 10b, 15, 19, 28, 29, 30, 37(?).

27 Tzaferis, 1992, p.11. Further evidence of this syncretism is seen in the discovery of the top of a small altar amid the ruins of the Pan Sanctuary dedicated to 'Jupiter Olybraeus' – a deity having connections with Cilicia (Isaac, in Ma'oz, forthcoming, no 11). The inscription is in Latin and may again point to a worshipper from the military.

28 See especially Meshorer 2, 1982, pl. 7:6, obverse with Augustus and Livia, reverse with temple and large 'theta' shaped object inside. We must theorise cautiously, because it is also possible that the temple depicted on the later coins had more than four columns on the front, and that these were not all shown on the coin in order to leave room for an adequate depiction of the cult statue.

29 Meshorer, 1984–85, nos 29, 30, e.g., and probably also Elagabalus, no 37.

30 This would create problems for locating the Augusteum at the mouth of the cave, of course, as well as the identification of the ashlar building presently designated as the 'Temple of Zeus'. Until further evidence is available, we must admit that the location of both buildings remains in the area of speculation.

31 As read by Isaac in Ma'oz, forthcoming, no 4. The inscription has deteriorated since its discovery in the nineteenth century and the date can no longer be read on it. Waddington no 1893; Brünnow-Domaszewski, 249,b; CIG 4537; Guérin, *Galilee* 2, 1880, p.311; IGR iii, 1109; pl. V. Hornum, 1993, gives numerous other examples of inscriptions to Nemesis *pro salute* the emperor, but in Latin, dating to the second century as well.

32 Ma'oz, 1994–99, p.93; 1991, p.60; Friedland, 1997, pp.31–32. See also Tzaferis, 1992, p.4 et passim.

33 Hornum, 1993.

34   Hornum, 1993, p.42.

35   Hornum, 1993, p.43.

36   Hornum, 1993, pp.50, 56.

37   Hornum, 1993, p.88.

38   Hornum, 1993, p.90.

39   *Jos., War* 7.37–38.

40   See Seyrig, 1932, pp.50–64. Among those cities listed as having Nemesis cults: Antheon, Antioch, Aradus, Balamie, Dura-Europos, Gerasa, Heliopolis/Baalbek, Jerusalem, Neapolis, Nicopolis, Palmyra, Ptolemais-Akko, and Sebaste. The evidence in almost every case dates to the third century (pp.50–51).

41   Under Commodus coins continue to be minted, but the types are exactly the same as those of his father. We presently have nothing else that can be confidently dated to his reign.

42   Dio *Roman History* 76.13.1.

43   Julia Domna (199 AD; Meshorer, 1984–85, nos 13–14); Geta (199 AD; Meshorer, 1984–1985, nos 15–18); Plautilla (201 AD; Meshorer, 1984–85, nos 25–28).

44   Meshorer, 1984–85, nos 29–30. It is these coins, by the way, which prove that the era of Banias begins in 3/2 BC, since their date (KC=220) can only be 217 AD.

45   Meshorer, 1984–85, nos 38, 41, 49, 50; Ma'oz, 1994–99, pp.96–97.

46   Meshorer, 1984–85, nos 32, 38, 39, 45.

47   Meshorer, 1984–85, nos 35, 44. The objects on each side of the cult statue may represent the sides of the cave, but may also be some sort of decorated columns.

48   Meshorer, 1984–85, nos 40, 40a, 42, 46, 47, 55.

49   Farnell, 1977, p.433.

50   Ma'oz, 1994–99, pp.93–94.

51   Cf. Meshorer, 1984–85, p.38, pl. 13; Ma'oz, 1994–99.

52   Berlin, 1999, pp.34–35.

53   Isaac, in Ma'oz, forthcoming, no 5. Waddington no 1894; CIG 4539 with addenda on p.1180, pl. VI. Note that five of the eight family members mentioned have names derivative of 'Agrippa'. This indicates, as Isaac notes, 'a tradition, among the local upper-class, of loyalty to the Herodian house, founders of the city'.

54   One fragment in Greek (Isaac, in Ma'oz, forthcoming, no 9) begins 'To Imperator Caesar Marcus Aurelius Antoninus Augustus Pius, L(ucius) Septimius Octavius (dedicated…)' – and can be attributed to either Caracalla or Elagabalus. An altar fragment, in Latin (Isaac, in Ma'oz, forthcoming, no 10), reads, 'For the good fortune of the Emperor [M(arcus) Aur(elius) An]toninus Aug(ustus) son of the Emperor Ant(oninus) Aug(ustus)'.

55   Found below Tel Dan by Zvi Ma'oz.

56   See Miller, 1917, Bowersock, 1983. Several sites are named which disappeared before 79 AD in the eruption of Vesuvius. Others are related directly to Scriptural or specifically Christian interests (Mt. Sinai, the Mt. Of Olives etc.) Bowersock connects this map with the one produced by Agrippa, displayed at the Porticus Vipsania and seen by Strabo before his death in AD 23 and also seen and used by Pliny in his *Natural History*. He believes that copies of the map were in circulation in the first century AD (Bowersock, 1983, pp.165–66).

57   Levi and Levi, 1967, pp.30–31, suggest a date around 260 AD.

58   Paneas, 'known in the days of the Herods as Caesarea or Caesarea Philippi' is called Caesarea Paneas on the map, a name change which took place 'afterward' and represents a 'transitional period, which included the second century, as we can tell from Ptolemy's *Geography* [5.14.17], it was called Caesarea Paneas' (Bowersock, 1983, p.169). All of this is consistent with the conclusion that the city name was changed to Caesarea Paneas, perhaps as early as the early second century, and certainly by the time of the production of the Peutinger Map, at least in the form it has come down to us.

59 Liebermann, 1946, p.365.

60 *Midrash Rabbah Genesis* 63:8 (Freedman and Simon 2, 1939, pp.563–64). Cf. *JT Terumot* 8:12.

61 Trattner, 1955, p.460. Cf. Bader, 1988, p.460.

62 See Tzaferis's forthcoming archaeological report for research on the ancient fortifications of the city.

63 Freedman and Simon 5, 1939, pp.432–33.

64 *JT Shebi'ith* 9.2, 38d, Liebermann (trans.) 1946, p.350.

65 Liebermann, 1946, p.351. Cf. Sperber, 1974, pp.179, 351. Sperber gives a number of parallels from other cities making the same threat.

66 Sperber, 1974, p.179.

67 These give 'interesting evidence of the elaborate land division carried out under the rule of Diocletian in connection with the reorganization of the empire' (Aharoni, 1955, p.112). Macalister reports on a stone found 'near the Gesr el-Ghajar bridge on the Banias road not far from Abil…It would appear as if Diocletian ordered a sort of Domesday Book, fixing the dimensions and value of landed possessions, as he endeavoured to decide the value of merchandise, by his edict "De pretiis rerum venalium"' (Macalister, 1908, pp.260–61).

68 So Aharoni, 1955, p.221.

69 Millar, 1993, p.535. Millar has listed 35 such inscriptions (pp.535–44). He notes that 'all of the known markers come from the east side of the Huleh Valley (or actually on the Golan Heights), and none from Galilee proper or Judaea' (p.535).

70 In this context, 'Roman Banias' is used to signify roughly the second and third centuries.

71 Isaac, forthcoming. Isaac lists seventeen Roman, six Greek, and five Semitic names on the inscriptions. However, five of the Roman names belong to one family. Two of the Semitic names are specifically patronymics.

72 Isaac, forthcoming.

73 Dar and Kokkinos, 1992.

74 Friedland, 1997, pp.15, 101.

75 Friedland, 1997, p.101; 1999, pp.21–22.

76 Friedland, 1997, p.108.

77 Gregg and Urman have published an inscription from Banias with a list of names that they suggest are 'a list of contributors to or builders of a structure, naming members of a commission (a local version of magistrates like the *quattuorviri*)'. Gregg and Urman, 1996, p.281 (Inscription no 238).

78 Waddington no 1894.

79 'Τοὺς ὑπὸ τῆς βουλῆς καὶ τοῦ δήμου ψηφισθέντας ἀνδριάντας Φιλίππου τοῦ Ἀντιπάτρου καὶ Ἀντιπάτρου τοῦ Φιλίππου τοῦ πατρὸς αὐτοῦ ἱερασαμένου καὶ ἐπιδόσεις ποιησαμένου καὶ γυμνασιαρχήσαντος ἐπισήμως τειμῆς ἕνεκα οὓς αὐτοὶ ἐκ τῶν ἰδίων ἀνέστησαν'. Haussoullier and Ingholt, 1924, no 7: pp.331–33. This inscription was probably first noticed by van Berchem in 1895, but was not published until 1924. It was found in reuse as the lintel of a doorway in a building near the banks of the Banias River and probably should be dated to the first half of the second century.

80 MacAdam's survey of inscriptions from the Late Roman and Byzantine Periods indicates that local leaders were still bearing the primary responsibility for public works and infrastructure in the towns of the region: 'The known inscriptions demonstrate clearly that the villages of southern Syria undertook (normally at their own expense) public works projects of every conceivable kind. Among these I note the construction of baths, basilicas, stables, refectories, temples, hotels, reservoirs, theatres, aqueducts, courtyards, fountains and public buildings of uncertain character known by a variety of names' (MacAdam, 1983, p.108). As we have noted, the responsibilities of local leadership eventually became so onerous that the *Midrash Rabbah* proposes this interpretation of Numbers 11:5 ('The Lord bless thee and guard thee'): '*The Lord bless thee* with

wealth *and guard thee* that thou not be compelled to take office in the province of Paneas and that no fine be imposed upon the district as a result of which they should say to you: "Give gold!"'

81 At least some of these individuals may have actually been members of the Herodian family, though it is also possible that they were descended from clients of the Herodian kings who had been allowed to take on the names of their patron.

82 Under the leadership of Rabbi Jose ben Kisma, among others. Bader, 1988, pp.286–87, and discussion below.

83 Alon, 1980, p.29f; Liebermann, 1946, p.365.

84 These black stones resemble those of the Cardo Maximus of Scythopolis-Beth Shean that are of later date. It is not yet possible to assign a definite date to the paving stones at Banias. Surviving stones from the street are found in reuse in many places throughout the site, particularly in structures dating from the Middle Ages, when the Cardo was apparently dismantled.

85 It should be remembered that the Augusteum played a primarily civic and political role in the life of the city and the region.

86 A bridge from medieval times survives at the spot, the waters of the Banias still rushing beneath it with a great roar.

87 Ma'oz, forthcoming, and 1993b, p.137.

88 Nineteenth-century travellers found this same street system still in use, including the southern bridge (across the Wâdî Sa'âr and the western bridge across the Nahal Hermon).

89 Ma'oz, forthcoming, and 1993b, p.137. Ma'oz notes parallels at Phoenician temples in Lebanon ('Amrit and Afqa). He suggests that vestiges of the pool above may have survived, e.g. the triple arched drain (*cloaca*) under the modern mill that may be seen at the site.

90 See Ma'oz, 1994–99, pp.97–99.

91 *SEG* 32 (1982), p.414, no 1499.

92 Ma'oz, 1993b, p.137.

93 A large channel, still open, has been found running from the area of the spring through the middle of the city, parallel to the Cardo Maximus, emptying into the Wâdî Sa'âr at the south edge of the centre. A branch of this system runs beneath the palace/public bathhouse, providing water for the baths and fountains, and eventually emptying into the river on the western edge of the centre.

94 See Berlin, 1999, p.31.

95 This variety survived and was grown in the area as late as the period of the British Mandate. Urman, 1985, p.144.

96 This according to the *JT Demai* 2:1 [22c] (Sarason, *TLI* 3, 1991, p.71).

97 Probably signifying 'λίτρα=pound (i.e., a unit of weight) 8'. These are now in the Beth Ussishkin, Kibbutz Dan. The objects cannot presently be dated more narrowly than 'Roman/Byzantine' though the absence of a royal name probably indicates a date after the death of Agrippa II. See Kushnir-Stein, 1995.

98 Hartal, 1985, pp.7–8. It should be noted, however, that many of the surviving villas date from the Late Roman or even Byzantine Periods. It is reasonable to assume that these neighbourhoods were inhabited by the most prosperous citizens in earlier times as well.

99 Discovered in Hartal's survey, Hartal, 1985, p.7.

100 Hartal, 1997, pp.5–8. 'The aqueduct was probably built when the town expanded in the late first century and early 2nd centuries CE. Repairs were made in the Mid-3rd century CE. A coin of Banias dated 211 CE was found in the plaster covering the pool's bottom. The system ceased to function 'in the course of the 6th century CE, when the city area shrank and the northwest suburb was abandoned' (Hartal, 1997, p.7).

101 Hartal, 1997, p.6.

102 A number of sites in the Golan that seem to have been within the Banias district have been surveyed by Urman and others. See Gregg and Urman, 1996. Inscriptions have been found in

the following: Hafar, Baidarus, Sukeik, Mumsiyye (El-Ghassaniyye), Surman (El-'Adnaniyye) and 'Ein Ziwan (El-Qakhtaniyye), Quneitra, Bab el-Wawa and Mansura, Tell esh-Sheikha and Buqa'ta. Excavation will be required to determine the precise dating and history of these sites. Some are too far away to be considered a part of 'greater Banias'.

103 *JT Shebi'ith* 9:2.
104 See Liebermann, 1946, p.350.
105 Freedman and Simon 5, 1939, pp.432–33. See Sperber, 1974, p.179; Liebermann, 1946, p.351.
106 Athens and Rome are well-known examples.
107 These were identified and surveyed by Hartal in 1983, Hartal, 1985, p.7.
108 Hartal, 1997, p.7. See plan, Fig.2, no 5. Another first- or second-century tomb, east of Banias at 'En el-Ghazlan (Wâdî Naqib) was excavated in 1985. Among the finds were many bronze objects, fragments of boxes, parts of a lock and key, cosmetic utensils, rings and butterfly shaped brooches; small glass bottle and two gold rings, one with a gem incised with the representation of a head, three bronze juglets, and four glass bottles. Hartal, 1985, p.26.
109 A large burial cave (first/second century) was excavated at Snir by D. Amir in 1973, along with several other tombs found during construction work. More burial caves were found on the slope below Snir in 1988–89, and excavated by Ma'oz.
110 Ma'oz, 1993b, p.142. The excavator also describes several other large tombs in the area, some with well-carved sarcophagi.
111 B. Isaac. Jeremias (trans.) 1932, pp.81–82, Fig.7–8.

CHAPTER 4

1   His own name means, 'gift of the Sun'.
2   Bernand, 1960, pp.161–62, no 69, pl. xxiv (D15); Bernand, 1969, pp.177–78, no 170, pl. 15.
3   Bernand, 1969, p.77; see notes 7, 8.
4   Perdrizet and Lefebvre, 1919, no 528; p.7, drawing on p.96; text on p.94.
5   The oracle of Bes was more important in the third and fourth centuries than in the second, enjoying great popularity during the Persian threat in Julian's time. Perdrizet and Lefebvre, 1919, p.xxi.
6   Perdrizet and Lefebvre, 1919, p.94.
7   'ζάθεος' there means 'very divine, sacred' and is also used to describe a city (*Iliad* 1.38). 'ἀρητήρ' (*Iliad* 1.11) is used in reference to an old priest.
8   See Farnell 5, 1977, pp.431–34 for an extended discussion, and especially Borgeaud, 1988. Also, see Herbig, 1949.
9   Farnell 5, 1977, p.432.
10 Farnell 5, 1977, pp.432–34. The phallus is also associated with Hermes, who is prominent in the pantheon of Banias as well.
11 Imhoof-Blumer, 1964, pp.128, 151.
12 Travlos, 1971, p.417. See Figs 538 (votive relief) and 539. For a detail of the roof of the cave and the rock-cut relief of Pan see Wycherley, 1978, Fig.50, p.173. Other shrines of Pan in the area are at Parnes, Penteli, Hymettos, Aigaleos, and Eleusis.
13 E.g. Wycherley, 1978, Fig.51, p.179.
14 See Richardson, 1992, pp.238–39.
15 Dionysius of Halicarnassus, *The Roman Antiquities* 1:32:5.
16 Dionysius of Halicarnassus, *The Roman Antiquities* 1.80.1 (Cary, *LCL* 1, 1937, pp.273–74). See also Plutarch's *Romulus* 21.4–10.
17 *Fasti* 2.267–85 (Frazer, *LCL*, 1989, pp.76–77).
18 Frazer, 1989, *LCL*, pp.389–94.

19   Berlin, 1999, pp.30–31.

20   Berlin, 1999, pp.31–34.

21   Kushnir-Stein has recently suggested an earlier date, perhaps 75/76 AD (forthcoming).

22   Meshorer, 1984–85, p.39; 1982, Vol. 2, p.256, pls 15:39, 41.

23   See Wycherley, 1978, Fig. 50, p.173, Travlos, 1971, Fig. 386–87, p.296.

24   Meshorer 2, 1982, p.212, n.91; p.88.

25   The earliest inscription found at the sanctuary dates to 63 AD, but it honours Asclepios, not Pan. See Isaac, no 6, in Ma'oz, forthcoming.

26   Kasher notes a 'renaissance' of pagan shrines dedicated to Phoenician gods on Mt. Hermon during the same period. Kasher, 1988, note 122, p.85.

27   Isaac, in Ma'oz, forthcoming, no 8.

28   See Tzaferis, 1992, p.200.

29   Imhoof-Blumer, 1964, pp.128, 151.

30   See Meshorer, 1984–85 for a complete catalogue of these types.

31   Iliffe, 1934, pp.165–66, lists several examples of this 'ugly Pan' in the museum collection which date from the first and second centuries, found in such places as Bir es Sammeil, ez Zib, and Ascalon (in the latter case in company with Dionysus).

32   Pliny, *Nat. Hist.* 34.64.

33   Helbig, 1963, no 566. Bieber, 1955, Fig. 86; p.38.

34   As noted above, elsewhere in Israel examples of the old Pan still appear. Examples have been discovered at Askelon and Nysa-Scythopolis (Beth Shean). A notable exception to the 'ugly Pan' iconography is the small (6 cm) bronze figurine found at Sepphoris (Nagy, 1996, p.171. Israel Antiquities Authority no 95–3887). The pointed ears and 5–7 reed syrinx in the figure's hand suggest that it should be identified as Pan. This object is dated to the second-third centuries AD, and is thus contemporary with the adoption of the new depiction of Pan at Banias. The Sepphoris figure, like the Banias type, does not have the lower limbs of a goat and represents an attractive young man. The bunch of grapes in his hand, however, indicates a closer connection with the cult of Bacchus or Dionysos at Sepphoris than at Banias. A number of statue fragments found at the Banias sanctuary seem to be from Pan figures or satyrs: a. a tree trunk with a syrinx hanging on it (Friedland, 1997, Cat. 18); b. hand holding a syrinx (Cat. 19); c. torso of a dancing satyr (Cat. 20); d. fragment of a base with human and animal feet (Cat. 29; satyr and panther?) but nothing has been found which seems to belong directly to the primary cult statue itself.

35   Philostorgius, *HE* 7.3, as epitomised by Photius (Walford, 1855, p.476). Note also this fragment: 'Herod the Great, in later times, built this city, and changed its name to that of Caesarea Philippi; now, however, it is called Paneas, from the statue of Pan which was placed within its confines' (Walford, 1855, p.522).

36   Porphyry, *Adversus Christianos,* Stern (trans.) 2, 1980, pp.461–62. Jerome, for example, uses the same phrase several times. Eusebius, locked in battle with those of his contemporaries who still worshipped Pan, seemed loath to call the city by its name in his own day, and avoided doing so by referring to it as 'Caesarea Philippi, called Paneas by the Phoenicians' (Williamson, 1965, p.310).

37   Claudius Ptolemy (c. 90–168 AD), *Geography* 5.14.17: 'The inland towns in Phoenicia are Arca, Palaeobyblus, Gabala, and Caesarea Panias'. It is true that the usual English translation of Josephus's *Ant.* 18.28 says that Philip 'made improvements at Paneas, the city near the sources of the Jordan' but the original text ('Φίλιππος δὲ Πανεάδα τὴν πρὸς ταῖς πηγαῖς τοῦ Ἰορδάνου κατασκευάσας ὀνομάζει Καισάρειαν…') may be understood in a manner more consistent with Josephus's usage of the term Paneas, which elsewhere always refers either to the district or to the area of the cave and spring and not to the city, which he always calls Caesarea or Caesarea Philippi. Philip, he suggests, improved the area called Paneas by creating a city there that he called Caesarea.

38 Pliny, *Nat. Hist.* 5.15.71. This statement does, however, suggest that one of the ways this Caesarea was distinguished from the one on the Mediterranean was by referring to its location in a sort of unofficial way as 'Caesarea in Paneas' or something of the sort.

39 Pliny, *Nat. Hist.* 5.16.74.

40 Isaac, in Ma'oz, forthcoming, nos 1a and 2. Victor describes himself as a priest, or, perhaps, simply as a supplicant.

41 For Maia on a coin of the city see Meshorer, 1984–85, pp.43–44.

42 Waddington no 1891. Isaac's translation. He notes that the inscription is metrical, consisting of two hexametres and a pentametre. The year is 150 in the era of Banias=148 AD.

43 This is Isaac's translation. Tzaferis suggests an alternative translation: 'The present goddess was dedicated to DioPan the sound-lover, by the priest Victor, the son of Lysimachos'. This results from a different interpretation of the word 'φιλευήχῳ' (as to whether the fifth letter should read as 'υ' or 'o'), and translation of 'διοπανί'. According to one tradition Pan is the son of Zeus (Borgeaud, 1988, 42f), so the unusual 'διοπανί' may simply mean 'son of Zeus'. Isaac notes legends of the Hellenistic period which depict Pan as the unsuccessful lover of Echo, though this kind of coupling of the two is not common (Borgeaud, 1988, pp.78f; *RE* v2, cols. 1926–30, esp. 1927f. s.v. Echo (Waser) with references to ancient literature that combines Pan and Echo).

44 Friedland, 1997, Cat. 11, suggests that a torso found by Ma'oz may have come from this statue, which served as a fountain figure, standing somewhere quite near the niche, but not in it.

45 See Berlin, 1999, pp.31–34.

46 Meshorer, 1984–85, nos 31,32, 38, 39, 45.

47 Meshorer, 1984–85, nos 38 (here both the niche and the circular colonnade are seen together), 41, 49, 50 (the goats appear inside the cave), cf. no 59. Meshorer thinks the goats share a single head, but Ma'oz questions this (Ma'oz, 1994–99, p.95).

48 Meshorer, 1984–85, no 35. Cf. no 44, where a Tyche figure is shown in a similar fashion. In this case an arch (of flowers?) can be seen stretched between the two columns.

49 Meshorer, 1984–85, nos 40, 42, 46, 47, and 55.

50 A coin of Elagabal in the name of Julia Maesa minted in Pella in Macedonia provides evidence that this interest in Pan extended beyond the city of Banias (*BMC* 39). Pan is depicted somewhat differently, seated on the tree stump instead of standing, holding the lagobola with his left arm, and apparently looking intently at a multi-reeded syrinx instead of playing a single reeded instrument. But he appears as an attractive nude young man, with none of the ugliness of the traditional Pan, and thus seems to belong to the same theological context as the Pan of Caesarea Paneas.

51 The first (Isaac, in Ma'oz, forthcoming, no 5) was discussed above. The second (Isaac, no 9) is an altar, dedicated by L(ucius) Septimius Octavius (whose name probably indicates that he received citizenship during the early years of the Severan Dynasty). The third (Isaac, no 10) is a fragment dedicated to 'the good fortune of the Emperor [Elagabalus]'.

52 Berlin, 1999, pp.36–41.

53 Farnell 5, 1977, pp.382, 432.

54 Herodotus, *The Histories* 6.105.

55 *Fasti* 2.267–85 (Frazer, *LCL*, 1989, pp.76–77).

56 *Jos., War* 7.37–38

57 Le Bas and Waddington, 1870, 1620 B., l. 42.

58 Moretti, 1953, no 72, p.210.

59 Robert, 1960, pp.441, 443. See Lifshitz, 1978, pp.3–30.

60 ἐν τᾷ πατρίδι αὐτοῦ Πά[νεια]. Robert, 1960, p.445. 'Ainsi nous reconnaissons à Didymes et à Rhodes deux athlètes originaires de Césarée Panias et vainqueurs dans les concours Paneia de cette ville' (Robert, 1960, 446).

61 Borgeaud, 1988, pp.42f, 100, 113, 182.

62 Isaac, in Ma'oz, forthcoming, no 7. See his discussion.

63 The inscription was found on a pillar in an Early Islamic dump; it is not possible to determine where it originally stood. Isaac's translation is as follows: 'To Heliopolitan Zeus, the father, for the salvation of our lords the emperors, Quadratus, also named Marcellus son of Selamanes, physician, dedicates (this statue of) Asclepios, having made a vow, with his wife and children. Year 65 [= AD63]'.

64 Isaac, in Ma'oz, forthcoming, no 8.

65 Sourdel, 1952, p.19.

66 Isaac, in Ma'oz, forthcoming, no 12. See *OGIS* 415.

67 Isaac, in Ma'oz, forthcoming. Another altar, found with this one, is dedicated to 'Jupiter Olybraeus' – a deity elsewhere identified as Cilician (Isaac, no 13).

68 Zeus is mentioned in the inscription of the priest Victor, son of Lysimachos (Isaac, in Ma'oz, forthcoming, no 1a), but only in connection with the circle of deities around Pan: the Nymphs, Hermes, and Maia. In this case he appears as the father of Hermes. Cf. Eusebius, *Preparation* 14:124d, quoting Porphyry, *Of the Philosophy Derived from Oracles*. Friedland believes that a life-size head found in the debris of the sanctuary may be that of Zeus (Cat. 4).

69 Meshorer, 1984–85, p.41; see e.g. nos 5, 5a, 6, 8, 10, 10a, 10b, 15, 19, 29, 30; etc. An unidentifiable object appears near his right leg in every case. Meshorer identifies this as a tree trunk, the same object as that on which Pan leans in coins depicting him. I see a shorter object of different form, possibly an altar with flames. It is on every Zeus type, including those showing the image inside a tetrastyle temple (nos 29–30) where is it placed directly under the *patera*. Thus, this object is probably not, as Meshorer suggests, a tree trunk, but a feature found in the *sanctum* of the Zeus temple, where the cult statue stood.

70 Tzaferis, 1992, p.11.

71 Meshorer, 1984–85, nos 29, 30.

72 Meshorer, 1984–85, no 37.

73 Compare, for example, Meshorer 2, 1982, pl. 7:6, obverse with Augustus and Livia, reverse with the temple and a large object (a shield?) placed between the two centre columns.

74 Note a very similar depiction of Zeus, with altar in front, on a coin of Trajan from Egypt. Milne, 1898, p.134, Fig.93. It is possible, of course that some existing columns may not be shown in order to provide a space to picture the cult statue, or simply to make the design of the coin more aesthetically pleasing. Such a phenomenon is common on coins depicting architecture. Columns on Philip's issues are equidistant with no cult statue.

75 Meshorer, 1984–85, no 25.

76 Meshorer, 1984–85, no 26.

77 Borgeaud, 1988, 78f.

78 A number of these may be seen in the National Museum at Athens. See the relief from Pendeli in Borgeaud, 1988 (Fig.11). See Borgeaud, 1988, pp.48f, 54f., and *passim*.

79 For examples of the Nemesis cult in Syria: Seyrig, 1950, pp.229–52. Examples are on pages 242–47. See also Seyrig, 1932, pp.50–64 for another Nemesis list.

80 Isaac, in Ma'oz, forthcoming, no 4; Waddington, 1870, no 1893.

81 Hornum, 1993, pp.42–43.

82 Hornum, 1993, pp.56, 88, 90. Hornum gives a number of examples of inscriptions to Nemesis *pro salute* of the emperor, all in Latin, which date to the second century and thus parallel the inscription of Valerios Hispanos at Banias, except that in the later case the language is Greek.

83 MND 416 (MA 3281).

84 Ovid, *Metamorphosis* 6.384–400.

85 Nonnos of Panopolis, *Dionysiaca* 19:315–27 (Rouse 2, *LCL*, 1940, p.113); see also 1.40–45; 10.232 (Rouse, *LCL*, 1940, pp.6–7, 345).

86 Banias was not a colony, of course. But its history as an independent royal capitol may have prompted certain pretensions among its citizens.

87 Friedland, 1997, Cat. 15. See Borgeaud, 1988, pp.17–19.

88 Friedland, 1997, Cat. 13, p.89. For another Aphrodite, found at Banias (Kibbutz Snir), see Dar, 1991, pp.116–18. The statue of Eros found at the sanctuary (Friedland, 1997, Cat. 22) probably was a subsidiary figure associated with the statue of Aphrodite (Friedland, p.91). A bronze shield portrait of a goddess in the National Museum of Damascus (no 16967) found at Banias in 1964 and dated 150–200 AD may also represent Aphrodite. The piece has two parts, a portrait with lead filling and shield that forms the frame. On the back are six pegs for hanging on a wall, or perhaps to be set in the centre of a gable, along with a series of images of gods and similar portraits. The piece is not life size (39 cm in diameter), and thus may be a votive object. The figure is dressed in a chiton with buttoned sleeves. The hairstyle and diadem are suggestive of Aphrodite and the rendering of the eyes suggests the dating. See a photo in Klengel, 1972, p.94. A somewhat similar object in the British Museum is identified as a medal awarded to a soldier to be attached to his ceremonial armour. If the Banias piece had a similar use it may be yet another indication of a military presence in the town.

89 Friedland, 1997, Cat. 7, 8, 12[?], 29 [?]; p.91.

90 Friedland, 1997, Cat. 23; p.93, n.62.

91 Friedland, 1997, Cat. 2, 6, 21, 25; p.95.

92 Thus, for example, the Tyche of the Decapolis city of Hippos (meaning 'horse') is shown on coins of the city standing beside a horse.

93 Meshorer, 1984–85, pl. 7:G.

94 Meshorer, 1984–85, no 11. Cf. nos 13, 20, 22, 33, 34, 52, 53.

95 Though strictly speaking, the statue seems to be standing under columns topped by a kind of floral arch or canopy in the coin depicting Elagabalus (Meshorer, 1984–85, no 44).

96 Meshorer, 1984–85, nos 44, 51, 58.

97 As suggested by Tzaferis, 1992, p.199.

98 Meshorer, 1984–85, nos 36, 57. The same seated figure, without the temple, appears in coin no 26, where it seems to be another rendering of Maia (cf. with no 25). The prototype is probably the famous Tyche of Antioch, with the Orontes personified as a swimmer at her feet.

99 Meshorer, 1984–85, no 56.

100 Jos., Ant. 15.363.

101 And perhaps games and gladiatorial contests as well. See discussion by Tzaferis, 1992, pp.196ff.

102 Jos., War 3.443–44.

103 Friedland, 1997, p.97.

104 Meshorer, 1984–85, nos 29, 30, 37.

105 Avnar Raban, one of the excavators of Caesarea Maritima, has suggested that the Augusteum there was converted into a temple of Tyche, giving as evidence a coin of Trajan which seems to show Tyche in a temple on the acropolis of that city, where the Augusteum had stood. See Rosenberger 2, 1975, no 19. The Tyche on the coin in question wears military garb, as does the Tyche of Banias in coins from that city, indicating that she is likely identified with Roma. Raban made this suggestion at a meeting of the American Schools of Oriental Research in 1997.

CHAPTER 5

1 Quoting Strabo who in turn quotes Timagenes, Josephus says, 'he added a country to them, and obtained a part of the nation of the Itureans for them, and bound them to them by the bond of circumcision'. Jos., Ant. 13:318–19.

2   Clearly, Josephus considered the Golan to be a part of the Galilee and rabbinic sources also regularly include Gamala, in the Golan, within Galilee (Gregg and Urman, 1996, p.306).

3   *Jos., Ant.* 17.27–28.

4   *Jos., Ant.* 17.29–31.

5   *Jos., Life*, 11. See Chapter 2.

6   *Jos., Life*, 11.

7   Even if Josephus's numbers are exaggerated. He may be referring to the entire Jewish population of the district, rather than the number of Jews in the city of Banias itself.

8   *Jos., War* 2.421; 4.81; *Life* 36.

9   See discussion in Chapter 2, and *Jos., Life* 74–76.

10   Or perhaps, given the city plan, they inhabited a fortified village in the immediate suburbs of Banias.

11   See Chapter 2, above.

12   Reed, 1999, argues that the old Israelite community in Galilee totally disappeared and that the 'Jewish' population of the region was entirely the result of immigration from the south during Hellenistic times. The unquestioned Northern associations found in 'Q' are thus attributed by him to 'one particular Galilean community's carefully crafted epic imagination to locate themselves on their social map' (p.107). This is a useful hypothesis; the case is not closed, however, despite the lack of archaeological evidence. What is still lacking is a clear motivation for the creation of such an imaginative epic. And why did these 'Northern Jews' feel such hostility toward their Southern origins? Furthermore, the Northern traditions were not only characteristic of the 'Q Community' but also appear within certain strands of apocalyptic Judaism not directly associated with earliest Christianity, though quite likely, as suggested above, a part of the matrix into which earliest Christianity was born. In certain cases they are intimately tied to specific geographical locations. It seems unlikely that such Northern traditions were maintained by the pagan population exclusively, and passed along from them to later Southern Jewish immigrants.

13   Biran, 1994.

14   Clermont-Ganneau, 1902, pp.346–66.

15   Nickelsburg, 1981, pp.583–84. See also Nickelsburg, 2001, especially p.245, where he notes the similarities between the myth of Pan and the Nymphs and the myth of the 'Watchers' in I Enoch.

16   Nickelsburg, 1981, p.584.

17   Nickelsburg, 1981, p.586. The continuation of these themes in Christian circles are discussed below.

18   Nickelsburg, 1981, pp.589–90.

19   For Banias as Rabbi Jose ben Kisma's home see Bacher 1, 1903, pp.397–400.

20   Rabbi Jose ben Kisma told this story: 'I was once walking by the way and a man met me and greeted me and I returned his greeting. He said to me, "Rabbi, from what place art thou?" I answered, "I come from a great city of Sages and scribes." He said to me, "If thou wilt dwell with us in our place I will give thee a thousand thousand golden denars and precious stones and pearls." I answered, "If thou gavest me all the silver and gold and precious stones and pearls in the world I would not dwell save in a place of the Law" [that is, in a place were the law is studied]', *Mishna Aboth* 6:9 (Danby, 1933, p.460–61). Banias might be the 'great city of Sages and scribes', in this story, but that is unlikely. After all, Rabbi Jose ben Kisma had been forced to move away from *that* city. Since, as the record indicates, he made his home in Banias, that city must therefore have been the one to which he moved. It must also have been a 'place of the Law', since he says he would not live elsewhere.

21   Bader, 1988, p.286.

22   *BT Sanhedrin* 98a (Epstein, 1935, p.665); see Bacher 1, 1903, p.402. Some rabbinical interpreters claimed Rabbi Jose was really referring to the gate of Tiberias, or even Rome (Bader, 1988, p.290).

NOTES ON THE TEXT

23   Bader, 1988, p.290.

24   Bader, 1988, pp.286–87.

25   So Strack and Stemberger, 1991, p.84. He was a student of Aqiba.

26   *BT Sukka* 27b (Epstein, 1938, p.121, n.2). The name used by the *Talmud* (*Kesariyon*) means 'little Caesarea' and is used to distinguish Banias from Caesarea Maritima, a larger and more important city.

27   Gregg and Urman, 1996, p.306.

28   *Midrash Rabbah Numbers* 12:3 (Freedman and Simon 5, 1939, p.455).

29   Urman, 1985, pp.22–24. Bethsaida, a significant part of the district of Banias, was also home to a large Jewish community and several famous sages during the second and third centuries, probably also benefiting from the influx of refugees after the Revolt of Bar Kochba. See Gregg and Urman, 1996, pp.306–7.

30   As far as we know, good relations continued between Rome and the Jews of Banias throughout the period of the Severan Dynasty as well. In general, the Jewish community 'enjoyed long periods of comfort and security' during this time. Liebermann, 1946, p.365. Severus and Caracalla (193–211 AD, 211–17 AD) were said to be especially fond of the Jews. Alon, 1980, p.29. Alexander Severus (222–35 AD) was friendly both to Judaism and Christianity. He was said to have had statues of Orpheus, Abraham, and Jesus, in his bedroom.

31   The Jordan issues from the cavern of Paneas. *BT Baba Bathra* 74b (Epstein 1935, p.297; *BT Seder Kodashim Bekoroth* 55a (Epstein, 1948, p.377).

32   *BT Seder Kodashim Bekoroth* 55a (Epstein, 1948, p.378).

33   *Mishna Para* 8:11 (Danby, 1933, p.707). Cf. Dalman, 1935, p.204.

34   *Midrash Rabbah Genesis* 33:4 (Freedman and Simon 1, 1939, p.264); cf. Neubauer, 1868, p.37.

35   *Mekhilta Amalek* 2.13.F-1 (Neusner 2:44, 1988). See also Ginzberg, 1938, p.884, n.884.

36   Neubauer, 1868, p.237; Epstein, *BT Sukkah* 2, 1938, p.121, n.2.

37   Neubauer, 1868, p.237.

38   *JT Demai* 2:1 [22c] (Sarason, *TLI* 3, 1993, p.71; Urman, 1985, pp.143–44). *Jonathan/Jerusalem Targum Numbers* 38:8: 'The two tribes and the half tribe have received their inheritance beyond the Jordan first. Their border goeth forth on the east from the plain of the Salt Sea to Kinnereth, the city of the Kingdom of the Amorites, and thence to the mountain of snow [Hermon], and to Hamatha of Lebanon; thence to Haba, on the northern side of Hainutha of Damasek, and from Hoba to [*Kiokinos Detarnegola*, 'the rooster shape'] of the snowy mount of Kisarion, eastward of Dan...' (Etheridge 2, 1862, p.466).

39   *JT Shebi'ith* 6:1 (36c). Schwab (trans.), 1932, p.379. See Urman, 1985, p.142 and Sussman, 1981, pp.146–53.

40   Biran, 1974, 1980, 1994.

41   See Etheridge 1, 1862, p.199; Carmoly, 1847, p.164. The *Jerusalem Targum* renders the word Dan as 'Dan of Kisrion' and never only Kisrion or Paneas (Neubauer, 1868, p.236). This implies knowledge of a town, Dan, in the district of Banias. The *JT* specifically speaks of 'Kefar Dan', the birthplace of Rabbi Yose, e.g. *Demai* 2:1 [22d] (Sarason, *TLI* 3, 1993, p.70). Cf. Neubauer, 1868, p.236.

42   *Midrash Rabbah Genesis* 94.9 Freedman and Simon 2, 1939, p.876.

43   *Pirke Rabbi Eliezer* 17 (Carmoly, 1847, p.164).

44   *BT Megillah* 6a (Epstein, 1938, p.29).

45   *BT Seder Kodashim Bekoroth* 55a (Epstein, 1948, p.377).

46   Eusebius, *Onomasticon* 76 (Freeman-Grenville et al., 2003, p.46); *HE* 7:18 (Williamson, 1966, p.302). A third-century milestone has been found on this road from Tyre to Damascus that specifically mentions Paneas. AE 1936, p.43, no 129.

47   Stewart, *PPTS* 2, p.12.

48   Jerome, *Onomasticon* 77 (Freeman-Grenville et al., 2003, p.46).

49   Jerome, *Commentary of Ezekiel* 27:19 (Migne, *PL* 25, Col. 258): Dan, 'ubi hodie Paneas, quae quondam Caesarea Philippi vocabatur'; *Comm in Amos* (Migne, *PL* 25.1084): 'Dan, in terminis terrae Judaicae, ubi nunc Paneas est'.

50   Jerome, *Comm. On Matt.* 16:13 (Bonnard 2, 1977, pp.11–12). Robinson points out that, though this tradition was passed on, 'the absurdity of this etymology is obvious' – the name simply being the Greek form of the Hebrew word Iarden – with no relation to the word Dan – which comes 500 years after the first occurrences of the word Jordan. Robinson, 1857, p.412, Note 5.

51   Jerome, *Onomasticon* 21 (Freeman-Grenville et al., 2003, p.20).

52   Rom. 16:23. 'Episcopi Paneadis. I. Erastus. Dorotheo Tyri Erastus, cujus Paulus (epistolae ad Romanos c.16.v.23) meminit, ecclesiae Hierosolymorum oiconomus primum fuit, deinde Paneadis episcopus. At cum bona venia eruditi Dorothei, dicam a Paulo *Erastum* quidem appellari arcarium civitatis, at illius ex qua scribebat, Corinthi scilicet, non Hierosolymorum' (Le Quien, Oriens, II, 1740, p.831). The tradition may preserve some memory of a connection between the Church in Banias and the Church in Jerusalem (see below). Erastus was a city official in Corinth. The tradition is identified as a 'local' one in Janin, 1953, Col. 210.

53   Acts 21:3–4; Acts 22:10–13.

54   Commenting on Mark 8:27–30, the text which sets the three stories in the district of Caesarea Philippi, Willi Marxen says: 'It is the same here as elsewhere in Mark. *The locales that he occasionally furnishes his pericopes derive entirely from his sources.* We must note the fact that at a very early stage local traditions were formed which may be associated with Christian Communities in these places. We must also reckon with the probability that the geographical data may be historically reliable', Marxen, 1969, pp.72–73.

55   Hengel, 1985, p.32, citing Schmitals, who identifies Mark 8:27 as the beginning of 'Ur-Markus' and agrees that from this point forward the reader is on 'rock hard historical ground'.

56   See Nickelsburg, 1985.

57   Much of the Synoptic tradition belonged to disciples in the area around Capernaum (both the action stories of Mark and the sayings of 'Q') and was presumably carried with them north as they fled the destruction wreaked by the Roman armies in Galilee during the early days of the Revolt. This destruction is probably reflected in the famous 'woes' pronounced on the cities of Galilee by Jesus (Matt. 11:20–24; Luke 10:13–15).

58   See Saldarini, 1994, where this thesis is worked out in detail.

59   Luke begins the cycle at Bethsaida, but omits all reference to Caesarea Philippi and thus the cycle is obscured: Luke 9:10; cf. 9:18.

60   Matthew also adds Jeremiah to the list of prophets whom some identify with Jesus, and the phrase 'the Son of the Living God' to his messianic title. Luke, besides stylistic changes, notably omits the reference to Caesarea Philippi, simply beginning: 'Once when Jesus was praying in private and his disciples were with them, he asked them… etc' (Luke 9:18–21).

61   Whether any credence whatsoever could be given to the idea that Jesus's allusion to the 'gates of Hell' is a reference to the Cave of Pan, and that the 'rock' which triggers Jesus's pun on the name of Peter is the red-rock bluff which forms the face of the cave, depend on whether this Matthean extension of Mark's more primitive account was ever tied to Caesarea Philippi. For the use of Matthew's gospel by Jewish-Christians in the area, see below. An early eighteenth-century missionary in Syria, Père Nacchi, found a local tradition still persisting which located Jesus's Admission of Messiahship at nearby Tel Dan. 'In the territory of Caesarea, near that city, there is an eminence about eight or ten feet high, and three quarters of a mile in compass; shaded with verdant oaks, sycamores, citron and orange trees. The tradition is that this was the place where Christ asked his disciples what both the people and themselves said of him', (Bousquet, 1852, pp.325–26. Green (trans.) 1736, p.59). This tradition appears from time to time in earlier pilgrim accounts, e.g., *The Pilgrimage of Saewulf to Jerusalem* (written

1102–3 AD): '…Caesarea, the city of Philip the Tetrarch, in the neighborhood of which Jesus came and asked his disciples, saying: 'Whom do men say that the Son of Man is?' as the Gospel relates. Brownlow, *PPTS* 4, p.22.

62   Sometimes the reference to 'after six days' is asserted to imply a journey of that length between Caesarea Philippi and Mount Tabor. But such a journey would not take six days, and besides, Luke's variation, 'about eight days', casts doubt on making too much of the time period between the events.

63   Cf. Matthew 17:1–2a; Luke 9:28–29a. Luke has reset both events, omitted the geographical reference and emphasising a prayer retreat 'in private' and on 'a mountain'. As noted above, he also extends the interval between the two events to 'about eight days'.

64   *Onomasticon* 21–22 (Freeman-Grenville et al., 2003, p.20).

65   Nickelsburg, 1981, p.590, with documentation, n.63.

66   Nickelsburg, 1981, p.598; 2001, pp.246–47.

67   Nickelsburg, 1981, p.599.

68   Taylor, 1968, pp.139–40.

69   *Orphica* 11, lines 4ff. (Abel, 1885, p.64).

70   Euripides *Medea* 1167–74 (Kovacs, *LCL*, 1994, p.403). Cf. Euripides, *Hippolytus* 141–44: 'Has some god possessed you, dear girl? Do your wits wander under the spell of Pan or Hecate, the august Corybantes or Cybele, the mountain mother?'

71   Trombley, 1993, p.286–87.

72   Banias retained its reputation as a site for healing, particularly of mental diseases, long after the disappearance of paganism. Khader, the Moslem 'saint' discussed in detail below, whose shrine still exists at Banias, was the greatest healer of mental troubles of all such saints (Canaan, 1980, p.119) and was known for his ability to heal fits, apoplexy, epilepsy, and convulsions (Canaan, 1980, p.124). Numerous healing shrines in Palestine are associated with him (Canaan, 1980, pp.120–22).

73   Eusebius, *HE* 3:5 (Williamson, 1966, p.111).

74   Eusebius's account, though sometimes questioned, is still generally accepted as having an historical basis.

75   *Panarion* 29, 7, 7–8 (Williams, 1987, Vol. 1, p.118). Of the Ebionites: 'They got their start after the fall of Jerusalem. For since practically all who had come to faith in Christ had settled in Peraea then, in Pella, a town in the "Decapolis" the Gospel mentions, which is near Batanaea and Bashanitis – as they had moved there then and were living there, this provided an occasion for Ebion, *Panarion* 30,2,7 (Williams 1, 1987, p.121). Caution must be exercised in evaluating Epiphanius's interpretation of events, of course. Klijn and Reinick question whether he had independent information or was simply speculating. 'From the tradition found in Eusebius about certain Christians leaving Jerusalem before its fall in 70, he concluded that all Jewish-Christians living to the east of the Jordan, such as the Nazoraeans and the Ebionites, originated among these Christians. We may repeat that all these observations were not the fruit of fresh information but the result of his desire to reconcile different sources' (Klijn and Reinick, 1973, p.72). In *Onomasticon* 172 (Freeman-Grenville et al., 2003, p.95) Eusebius describes the town 'on the left of Damascus' (and thus toward Banias) called 'Choba', located 'in those parts where there are Hebrews who believe in Christ, called Ebionites'.

76   *Panarion* 30,18,1 (Williams 1, 1987, p.133). Harnack 2, 1908, p.102 thinks 'Nabatea' should be read 'Batanea'. He also suggests that the Christians scattered in consequence of the revolt went to Pella, Kochaba in Basanitis (the modern Kharaba, 8 k sw of Bostra), and Berea (Coele-Syria). 'Epiphanius, it is true, adds Batanea, Paneas, and Moabitis, but we cannot be sure that the dispersed Jewish-Christians reached these districts at the same early period' (Harnack 2, 1908, p.103). He does not indicate his reasons for this conclusion.

77   *Panarion* 53:1 (Williams 2, 1987, p.70).

78   *Panarion*, 19,1,1 (Williams 2, 1987, p.44).

79   Jerome, *Liber de Viris Illustribus* 3 (Migne, *PL* 2, Col. 613). The testimony of the Fathers to the use of the gospel of Matthew, in some form, by these Jewish-Christian sects raises interesting questions about the possible movement of the so-called 'Q community' – itself a kind of Jewish-Christian sect, from Galilee northeast into Syria.

80   White, 1991, pp.211–47. White claims Matthew was written in 'a Palestinian location but a settlement somewhere in the border region between lower Galilee (whose border cities such as Chorazim, Bethsaida, and Capernaum Matthew criticises for being unresponsive to Jesus)...and Syria.' Here, he contends, the identity crisis triggered for both Judaism and Jewish-Christianity by the calamity of the Jewish war would have been most acutely felt. Saldarini, 1994, p.26, locates the group 'somewhere in Syria or Coele Syria' or in Galilee or 'somewhere contiguous in south Syria, Peraea, Gaulanitis, or along the Mediterranean coast' (Saldarini, 1998, p.149).

81   In a letter to the editor (*BAR* 24:5; 1998; p.16), Anson Rainey says: 'the route from Abel-beth-maacha to Tyre was well used until 1922, when the area was split between the mandates of Britain and France. It is the famous road from Paneas (Caesarea Philippi = Banias) to Tyre, marked by the milestones found in Lebanon and the north Hula Valley. It is undoubtedly the Way of the Sea mentioned in Isaiah 9:1 (English) and the Gospel of Matthew. Jesus used that road when he visited the "region of Tyre and Sidon" (Mark 3:8; Matthew 15:21) and probably when he came to the "region of Caesarea Philippi" (Mark 8:27; Matthew 16:13). There is no other Way of the Sea (or Via Maris) in the Holy Land, contrary to modern tour-guide mythology.' Saldarini notes that apart from his trips to the nearby districts of Tyre and Sidon, and an event in the also nearby 'district of the Gadarenes', Jesus's ministry in Matthew is confined to 'the northeast corner of lower Galilee' (Saldarini, 1998, p.150), and thus the territories of Philip the Tetrarch.

82   Klijn, 1992, p.37.

83   Klijn, 1992, pp.38, 42.

84   The author of the Gospel of Matthew represents one of the small groups within the Jewish tradition who sought another way of defining and leading Israel, a way which was rejected by the larger Jewish community, but who had enormous influence on the growing number of gentile believers-in-Jesus and the emerging Christian church (Saldarini, 1994, p.123). The first clear indication of Byzantine Christianity in Banias comes only at the time of the Council of Nicaea.

85   Dauphin, 1982, pp.129–42, has suggested that the two communities lived in relative peace with each other, citing evidence from the nearby Golan. Ma'oz disagrees, suggesting that where possible the two communities practiced 'segregation and ethnic exclusion' (Ma'oz, 1985, pp.59–68).

86   A large number of scholars hold that Edessa was the cradle of Syriac Christianity, thereby accepting that there is some value in the tradition enshrined in the Syriac *Doctrine of Addai*, which tells how Christ sent the legendary Addai, one of the Seventy Disciples, to King Abgar of Edessa. This document, in the form we now have it, can hardly be earlier than the fifth century; though a form of the legend is recorded by Eusebius, *HE* 1.13 (Williamson, 1966, p.65) in connection with the Apostle Thaddaeus, it is extremely hard to assess what historical kernel the tradition has (Murray, 1975, p.4). Murray notes the strong Jewish element in Christianity in Edessa (pp.5–7) and that Mani, 'came from the Jewish-Christian Elkesaites in southern Mesopotamia' (p.8).

87   See Phillips, 1876. Another fragment from *The Epistle of Addaeus* says: 'Addaeus preached at Edessa and in Mesopotamia (he was from Paneas) in the days of Abgar the King. And when he was among the Zophenians, Severus the son of Abgar sent and slew him at Agel Hasna, and also a young man his disciple.'

CHAPTER 6

1 Eusebius, *HE* 6.16–17 (Williamson, 1966, p.310).
2 A fragment of this work is preserved by Photius, Tardieu (trans.) Frag. 6:6a: 'Parmi les offrandes qu'on jette à l'eau, les unes coulent à pic, même si elles sont légères. C'est un signe que ceux qui les font sont en faveur auprès de la divinité. Dans le cas contraire, ces même si elles sont très pesantes, restent à la surface et sont rejetées au dehors d'une façon étonnante' (pp.45–46). Tardieu, 1990, cites several parallels that indicate the old Semitic roots of the ceremony, pp.65–66.
3 The others are Tyre, Ptolemais, Damascus, Sidon, Tripoli, Berytus, Palmyra, Alassu, and Emesa. Together they comprise the 'Province of Phoenicia'. See Gelzer, 1898, p.12; Honigmann, 1925.
4 Eusebius, *The Life of Constantine* 3.54 (Cameron and Hall, 1999, pp.143–44).
5 Eusebius, *The Life of Constantine* 3.55 (Cameron and Hall, 1999, pp.144–45).
6 'We have reason for thinking that the Pan-worship was orgiastic, and therefore specially attractive to women' (Farnell, 1977, p.433). 'The herdsmen of Arcadia, clad in goat-skins as votaries of Pan, may have danced ritual-dances in spring to commemorate the awakening of the earth-goddess' (Farnell, 1977, p.433). 'The phallos, the fetish of life, may have belonged to Pan-cult as to Hermes-cult in Arcadia and elsewhere' (Farnell, 1977, p.433–34).
7 Eusebius, *The Life of Constantine* 3.54 (Cameron and Hall, 1999, pp.143–44), Farnell, 1977, p.163.
8 Fox, 1987, p.673.
9 Berlin, 1999, p.41, provides the evidence: 1) the last inscriptions are from the third century; 2) the last sculptural dedications date from the fourth century; 3) Ceramic dedications do not persist after the fifth century. Meanwhile, building stops within the city itself and existing buildings begin to be abandoned.
10 Plutarch, *Moralia* 419.17.
11 Taylor, 1968, pp.139–40.
12 Fox, 1987, pp.130–31, p.673. A statue of Pan on the Island of Aegina, erected by Ampelius, a governor of Achaia, is dated 359–60 AD (Chuvin, 1990, p.5).
13 Two other pagan writers of the third century, Solinus (*Collectanea Rerum Memorabilium* 31:1; Mommsen, 1864, p.161) and Porphyry (Stern, 1980, p.462), mention Banias, but without adding to our knowledge of the city during that time.
14 Quoted by Eusebius *PE* 3.11.115 a (Gifford, 1981, p.125).
15 Quoted by Eusebius *PE* 3.14.124 a (Gifford, 1981, p.136). Coggan, 1992, points out that Eusebius has taken two terms, 'Pan', and 'daemon', which had complex and ambiguous connotations in pagan literature and 'transformed them into flat, univocal meanings which were exclusively negative', Thus, the complex and ambiguous deity Pan begins to be transformed into the Christian Devil, and the complicated and ambiguous demons become the evil spirits (demons) of the gospels. Note the conflict between the disciples and the demon who controls the epileptic boy in the Synoptic story (Matthew 17:14–20; cf. Mark 9:17–29; Luke 9:37–43).
16 Eusebius *PE* 6.190 b-c (Gifford, 1981, p.208).
17 Eusebius *PE* 5.5.189 d (Gifford, 1981, p.208).
18 Plutarch, *Moralia* 419.17.
19 Eusebius, *PE* 5.18.207d–208a (Gifford, 1981, p.225). See Coggan, 1992.
20 Note the healing of the boy with the 'demon' in the vicinity of Banias in the 'Banias Cycle' of stories in the gospels, discussed above.
21 Shenute, a monk (*ca.*450–89 AD), smashed the idols in the village. The priests of Pan hauled him into court over the incident. See Trombley 2, 1993, p.207ff.
22 Irenaeus (writing 181–89), *Against Heresies* 16:1:2b–3a (Migne, *PG* 7): 'The Valentinians, again, maintain that the dispensational Jesus was the same who passed through Mary, upon whom that Saviour from the more exalted [region] descended, *who was also termed Pan*, because He

possessed the names (vocabula) of all those who had produced Him...' As we have seen, this use of the term Pan as a play on its Greek meaning 'all' was characteristic of certain Pagan philosophers as well.

23 The Jews were apparently not involved in the struggle between Constantine's Christian mobs and the pagans. 'Religious persecutions, the main cause which prompted the Jewish masses to revolt, did not exist in the third and fourth centuries' (Liebermann, 1946, p.341). The reign of Constantine was bad for Jews, but not because of religious persecution. Rather it was the rapacity of the tax-collectors who oppressed them (Liebermann, 1946, p.344). A similar situation had existed in pre-Christian times, under Diocletion, and specifically at Banias (Liebermann, 1946, pp.350–51).

24 Luke 8:43–48. The Markan account (5:21–43), which is probably Luke's source, is faithfully excerpted by Luke. It is even further shortened in Matthew (9:18–26).

25 Eusebius, *HE* 7:18 (Williamson, 1966, pp.301–2). A very similar account also appears in Eusebius *Commentaria in Lucam* (8:43ff), Migne *PG* 24.542c–544a. This account, however, shows signs of later editing, particularly its reference to Maximius.

26 Eusebius's attitude may have reflected his general concern about the misuse of images in Christian devotion. In a letter to Constantine's sister, he rebuked her for placing too much importance on a likeness of Christ. This letter was later cited by the Council of Constantinople (754 AD) during the Iconoclastic Controversy. See Drake, 1975, p.153, n.50.

27 Luke 8:43–48 (New International Version).

28 Knowledge of this particular project may have prompted Asterius of Amaseia to say that the statue had in fact been destroyed by Maximinus. But if this were true, Eusebius could not have seen the statue still in place, as he claims. Asterius, in order to accept the statue's authenticity, was forced to ignore Eusebius's testimony. See M. de Beausobre, 1727, pp.60–61.

29 Macarius Magnes, a near contemporary of Eusebius, as quoted in Nicephorus, Patriarch of Constantinople's, *Antirrhetica* (a ninth-century defence of use of images), thinks the woman's name was Berenice, and that she was the ruler of Edessa. Leclercq, *DACL* 6.2, s.v. 'Hémorroïsse', Cols. 2203–4.

30 E.g. Macarius Magnes.

31 An inscription on a column found at the Pan sanctuary seems to indicate that a statue of Asclepios once stood there. Isaac, in Ma'oz, forthcoming, no 6. Eisler, 1930, p.27, emphasising the inscription said to have been found with the statuary group in an insertion in one manuscript of Josephus ('For the healing of all diseases') identifies the figures as Asclepios and Panacea. He thinks the Lateran sarcophagus depicts the resurrected Christ appearing to Mary Magdalene (p.18). The historical validity of the manuscript evidence given is highly questionable, however. As we have noted, the inscription more likely included only terms of honour for the reigning emperor. Keel, 1994, pp.155–65, thinks the statue is Asclepios. But the assertion is not very seriously researched.

32 For an extensive bibliography of works on the statue, see Leclercq, *DACL* 6.2, s.v. 'Hémorroïsse', Col. 2203, Note 1.

33 The book is lost, but epitomised by Photius. English Translation: Walford, 1855.

34 Philostorgius, *HE* 7.3 (Walford, 1855, p.475).

35 See discussion above of the public nature of the city centre in Banias.

36 Gieseler, 1868, p.71.

37 Leclercq, *DACL* 13.1, s.v. 'Panéas', Cols. 1014–15.

38 Harnack, 1924, p.146. See also Keel, 1994, pp.155–65.

39 Perate, 1885, p.306.

40 Beausobre, 1727, pp.83–86.

41 It might be argued that Eusebius, who saw the statue, would have known if it were Hadrian and not Jesus. In fact, he may have suspected precisely that identification, and thus the hint of

scepticism noted above. See Perate, 1885, p.305. Mattingly, 1926, lists series of 'restitutor' coins of Hadrian in gold (pp.377–78) and bronze (pp.463–67). Several have 'Hadrian, togate, standing r., holding roll in l. hand and extending r. to raise up kneeling figure of province in front of him' or 'similar, but Hadrian standing l. Varieties occur in dress and attributes of province, details in field etc.' (p.463). See plate XVI: 328 for example (Galliae). These were minted in Rome, AD 134–38. The adventus, exercitus and restitutor types do not include Syria; those of Palestine use woman and children standing, not the type noted here. This could mean that the statue is not of Judaea capitulating, but of Syria accepting Hadrian's largess.

42 Museum Number 174. Von Matt, 1961, p.xv. Photographs of the sarcophagus may be found in Von Matt, 1961, pls 36–38.

43 Perate, 1885, p.311. Leclercq, *DACL* 6.2, s.v. 'Hémorroïsse', Col. 2206. The sarcophagus has been damaged and repaired. However, a drawing of the original made in the sixteenth century by Philippe de Winghe, before the damage was done, shows that the restoration was true to the original, except for the treatment of the head of the male figure, which seems to be laureated in the drawing, but not on the restored sarcophagus. The drawing is in the Vatican collection (Cod. Vat. Lat. 10545, Fol. 193). See Wilpert, 1924, p.298; Leclercq, *DACL* 13.1, s.v. 'Panéas', Col. 1014; Fig. 9579.

44 Von Matt, 1961, p.xv. Though the Christ depicted on the front is still shown as the traditional Apollo-like figure.

45 Von Matt, pl. 36. Leclercq, 1907, p.250.

46 Leclercq, *DACL* 8.2, s.v. 'Latran', Fig. 6897.

47 Leclercq, *DACL* 8, Part 2, s.v. 'Latran', Fig. 6897; Leclercq, *DACL* 2.2, s.v. 'Moise', Cols. 1661–67. The tree is rare in ancient depictions of this scene, but can be seen in some catacomb frescos (see Fig. 8258). Parallels may also be found for the supplicant (Fig. 8259, 8260 – two supplicants).

48 This feature is most clearly seen in the de Winghe drawing. See Wilpert, 1924, p.298; Leclercq, *DACL* 13.1, s.v. 'Panéas', Col. 1014; Fig. 9579.

49 E.g. Leclercq, *DACL* 6, Part 2, s.v. 'Hémorroïsse', Fig. 5642 (a third-century fresco); see also Figs 5643, 5644, 5645.

50 Leclercq, 1907, p.250. Leclercq 6, Part 2, s.v. 'Hémorroïsse', Cols. 2205–6.

51 Leclercq, 1907, p.249, summarises Bottari's argument. See also Perate, 1885.

52 Eusebius, *HE* 6.18 (Williamson, 1966, pp.301–2).

53 See also St Laurenti, p.215.

54 Leclercq is the principal proponent of this position. *DACL* 6.2, s.v. 'Hémorroïsse', Col. 2205.

55 This sarcophagus may be compared to another from the same period, also found in the Vatican Grottos. In this case the woman seems to be looking at the hem of Jesus's robe, not reaching up to him. The buildings are lacking in the background, and Jesus is shown as young and beardless. This is the more traditional rendering, based on the Gospel story on one hand, and current iconography on the other. Von Matt, 1961, pl. 30, note on p.xv.

56 Leclercq, 1907, p.249. This resemblance is much clearer in de Winghe's drawing. The drawing usually reproduced in the literature more nearly resembles modern conventional 'portraits' of Jesus. We are tempted to attribute this rendering to the fancy of either those artisans who repaired the sarcophagus, or the artist who drew it for publication, that is was indeed a 'portrait of Jesus'.

57 For example, the bust of Antinous. See Friedland, 1997.

58 Perate, 1885, pp.307–8; Leclercq, *DACL* 3.2, s.v. 'Coq', Col. 2891; Fig. 3288.

59 Leclercq, *DACL* 3.2, s.v. 'Coq', Col. 2891. Such a statue also stood in St John Lateran in Rome, leading some other scholars to think the buildings depicted on the left panel of the Lateran sarcophagus were actually to be found in Rome. Leclercq, *DACL* 8.2, s.v. 'Latran', Col. 1741.

60 The Santa Pudenziana church was begun in *ca.* 387 and completed *ca.* 390 AD. The fresco which depicts buildings in Palestine is dated between 401–17 AD. See Mancinelli, 1981, p.58.

61   Perate, 1885, p.312. See Leclercq, *DACL* 2.2, s.v. 'Basilique', Cols. 527–602, esp. Col. 591.

62   Leclercq, *DACL* 8.2, s.v. 'Latran', Cols. 1737–41, Fig.6897. Or perhaps the one on the left belongs to the part of the panel depicting Moses striking the rock. Leclercq, *DACL* 2.2, s.v. 'Moise' Cols. 1661–67. The tree is a rare addition in this scene otherwise rather common scene. The Apostle Paul places a Christological interpretation on this event: '...for they drank from the spiritual rock that accompanied them, and that rock was Christ' (1 Corinthians 10:4). Perhaps the sculptor sees some connection between the water, the rock (cf. Matthew 16:20), and Jesus's visit to the 'region of Caesarea Philippi', or even to the Transfiguration on nearby Mt. Hermon, where Jesus is proclaimed to supercede Moses. And perhaps the building directly behind this scene represents a church somehow symbolised by the scene. Perate, 1885, p.312: 'Ces constructions – là n'ont pas l'air d'un simple ornement; elles ont du exister quelque part. Il est agréable, en les voyant, de nous transporter à Panéas; et ce premier temple, le plus proche, serait donc l'ancienne maison de l'hémorroisse, conservée, nous dit Eusèbe, mais conservée sous forme de temple.'

63   See the excavation report, Tzaferis, forthcoming.

64   Crowfoot, 1941, p.5.

65   Eusebius, *HE* 8.1 (Williamson, 1966, p.328).

66   Crowfoot, 1941, p.61. Closest parallels are temples like those at Musmiya, Sanamen, and Slem (see Butler, 1930, pp.317 and 357).

67   'The statue of Christ was dragged around the city and mutilated by the pagans; but the Christians recovered the fragments, and deposited the statue in *the church in which it is still preserved*', Sozomen *HE* 5.21 (Hartranft, 1891, pp.342–43).

68   He repeats the story of Constantine's demolition of temples and idols, adding, 'many other cities about this time, without any command of the emperor, *destroyed the adjacent temples and statues, and erected houses of prayer*', Sozomen *HE* 2.5 (Hartranft, 1891, p.262).

69   Eusebius, *The Life of Constantine* 3.58.3 (Cameron and Hall, 1999, p.146).

70   M. Guidi, *Un Bios di Costantino*, Rome, 1908.

71   Meliara (eleventh century) and Xanthopoulos (Nikephaoros Kallistos, d.c. 1335): Kopp, 1963, p.235.

72   Kopp, 1963, p.235.

73   Or, since later writers tended to attribute all churches of the period to Queen Helena, there may have been no historical connection at all.

74   Macarius's work *Apocriticus* is quoted in the *Antirrhetica*, a ninth-century defence of the use of images by Nicephorus, Patriarch of Constantinople, and by Photius, *Bibl.* Cod. 271 (Migne *PG* 104: 223–24). See Crafer, 1919, p.31, for an English translation of the fragment as preserved by Nicephorus.

75   Macarius says that the woman 'having had the record of the deed itself nobly represented in bronze, gave it to her son, as something done recently, not long before ...' Crafer, 1919, p.31.

CHAPTER 7

1   Jackson, 1892, p. 147.

2   The original work by the Arian historian Philostorgius is lost, but was fortunately epitomised by Photius sometime before 895 AD.

3   'On either side of the single apse many churches have two rooms known as the *pastophoria*. One of the rooms served as a robing room for the clergy. It was known as the *diaconicon*. The *prothesis* was the other room; it was used for the presentation and preparation of offerings. These rooms were in use until the sixth century when developments in the liturgy made them

obsolete' (Hoppe, 1994, p.65). 'Diaconicon – The room used by the priests and their assistants (deacons) to store offerings brought to the church, their robes, and cultic artifacts. Initially it adjoined the church's hall or atrium, but in later periods it was the sacristy of the church located south of the central apse' (Tsafrir, 1993, p.351). One of the rooms beside the apse in the church in Banias has survived, but it is located on the *North* side of the apse.

4   Tzaferis, forthcoming excavation report.

5   Philostorgius, *HE* 7.3 (Walford, 1855, p.476).

6   Wilkinson, 1977, p.3.

7   Sozomen, *HE* 2.5 (Hartranft, 1891, p.262).

8   Sozomen, *HE* 7.15 (Hartranft, 1891, p.386).

9   Sozomen, *HE* 7.15 (Hartranft, 1891, p.386).

10 He continues: 'Eusebius relates, that at the base of this statue grew a herb which was unknown to the physicians and empirics, but was efficacious in the cure of all disorders. It does not appear a matter of astonishment to me, that, after God had vouchsafed to dwell with men, he should condescend to bestow benefits upon them.' Sozomen, *HE* 5.21 (Hartranft, 1891, pp.342–43).

11 Libanius, *Oration* 18.126–28 (Norman, 1969, pp.361–62).

12 Libanius, *Oration* 18.304 (Norman, 1969, p.393).

13 Gregory of Nazianzos, *First Invective Against Julian*, Sections 80–81 (King, 1888, pp.48–49).

14 Gregory of Nazianzos, *First Invective Against Julian*, Section 77 (King, 1888, p.46).

15 Libanius, *Oration* 18.171 (Norman, 1969, p.393). Heracleius the Cynic wrote against Julian, who 'composed an elaborate reply in which the poor Cynic was presented as not really knowing his business. Heracleius had compared Julian with the goat-like Pan. The shaft had struck home' (Bowersock, 1978, p.19). Julian's reply was a 'long myth with which…he concluded his address to the Cynic Heracleius …' (p.17).

16 Preger, 1901, 1975, pp.53–54. The *Parastaseis Syntomoi Chronikai* is an anonymous work preserved in a single ms. of the eleventh century. It was written in the eighth or ninth century in the context of the iconoclastic controversy, preserving stories of harmful miracles done by pagan statues. See Cameron and Herrin, 1984, and Mango, 1959, p.109.

17 Cameron and Herrin suggest that this document does not quote Eusebius directly, but via some compendium; and that it is mistaken in attributing any part of the account to John Diakrinomenos, since his history deals with the period from 431 to 471 AD (Cameron and Herrin, 1984, p.39).

18 It is significant that Julian is said to put up a pair of statues, male and female. Is there some reminiscence here of the original work, which included a female statue?

19 Θεῷ Διὶ παντεπόπτῃ . Ἰουλιανὸς Πανεάδι εἰς δῶρον ἄγει.

20 Cameron and Herrin, 1984, pp.124–27.

21 Cameron and Herrin are also sceptical of the historicity of this martyrdom, and suggest that once again the document does not quote Eusebius directly, but via some compendium.

22 Ammianus Marcellinus, *History* 22.11.3–11.

23 Negev, 1969, p.173. See Bowersock, 1978, pp.123–24. This inscription may now be seen in the Ussiskin Museum located near the entrance to the site of ancient Dan.

24 Bowersock, 1978, p.124.

25 Sozomen *HE* 5.21 (Hartranft, 1891, p.343).

26 See Russell, 1980, pp.50–51. 'Harvard Syriac 99' was translated and published by Brock, 1977, pp.267–86, and 1976, pp.103–7. For the hour and day of the earthquake see Brock, 1977, 276. 'Judging by the damage noted at Tiberias and Paneas, the Safed epicenter…was…involved' (Russell, 1980, p.49).

27 E.g., in Alexandria, according to Theodoret, the temple of Serapis was destroyed and the cult statue beheaded. 'Serapis was broken into small pieces of which some were committed to the flames, but his head was carried through all the town in sight of his worshippers, who mocked

the weakness of him to whom they had bowed the knee. Thus all over the world the shrines of the idols were destroyed' (Jackson, 1892, p.147–48).

28 Sozomen, *HE* 5.21 (Hartranft, 1891, p.343).

29 Tsafrir, 1986, p.129.

30 'Marosa' is the name the Greek church gave the woman, a term created from the phrase in Matthew 9:20: γυνὴ αἱμορροοῦσα.

31 Bernard, *PPTS* 2, p.8.

32 As implied by the Jeffreys, Jeffreys, Scott translation. John Malalas lived c. 490–c. 570. The *Chronicle* was written around 565–75 AD. See: Spinka and Downey, 1940; Jeffreys, Jeffreys, and Scott, 1986. Citations in the text are from the latter.

33 During the second to fourth centuries, even Christian centres like Bostra did not have a majority, and '…the new religion had made still less headway in the old centres of paganism', i.e. Gaza, Ascalon, Paneas and Sebaste (Avi-Yonah, 1984, pp.189–90). For an overview of the transition from paganism to Christianity in Palestine, particularly emphasising the situation at Beth Shean-Scythopolis, see Tsafrir, 1998.

34 Jackson, 1892, p.147.

35 *Codex Theodosanius* 9.16.1–12 (Pharr, 1952, pp.237–39).

36 Jackson, 1892, p.147.

37 For example, he describes the attempt by Marcellus, bishop of Apamea, to destroy the temple of Jupiter. In Alexandria, as already noted, the temple of Serapis was destroyed and the cult statue beheaded, in a manner reminiscent of the Banias story. Jackson, 1892, pp.146–48. But, despite these events, as late as 453 AD the temple of Isis at Philae was still in operation. Milne, 1898, pp.97, 100.

38 *HE* 29 (Jackson, 1892, p.152).

39 Marcus the Deacon, *Life of Saint Porphry* 41 (Hill, 1913, p.51).

40 Libanius, *Oration* 18.126 (Norman, 1969, p.361).

41 Libanius, *Oration* 18 (King, 1888, p.212).

42 *Codex Theodosanius* 15.1.36 (Pharr, 1952, p.427).

43 Judging from inscriptional evidence, 'the bottomlands of the Beka'a valley were being Christianised in the early fifth century, a periodisation consistent with other parts of Syria such as the Apamene' (Trombley 2, 1993, p.157). However, 'the accumulated evidence suggests… that the countryside of early fifth-century Syria was in many places hardly Christianised' (Trombley 2, 1993, p.163).

44 Bowersock, 1990, p.36.

45 Trombley, 1981, p.77.

46 Chuvin, 1990, pp.144ff.

47 Devreesse, 1945, p.199, p.130; Janin, 1953, p.210, citing Mansi 3, 586c; Le Quien, p.831. Mansi 6, p.1178 lists Bracchus Paneadensis; and cites these variations in other manuscripts: Bracheus or Batrachus.

48 See the forthcoming Ma'oz' excavation report and Berlin, 1999.

49 See Dussaud, 1900, pp.51, 127.

50 Cook, 1930, p.9; Paton, 1925, I, 60; Frazer, 1919, pp.37, 46.

51 Thomson, 1911, p.596.

52 Meshorer, 1984–1985.

53 Both are honoured on the same day, April 23.

54 Dussaud devotes a whole chapter to the Nusāriyeh form of the cult: Dussaud, 1900, pp.128–35. He calls Khader the reappearance of 'une divinité phénicienne' (p.132). In the West, this mysterious Khader/George becomes the famous 'Green Man' whose image appeared on the walls of European churches (including Canterbury Cathedral) for hundreds of years, peering down on the worshippers from arched corners or up from under shelves and benches.

The Green Man, partially of human and partially of plant form, is still remembered in certain Spring rituals in the English countryside. For a full account of this remarkable phenomenon, see Anderson, 1990, especially pp.29, 75.

55   Dussaud, 1900, pp.134–35.

56   See Canaan, 1980, esp. pp.120–22.

57   II Kings 2:11.

58   Guérin, 1880, p.308. 'On y remarque plusieurs colonnes, provenant d'un édifice ancien, dont l'une est surmontée d'un chapiteau corinthien, et un petit baptistère de forme carrée, orné aux quatre faces d'un fronton triangulaire décoré de fleurs; il repose sur une base élégante, qui imite une corbeille tressée à jour.'

59   Trombley, 1981, p.182, with documentation.

60   Trombley, 1981, p.77.

61   Trombley, 1981, p.119.

62   An interesting parallel from the same period in Arabia may be cited. 'In 515 at Zoara, an Arabian locality just south of the Dead Sea, Theandrites, a god venerated by Proclus and Isidorus, was replaced by Saint George. Stones bearing ex-votos to the fallen god were used again in the new masonry, and an inscription dated 22 March 515, lyrically evokes the transformation of the temple into a church: "God has his dwelling where there was once a hostel of demons; redeeming light now shines where once darkness spread its veil; where once sacrifices were made to idols, angels now dance".' OGIS 610; see Chuvin, 1990, p.141; citing Marinus, *Life of Proclus*, 19. A church was dedicated to St George in the fifth century at Mumsiyye (El-Ghassaniyye) in the Golan, in the district of Banias (Gregg and Urman, 1996, pp.213–14).

63   Bliss, 1912, p.10.

64   *Panarion* 19,1,1 (Williams 1, 1987, p.44); 53,1 (Williams 2, 1994, p.70). Epiphanius's use of the term 'Iturean' obviously refers to an area east of the Jordan, including Banias, and not to the ancient kingdom of Iturea in Lebanon.

65   *Pananion* 30,18,1 (Williams 1, 1987, p.133).

66   At villages like Farj and Er-Ramthaniyeh, Dauphin found stones with carved symbols belonging to both religions such as a lulav, fish, or ship, as well as symbols associated specifically with Jewish-Christians such as a cross superimposed on a ship's mast. Dauphin, 1982, pp.129–42. Ma'oz points out the likelihood that these should be attributed to Jewish-Christian sects. Ma'oz, 1985, pp.59–68.

67   Daftary, 1990, pp.142–43.

68   See *Onomasticon* 77 (Freeman-Grenville et al., 2003, p.46). Here, depending on Eusebius, he distinguishes between Dan and Paneas. But in *Comm in Ezech* 27:19 he identifies Dan with Paneas: 'Dan, Quae hodie appellatur Paneas' (Migne, *PL* 25.258). Archer, 1958, p.126. Eucharius (c. 440 AD) a near contemporary of Jerome, states the matter correctly: 'Dan is a little village on that frontier of Judaea which looks towards the north, at the fourth milestone from Paneas as you go towards Tyre' (Stewart, *PPTS* 2, p.12).

69   Robinson, 1857, p.412, note 5.

70   Thus Kopp, 1963, p.233.

71   Philostorgius *Fragment* (Walford, 1855, p.522).

72   Here is Philostorgius's full statement on the 'history' of Dan-Paneas, which furnished a good summary of what was probably the popular version of his day: 'At the farthest confines of Palestine, near where Phoenicia commences, there is situated a city formerly called Dan, after the tribe to which it belonged. Here some wanderers, cut off from the rest of their race at a distant period, settled down for some time, taking possession of the district around, built a town at its extreme border, and assumed to themselves the name of Phylarchs. This was the farthest point of Judaea on the side of Phoenicia. Herod the Great, in later times, built this

city, and changed its name to that of Caesarea Philippi; now, however, it is called Paneas, from the statue of Pan which was placed within its confines. In this town of Paneas rises one of the two fountains of the Jordan, (for it has two sources,) which is even now called "Dan", after the ancient name of the place. The other fountain, which is called "Jor", is about 160 stadia distant, and takes its rise out of the side of a hill. From each of these fountains flows a river, the one called Jorates and the other Danites. Descending from their hills, these rivers descend into a plain, where they join their waters, and flowing in a single channel, form the river Jordan' (Philostorgius *Fragment*, Walford, 1855, p.522).

73   Philostorgius, *Fragment* (Walford, 1855, p.522).
74   Philostorgius, *HE* 3.11 (Bidez, 1981, p.41:5–16), responding to this concept as presented in Servius's Fourth Century commentary on Vergil.
75   Martianus Capella (c. 400) also mentions the city, drawing on Pliny and Solinus as his sources: 'the river Jordan, which river rises from the spring Panias …' (Stern 2, 1974, p.653).
76   Wilkinson, 1977, p.4.
77   Tsafrir, 1986, pp.135–36. Tsafrir believes that Theodosius got his information not from a civil itinerary but from a Christian map produced especially for pilgrims and that the Madeba Map used the same source. He suggests that Paneas was the last town depicted on the northeast border of the map, p.139.
78   Wilkinson, 1977, p.63.
79   Stewart, *PPTS* 2, p.35, p.6.
80   This is certainly true of Theodosius. Tsafrir, 1986, p.130.
81   *Life of Sabas* 108 (Price, 1991). Written c. 557 AD.
82   *Malalas* 10.12 [237–39] (Jeffreys, Jeffreys, and Scott, 1986, pp.126–27). The entire account goes as follows: 'King Herod II, the son of Philip, grieving for John [the Baptist], came from the city of Sebaste to the city of Paneas in Judaea. A very wealthy woman, named Veronica, who lived in the city of Paneas, approached him, wishing to erect a statue to Jesus since she had been healed by him. As she did not dare to do this without imperial permission, she addressed a petition to the emperor Herod, asking to erect a statue to our Saviour Christ in that city. The petition ran as follows: To the august toparch Herod, lawgiver to Jews and Hellenes, emperor of the land of Trachonitis, a humble petition from Veronica, a dignitary of the city of Paneas… [She describes her healing by Jesus of haemorrhage, asks permission to erect the statue.] When the emperor Herod heard the contents of this petition, he was amazed by the miracle and, fearing the mystery of the cure, said, "This cure, woman, which was worked on you, is worthy of a greater statue. Go then and erect whatever kind of statue you wish to him, honouring by the offering him who healed you." Immediately Veronica, who had formerly suffered from a haemorrhage, set up in the middle of her city of Paneas a bronze statue of beaten bronze, mixing it with a small quantity of gold and silver, to our Lord God Jesus Christ. This statue remains in the city of Paneas to the present day, having been moved many years ago from the place where it stood in the middle of the city to a holy chapel. I found this document in the city of Paneas in the house of a man called Bassus, a Jew who had become a Christian. Included in it were lives of all the emperors who had formerly reigned over the land of Judaea.'
83   Wilkinson, 1977, p.81.
84   For example, from early sixth-century Constantinople: *Theodoros Anagnostes: Epitome* 139, lines 14–22 (Hanson, 1995, p.60, l.14ff).
85   See Tzaferis, forthcoming excavation report.
86   Berlin provides documentation for this at Beth Shearim, Beth Shean, and Hammat Gader, all to the south of Banias. Berlin, 1999, p.42.
87   Adan-Bayewitz, 1993, notes ceramic evidence for a general decline through the Hula Valley and eastern Galilee from the mid-fourth century on.

88 Hartal, 1989, pp.117–38. Though there were fewer settlements in the Byzantine period, the surviving settlements were larger, probably indicating that the population was gathering together for mutual protection against raids etc.

89 The quake probably originated from the Safad/Reina hexametres in Galilee. See Russell, 1985, pp.43–44.

90 Russell, 1985, pp.44–45.

91 *SEG* 7 (1934), pp.54–55, no 327.

92 George of Cyprus, *Descriptio Orbis Romani* (Gelzer, 1890, pp.49–50). This work dates from the sixth or early seventh century and is preserved in a ninth-century compilation. It lists metropolitan sees, archbishoprics and bishoprics, and probably reflects the political organisation of the area at the end of the Byzantine domination as well. George does not designate towns as 'πόλεις', but specifies only those bearing the name 'κώμη' (village). Thus, he implies that Paneas is a 'πόλις' at this time. We cannot be sure, however, that his information is up-to-date. Elsewhere he lists Damascus under the jurisdiction of Emesa (Gelzer, p.50) a possible indication of severe decline in the area. See also Jones, 1971, pp.281–88; Table VI, p.544; Honigmann, 1925, pp.77, 88.

93 Nau, 1909, p.215.

94 Tsafrir, 1986, p.139.

95 Kennedy, *Polis*, 1985.

96 Zeyadeh, 1992, p.108.

97 Zeyadeh, 1992, p.109.

98 Kennedy, *Polis*, 1985, p.5.

99 See also Bowersock, 1990, p.40.

100 Kennedy, *Polis*, 1985, p.18.

101 Hartal, 1985, pp.7–8. A salvage excavation in 1984 discovered a large house from late Roman/Byzantine times, probably with a bathhouse attached (p.9).

102 For a summary of the archeological and numismatic evidence for this invasion, see Russell, 2001, pp.42–57.

103 Bedrosian, 1985, p.95.

104 Hitti, 1961, pp.105–6.

105 Schick, 1995, pp.21, 26–31.

106 *BT Sanhedrin* 98a (Epstein, 1935, p.665).

107 For an account of this and following period see al-Balādhurī's *Futāh al-Buldān* (Hitti, 1961).

CHAPTER 8

1 Hitti, 1961, pp.412ff.

2 See Kennedy, *The Prophet*, 1985, pp.60–61; Hitti, 1961, p.414; note 5.

3 Hitti, 1961, p.415; *CMH* 2, p.343.

4 *EI 1, s.v. Baniyās*, p.1017. Kaegi, 1992, reports that just before the battle, 'Byzantine forces under Theodore Trithurios advanced through the Beqa' Valley and then across the Golan Heights and encamped at or near Jilliq, which is modern Kisme' (p.119).

5 See Ibn 'Asākir, Vol. I, p.163; al-Balādhurī, p.137; tr. p.210; cf. Al-Tabarī, Vol. 1, pp.2395–96 for Moslem accounts.

6 Hitti, 1961, p.416.

7 Kennedy, *The Prophet*, 1985, pp.117–18; Hitti, 1961, p.417; *CMH* 2, p.345.

8 Hitti, 1961, pp.422–23.

9 Hitti, 1961, p.424.

10   *EI 1, s.v. Baniyās*, p.1017.

11   Hartal, 1985, p.8.

12   Wilkinson, 1977, p.39.

13   See Ilisch, 1993, p.26, pl. 9, nos 254–57. This identification has been rejected by Ariel Berman, however.

14   Hitti, 1961, p.484.

15   Necephorus Calliste, *HE* 14.39: 'Nam Sophronio defuncto, in locum eius Athanasius Caesareae Philippi Episcopus suffectus est. Cujus sedem Gabriel quidem Caesareae Philippi, et ipse nuper Episcopus renuntiatus, dolo rapuit: et paulo post fatis concedens, vel invitus eam rursus Athanasio priori reliquit' (Migne, *PG* 146.1198).

16   Michael the Syrian, *Chronique* 2 (Chabot, 1924, p.459: 'John of Paneas', p.461: 'John of the Golan').

17   Hitti, 1961, p.439.

18   Wilkinson, 1977, p.107. See also p.4.

19   Kennedy, *The Prophet*, 1985, p.118; Hitti, 1961, p.414.

20   Hitti, 1961, p.440.

21   Hitti, 1961, p.499.

22   [*Quoting John Malalas*]: 'Berenice the sick woman of yore set up in the midst of her own city of Paneada a monument in bronze adorned with gold and silver. It is still standing in the city of Paneada. Not long ago it was taken from the place where it stood to the middle of the city, and placed in a house of prayer. One Batho, a converted Jew, found it mentioned in a book which contained an account of all those who had reigned over Judaea', *De imaginibus Oratio* 3 (Migne, *PG* 94.1369–74); Allies, 1898, pp.125–26.

23   Hitti, 1961, p.591.

24   John also quotes the passage from Eusebius concerning the statue. See Anderson, 1997, pp.94–95.

25   Germanus, writing c. 725 AD, seems to base his information on Eusebius. Migne *PG* 98.185–88; Grumel, 1936, p.4: no 330. Germanus claims the healing power of the statue at Paneas proves the validity of such. A similar point is made in the *Life of Saint Stephen the Younger* (Migne, *PG* 100.1085); Grumel, 1936, p.5: no 331.

26   This date is accepted by Wilkinson, 1977, p.128, and Kopp, 1963.

27   Wilkinson, 1977, p.128; cf. Thomas Wright, 1848, p.17.

28   Kopp, 1963, p.234. Brownlow, *PPTS* 3, p.17, translates the verb as present tense ('*is* a church'). Wilkinson, in the version quoted in the text above, retains the ambiguity, 'which had a church…'

29   Kopp, 1963, p.234.

30   See Tzaferis's excavation report, forthcoming.

31   See M. Guidi, *Un Bios di Costantino* (Rome: 1908).

32   Since the statement in the Life of Constantine is based on Epiphanius the Monk's Account, 'its topographical information refers to a time between 715 and 1009 AD', Wilkinson, 1977, p.202. The passage in Epiphanius merely says: 'About a mile further on [from Capernaum] stands a stone marked with the sign of the cross. That is where he healed the woman with the issue of blood', Wilkinson, 1977, p.120. There is no mention of a church. *The Life* apparently used a late version of Epiphanius, written sometime after 714 and before 1009 AD.

33   Wilkinson, 1977, p.203.

34   Meliara and Xanthopulos. Also mentioned by Nicephoros Callistos (d. *ca.* 1335 AD). Kopp, 1963, p.235.

35   Kopp, 1963, p.235.

36   Who in fact never travelled further north than Tiberias.

37   Watt 20, 1960, p.136, para 320.

38   Kopp, 1963, p.234.

39   Mango and Scott, 1997, p.79.

40   A work which may be characterised as 'pious fiction', by an otherwise unknown author called 'John the Monk' (claimed by some to be John of Damascus). It uses Philostorgius extensively for historical details. Artemius lived in the fourth century and was probably a friend of Constantius. The work may be found in English translation (by Mark Vermes) in Lieu and Montserrat, 1996, pp.224–56. The relevant passage (Section 57, pp.247–48) reads: 'There was a statue of the Saviour in the city of Paneas, magnificently erected by the haemorrhaging woman whom Christ cured, and set up in a prominent place in the city. After a time it became well-known from the miracle of the grass growing out of it. The Christians removed it and established it in the sacristy of the church. This statue the pagans pulled down and they fastened ropes to its feet and dragged it to the marketplace until it gradually broke up and disappeared. Only its head was left and was carried off by someone in the confusion raised by the pagans, while they addressed blasphemous and wholly inappropriate words to our Lord Jesus Christ such as no one had ever heard.'

41   Since he wrote mostly about the conquest of the northern coastal areas, some think he might really be from the 'other' Banias on the coast. But according to Donner, 1987, pp.12–13, this place was never called Banias until much later (first by Ibn al-Athīr), before this time being called Bulunyas.

42   Hitti, 1961, p.543.

43   Wilkinson, 1977, p.1.

44   Al-Ya'qūbī, *Kitāb al-buldān*, pp.326-29; Schick, 1995, pp.148–50; Gil, 1992, p.214.

45   Marmardji, 1951, p.13.

46   Gil, 1992, p.214, suggests that al-Ya'qūbī may have copied this information 'from an older source, from the time of the Umayyads'. The idea of such a complete transformation in the nature of the town's population, occurring so early, would be indeed remarkable, but is certainly not out of the question.

47   Friedland, 1997, p.38.

48   Salibi, 1977, p.51.

49   In April, 975 John Zimisces marched south from Antioch and reconquered the northern part of the Holy Land (Damascus, Tiberias, Nazareth, Acre, Sidon, Beirut etc., as far as Caesarea). Apparently his conquests did not include Banias. He did not hold the territory; these places were soon back in the hands of the Fatimids. See also Kennedy, *The Prophet*, 1985, p.279–80.

50   Collins, 2001, p.136; Le Strange, 1896, pp.24–25.

51   As we shall see, they seem to have brought some non-Moslems with them. Gil, 1992, p.214, reads Muqaddsī to say that the majority of the inhabitants *of Banias* were refugees, rather than that the majority of all the refugees fled to one place, namely Banias (the impression given by Collins' and Le Strange's translations). Gil's interpretation seems more likely.

52   See Kennedy, *The Prophet*, 1985, pp.287–92.

53   See Bianquis, 1986, pp.374–75: Ibrâhim b. Sa'id al Hasani al-Zahid, 'Asākir 2.207–10

54   Bianquis, 1986, p.50.

55   Bianquis, 1986, pp.70, 89, 166, 292.

56   Gil, 1997, p.22; Bianquis, 1986, pp.88–89. Ibn al-Athīr, *al-Kamil RHCHO* 8, p.640.

57   Bianquis, 1986, p.55. For a list of notables connected with the school at Banias see Bianquis, 1974, note 2, p.58.

58   See Daftary, 1990, pp.182–83.

59   Collins, 2001, p.41.

60   Collins, 2001, p.157; Le Strange, *PPTS* 3, p.85.

61   Collins, 2001, p.136; Le Strange, *PPTS* 3, p.24.

62   Collins, 2001, p.132; Le Strange, *PPTS* 3, p.10.

63   Collins, 2001, p.160; Le Strange, *PPTS* 3, p.94.

64   Collins, 2001, p.161; Le Strange, *PPTS* 3, p.95.
65   Collins, 2001, p.136; Le Strange, *PPTS* 3, p.24.
66   Collins, 2001, p.155; Le Strange, *PPTS* 3, p.82.
67   Collins, 2001, p.137; Le Strange, *PPTS* 3, pp.24–25.
68   As translated by Le Strange, *PPTS* 3, p.81. That is, with effects on the stomach and digestive system which are still familiar to those who may venture to drink water directly from the springs, rivers, or standing pools in these parts. Collins, 2001, p.155: 'purgative'.
69   Collins, 2001, p.137; Le Strange, *PPTS* 3, pp.24–25.
70   Le Strange, *PPTS* 3, pp.24–25.
71   See Kennedy, *The Prophet*, 1985, pp.330–37.
72   Kennedy, *The Prophet*, 1985, pp.336–37.
73   Ibn Tagri Birdi, citing Sibt ibn al-Gawzi, claims that this was a cynical act on the part of Al-Hākim to gain support among the people of the mountains: 'Al-Hākim secretly sent money to Darazi and said to him, "Do this in order to gain Syria! Disseminate your doctrine in the mountains; the people there are gullible". So he went to Syria and settled in the Wâdî al-Taym, west of Damascus, in the region of Banias' (Bianquis, 1986, p.368).
74   We are reminded that Neo-Platonism held on for centuries in these very regions as a defiant last alternative to Christianity.
75   Bliss, 1912, pp.10–11.
76   Betts, 1988, p.13; Daftary, 1990, p.198. See Hitti, 1961, pp.583ff.
77   Gil, 1992, p.429 (citing Ibn 'Asākir 3.406, and 6.446).
78   According to Ibn al-Jawzi, *Muntazam* 9.69. Cited by Gil, 1992, pp.215–16.
79   Mann 1, 1920, p.157; original text in 2, pp.176–78.
80   It is unfortunate that the celebrated eleventh-century traveller Nâsir i-Khusran (1035–47 AD) never visited Banias, always taking other routes between the coast and Damascus, and perhaps in so doing demonstrating concern for the dangers of the area.
81   Amiran, et al., 1995, p.269; Bianquis, 1986, p.637. Other sources date the event to 20 April 1067.
82   Wechter, 1945, p.201.
83   Assaf, 1938, p.III, English summary; Gil, 1992, pp.214–15, cf. p.624. A manuscript of the eleventh century in Cambridge mentions Jewish inhabitants of Banias. See Braslavski, 1938, pp.128–31, [in Hebrew, English summary]. See also Assaf, 1938, pp.16–19 [In Hebrew, English summary]. Assaf presents the full text of this document with the comment: 'from which it would appear that the Jewish community in Baneas was under the jurisdiction of Damascus'.
84   *EJ* 4, p.163. Mann 1, 1920, p.157; original text in 2, pp.202–3. Mann notes that the Geniza fragment describing the two communities, 'clearly dates from the beginning of the twelfth century since Moses Nagid, the son of Meborak, is mentioned therein'. Nagid is known from other documents to have lived at this time.
85   Gil, 1992, p.214.
86   Gil, 1992, p.214. 'Haver' is an honorific title, roughly equivalent to the loose use of the English 'Esq.'
87   Gil, 1992, pp.214–15, cf. p.624. Gil suggests that the name Qitos: 'obviously of Greek origin, perhaps confirms Muqaddasi 's remarks about the origins of the inhabitants of Baniyas from the coastal towns of Syria, where the tradition from Byzantine times was perhaps stronger, particularly in the sphere of terms and names' (p.216).
88   Gil, 1992, p.215.
89   Oxford MS. Heb. d. 75, fol. 13. See Mann 2, 1920, pp.202–3 and Gil, 1992, p.215.
90   Runciman 2, 1951, pp.121–23.
91   Gil, 1992, p.411.
92   Daftary, 1990, p.207. Though the Fatimids did gain brief control over Jerusalem in 1096 AD, only to lose it to the Crusaders less than three years later. See Hitti, 1961, pp.574ff.

CHAPTER 9

1   The Wâdî Sa'âr 'divides the Golan from Mount Hermon's massif' and is the northern geographical boundary of the Golan. The massif is limestone; the other side of the wâdî is basalt, thus 'a geological seam'. Of note is the rapid descent of Wâdî Sa'âr from the Druze village of Mas'ada to Banias: 'from 950 m. to 340 m. where it joins Nahr Banias – a descent of more than 600 m. in a distance of only seven kilometres (a slope of 86%)' Urman, 1985, pp.31–32.

2   See Tzaferis's excavation report, forthcoming. He suggests that given the frontier nature of the city, it may have had actual defensive walls, though no archaeological proof has yet been discovered. During the Byzantine Period, walls were constructed to include the new suburbs to the south of Wâdî Sa'âr, portions of which have survived.

3   See Benvenisti, 1970, for an extensive discussion of the fortifications.

4   Ryan, 1969, p.133.

5   'A day's journey to the north-east of Tiberias is Mount Libanus, at the foot of which the river Jordan boils out from two fountains, of which one is called Jor, and the other Dan; the streams of which, joining in one, become a very rapid river, and take the name Jordan. Its origin is near Caesarea, the city of Philip the Tetrarch, in the district where Jesus, as is related in the Gospel, interrogated his disciples, saying, "Whom do men say that I, the Son of Man, am?" Now the river Jordan, flowing from its spring with a very rapid course, falls into the sea of Galilee...' Wright, 1848, p 47; Brownlow, *PPTS* 4, p.22.

6   Wilkinson, 1988, p.160. See also Brownlow, *PPTS* 4, pp.54, 66.

7   Ryan, 1969, p.133; see also p.262. Jerome, *Comm in Amos* (Migne *PL* 25.1084): 'Dan, in terminis terrae Judaicae, ubi nunc Paneas est'.

8   Runciman 2, 1951, p.95.

9   Ryan, 1969, p.205.

10 Scheiber, 1954, p.33.

11 Goitein, 1953, p.75.

12 Goitein, 1953, p.77; Mann, 1935, p.42.

13 Goitein, 1953, p.84.

14 Gil, 1992, p.215.

15 Runciman 2, 1951, p.170.

16 Daftary, 1990, pp. 142–43.

17 See Franzius, 1969; Daftary, 1990, p.375; Runciman 2, 1951, p.179. On Bahrām's activities in Damascus and Banias, see Gibb [Ibn al-Qalânisî], 1932, pp.179–80.

18 Gibb, 1932, p.187.

19 Gibb, 1932, p.187.

20 Ilisch, 1993, p.27 (pl. number 9: Coin number 258).

21 See Berman in forthcoming excavation report.

22 Daftary, 1990, pp.375–76.

23 Paul Deschamps, 1939, pp.146–47. See Ibn al-Athîr, *Kamel-Altevarykh*, *RHCHO* 1, pp.367, 382–84, 789; Gibb [al-Qalânisî], 1932, pp.179–80; Abū'l-Fedā, *Annals*, *RHCHO* 1, pp.17–18.

24 Gibb [al-Qalânisî], 1932, pp.191–95; see also Ibn al-Athîr, pp.384–86.

25 Schlumberger, 1964.

26 See Rey, 1869, p.245 for further family history.

27 Arabic Ms. no1466, cited by Deschamps, 1939, p.217.

28 E.g. Deschamps, 1939, p.147.

29 Benvenisti, 1970, pp.147–48: 'a thorough examination of the sources shows that this assertion is not firmly based: the sources do not mention the existence of a separate citadel in the vicinity of Banias, but always refer to a citadel within the walls of the city, specifying a separate

defensive unit within the city defences…The citadel of Banias was thus a separate defensive unit, within the fortifications, and resembled the defensive arrangements of Jerusalem, Arsuf, Caesarea and Tyre. It is possible that Subeibe was indeed not the citadel of Banias, but an independent Frankish castle, though this is doubtful since no such castle is mentioned in the sources…The first Frankish source to mention the name Subeibe was Joinville, in his account of the attempt to capture it in 1253…The only thing which is clear today is that Subeibe was not the citadel of Frankish Banias and that in its present form it is an Ayyûbid-Mamlûk structure.' Berchem thought that the southern and northern faces of Subeibe were Crusader (1888, p.19), and that they were probably built while Banias was held by Crusaders without interruption (between 1139–64). Recent studies also cast doubt on this theory. See below.

30 See Gibb, 1932 [al-Qalânisî], pp.216–17; Ibn al-Athîr, *Kamel-Altevarykh*, RHCO 1, pp.396–97, 792; Kemal ed-Dîn, *Extraits du Dictionnaire Biographique*, RHCO 3, p.696; Abū'l-Fedā, *Annals*, RHCO 1, p.20; and William of Tyre, Babcock and Krey 2, 1943, p.74.

31 Gibb, 1932, [al-Qalânisî], p.218.

32 Babcock and Krey 2, 1943, p.74.

33 Wilkinson, 1988, p.79.

34 MacPherson, *PPTS* 5, p.24. 'Twenty-four miles from Damascus is Paneas, at the foot of Lebanon, towards the south, an eminent city, which is called Belinas, from Bilina, on account of the beauty of its site – and Cesarea Philippi, receiving from Caesar his own name.'

35 Wilkinson, 1988, pp.189–92. This work also describes a great fair in the plain where the 'Dan' becomes visible (after running underground) at a place called Meddan. 'Every year a countless crowd of people gathers in the plain, bringing anything it wants to sell, and stays there. A great army of Parthians and Arabs looks after the people as they feed their flocks in the lavish pastures.' This is in the province of 'Sueta' and Job's tomb is there (p.191).

36 Babcock and Krey 2, 1943, p.77; Gibb [Ibn al-Qalânisî], 1932, pp.216–17; Ibn al-Athîr, RHCO 1, pp.401–2.

37 Babcock and Krey, 1943, p.77.

38 Renier apparently never had children. Agnes, after his death, married Gerard of Sidon and had a son by him, named Renaud, who was lord of that city at the time William of Tyre was writing. At Renier's death the *seigneurie* of Banias passed to his cousin, Humphey of Toron. Babcock and Krey 2, 1943, p.77; Schlumberger, 1964, p.119; Rey, 1869, p.470.

39 See Moshe Sharon, 'The Arabic Inscriptions of Baniyas', forthcoming.

40 For a summary of the career of Zengî see Alptekin, 1978.

41 Abū'l-Fedā, *Annals*, RHCO 1, p.23; Ibn al-Athîr, *Kamel-Altevarykh*, RHCO 1, p.424; W.B. Stevenson, 1907, p.139.

42 Gibb [Ibn al-Qalânisî], 1932, pp.256–59; Benvenisti, 1970, p.149; Runciman 2, 1951, p.227.

43 Babcock and Krey, 1943, p.107.

44 Babcock and Krey, 1943, p.107.

45 Gibb [Ibn al-Qalânisî], 1932, pp.270–73. Kemal ed-Dîn, *Extraits de la Chronique d'Alep*, RHCO 3, p.682.

46 Gibb [Ibn al-Qalânisî], 1932, pp.270–73; Ibn al-Athîr, *Kamel-Altevarykh*, RHCO 1, p.436, identifies the defenders as including 'plusieurs habitants du Becaa et des campagnes voisines'.

47 Babcock and Krey 2, 1943, p.108.

48 Babcock and Krey, 1943, p.108.

49 Gibb [Ibn al-Qalânisî], 1932, pp.270–73.

50 Babcock and Krey, 1943, p.109.

51 Babcock and Krey 2, 1943, p.109.

52 Prawer, 1972, p.124, describes the use of these towers.

53 Babcock and Krey 2, 1943, p.111.

54 See Tzaferis, forthcoming excavation report.

55 Babcock and Krey, 1943, p.113.

56 Hitti, 1929, pp. 28–29.

57 Babcock and Krey, 1943, p.112.

58 Hitti, 1929, p.3.

59 Hitti, 1929, p.161.

60 Hitti, 1929, p.116. The tent was likely located relatively near the Banias River, in the fields now cultivated by the residents of Snir.

61 Hitti, 1929, pp.93–94. Usama also hunted with comrades in the forest of Banias, which abounded in game. While living in Damascus, he says, 'I took part, during the day of Shihab-al-Dîn Mahud ibn-Taj-al-Mulûk, in the chase of birds, gazelles, wild asses and roes. One day I saw him as we went out together to the forest of Baniyas, where the ground was thickly covered with grass. After killing a number of roe deer, we pitched our tents in the form of a circle and encamped. A roe deer which was sleeping in the grass now appeared in the midst of the enclosure. It was seized among the tents.' Hitti, 1929, p.214.

62 Babcock and Krey 2, 1943, p.186.

63 Gibb [Ibn al-Qalânisî], 1932, pp.297–300; Ibn al-Athīr, *Kamel Altewaryk*, RHCO 1, pp.469, 540; Ibn al-Athīr, *History of the Atabeks of Mosul*, RHCO 2:2, p.161; Abū'l-Fedā, *Annals*, RHCO 1, p.28.

64 Gibb [Ibn al-Qalânisî], 1932, p.311; Abû Chama, *The Two Gardens*, RHCO 4, pp.74–75.

65 Runciman 2,1951, p.340; Gibb, 1932 [al-Qalânisî], pp.315–16; Deschamps, 1939, p.154.

66 Abû Chama, *The Two Gardens*, RHCO 4, p.77.

67 Aleppo, Harran, Tripoli, Beirut, Tyre, Homs, Am'arra, Hama Shayzar etc. Runciman 2, 1952, p.343; Maalouf, 1984, p.154; Abû Chama, *The Two Gardens*, RHCO 4, p.84; Ibn al-Athīr, *Kamel-Altevarykh*, RHCO 1, p.503.

68 'About this time an immense company of Arabs and Turkomans, in far larger numbers than every before, had assembled in a forest near the city of Banyas. These people, like the Arabs, habitually live in tents and sustain life on milk. The forest is now generally known as the forest of Banyas from the city of that name, but in olden time the entire tract, including those parts which extend toward both north and south as well as that which covers Lebanon itself, was called the forest of Lebanon…' Babcock and Krey 2, 1943, p.255.

69 Apparently Renier had no male heir and the *seigneurie* went to Humphrey (II), who had married one of Renier's daughters. See Rey, 1869, p.470. A bulla of Humphrey, found in Tyre, may be seen in Briailles, 1950, pp.287–88, pl. XIII:5.

70 Babcock and Krey 2, 1943, p.256.

71 Babcock and Krey, 1943, p.256..

72 Abû Chama, *The Two Gardens,* RHCO 4, pp.84–85; see Deschamps, 1939, p.156.

73 Gibb [Ibn al-Qalânisî], pp.340–42. See also Abû Chama, *The Two Gardens*, RHCO 4, pp.85–91.

74 Babcock and Krey, 1943, p.258.

75 See Tzaferis, forthcoming excavation report.

76 Apparently under the impression that the citadel in this story is Subaybah, Gabrieli, 1969, p.66, causes Al al-Qalânisî to say 'the walls of the *lower city* were in ruins'. Gibb, correctly translates, 'the wall of Banyas and the dwellings of its inhabitants were entirely in ruins' (p.335). It is very unlikely that Subaybah was in existence at this time. See below.

77 Babcock and Krey, 1943, p.259.

78 Babcock and Krey, 1943, p.261.

79 'Rey propose d'identifier ce lieu avec Ain Belatha, dans la vallée du Bahr-Hulé' (Deschamps, 1939, p.159, n.3).

80 Babcock and Krey 2, 1943, p.264.

81 Babcock and Krey 2, 1943, p.310. He admits, however, 'we have no trustworthy information on these points'.

82   Humphrey continued to control Toron and Chateau-de-Neuf. In 1179 he was wounded in an engagement near Banias and died ten days later. He was buried at Toron. Briailles, 1950, p.288; Rey, 1869, pp.468–76.

83   Ibn al-Athīr, *History of the Atabeks of Mosul*, RHCO 2:2, pp.233–34; Deschamps, 1939, p.161.

84   Ibn al-Athīr, *Kamel Altevaryk*, RHCO 1, p.542, 'Aujourd'hui, Dieu a refraichi la peau de ton père en le tirant du feu de la gehenne'.

85   Ibn al-Athīr, *Kamel Altevaryk*, RHCO 1, p.541.

86   Sandoli, 1974: 'a. Pietro (no 402): Sigillo di cera a navetta, alto 55 mm. x 38…Retto. Nel Centro: Il vescovo, vestito pontificalmente, benedice collo destra, regge il pastorale colla sinistra. Tra i due cerchi concentrici si legge: b. Natale (no 403): Sigillo de cera rossa del diathetro di 30 mm…' (depicted on p.298, Fig.128).

87   A complete list of Crusader coins found at the site may be found in Bermann, forthcoming excavation report.

88   It must be remembered, however, that the *fleur de lis* was also a Mamlûk device.

CHAPTER 10

1   Bah' al-Dîn, *Saladin* 45 (Richards, p.47).

2   See Babcock and Krey, 1943, pp.60–61.

3   Ibn al-Athīr *Kamel Altevaryka*, RHCO 1, pp.610–11; Abû Chama, *The Two Gardens*, RHCO 4, pp.161–62; Runciman 2, 1951, p.399.

4   Deschamps, 1939, p.162; Newby, 1983.

5   Runciman 2, 1951, p.418.

6   Broadhurst, 1980, pp.59–60; Ibn al-Athīr, *Kamel Altevarykh*, RHCO 1, p.636.

7   Runciman 2, 1951, p.434.

8   Ibn Jubair, *Extrait du Voyage d'ibn Djobeir*, RHCHO 3, pp.439–40; Le Strange, 1896, p.418. It is significant that the fortress of Subaybah, which stands on the hill behind Banias, and is later called the 'fortress of Banias', is not mentioned by Ibn Jubair. The strong implication is that no fortress existed yet at that location. In addition to the streams that surround the town's fortifications, water runs even today through a channel along what was once the main street of the town, pouring out of the medieval gate which has survived from Ayyûbid times, just as it did when Ibn Jubair visited the place.

9   Marmardji, 1951, pp.13–14.

10   Humphreys, 1977, p.77.

11   Runciman 2, 1951, pp.452–53.

12   Stewart, *PPTS* 11, p.105.

13   Stewart, *PPTS* 5, p.35.

14   Stewart, *PPTS* 6, p.31.

15   La Monte, 1932, p.147. 'Humphrey's lands were in the hands of the enemy. Josecelin was to have them if they were recovered.'

16   Humphreys, 1977, p.77.

17   Runciman 2, 1951, pp.452–453.

18   Bah' al-Dîn, *Saladin* 97 (Richards, p.90); Wilson and Condor, *PPTS* 13, pp.141–42.

19   Bah' al-Dîn, *Saladin* 102 (Richards, p.96); Wilson and Condor, *PPTS* 13, p.153.

20   Abû Chama, *The Two Gardens*, RHCO 4, pp.399–40. The prisoner was kept in the administrative quarters located in the town itself, 'au château de Banyas'. The fortress Subaybah had not yet been built.

21   Wechter, 1945, p.201ff.

22   A Persian word meaning 'four persons'.

23   Broadhurst, 1980, p.101.

24   Broadhurst, 1980, pp.103–4.

25   Broadhurst, 1980, p.111.

26   See an amusing instance in Broadhurst, 1980, p.112.

27   Broadhurst, 1980, p.122; note 22, p.324.

28   Broadhurst, 1980, p.130.

29   Broadhurst, 1980, pp.132–35; Humphreys, 1977, pp.110–12.

30   Broadhurst, 1980, pp.138–39.

31   Broadhurst, 1980, p.137. See also Gottschalk, 1958, p.29; Abû Chama, *The Two Gardens*, RHCO 5, p.124–25.

32   Humphreys, 1977, pp.77, 142.

33   Humphreys, 1977, p.137.

34   Abû Chama, *The Two Gardens*, RHCO 5, 1898, p.146.

35   Amiran, et al., 1995, p.270; Humphreys, 1977, p.147. Maqrizî mentions a great earthquake over 'most of Egypt, Syria' etc., dated in the year 1203/4. Broadhurst, 1980, p.146. This is most likely a mistake – perhaps confusion with the earthquake of 1020 mentioned above. Current earthquake research does not include one for this date.

36   As corrected by Sharon. See forthcoming excavation report.

37   Broadhurst, 1980, p.146.

38   Broadhurst, 1980, pp.153f.

39   So Humphreys, 1977, p.143; Maqrizî dates the death to 607H=1210–11.

40   Humphreys, 1977, p.143.

41   Adler, 1930, p.110; Carmoly, 1847, p.136.

42   See Guérin, 1880, p.321; Carmoly, 1847, p.165. Carmoly maintains that this Iddo 'the Prophet' is in fact a different person from the Iddo 'the Seer' mentioned in the biblical text.

43   Another Jewish 'Visitor' (1215–60): *The Forged Itinerary of R. Menahem of Hebron*. This thirteenth-century forgery bears a fictitious name and consists of pieces of real itineraries assembled in France (Prawer, 1988, p.227). The itinerary has the 'author' going to Dan where 'there is a large community and very important people therein and I remained there for four days and walked to the east of the city with the city's inhabitants and they showed me the Cave of Paneas [written Aspamia instead of the usual Pamias, i.e. Banyas] and the spring of the Jordan coming out and flowing out from beneath the cave' (Quoted and translated by Prawer, 1988, p.225). Prawer notes that 'though it is known that Jerusalem had a Jewish community at that time, there is no proof whatsoever of the existence of a Jewish community in Banyas' (Prawer, 1988, p.226). Another Rabbi visited Banias a few years later: R. Jacob, the 'Messenger of the Yeshiva of Acre' (c. 1258–70). In his 'Description des Tombeaux Sacrês' he calls it 'Pameas', confusing it with Dan. 'A Pameas, qui est Dan, se trouve enterré Iddo, le prophete, avec lequel soit la paix!' (Carmoly, 1847, p.183). R. Jacob was 'a kind of professional fund-raiser on behalf of the Academy in Acre' (Prawer, 1988, p.230). He apparently left this itinerary in France, where it was edited by someone else.

44   See Broadhurst, 1980, p.155; cf. Humphreys, 1977, p.164.

45   Broadhurst, 1980, p.155.

46   Humphreys, 1977, p.164.

47   Gottschalk, 1958, pp.55–56.

48   Ziadeh, 1953, p.56; Abû Chama, *The Two Gardens*, RHCHO 5, p.171; Gottschalk, 1958, p.88.

49   Gottschalk, 1958, p.88.

50   Yāqūt, *Mu'jam al buldān* (Humphreys, 1977, p.223). Date 1228.

51   E.g. Ernoul, writing c. 1220: 'Now we have told you of the Mount of Niban, whence the fountains spring at its feet. Now we tell you of a city below the slope of the mountain above the fountains, which is called Belinas. It was already Christian in the time of Godfrey of

Bouillon, but I cannot tell you in the time of which king it was lost by them. But afterwards they fortified two castles near to it: the one is call Toron… four leagues from the city of Belinas…the other is called Saphet' (Condor, *PPTS* 6, p.51).

52 See Clermont-Ganneau, 1888, p.242; Berchem, 1888.
53 Though it has been often asserted that Subaybah was built by the Crusaders, strong evidence suggests that it was built by the Moslems instead. See e.g. Ellenblum, 1989.
54 Ellenblum points out that there are only two witnesses to the idea that the Crusaders built Subaybah, both from the thirteenth century, and both highly suspect. There are none at all from the twelfth century. William of Tyre does not mention the fortress, speaking instead of a 'praesidium' inside the town of Banias. Ibn Jubair, visiting in 1184, notes the fort at Hunîn, but not Subaybah, suggesting that it was not in existence at that time. Ibn Jubair, *Extrait du Voyage d'ibn Djobeir*, *RHCHO* 3, pp.440. Sibt ibn al-Jawzī (d.645 or 1256) plainly says, 'al-'Azîz 'Uthmân was the ruler of Banias…and he built al Subaybah' (Mi'rat al-Zaman 8:678 – cited by Ellenblum, 1989, p.108).
55 Broadhurst, 1980, p.201. Shortly thereafter, al Kamil removed the young prince and put his own brother Ashrat Musa in his place in Damascus. He also proposed to take over Palestine and Southern Syrian directly and move 'Uthmân to Baalbek. But the inscription on the gate of Banias seems to show that this did not happen. See Clermont-Ganneau, 'Inscription …' 1888, p.242.
56 Broadhurst, 1980, p.209.
57 Humphreys, 1977, pp.194–95.
58 Broadhurst, 1980, p.219.
59 Berchem, 1888, p.7.
60 Broadhurst, 1980, p.273.
61 Broadhurst, 1980, p.274.
62 Al-Sa'id was granted an *iqta* in Egypt instead, nearly equal in importance to Banias. But apparently he never actually possessed it (Humphreys, 1977, pp.292, 310).
63 Gottschalk, 1958, pp.29–30; Broadhurst, 1980, p.284.
64 Show, 1963, p.307. 'In this city there rises a spring called Jor, and in the middle of the plain outside the city there arises another very beautiful spring call Dan. Now it so happens that when the streams from these two sources meet, they become the river which is called the Jordan …' This is a typical etymology of the day, though this time coming from one who had actually seen both streams.
65 Show, 1963, p.308.
66 Show, 1963, p.308.
67 Show, 1963, p.308.
68 Show, 1963, p.308.
69 Show, 1963, p.309.
70 Show, 1963, p.309.
71 Show, 1963, p.310.
72 Humphreys, 1977, p.348.
73 Holt, 1995, p.3.
74 *Encyc. of Islam* 1:1017a (with documentation from Arabic sources); Ziadeh, 1953, p.13.
75 Though perhaps not as many as 200, as claimed by al-Zahîr (b. 1410). Ziadeh, 1953, pp.70–72; Bakhit, 1982, p.67.
76 See Ziadeh, 1953, pp.53, 55–56.
77 Gaudefroy-Demombynes, 1923, pp.179–80.
78 See Dar and Kindler, 1988–89, p.129.
79 Sadeque, 1956, pp.117–18. Cf. Holt, 1995, p.4.
80 Hartal, 1997.

81   From *Sirat al-Malik al-Zahîr*; Sadeque, 1956, p.111.

82   Holt, 1995, p.107. There is some evidence for this being the case. Baybars himself seems to have used Banias in this way. See Lyons [Ibn al-Furat], 1971, p.116.

83   Lyons [Ibn al-Furat], 1971, p.90.

84   Lyons [Ibn Al-Furat], 1971, p.164.

85   Holt, 1995, p.76.

86   See Janin, 1953, Col. 211.

87   In *Pars Quarta: Mathematicae in Divinis Utilitas* ('Mathematics in the Service of Theology'), Sect. 338.

88   Stewart, *PPTS* 12, p.97.

89   Sauvaget, 1949, p.27, quoting al-Jazari no 149.

90   Sauvaget, 1949, p.82, quoting al-Jazari no 506; Abû l Feda, *Memoirs*, pp.33–34. Qara Sunqur was governor, at various times, of several important Syrian cities, and involved in many of the intrigues and political infighting of the period, including involvement in the assassination of the Sultan al-Malik al-Ashraf in 693 (1293–94). (See Abû l Feda, *Memoirs*, p.22 etc.)

91   Marmardji, 1951, p.14.

92   Le Strange, 1896, p.419.

93   Le Strange, 1896, pp.418–19.

94   Wechter, 1945, pp.201ff. Names include Sabbas (under Alexander Comnenus); Gabriel Broulasuers (1320); and Euthyme (1377–78). Janin, 1953, Cols. 210–11.

95   Condor, *PPTS* 13, pp.12–13; Stewart, *PPTS* 12, p.19.

96   Stewart, *PPTS* 12, p.128. Carmoly records a supposed visit by a Jewish pilgrim, Rabbi Isaac ben Joseph ibn Chelo, in 1333. Adler, 1930, pp.149–50; Carmoly, 1847, p.264. He makes no mention of any Jewish pilgrimage sites there, though he usually mentions such places. However, Prawer, 1988, p.227, says this itinerary is a 'clever forgery' created by Carmoly.

97   Robinson, 1857, p.412. It is certain, however, that some missionaries or pilgrims from the West, or at least certainly Russia, did visit Banias prior to the nineteenth century.

98   Gaudefroy-Demombynes, 1923, pp.179–80.

99   'Baniyas (Belinas) is the city of the district of Jaulan, and it has a citadel known as al-Subaiba which was built by the Franks after the year 500 (1106–7)' (Lyons, 1971, p.47). Ibn al-Furat's citation of the earlier history reads: 'He said that the town was surrendered to Yanal al-Tajji in the year 501 (1107–8), but he did not mention from whom he took it. Then Tancred (Tankrid), the lord of Antioch, came down against it when there were very few provisions in it and plundered it without resistance, after which he then left it…The na'ib of Khwaja Bahrām Isma'il, remained in Baniyas and surrendered it to the Franks. He stayed there under their authority until he was killed in the year 524 (1129–30). The Franks then continued to hold the place until Shams al-Mulûk Isma'il marched there and came down against it on Wednesday, the 24th of Muharram in the year 527 (5 December 1132). Some historians have said that the citadel of as-Subaiba was built after the Franks took the town in the year 524 (1129–30) and that it was they who constructed it. Shams al-Mulûk took it by force in one day after attacking and encircling it and it stayed in his hands and in those of his brother Shihab al-Dîn Mahmud after him until Shihab al-Dîn surrendered it to Fulk, son of Fulk the Frank, the ruler of Jerusalem, in the year 534 (1139–40). The Franks continued to hold it until Nūr ad-Dîn came down against it and took it on Monday, the first day of Dhu'l-Hijja in the year 559 [October 1164]' (Lyons, 1971, p.47).

100 al-Zahîr, 1896, pp.46–47.

101 Ellenblum, 1989, p.105.

102 Laoust, 1952, pp. 95–96, quoting the *Annals of Muhammad Ibn Tulun*.

103 Stewart, 1892–93, p.23.

104 'Ye cytie yt now is called Belenas was sometyme called Dan, after ye name of ye sayd well [i.e. "Jor"], for it stondeth fast therby, at ye fote of the sayd Moute Libani; and at this towne of Dan,

otherwyse called Belenas, begynneth ye lode of promyssion [land of promise] northwarde…
Belenas is otherwyse called Cesaria Philippi' (Ellis, 1851, pp.48–49).

105   Bakhit, 1982, p.67.

106   Hitti, 1961, pp.668–69.

107   Van Egmont 2, 1769, p.266.

108   Luke, 1927, p.19. This traveller did know the name 'Banias' and passed rather close to the site, but did not connect it with Caesarea Philippi. His itinerary from Damascus to Jerusalem was via 'Ebbrech' (Khan al-Bureij?), across the river 'Nharlariac' (Nahr al-'Arni), to 'Sasia' (Sa'sa) 'where is paid by the Frank Christians a certain tax'. Then to Oinirti, Pergie, and Sumaea, 'and on our way we saw at the foot of the Snowy Mountain (Hermon) certain towns where are produced [raisins]…On the third day we came to the mountains of Caphet (Safet) in Upper Galilee…but before reaching these mountains we saw not far from them, in a certain valley, a lake which these people call Lake Melhec (Hulah), formed by the waters of the [Jor?] and the Dan descending Mount Lebanon or, *as these people say descending from the mountains of Banias*.' He crossed the Jordan at Jacob's Bridge (Khan Yubb Yusuf) (Luke, 1927, pp.17–18).

109   See Condor, *PPTS* 13, p.15.

110   See Carmoly, 1847, p.564.

111   Cf. II Chron. 12:15; 13:22 ('Iddo the Prophet').

112   According to I Chron. 6: 62, 71, the 'Gershomites' were alloted 'Golan in Bashan'.

113   Carmoly, 1847, p.183. R. Jacob was 'a kind of professional fund-raiser on behalf of the Academy in Acre' (Prawer, 1988, p.230). This itinerary was apparently left by him in France, where it was edited by someone else.

114   A Geniza fragment (no 2699) in the E. Adler collection. See Prawer, 1988, pp.176ff. 'The author…is an Oriental Jew who went on a pilgrimage to the Holy Land under Crusader rule in the twelfth century' (Prawer, 1988, p.178). He visited Kadesh Naftali 'on the road to Banias, and finally to Lebanon' (apparently actually passing through Banias, see map, p.183). According to Prawer, this work was plagiarised in the fifteenth century, at which time the statement 'Iddo [the Seer] is buried in Dan', has added to it. Prawer, 1988, p.184.

115   Carmoly, 1847, p.449.

116   A document dated 1624 mentions the murder of a Jewish physician named 'Elijah ha-Kohen of Banias' by an Arab sheikh. *EJ* 4, p.163: Ben Zvi, in *Tarbiz* 3 [1932], p.442.

CHAPTER 11

1   Hitti, 1965, p.163.

2   Hitti, 1965, p.161, Sandys, 1610, p.212.

3   Sandys, 1610, p.212.

4   Abû-Izzeddin, 1984, p.85.

5   And declaring them 'impregnable', Abû-Izzeddin, 1984, p.188.

6   Thomas Fuller, in his famous book *A Pisgah Sight of Palestine* (1650) obviously relies on literary sources such as Josephus, Philostorgius etc. P. Pesenti, *Pellegrinaggio de Gierusalemme* (1615) goes across Jordan by way of a bridge 'with three arches' on the way from Damascus (the 'Bridge of Jacob's Daughters' near the Sea of Galilee, near Capernaum, which he visits just after crossing). Francisco Quaresmii's, *Elucidato Terrae Sanctae* (1635) simply skips from Lake Merom to the 'Road to Damascus' (i.e., the location of Paul's conversion), without reference to Banias. M.I. Douban, *Le Voyage de la Terre-Sainte* (Third Ed., 1666) did not visit Banias (or Damascus) though he travelled widely in Galilee and the coast of Lebanon.

7   Book 12, Line 144.

8   Two Jesuit missionaries attended a Synod of Maronite church leaders on 30 September 1736. Among those attending was 'Michel, archeveque de Banias' – but most likely this cleric held only a titular bishopric. Bousquet 1, 1852, p.144.

9   Pere Nacchi was 'Superior general des Missions de la Compagne de Jésus en Syria et en Egypte'. The report is reprinted in Bousquet 1, 1852, p.325. This account became available in Great Britain when it was translated and included by John Green in his *A Journey from Aleppo to Damascus* (1736). Green also provides a map, which he claims is the first really accurate one of the area. It indeed shows Paneas in approximately the correct position *vis à vis* the three 'sources of the Jordan', with a road shown from Sidon, across the Anti-Lebanon, slightly SE to Paneas, then NE to Damascus. The map is not entirely accurate, however. Only two sources of the Jordan are shown, with Banias located halfway along the easternmost one. Green may be trying to create a map based on Nacchi's description (below) and thus confusing Dan with Banias.

10 'In the territory of Caesarea, near that city, there is an eminence about eight or ten feet high, and three quarters of a mile in compass; shaded with verdant oaks, sycamores, citron and orange trees. The tradition is that this was the place where Christ asked his disciples what both the people and themselves said of him. At the foot of this eminence, the two fountains Jor and Dan break forth, at about thirty paces one from the other, and fifty paces from thence meeting, form the famous river of Jordan. The Christians make their sick people drink its waters, which often prove an immediate remedy' (Green, 1736, p.59).

11 Stavrou and Weisensel, 1986, pp.59–60, 71–73.

12 Thompson, 1798, p.267, describes a trip made around 1733 via Tripoli-Baalbek-Damascus-Tripoli and then Beyrout-Sidon-Tyre-Accho. His comments on the sources of the Jordan obviously have their origin in the hopelessly confused accounts of ancient authors: 'The true source or head of the Jordan is now agreed to be the little lake called Phiala, near the mountains of Anti-Lebanus. Josephus indeed makes mention of a lesser Jordan, whose fountain he places about Panion, while he derives the other, or greater Jordan, from Mount Lebanus. However, he is not to be understood here as meaning two distinct rivers, but as dividing the same into two parts, which he denominates differently, and perhaps improperly, according to their distance from the original spring.' Thus, Thompson thinks there is one stream that passes from Phiala via Banias and Merom to the Sea of Galilee!

13 Rafeq, 1966, p.244.

14 Bausman, 1857, p.471.

15 This according to Buckingham, who was told this during his visit some four years later. Buckingham, 1822, p.40.

16 Seetzen, 1810, p.8. It is interesting that as a reader of Arabic, he could not find anything even among the Arabic libraries in Damascus regarding the area.

17 Seetzen, 1810, p.9.

18 Most early nineteenth-century travellers took care to avoid the area. Henry Light, for example went from Beirut up to the 'Cedars of Lebanon' area and returned, visiting neither Banias nor Damascus (*Travels in Egypt, Nubia, Holy Land, Mount Lebanon and Cyprus in the Year 1814*. London: 1818). John Bramson (1813–15) visited only Jaffa, Jerusalem, and Accho, staying carefully near the coast. William Jowett (1815–29) travelled extensively in 'Mount Lebanon' from Beirut, but did not cross the mountains, or go to Banias. In 1817, he visited the Sea of Galilee, but again did not attempt to go to Banias. Jowett, 1824, pp.442–43. James Connor (1819–20) says, 'It was my intention to go direct from Jerusalem to Damascus, by way of Napolose and Tiberias; but the disturbed state of the country about Napolose, occasioned by the presence of the Pacha of Damascus, who was making his rounds to collect the tribute, caused me reluctantly to alter my plans…' Later he went to Damascus, but from Mar-Hanna, and the Beka'a. Even more serious than the disruption caused by the tax collection was the continuing threat of robbery and violence on the roads. Buckingham made several unsuccessful

attempts to get from Nazareth to Damascus. On one occasion, at the ruins of Capernaum on the shore of the Sea of Galilee, he met a party from Tiberias that had tried to make the trip. Though there were six in the party, and all armed, they were attacked by a gang that included several soldiers. They were 'stripped both of their money and arms, and some of those who were well-dressed, had their clothes taken from them'. Two were so severely beaten that they were left behind. 'These men conjured us by every thing sacred not to proceed any farther, but to return with them to Tiberias, as we were certain of being plundered at best, and perhaps murdered also' (Buckingham 2, 1822, pp.351–52).

19   It is almost certain that other Europeans had visited the town, but documentary evidence is lacking. Most of Seetzen's own diaries were unpublished until almost fifty years after his journey (Seetzen, 1854). However, some of Seetzen's letters concerning his journey were published in French in the *Moniteur*. These in turn were sent by members of the National Institute of Paris to Sir Joseph Banks, who gave them to the Palestine Association of London. The Association published a letter which Seetzen wrote from Akko to a Mr. Zach, 'Grand Marshall of the Court of Saxe-Gotha', dated 16 June 1806, under the title *A Brief Account of the Countries Adjoining the Lake of Tiberias, the Jordan, and the Dead Sea*. The editor notes in his preface that 'Few countries are so completely unknown to all Europeans, as those parts of the land of Judaea which have been visited by Mr. Seetzen', and that most travellers have followed 'the beaten track from Jaffa, or Akka to Jerusalem and Bethlehem', leaving 'all the rest of the country…to complete obscurity'. By this circuitous route Seezten's daring journey and his discoveries became known.

20   Seetzen, 1810, p.16.

21   Seetzen left a paper on the wall at the convent of Mt. Sinai dated 9 April 1807, seen by Burckhardt, 1822, p.553: 'U. J. Seetzen, called Mousa, a German traveller, M.D. and recorder (Assesseur) of the College of H. M. the Emperor of all the Russias in the *seigneurie* of Jever in Germany, came to visit…[lists places he went]'. He died of poison in 1811 in Arabia. Bliss, 1906, pp.173–74.

22   Burckhardt, 1822, p.37.

23   Thomson (1846, pp.195–96) comments on Burckhardt's visit, 'the whole description of this place, by this in general most accurate traveller, is not only confused and imperfect, but in some places quite erroneous. He visited Banias in very cloudy and rainy weather, and evidently did not examine the walls of the city.'

24   Oliphant, 1880, p.23.

25   See Amiran et al., 1995, p.263.

26   According to John Wilson, 1847, p.146.

27   Van de Velde, 1854, p.425.

28   Kitchener, 1877, p.172.

29   The second bridge he mentions may in fact be the bridge across Wâdî Sa'âr.

30   Giekie 2, 1898, p.393.

31   The Scotsman John Wilson recorded the names of six of these towers during his visit to Banias in 1843: the *Birj el-Bawadi* (the southern gate where the bridge crossed Wâdî Sa'âr); the *Birj el-Huran* ('now fallen'); the *Birj el-Atlas* ('fallen to the plinth and having old bevelled stones'); and along the mote on the east, the *Birj el-Atilah*, the *Birj ed-Daulah*, and the *Birj el-'Ali*. Wilson, 1847, pp.175–76.

32   Thomson, 1846, p.188.

33   Lynch, 1850, pp.473–74.

34   Kean, 1893, pp.284–85.

35   Kitchener, 1877, p.172.

36   Twain, 1870, pp.470–77.

37   Libbey and Hoskins, 1905, p.97.

38 In 1854, Guérin saw so many fragments of monolithic columns lying in the same general direction that he concluded that one of the streets of the ancient city had been 'ornamented with a double row of columns' (p.336). Recent excavations have definitely located the route of the main north-south street through the ancient town. Unfortunately, the destruction of the village by the Israelis following the 1967 War has made it impossible to know whether a reconstruction of the *cardo*, based on the placement of the fragments as seen by Guérin, might have been possible.

39 Robinson, 1857, p.409; Guérin, 1880, p.309; McGarvey, 1881, p.336; Twain, 1870, p.470ff; Condor and Kitchener, 1881, p.110; De Saulcy, 1854, p.497.

40 Tristram, 1866, p.587.

41 Giekie, 1898, p.394.

42 Buckingham, 1825, p.404.

43 Porter, 1870, p.115. Bayard's party (1852) was warned about the Druze uprising ('on account of the conscription') and the fact that they were infesting the road to Damascus. The sheikh of Banias gave the group one armed guard to accompany them (pp.113–19). Since Tristram found that the villagers did not carry arms and were a 'harmless lot' during his visit in 1863, and that 'law and order reigned' and that there was both a village policeman and a 'Kadi from Damascus' (Tristram, 1866, p.587) it appears that the Sheikh's right to have his own militia had been curtailed. This may have been in consequence of his attempts to 'shake down' European visitors, or it may indicate that the central government was now taking more interest in maintaining order in the area, particularly in view of Druze unrest and other destabilising factors.

44 Beaufort, 1874, p.288.

45 Coleman, 1892, pp.374–75.

46 McGarvey, 1881, pp.336–37.

47 Bausman, 1861, p.466.

48 Macgregor, 1870, pp.230, 233.

49 Hodder, 1873, p.293.

50 Coleman, 1892, p.381.

51 Tristram, 1866, p.587.

52 Macalister, 1868, p.369. Finn's act of kindness was remembered, and when he returned to Banias in 1855 the sheikh immediately sent his son out to invite him to be his guest.

53 Newbold, 1856, p.26. A list of the villages under the control of Hasbeya, including Banias, may be found in Burckhardt, 1822, p.33.

54 The sheikh of Banias brought some 'relatives from Hasbeyah' to the Finn party for medical treatment. Macalister, 1868, p.369.

55 De Saulcy, 1854, p.488.

56 Taylor, 1857, p.113. John Macgregor ('Rob Roy') says that the sheikh told him (1869) that straw had been put in the water at Sheba and had appeared in the spring at Banias. Macgregor recognised this as a corruption of the old story about King Philip told by Josephus. Macgregor, 1870, pp.229–30.

57 Wortabet, 1856, pp.297–98.

58 Oliphant, 1880, pp.24–25.

59 Bausman, 1861, p.466.

60 '...the family of Hajj Ismail el arkawy', Libbey and Hoskins, 1905, pp.98–99.

61 Thomson, 1846, pp.188–89.

62 Lynch, 1850, pp.373–74.

63 Taylor, 1857, p.113.

64 De Saulcy, 1854, pp.486–87.

65 Taylor, 1857, p.114.

66 Curtis, 1852, p.246.

67 Regarding the Metoulai, he comments, 'The Metouali, as far as I could yet learn, are them-selves a sect of Mohammedans, who admit the Koran, and perform the same prayers and ablutions as the rest; but pay some marks of respect to Hussein and Ali, and have particular opinions on the succession of the caliphs, like the Mohammedans of Persia' (Buckingham, 1822, p.404). Newbold thought that they 'descended from the Assassins'.

68 M. Poussou, the Roman Catholic prefect apostolic, in a letter dated 10 November 1837, sent from Damascus as missionary report. Poussou, 1838, pp.130–39.

69 Bausman, 1861, p.474.

70 *Nusayris*: named after Muhammad b. Nusayr (d. 270 or 883), are 'still found in Syria, where for centuries they have maintained rivalries with their Nizari Ismā'īli neighbours, worship 'Ali as God and maintain that Muhammad was his prophet'. Their esoteric theology shows Gnostic influences. Daftary, 1990, p.101.

71 Newbold, 1856, p.29. Compare a similar list in Robinson, 1857, p.136, Appendix 11, and the note that idolatrous worship, 'which prevailed so greatly over the whole of the northern districts of Palestine, may be traced to this day in the secret rites of the Nosairi and Druze sects, in the vicinity' (p.27).

72 Wilson 2, 1847, p.176.

73 For a discussion of this practice in Southern Turkey, see Russell, 'The Archaeological Context of Magic...', 1995.

74 Bliss, 1912, p.10: 'Vestiges there are to-day of the old cults, and neither faint nor innate, though 1500 years have passed away since the edicts of Theodosius the Elder...The Cult of the Shrines, common to-day to Moslems, Christians, and Jews, is essentially the old cult of the High Places. In monasteries where the Christians vow to Elijah or to St. George, there the Moslems vow to the mysterious Khudr, the Ever Green or Ever Living One, whom they identify with both. At the Moslem Shrines of the Khudr Christians invoke St. George.' We have already noted the pagan connections in the theological and philosophical systems of the Nosairis and the Druze.

75 Melchites are Christians of the Greek rite who accept the supremacy of the Pope of Rome.

76 Greek bishops of Banias are mentioned during Mamlûk times, but they were probably merely titular e.g. Sabbas, under Alexis Commenus, Gabriel Broulasuers (1320), and Euthyme (1377–78). Janin, 1953, Cols. 210–11.

77 Titular bishops of Banias were appointed by the Roman Catholic Church, particularly during the sixteenth century when European contacts and influence raised hopes for the re-establishment of a viable Latin hierarchy. Janin lists a Bishop Germain (1599), Bishop Callinique (1645), and a Bon Rousseau (1658–68), for example. A few names are also listed from the early nineteenth century (such as Athanasius, 1827). Janin, 1953, Col. 211.

78 Libbey and Hoskins, 1905, pp.102–3.

79 'He then attempted to purchase Tell el Kady, the supposed site of ancient Dan, for an orphan agricultural school, but even after many preliminaries had been agreed upon he was forced to give up the location and build his orphanage just above the Merj Aiyun and not far from Jedeideh. This latter location is a much more salubrious one than Tell el Kady ever could have been and the large structure with its galvanised roof and American windmill nearby is a worthy tribute to the energy and ability of this man' (Libbey and Hoskins, 1905, p.102). The diocese numbered about 5,000 communicants and 10 priests. Janin, 1953, Col. 211. A church was eventually built in Banias, during the French Mandate, and stands today, empty, on the road that enters the site from the east. The building is on high ground, overlooking the moat and the line of ruined medieval towers that formed the ancient eastern wall.

80 Along with the 'directors of Catholic missions'. Cuinet, 1896, p.305.

81 Lewis G. Leary provides an extensive and highly sympathetic account of the life of Bishop Butrus and his curious funeral in 1902, to which he was an eyewitness. Leary, 1913, pp.156–62. The bishop's immediate successors were Clement Malouf (1901–41) and Leon Kilzi.

EPILOGUE

1   'In the territory now known as Syria there were two main pre-war districts: Damascus and Haleb. In A-Shams (Damascus) are included the districts of Hama, Damascus, Houran and the Karah. The Houran district included the Ajloun, or Irbid, area – which now belongs to the Kingdom of Jordan – while Quneitra belonged to the Damascus district, as did the areas of Hatzbaya, Ba'albek, Beka'a'a and Rashiya (now in Lebanon)...West of the Damascus province was the province of Beirut, containing the districts of Latakiya (Syria), Trablus/Tripoli, Beirut (Lebanon), Acre (Israel) and Nablus – the western part lies within Israel, and the political future of the eastern part is uncertain; Israel now controls both areas...This illustrates that no reference to the Ottoman period corresponds to the current definitions of Syria or the Land of Israel' (Biger, 1995).

2   Yadin Roman, 'The Making of a Border', *Eretz Magazine*.

3   The interesting context of this statement is as follows: 'What...is the natural draining area of the tributaries on the north side? Clearly all that lies between the Lebanon, the Litany, and Mount Hermon. The coast region north of Acre is of comparatively little importance to Palestine; on the other hand, Baneas, the old Dan, must, by reason of its immense military importance, be included with Palestine. The whole trade of this region drains naturally down to Esdraelon. East of Jordan Mount Hermon is the physical, as well as the economic, watershed, and the prolongation of the watershed to the east in the low hills of Jebel el Aswad makes a fairly good natural boundary for Palestine along the Damascus road. Thence the boundary should be the cultivable edge of the desert by Jebel Druz to Gilead. That is the true economic frontier of Palestine' (*Palestine*, 1919, p.198).

4   *EJ* 4, p.163.

5   Ben-Yaacov, 1967, p.273.

6   Ben-Yaacov, 1967, p.252.

7   Hitti, 1961, p.533.

8   For a detailed account of the issues related to water see Libiszewski, 1995.

9   In November 1964 UN observers reported seeing a huge crater and large unexploded bomb on the western edge of the village (Ben-Yaacov, 1967, p.249).

10 Ben-Yaacov, 1967, p.143.

11 Ben-Yaacov, 1967, p.147.

12 See Libiszewski, 1995.

13 Ben-Yaacov, 1967, p.147. See map, p.150.

14 See Libiszewski, 1995.

15 *EJ* 14, pp.1637–38.

16 See Chapter 1, pp.xx.

17 The details and precise events of those two fateful days are, not surprisingly, difficult to determine. Each side has its own own version of the story. For an Arab interpretation see Mara'i and Halabi, 1992.

18 Deut. 3:9; I Chron. 5:23; Cant. 4:8; Ezek. 27:5.

19 Though only a few hundred yards from Banias, this settlement itself was, according to the Israeli understanding, on land that had been allotted to Israel in the 1948 Armistice Agreement. Ilan, 1969, p.14.

Bibliography

ABBREVIATIONS

AE	*L'Année Épigraphique*
Ant.	*Antiquities*
BAR	*Biblical Archaeology Review*
BMC	*A Catalogue of Greek coins in the British Museum*
BT	*Babylonian Talmud*
CMH	*The Cambridge Medieval History*
EI	*The Encyclopaedia of Islam. New Edition*
EJ	*Encyclopaedia Judaica*
DACL	*Dictionnaire d'Archéologie Chrétienne et de Liturgie*
ESI	*Excavations and Surveys in Israel*
Geog.	*The Geography of Strabo* (H.L. Jones)
HE	*Ecclesiastical History*
IEJ	*Israel Exploration Journal*
INJ	*Israel Numismatic Journal*
JT	*Jerusalem Talmud*
Jos.	*Josephus*
LCL	*Loeb Classical Library*
OGIS	*Orientis Graeci Inscriptiones Selectae* (Dittenberger)
PEQ	*Palestine Exploration Quarterly*
PE	*The Preparation for the Gospel (Evangelicae Praeparationis)*
PG	*Patrologia Graeca*
PL	*Patrologia Latina*
PPTS	*The Library of the Palestine Pilgrims' Text Society*
RHCHO	*Recueils des Historiens des Croisades. Historiens Orientaux*
RPC	*Roman Provincial Coins*
SEG	*Supplementum Epigraphicum Graecum*
TLI	*Talmud of the Land of Israel*
War	*The Jewish War*

PRIMARY SOURCES

Abel, Eugenius (ed.). *Orphica*. Prague/Leipzig: 1885.
Académie des Inscriptions et Belles-Lettres. *Recueils des Historiens des Croisades. Historiens Orientaux*. 5 Vols. in 6 parts. Paris: 1872–1906.
al-Zahîr, Khalil b. Shahin. *Kitāb Zubdat Kashf al-Mamalik*. p.Ravaisee (eds). Paris, 1896.
Anderson, David (trans.). *St. John of Damascus, On the Divine Images*. New York, 1997.
Archer, Gleason L. (trans.). *Saint Jerome. Commentary on Daniel*. Grand Rapids, MI: 1958.
Babcock, Emily Atwater, and Krey, A.C. (trans.). *William of Tyre. A History of Deeds Done Beyond the Sea*. 2 Vols. *Records of Civilisation. Sources and Studies* 35. New York: 1943.

Bedrosian, Robert (trans.). *Sebeos' History*. New York: 1985.

Bernand, Andre, and Bernand, Etienne. *Les Inscriptions Greques et Latines du Colosse de Menmon*. Paris: 1960.

Bernand, Andre. *Le Paneion d'El-Kanaïs: Les Inscriptions Grecques*. Leiden: 1972.

Bernand, Etienne. *Les Inscriptions Greques et Latines de Philae*. Vol. 2. Paris: 1969.

Bidez, Joseph (ed.). *Philostorgius Kirchengeschichte*. Berlin: 1981.

Bonnard, Émile (trans.). *Saint Jérôme. Commentaire sur S. Matthieu*. 2 Vols. Paris: 1977.

Broadhurst, R.J.C. (trans.). *A History of the Ayyubid Sultans of Egypt*. Translated from the Arabic of al–Maqrizî. Library of Classical Arabic Literature 5. Boston: 1980.

Burnett, Andrew, Amandry, Michel, and Ripolles, Pere Pau. *Roman Provincial Coinage*. Vol. 1: *From the Death of Caesar to the Death of Vitellius (44 BC–AD 69)*. London and Paris: 1992.

Cameron, Averil, and Hall, Stuart G. (trans.). *Eusebius: Life of Constantine*. Oxford: 1999.

Cary, E. (trans.). *Dio's Roman History 6–7*. LCL. London: 1924.

— (trans.). *The Roman Antiquities of Dionysius of Halicarnassus*. LCL. 7 Vols. Cambridge, MA: 1937.

Chabot, Jean-Baptiste (ed. and trans.). *Chronique de Michel le Syrian*. Paris: 1899.

Collins, Basil (trans.). *Al-Muqaddasî, The Best Divisions for Knowledge of the Regions (Ahsan al-Taqā sīm fī Ma'rifat al-Aqālīm)*. Reading: 2001.

Cotovicus, Joannes. *Itinerarium Hierosolymitanum et Syriacum*. Antwerp: 1619.

Crafer, Thomas W. (trans.). *The Apocriticus of Macarius Magnes. Translations of Christian Literature. Series I: Greek Texts*. London: 1919.

Danby, Herbert (trans.). *The Mishna*. Oxford: 1933.

De Boor, Carl Gotthard (ed.). *Theophanis Chronographia*. Vol. 1. Leipzig: 1883.

Dittenberger, Wilhelm (ed.). *Orientis Graeci Inscriptiones Selectae*. Lipsiae: 1903–1905.

Epstein, I. (ed.). *The Babylonian Talmud*. London: 1935–.

Etheridge, J.W. (trans.). *The Targums of Onkelos and Jonathan ben Uzziel on the Pentateuch; with the Fragments of the Jerusalem Targum: from the Chaldee*. 2 Vols. London: 1862.

Evelyn-White, Hugh G. (trans.). *Hesiod. The Homeric Hymns and Homerica*. LCL. Cambridge, MA: 1959.

Frazer, James George (trans.). *Ovid's Fasti*. LCL. (2nd Edition). New York: 1989.

Freedman, H., and Simon, Maurice (eds). *Midrash Rabbah. Translated into English with Notes, Glossary and Indices*. 10 Vols. London: 1939.

Freeman-Grenville, G.S.P., Chapman, Rupert L. III, and Taylor, Joan E. *The Onomasticon by Eusebius of Caesarea*. Jerusalem: 2003.

Freese, J.H. (trans.). *The Library of Photius*. Vol. 1. New York: 1920.

Gabrieli, Francesco (trans.). *Arab Historians of the Crusades. Selected and Translated from the Arabic Sources*. Trans. from Italian by E.J. Costello. Berkeley: 1969.

Gelzer, Henricus (ed.). *Georgii Cyprii, Descriptio Orbis Romani. Bibliotheca Scriptorum Graecorum et Romanorum Teubneriana*. Lipsiae: 1890.

Gibb, H.A.R. (trans.). *The Damascus Chronicle of the Crusades. Extracted and Translated from the Chronicle of Ibn al-Qalānisī*. University of London Historical Series. Vol. 5. London: 1932.

Gifford, Edwin H. (trans.). *Eusebius of Caesarea. Preparation for the Gospel*. 2 Vols. Grand Rapids, MI: 1981. (Reprint of 1903 Edition.)

Godley, A.D. (trans.). *Herodotus*. LCL. 4 Vols. Cambridge, MA: 1928.

Grumel, V. *Les Regestes des Actes du Patriarcat de Constantinople*. Vol. 1: *Les Actes des Patriarches. Fasc. II: Les Regestes de 715 a 1043*. Istanbul: 1936.

Hall, Clayton Morris. *Nicolaus of Damascus' Life of Augustus. A Historical Commentary Embodying a Translation*. Smith College Classical Studies 4. Northampton, MA: 1923.

Hanson, Gunther Christian (ed.). *Theodoros Anagnostes, Kirchengeschichte. Die Griechischen Christlichen Schriftsteller der Ersten Jahrhunderte. n.F., Bd. 3*. Berlin: 1995.

Hartranft, C.D. (trans.). 'The Ecclesiastical History of Sozomen', in Philip Schaff and Henry Wace, *A Select Library of Nicene and Post Nicene Fathers*. Second Series. Vol. 2. New York: 1891.

Hill, G.F. (trans.). *The Life of Porphyry Bishop of Gaza by Mark the Deacon*. Oxford: 1913.

Hitti, Philip K. (trans.). *An Arab-Syrian Gentleman and Warrior in the Period of the Crusades. Memoirs of Usāmah Ibn-Munqidh (Kitāb al-I'tibār)*. New York: 1929.

— (trans.). *Ahmad ibn Jâbir Al-Balādhurī: The Origins of the Islamic State. Columbia College Studies in History, Economics and Public Law*. Vol. 68. New York: 1961.

Holt, Peter M. (trans.). *The Memoirs of a Syrian Prince; Abû al-Fidā', Sultan of Hamāh (672–732/ 1273–1331)*. Freiburger Islamstudien Band IX. Wiesbaden: 1983.

Jackson, B. (trans.). 'The Ecclesiastical History, Dialogues and Letters of Theodoret', in Philip Schaff and Henry Wace, *A Select Library of Nicene and Post Nicene Fathers*. Second Series. Vol. 3. New York: 1892, pp.33–159.

Jackson, John (trans.). *Tacitus. The Histories*. 3 Vols. LCL. London: 1931.

Jeffreys, Elizabeth, Jeffreys, Michael, and Scott, Roger (trans.). *The Chronicle of John Malalas*. Melbourne: 1986.

Jones, Horace Leonard (trans.). *The Geography of Strabo*. 8 Vols. LCL. Cambridge, MA: 1954.

King, Charles William (trans.). *Julian the Emperor, Containing Gregory Nazianzen's Two Invectives and Libanius' Monody, with Julian's Extant Theosophical Works*. London: 1888.

Kline, Galen R. *Bertrandon de la Broquière: The Voyage d'Outremer*. (Translated, edited and Annotated with an Introduction and Maps.) New York: 1988.

Klostermann, Erick (trans.). *Eusebius of Caesarea. Das Onomastikon der Biblischen Ortsnamen*. Hildesheim: 1977. (Reprint of 1904 Edition.)

Kovacs, David (trans.). *Euripides. Cyclops, Alcestis, Medea*. LCL. London: 1994.

Laoust, Henri (trans.). *Les Gouverneurs de Damas sous les Mamlouks et les Premiers Ottomans (658–1156/1160–1744). Traduction des Annales d'Ibn Tulun et d'Ibn Gum'a*. Damascus: 1952.

Le Bas, Ph., and Waddington, W.H. *Inscriptions greques et latines recueillies en Asie Mineure*. Paris: 1870. Reprint Hildesheim: 1972.

Lyons, U. and M.C. (trans.). *Ayyubids, Mamlukes and Crusaders. Selections from the Tarikh al-Duwal wa'l-Mulûk of Ibn al-Furat*. Vol. 2. Cambridge: 1971.

Maalouf, Amin. *The Crusades Through Arab Eyes*. New York: 1984.

Mango, Cyril, and Scott, Roger (trans.). *The Chronicle of Theophanes Confessor. Byzantine and Near Eastern History AD 284–813*. Oxford: 1997.

Marmardji, Le R.P.A.S. *Textes Géographiques Arabes sur la Paléstine. Recueillis, Mis en Ordre Alphabétique et Traduits en Français*. Paris: 1951.

Meynard, A.C. Barbier de (trans.). *'Abd al-Rahman Ibn Ismā'īl, called Abû Shamah. Le Livre des Deux Jardins. Histoire des deux règnes, celui de Nour ed-Dîn et celui de Salah ed-Dîn. RHCHO* 4. Paris: 1898.

Migne, Jacques Paul (ed.). *Patrologiae Cursus Completus*.

Mommsen, Theodor (ed.). *C. Lulii Solini, Collectanea Rerum Memoirabilium*. Berlin: 1864.

Moore, Clifford H. (trans.). *Tacitus the Histories*. 2 Vols. LCL. London: 1925.

Moretti, Luigi. *Iscrizioni Agonistiche Greche. Studi Publicata dall'Istituto Italiano per la Storia Antica* 12. Rome: 1953.

Necephorus Callistus. *Ecclesiasticae Historiae*. Vol. 2. Paris: 1630.

Neusner, Jacob (ed.). *The Talmud of the Land of Israel*. Chicago: 1991–.

— (trans.). *Mekhilta According to Rabbi Ishmael. An Analytical Translation*. Vol. 2. Brown Judaic Studies 15. Atlanta, GA: 1988.

Norman, A.F. (trans.). *Libanius. Selected Works*. Vol. 1. LCL. London: 1969.

Palestine Pilgrims Text Society. *Library of the Palestine Pilgrims Text Society*. London: 1890ff.

Paton, W.H. (trans.). *Polybius The Histories*. 6 Vols. LCL. London: 1926.

Pharr, Clyde (trans.). *The Theodosian Code and Novels and the Sirmondian Constitutions*. Princeton: 1952.

Phillips, George. (ed. and trans.). *The Doctrine of Addai, the Apostle*. London, 1876.

Preger, Theodor (ed.). *Scriptores Originum Constantinopolitanarum 1*. Leipzig: 1901. Reprinted by Arno Press, New York: 1975.

Price, R.M. (trans.), *Lives of the Monks of Palestine by Cyril of Scythopolis*. Cistercian Studies 114. Kalamazoo, MI: 1991.

Ramsey, G.G. (trans.). *Juvenal and Persius. LCL*. London: 1950.

Richards, D.S. (trans.). *The Rare and Excellent History of Saladin, or al-Nawādir al-Sultāniyya wa'l-Mahāsin al-Yūsifiyya by Bahā' al-Dīn Ibn Shaddād. Crusader Texts in Translation 7*. Aldershot, England: 2001.

Ryan, Frances Rita (trans.). *Fulcher of Chartres: A History of the Expedition to Jerusalem 1095–1127*. Knoxville: 1969.

Sadeque, Syedah Fatima (trans.). *The Slave King. Baybars I of Egypt*. [Translation of Ibn 'Abd al-Zahîr (1223–52 AD), Sirat al-Malik al-Zahîr.] Oxford: 1956.

Sandoli, Sabino de (ed.). *Corpus Inscriptionum Crucesignatorum Terrae Sanctae 1099–1291*. Pubblicazioni dello Studium Biblicum Franciscanum. No 21. Jerusalem: 1974.

Sarason, Richard S. (trans.). *TLI 3: Demai*. Chicago: 1993.

Sauvaget, J. (trans.). *Muhammad Ibrâhim Ibn Abû Bakr: Chronique de Damas d'Al-Jazari (689–98 H)*. Paris: 1949.

Schwab, Moise (trans.). *Le Talmud de Jérusalem*. Vol. 2. Paris: 1932.

Show, M.R.B. (trans.). 'The Life of St. Louis by Joinville', in M.R.B. Show, *Joinville and Villehardouin: Chronicles of the Crusades*. New York: 1963.

Spinka, Matthew, and Downey, Glanville (trans.). *Chronicle of John Malalas: Books VIII–XVIII*. Chicago: 1940.

Stewart, Aubry (trans.). *Felix Fabri, Wanderings in the Holy Land*. 2 Vols. *PPTS* 7–10. London: 1892–93.

Supplementum Epigraphicum Graecum. Lugduni Batavorum, 1923–.

Taylor, Thomas (trans.). *Iamblichus on the Mysteries of the Egyptians, Chaldeans, and Assyrians*. 3rd Edition. London: 1968. First published 1821.

Thackeray, H. St. J., Martin, Ralph, and Feldman, L.H. (trans.). *Jos. LCL*, 10 Vols. Cambridge, MA: 1956–65.

The Greek Ecclesiastical Historians of the First Six Centuries of the Christian Era. Vol. 1. London: 1845.

Waddington, W.H., and La Bas, Philippe. *Inscriptions Grecques et Latines de la Syria. Recueillées et Expliquées*. Paris: 1870.

Walford, Edward (trans.). 'Epitome of the Ecclesiastical History of Philostorgius, Compiled by Photius, Patriarch of Constantinople', in *The Ecclesiastical History of Sozomen*. Bohn Ecclesiastical Library. New York: 1855.

Watt, M. (trans.). *Eutychius of Alexandria. The Book of the Demonstration (Kitāb al-Burhan)*. Part I. *Corpus Scriptorum Christianorum Orientalium, Scriptores Arabici 21*. Louvain: 1960.

Williams, Frank (trans.). *The Panarion of Epiphanius of Salamis*. 2 Vols. Leiden: 1987, 1994.

Williamson, G.A. (trans.). *Eusebius of Caesarea. The History of the Church from Christ to Constantine*. Minneapolis: 1965.

SECONDARY SOURCES

Abdul-Hak, Selim, and Abdul-Hak, Andrée. *Catalogue Illustré du Département des Antiquitiés Greco-Romaines au Musée de Damas*. Vol. 1. Damascus: 1951.

Abû-Izzeddin, Nejla M. *The Druzes*. Leiden: 1984.

Adan-Bayewitz, D. *Common Pottery in Roman Galilee. A Study of Local Trade.* Ramat Gan: 1993.

Adler, Elkan Nathan. *Jewish Travelers in the Middle Ages.* London: 1930.

Aharoni, Y. 'Three New Boundary Stones from the Western Golan', '*Atiqot.* Vol. 1 (1955), pp.109–14.

Alon, Gedaliah. *The Jews in Their Land in the Talmudic Age (70–640 C. E)*: Vol. 1. Translated by Gershon Levi. Jerusalem: 1980.

Alouf, Michel M. *History of Baalbek.* 24th Edition; 12th English Edition. Harissa, Lebanon: 1956.

Alptekin, Coskun. *The Reign of Zangi (521–41/1127–49).* Erzurum, Turkey: 1978.

Amir, David. *Banias – From Ancient till Modern Times. Introduction to the Geography and Natural History of the Area by Dan Perry.* Dan, Israel: 1968. (Hebrew)

Amiran, D.H.K., Arieh, E., and Turcotte, T. 'Earthquakes in Israel and Adjacent Areas: Macroseismic Observations Since 100 B.C.E.', *IEJ* 44 (1995), pp.260–305.

Anderson, William. *Green Man: The Archetype of Our Oneness with the Earth.* London: 1990.

Anonymous. 'The Eastern Frontiers of Palestine', *Palestine. The Organ of the British Palestine Committee.* Vol. 5, No 25 (2 August 1919), pp.195–98.

Assaf, S. 'Dallata, Kades, and Banias', *Bulletin of the Jewish Palestine Exploration Society* 1 (1938), pp.16–19. [Hebrew, English summary].

Athanassiadi, Plymnia. 'Persecution and Response in Late Paganism: the Evidence of Damascius', *Journal of Hellenic Studies* 113 (1993), pp.1–29.

Avi-Yonah, M. 'Syrian Gods at Ptolemais-Accho', *IEJ* 9 (1959), pp.1–12.

— *The Jews under Roman and Byzantine Rule. a Political History of Palestine from the Bar Kokhba War to the Arab Conquest.* Jerusalem: 1984.

Bader, Gershom. *The Encyclopedia of Talmudic Sages.* Translated by Solomon Katz. London: 1988.

Bakhīt, Muhammad. '*Adnān. The Ottoman Province of Damascus in the Sixteenth Century.* Beirut: 1982.

Balch, David. *Social History of the Matthean Community: Cross-disciplinary Approaches.* Minneapolis: 1991.

Balog, Paul. *The Coinage of the Mamluk Sultans of Egypt and Syria. Numismatic Studies* No 12. New York: 1964.

Barag, Dan. 'King Herod's Royal Castle at Samaria-Sebaste', *PEQ* 125 (1993), pp.3–18.

Baramki, Dimitri. *Phoenicia and the Phoenicians.* Beirut: 1961.

Barkay, G., Ilan, Z., Kloner, A., Mazar, A., Urman, D. 'Archaeological Survey in the Northern Bashan (Preliminary Report)', *IEJ* 24 (1974), pp.173–84.

Bar-Kochva, Bezalel. *The Seleucid Army.* Cambridge: 1976.

Bacher, Wilhelm. *Die Agada der Tannaiten.* 2nd Edition. Strassburg: 1903.

Bausman, Benjamin. *Sinai and Zion; or, A Pilgrimage through the Wilderness to the Land of Promise.* Philadelphia: 1861.

Beaufort, Emily A. *Egyptian Sepulchres and Syrian Shrines.* London: 1874.

Beausobre, M. De. 'Dissertation sur la Statue du Paneade', *Bibliotheque Germanique* 13 (1727), pp.1–91. Amsterdam: 1727.

Benvenisti, Meron. *The Crusaders in the Holy Land.* Jerusalem: 1970.

Ben-Yaacov, Nissim. *The Israel-Syrian Armistice: Problems of Implementation, 1949–66.* Jerusalem: 1967.

Berchem, M. van. 'Le Château de Baniyas et ses Inscriptions', *Journal Asiatique* (1888), pp.440ff.

Berlin, Andrea M. 'Between Large Forces: Palestine in the Hellenistic Period', *Biblical Archaeologist* 60 (1997), pp.2–51.

— 'The Archaeology of Ritual: The Sanctuary of Pan at Banias/Caesarea Philippi', *Bulletin of the American Schools of Oriental Research*, No 315 (August, 1999), pp.27–45.

Betts, Robert Brenton. *The Druze.* New Haven: 1988.

Bianquis, Thierry. 'Ibn al-Nabulusi, un martyr Sunnite au IVe siècle de l'Hégire', *Annales Islamologiques* 61 (1974).

Bianquis, Thierry. *Damas et la Syria sous la Domination Fatimide. 359–468/969–1076*. 2 Vols. Damascus: 1986–89.

Bieber, Margaret. *The Sculpture of the Hellenistic Age*. New York: 1955.

Biger, Gideon. 'They Asked the Sheikh and Moved the Border', *Ha-aretz*, 13 June 1995.

Biran, Avraham. 'Tel Dan', *Biblical Archaeology* 37 (1974), pp.26–51; 43 (1980), pp.168–82.

— 'To the God Who is in Dan', in A. Biran (ed), *Temples and High Places in Biblical Times*, pp.142–51. Jerusalem: 1981.

— *Biblical Dan*. Jerusalem: 1994.

Birley, Anthony R. *Hadrian, The Restless Emperor*. London and New York: 1997.

Bliss, Frederick J. T*he Development of Palestine Exploration*. London: 1906.

— *The Religions of Modern Syria and Palestine*. Edinburgh: 1912.

Boas, Adrian J. *Crusader Archaeology. The Material Culture of the Latin East*. London: 1999.

Borgeaud, Philippe. *The Cult of Pan in Ancient Greece*. Chicago: 1988.

Bousquet, P.A. *Les Actes des Apôtres Modernes. Relations Épistolaires et Authentiques des Voyages Entrepris par les Missionnaires Catholiques*. Paris: 1852.

Bowersock, G.W. *Julian the Apostate*. Cambridge: 1978.

— *Hellenism in Late Antiquity*. Cambridge: 1990.

— *Roman Arabia*. Cambridge: 1983.

Braslavski, I. 'Geniza Fragments with Mentions of Dallata, Kedesh, 'Ammata and Baneas', *Bulletin of the Jewish Palestine Exploration Society* 4 (1938), pp.128–31. [Hebrew, English summary].

Briailles, Chadon de. 'Bulles de l'Orient Latin', *Syria* 27 (1950), pp.284–300.

Brochuiere, Bertrandon de la. *The Travels of B. de La Brocquière to Palestine, and His return from Jerusalem Overland to France during the Years 1432 and 1433*. Translated by Thomas Johnes. Hafod: 1807.

Brock, S.P., 'The Rebuilding of the Temple under Julian: A New Source', *PEQ* 108 (1976): 103–7.

— 'A Letter Attributed to Cyril of Jerusalem on the Rebuilding of the Temple', *Bulletin of the School of Oriental and African Studies* 40 (1977): 267–86.

Buckingham, James S. *Travels in Palestine, Through the Countries of Bashan and Gilead, East of the River Jordan*. Vol. 2. 2nd Edition. London: 1822.

— *Travels Among the Arab Tribes Inhabiting the Countries East of Syria and Palestine*. London: 1825.

Burckhardt, John Lewis. *Travels in Syria and the Holy Land*. London: 1822.

Burnett, A. 'The Coinage of King Agrippa I of Judaea and a New Coin of King Herod of Chalcis', pp.25–28 in H. Huvelin et al. (eds), *Melanges p.Bastien*. Wetteen: Numismatique Romaine, 1987.

Burrell, Barbara, 'Palace to Praetorium: The Romanization of Caesarea', pp.228–47 in Avner Raban, and Kenneth G. Holum, (eds), *Caesarea Maritima: A Retrospective after Two Millennia*. Leiden: 1996.

Butler, Howard Crosby. 'Section B The Expedition of 1909 in Syria', in *Publications of the Princeton University Archaeological Expeditions to Syria in 1904–5 and 1909*. Division 1. Leyden: 1930.

Cabrol, Fernand, and Laclercq, Henri (eds). *Dictionnaire d'Archéologie Chrétienne et de Liturgie*. 15 Vols. Paris: 1903–52.

Cameron, Averil, and Herrin, Judith (trans.). *Constantinople in the Early Eighth Century: The Parastaseis Syntomoi Chronikoi. Columbia Studies in the Classical Tradition* 10. Leiden: 1984.

Canaan, Tewfik. *Mohammedan Saints and Sanctuaries in Palestine*. Jerusalem: 1980 (Reprinted from the Journal of the Palestine Oriental Society, 1927).

Carmoly, E. I*tinéraires de la Terre Sainte les xiiie, xive, xve, xvie, et xviie Siècles, Traduits de l'Hébreu*. Brussels: 1847.

Chuvin, Pierre. *A Chronicle of the Last Pagans. Revealing Antiquity* 4. Cambridge, MA: 1990.

Clemens, Samuel (Mark Twain). T*he Innocents Abroad, or The New Pilgrims' Progress*. Hartford, CT: 1870.

Clermont-Ganneau, Charles. 'Inscription Arabe de Banias', *Recueil d'Archéologie Orientale* 1 (1888), pp.241–52.

— 'Les Seigneurs de Banias et de Soubeibe', *Recueil d'Archéologie Orientale* 1(1888), pp.253–76.

— 'Le Mont Hermon et son Dieu d'après une Inscription Inédite', *Recueil d'Archéologie Orientale* 5 (1902), pp.346–66.

Coggan, Sharon Lynn. *Pandaemonia: A Study of Eusebius' Recasting of Plutarch's Story of the 'Death of the Great Pan.'* Ph.D. Dissertation, Syracuse University, 1992.

Coleman, Henry R. *Light from the East*. Louisville, KY: 1892.

Condor, Claude R., and Kitchener, H.H. *The Survey of Western Palestine*. Vol. 1: Galilee. London: 1881.

— *The Prince's Visit to the Holy Land*. London: 1882.

— *The World's Greatest Explorers and Explorations: Palestine*. London: 1889.

Cook, Stanley A. *The Religion of Ancient Palestine in the Light of Archaeology*. London: 1930.

Crook, John A. 'Titus and Berenice', *American Journal of Philology* 72 (1951): pp.162–75.

Crowfoot, J.W. *Early Churches in Palestine*. College Park: 1941.

Crowfoot, J.W., Kenyon, Kathleen M., and Sukenik, E.L. *The Buildings at Samaria. Samaria-Sebaste. Reports of the Work of the Joint Expedition in 1931–1933 and of the British Expedition in 1935*, No 1. London: 1942.

Cuinet, Vital. *Syrie Liban et Paléstine, Géographie Administrative, Statistique, Descriptive et Raisonnée*. Paris: 1896.

Curtis, George William. *The Howadji in Syria*. New York: 1852.

Daftary, Farhad. *The Ismā'īlīs: Their History and Doctrines*. Cambridge: 1990.

Dalman, Gustaf. *Sacred Sites and Ways. Studies in the Topography of the Gospels*. London: 1935.

Dar, Shimon. 'A Relief of Aphrodite from Paneas, Israel', *Journal of the British Archaeological Society* 144 (1991), 116–18, pl. 16.

— *Settlements and Cult Sites on Mount Hermon, Israel. Iturean Culture in the Hellenistic and Roman Periods. BAR International Series* 589. Oxford: 1993.

Dar, Shimon, and Kokkinos, Nikos. 'The Greek Inscriptions from Senaim on Mount Hermon', *PEQ* 124 (January-June 1992), pp.9–25.

Dar, Shimon, and Kindler, Arie. 'The Coins from the Mamluk Enclosure at Nebi Hazuri', *INJ* 10 (1988–1989), pp.129–36.

Dauphin, Claudine M. 'Jewish and Christian Communities in the Roman and Byzantine Gaulanitis: A Study of Evidence from Archaeological Surveys', *PEQ* 114 (1982), pp.129–42.

De Beausobre, M. 'Dissertation sur la Statue du Panéade', *Bibliothèque Germanique* 13 (1727), pp.1–91. Amsterdam: 1727.

De Ridder, A. et al. *Collection de Clercq 4: Les Marbres, les Vases Peints et les Ivoires*. Paris: 1906.

De Saulcy, F. *Narrative of a Journey Round the Dead Sea and in the Bible Lands; in 1850 and 1851*. Vol. 2. London: 1854.

Deschamps, Paul. *Les Châteaux des Croisés en Terre Sainte II: Le Défense du Royaume de Jérusalem. Bibliothèque Archéologique et Historique* 34. Paris: 1939.

De Scheyb, Francisco Christophero. *Peutingeriana Tabula Itineraria*. Vindobonae: 1753.

Devambez, P. 'La 'Grotte de Pan' a Thasos', pp.117–23 in *Mélanges d'Histoire Ancienne et d'Archéologie Offerts à Paul Collart*. Lausanne, 1976.

Devreesse, Robert. *Le Patriarcat d'Antioche depuis la Paix de l'Église jusqu'à la Conquête Arabe*. Paris: 1945.

Donner, Fred M. 'The Problems of Early Arabic historiography in Syria', in Muhammad Adnon Bakhit (ed.), *Proceedings of the Second Symposium on the History of Bilād at-Shām During the Early Islamic Period Up to 40 A.D./640 A.D.* Amman: 1987. Vol. 1: pp.1–27.

Drake, H.A. *In Praise of Constantine, a Historical Study and New Translation of Eusebius' Tricennial Orations*. Berkeley: 1975.

Dussaud, René. *Histoire et Réligion des Nosairis. École Pratique des Hautes Études. Bibliothéque* 29. Paris: 1900.

— *Topographie Historique de la Syrie Antique et Mèdièvale*. Paris: 1927.

— 'Cultes Cananéens aux Sources du Jourdain. D'Après les Textes de Ras Shamra', *Syria* 17 (1936), pp.283–95.

Eisler, Robert. 'Le Prétendue Statue de Jésus et de l'Hémorroise a Panéas', *Revue Archeologique. Cinquiéme Série, Tom.* 30 (1930), pp.18–27.

Elisséeff, Nikita. *Nūr-ad-Dīn. Un Grand Prince Musulman de Syrie au Temps des Croisades, 511–569 H., 1118–74*. 3 Vols. Damascus: 1967.

Ellenblum, Ronnie. 'Who Built Qal'at al-Subayba?' *Dumbarton Oaks Papers*, No 43 (1989), pp.103–12.

Ellis, Henry (ed.). *The Pylgrymage of Sir Richard Guylforde to the Holy Land, A.D. 1506*. London: 1851.

Encyclopaedia Judaica. Jerusalem: 1971–72.

Farnell, Lewis Richard. *The Cults of the Greek States*. Vol. 5. New Rochelle, NY: 1977. (First published, 1909.)

Field, Henry M. *Among the Holy Hills*. 6th Edition. New York: 1895.

Fischer, Moshe L., and Stein, Alla. 'Josephus on the Use of Marble in Building Projects of Herod the Great', *Journal of Jewish Studies* 45 (1994), pp.74–85.

Foerster, Gideon. 'A Cuirassed Bronze Statue of Hadrian', *'Atiqot*, English Series 17 (1985).

Foss, Clive. 'Dead Cities of the Syrian Hill Country', *Archaeology* 49:5 (1996), pp.48–53.

Fox, Robin Lane. *Pagans and Christians*. New York: 1987.

Franzius, Enno. *History of the Order of Assassins*. New York: 1969.

Frazer, James George. *Folk-lore in the Old Testament*. Vol. 3. New York: 1919.

Friedland, Elise Anne. *Roman Marble Sculpture from the Levant: The Group from the Sanctuary of Pan at Caesarea Philippi (Panias)*. Unpublished Ph.D. Dissertation, The University of Michigan (1997).

— 'Graeco-Roman Sculpture in the Levant: The Marbles from the Sanctuary of Pan at Caesarea Philippi (Banias)', in J.H. Humphrey (ed.), *The Roman and Byzantine Near East*. Vol. 2: *Some Recent Archaeological Research. Journal of Roman Archaeology Supplementary Series* No 31. Portsmouth, RI: 1999.

Fuller, Thomas. *A Pisgah Sight of Palestine*. London: 1650.

Garnsey, Peter. *Famine and Food Supply in the Graeco-Roman World. Responses to Risk and Crisis*. Cambridge: 1988.

Gaudefroy-Demombynes, Maurice. *La Syrie a l'Époque des Mamelouks. Bibliothèque Archéologique & Historique*. Vol. 3. Paris: 1923.

Geikie, Cunningham. *The Holy Land and the Bible*. Vol. 2. London: 1898.

Gelzer, Henricus. *Patrum Nicaenorum. Scriptores Sacri et Profani, Fasc. 2*. Leipzig: 1898.

Geyer, Paul. *Itinera Hierosolymitana Saeculi IIII–VIII. Corpus Scriptorum Ecclesiasticorum Latinorum 39*. Vienna: 1898.

Gibson, Shimon, Ibbs, Bridget, and Kloner, Amos. 'The Sataf Project of Landscape Archeology in the Judean Hills', *Levant* 23 (1991), pp.29–54.

Gieseler, John C.L. *A Text-Book of Church History*. Vol. 1 (American Edition). New York: 1868.

Gil, Moshe. *A History of Palestine, 634–1099*. Trans. Ethel Broido. Cambridge: 1992.

— 'The Political History of Jerusalem During the Early Muslim Period', pp.1–35, in Joshua Prawer and Haggie Ben-Shammai (eds), *The History of Jerusalem, the Early Muslim Period, 638–1099*. New York: 1997.

Ginzberg, Louis. *Legends of the Jews*. Vol. 6. Philadelphia: 1938.

Gitler, Haim. '14. The Coins', in Shelly Wachsmann, *The Excavations of an Ancient Boat in the Sea of Galilee (Lake Kinneret)* (*'Atiqot*. English Series 19: 1990), pp.101–6.

Goitein, S.D. 'Obadyah, a Norman Proselyte', *The Journal of Jewish Studies* 4 (1953), pp.74–84.

Gottschalk, Hans L. *Al-Malik al-Kāmil von Ägypten und Seine Zeit. Eine Studie zur geschichte vorderasiens und Ägyptens in der Ersten Hälfte des 7./13/ Jahrhunderts*. Wiesbaden: 1958.

Grabois, Aryeh. 'Le Cité de Baniyas et le Château de Subeibeh pendant les Croisades', *Cahiers de Civilisaton Mediévale* 13 (1970), pp.43–62.

Gracey, M. H. 'The Armies of the Judaean Client Kings', pp.311–23 in Philip Freedman, and David Kennedy (eds), *The Defence of the Roman and Byzantine East*. Vol. 1. *BAR International Series* 297. Oxford: 1986.

Grainger, John D. *Hellenistic Phoenicia*. Oxford: 1991.

Green, John. *A Journey from Aleppo to Damascus with a Description of Those Two Capital Cities and the Neighbouring Ports of Syria*. London: 1736.

Gregg, Robert C., and Urman, Dan. *Jews, Pagans, and Christians in the Golan Heights. Greek and Other Inscriptions of the Roman and Byzantine Eras. South Florida Studies in the History of Judaism* 140. Atlanta: 1996.

Grimouard de St. Laurenti, Henri Julien. *Guide de l'Art Chrétien. Études d'Esthétique et d'Inconographie*. Vol. 2. Paris: 1872–75.

Grumel, Venace. *Les Regestes des Actes du Patriarcat de Constantinople*. Vol. 1: *Les Actes des Patriarches. Fasc. 2: Les Regestes de 715 a 1043*. Istanbul: 1936.

Guérin, M.V. *Description Géographique, Historique et Archéologique de la Paléstine. Troisième Partie. Galilée 1*. Paris: 1880.

Hajjar, Youssef. 'Dieux et cultes non heliopolitains de la Beqa, de l'Hermon et de l'Abliene a l'epoque romaine', pp.2509–604, in Wolfgang Haase (ed.), *Aufstieg und Niedergang der Römischen Welt. Principat 18:4*. New York: 1978.

Hamilton, Robert W. *Guide to the Historical Site of Sebastieh*. Jerusalem: 1936.

Hanauer, J.E. *Folk-Lore of the Holy Land, Moslem, Christian and Jewish*. London: 1907.

Harnack, Adolf. *The Mission and Expansion of Christianity in the First Three Centuries*. 2 Vols. Translated by J. Moffatt. New York: 1908.

Harper, George McLean. *Village Administration in the Roman Province of Syria*. Princeton: 1928.

Hartal, Moshe. 'Banias Survey', *ESI* 4 (1985), pp.7–8.

— 'Banias, The Aqueduct', *ESI* 4 (1985), p.8.

— 'En el-Ghazlan (Wâdî Naqib)', *ESI* 4 (1985), p.26.

— 'Banias, The Aqueduct', *ESI* 13 (1993), pp.1–2.

— 'Banias, the Aqueduct', *ESI* 16 (1997), pp.5–8.

— 'Namrud Fortress', *ESI* 16 (1997), pp.1–5.

Hartal, Moshe, and Ma'oz, Zvi. 'Banias Salvage Excavation – 1984', *ESI* 4 (1985), pp.8–9.

Haussoullier, Bernard, and Ingholt, Harold. 'Inscriptions Grecques de Syrie', *Syria* 5 (1924), pp.316–41.

Herbig, Reinard. *Pan. Der Griechisch Bocksgott. Versuch einer Monographie*. Frankfurt am Main: 1949.

Helbig, Wolfgang. *Führer durch die öffentlichen Sammlungen klassischer Altertümer in Rom*. 4th Edition. Vol. 1: *Die Päpstlichen Sammlungen im Vatikan und Lateran*. Tübingen, 1963.

Hettger, Henry T. 'Pulius Aelias Hadrianus', *World Coin News* (2 February 1988), p.14.

Hengel, Martin. *Judaism and Hellenism. Studies in Their Encounter in Palestine during the Early Hellenistic Period*. Vol. 1. London: 1974.

— *Studies in the Gospel of Mark*. London: 1985.

Hill, G.F. 'Adonis, Ball, and Astarte', *Church Quarterly Review* 66 (1908), pp.141.

Hitti, Philip K. *The Near East in History: A 5000 Year Story*. Princeton, N.J.: 1961.

— *A Short History of Lebanon*. New York: 1965.

Hodder, Edwin. *On Holy Ground or, Scenes and Incidents in the Land of Promise*. New York: 1873.

Holladay, Carl R. *Fragments from Hellenistic Jewish Authors*. Vol. 3: Aristolbulos. Atlanta: 1995.

Holleaux, Maurice. *Lagides et Séleucides*. Vol. 3 of Louis Robert (ed.), *Études d'Épigraphie et d'Histoire Grecques*. Paris: 1942.

Holscher, G. 'Paneas', pp.594–599 in George Wissowa (ed.), *Paulys Real-Encyclopädie der Classischen Altertumswissenschaft 18*, Part 3. Stuttgart: 1949.

Holt, Peter M. *Early Mamluk Diplomacy (1260–1290). Treaties of Baybars and Qalāwūn with Christian Rulers. Islamic History and Civilisation. Studies and Texts* 12. Leiden: 1995.

Holum, Kenneth. 'Iter Principis: Hadrian's Imperial Tour', *Biblical Archaeology Review* 23:6 (November/December 1997), pp.50–51, 76.

Honigmann, E. 'Studien zur Notitia Antiochena', *Byzantinische Zeitschrift* 25 (1925), pp.60–88.

Hoppe, Leslie J. *The Synagogues and Churches of Ancient Palestine*. Collegeville, MN: 1994.

Hornum, Michael B. *Nemesis, the Roman State, and the Games. Religions in the Graeco-Roman World* 117. Leiden: 1993.

Horvitz, Peter S. 'A Jewish Isolde in Chalcis', *The Celator* 10:8 (August, 1996), pp.38–39.

Humphreys, R. Stephen. *From Saladin to the Mongols. The Ayyubids of Damascus, 1193–1260*. Albany, NY: 1977.

Hütteroth, Wolf-Dieter, and Abdulfattah, Kamal. *Historical Geography of Palestine, Transjordan and Southern Syria in the Late 16th Century*. Erlanger Geographische Arbeiten, Sonderband 5. Erlangen: 1977.

Ilan, Zvi. *The Golan Was Always Jewish*. Tel Aviv: 1969.

Iliffe, J. H. 'A Bust of Pan', *The Quarterly of the Department of Antiquities of Palestine* 3 (1934), pp.165–66.

Ilisch, Lutz. *Sylloge Numorum Arabicorum Tübingen: Palästina*. Tübingen: 1993.

Imhoof-Blumer, R.W., and Gardner, Percy. *Ancient Coins Illustrating Lost Masterpieces of Greek Art. A Numismatic Commentary on Pausanias*. Chicago: 1964. (Reprint of 1887 Edition.)

Irby, Charles, and Mangles, James. *Travels in Egypt and Nubia, Syria, and the Holy Land*. London: 1844.

Janin, R. 'Cesaree de Philippe', in Alfred Baudrillart et al., *Dictionnaire d'Histoire et de Géographie Ecclésiastique* 12, Cols. 209–11. Paris: 1953.

Jeremias, Joachim. 'Ein Grabepigramm aus Caesarea Philippi', *Palästinajahrbuch* 28 (1932), pp.81–82.

Jones, A.H.M. 'The Urbanization of the Ituraean Principality', *Journal of Roman Studies* 21 (1931), pp.265–75.

— *The Cities of the Eastern Roman Provinces*. 2nd Edition. Oxford: 1971.

Jordan, Ruth. *Berenice*. New York: 1974.

Joudah, Ahmad Hasan. *Revolt in Palestine in the Eighteenth Century. The Era of Shaykh Zahir al-'Umar*. Princeton: 1987.

Jowett, William. *Christian Researches in the Mediterranean from 1815 to 1820*. 3rd Edition. London: 1824.

Kaegi, Walter Emil. *Byzantium and the Early Islamic Conquests*. Cambridge: 1992.

Kahn, Lisa C. 'King Herod's Temple of Roma and Augustus at Caesarea Maritima', pp.130–45 in Avner Raban, and Kenneth G. Holum (eds), *Caesarea Maritima: A Retrospective after Two Millennia*. Leiden: 1996.

Kasher, Aryeh. *Jews, Idumaeans, and Ancient Arabs*. Tübingen: 1988.

— *Jews and Hellenistic Cities in Eretz-Israel. Texte und Studien zum Antiken Judentum* 22. Tübingen: 1990.

Kean, James. *Among the Holy Places*. London: 1893.

Keel, O. 'Antike Statuen als historische Monumenten für biblische gestalten', pp.155–65 in Andreas Kessler, Thomas Ricklin, and Gregor Wurst (eds), *Peregrina curiositas. Eine Reise durch den Orbis Antiquus zu Ehren von Kirk van Damme. Novum Testamentum et Orbis Antiquus* 27 (1994).

Kennedy, Hugh. 'From Polis to *Madina*: Urban Change in Late Antiquity and Early Islamic Syria', *Past and Present* 106 (February, 1985), pp.3–27.

— 'The Last Century of Byzantine Syria: A Reinterpretation', *Byzantinische Forschungen* 10 (1985), pp.141–84.

— *The Prophet and the Age of the Caliphates. The Islamic Near East from the Sixth to the Eleventh Century*. London: 1985.

Kindler, Arie. 'A Coin of Herod Philip – the Earliest Portrait of a Herodian Ruler', *IEJ* 21 (1971), pp.161–63; pl. 32.

Kindler, Arie, and Stein, Alla. *A Bibliography of the City Coinage of Palestine from the 2nd Century B.C. to the 3rd Century A.D. BAR International Series* 374. Oxford: 1987.

Kitchener, H.H. *Palestine Exploration Fund. Quarterly Statement for 1877*. London: 1877.

Klengel, Horst. *The Art of Ancient Syria*. New York: 1972.

Klijn, A.F.J., and Reinink, G.J. *Patristic Evidence for Jewish-Christian Sects*. Leiden: 1973.

— *Jewish-Christian Gospel Tradition*. Leiden: 1992.

Kokkinos, Nikos. *The Herodian Dynasty: Origins, Role in Society and Eclipse. Journal for the Study of the Pseudepigrapha. Supplement Series* 30. Sheffield: 1998.

Kopp, Clemens. *The Holy Places of the Gospels*. New York: 1963.

Kuhn, Heinz-Wolfgang, and Arav, Rami. 'The Bethsaida Excavations: Historical and Archaeological Approaches' in Birger A. Pearson (ed.), *The Future of Early Christianity: Essays in Honour of Helmut Koester*, 1991, pp.91–106.

Kushnir-Stein, Alla. 'Two Inscribed Weights from Banias', *IEJ* 45 (1995), pp.48–51.

La Monte, John F. *Feudal Monarchy in the Latin Kingdom of Jerusalem 1100 to 1291. Publications of the Mediaeval Academy of America* 4. Cambridge: 1932.

Landau, V.H. 'A Greek Inscription Found Near Hefzibah', *IEJ* 16 (1966), pp.54–70.

Lane-Poole, Stanley. *A History of Egypt in the Middle Ages*. 2nd Edition, Revised. London: 1914.

Lauffray, Jean. 'Forums et Monuments de Béryte', *Bulletin de Musée de Beyrouth* 7 (1944–45), pp.13–80.

Leary, Lewis Gaston. *Syria: The Land of Lebanon*. New York: 1913.

Leclercq, Henri. *Manuel D'Archéologie Chrétienne Depuis Les Origines Jusqu'au VIIIe Siécle*. Vol. 2. Paris: 1907.

— 'Paneas', *DACL* 8, Part 2, Cols. 1737–41. Paris: 1929.

Le Quien, Michael. *Oriens Christianus in Quatuor Patriarchatus Digestus* 2. Paris: 1740.

Levi, Annalina and Mario. *Itineraria Picta: contributo allo Studio della Tabula Peutingeriana, Studi e materiali del Museo dell'Impero Romano 7*, Ora Museo della Civiltà Romana. Rome: 1967.

Libbey, William, and Hoskins, Franklin E. *The Jordan Valley and Petra*. Vol. 1. New York: 1905.

Libiszewski, Stephan. *Water Disputes in the Jordan Basin Region and their Role in the Resolution of the Arab-Israeli Conflict. ENCOP Occasional Paper* No 13. Zurich/Berne: 1995.

Liebermann, Saul. 'Palestine in the Third and Fourth Centuries', *The Jewish Quarterly Review* 36 (1946), pp.329–70.

Lieu, Samuel N.C., and Montserrat, Dominic (eds). *From Constantine to Julian: Pagan and Byzantine Views*. London: 1996.

Lifshitz, Baruch. 'Etudes sur l'Histoire de la Province Romaine de Syrie', pp.3–30 in Hildegard Temporini, and Wolfgang Haase (eds), *Aufstieg und Niedergang der Römischen Welt*. Principat 8. New York: 1978.

Littmann, Enno. *Syria. Publications of the Princeton University Archaeological Expeditions to Syria in 1904–1905 and 1909. Division IV Semitic Inscriptions. Section A Nabatean Inscriptions from the Southern Hauran*. Leyden: 1914.

Lortet, Louis. *La Syrie d'Aujourd'hui. Voyages dans la Phénicie, le Liban et la Judée, 1875–1880*. Paris: 1884.

Lowe, Malcolm, and Flusser, David. 'Evidence Corroborating a Modified Proto-Matthean Synoptic Theory', *New Testament Studies* 29 (1983), pp.25–47.

Luke, Harry Charles. *A Spanish Franciscan's Narrative of a Journey to the Holy Land*. London: 1927.

Lynch, W.F. *Narrative of the United States' Expedition to the Jordan River and the Dead Sea*. 2nd Edition, Revised. London: 1850.

MacAdam, Henry Innes. 'Epigraphy and Village Life in Southern Syria During the Roman and Early Byzantine Periods', *Berytus* 3 (1983), pp.103–15.

Macalister, R.A.S. 'Gleanings from the Minute-books of the Jerusalem Literary Society', *Palestine Exploration Fund Quarterly Statement* 1908, pp.116–25. London: 1908.

Macgregor, John. *The Rob Roy on the Jordan*. 2nd Edition. London: 1870.

Maltiel-Gerstenfeld, Jacob. 'A Portrait Coin of Berenice, Sister of Agrippa II?' *INJ* 4 (1980), pp.25–26.

Mancinelli, Fabrizio. *Catacombs and Basilicas. The Early Christians in Rome*. Florence: 1981.

Mandeville, John. *The Travels of Sir John Mandeville; The Version of the Cotton Manuscript in Modern Spelling*. London: 1900.

Mango, Cyril A. *The Brazen House*. Copenhagen: 1959.

Mann, Jacob. *The Jews in Egypt and in Palestine under the Fatimid Caliphs*. Vols 1–2. London: 1920.

— *Texts and Studies in Jewish History and Literature*. Vol. 2. Philadelphia: 1935.

Mansi, Joannes Dominicus. *Sacrorum Conciliorum Nova, et Amplissima Collectio*. Forence: 1761.

Ma'oz, Zvi. 'Comments on Jewish and Christian Communities in Byzantine Israel', *PEQ* 117 (1985), pp.59–68.

— 'Banias, Temple of Pan (1988)', *ESI* 7–8 (1989), p.11.

— 'Banias, Temple of Pan – 1990', in *ESI* 10 (1990), pp.59–61.

— 'Banias, Temple of Pan – 1991/1992', *ESI* 13 (1993), pp.2–7.

— 'Banias', in Ephraim Stern (ed.), *The New Encyclopedia of Archaeological Excavations in the Holy Land*. 4 Vols. New York: 1993: 1:pp.136–43.

— 'Coin and Temple–The Case of Caesarea Philippi-Paneas', *INJ* 13 (1994–99), pp.90–102.

Ma'oz, Zvi et al. *Panion I: Excavations in the Sanctuary of Pan at Caesarea-Philippi, Banyas*. Jerusalem: forthcoming.

Mara'i, Tayseer, and Halabi, Usama R. 'Life Under Occupation in the Golan Heights', *Journal of Palestine Studies*. Vol. 22: 1 (1992), pp.78–93.

Marxen, Willi. *Mark the Evangelist*. Nashville: 1969.

Masterman, Ernest W. Gurney. *Studies in Galilee*. Chicago: 1909.

Mattingly, Harold, and Sydenham, Edward A. *The Roman Imperial Coinage:* Vol. 2: *Vespasian to Hadrian*. London: 1926.

Maude, Mary Fawler. *Scripture Topography*. 5th Edition. London: 1856. (First published in 1843).

McCullough, W. Stewart. *A Short History of Syriac Christianity to the Rise of Islam*. Chico, CA: 1982.

McGarvey, J.W. *Lands of the Bible*. Philadelphia: 1881.

Mély, F. de. 'Figures du Christ', *Revue Archéologique. Cinquiéme Série-Tome* 32, (1930), pp.145–50.

Merrill, Selah. 'Caesarea Philippi and the Highlands of Galilee', in Charles W. Wilson (ed.), *Picturesque Palestine*. Vol. 2. London: 1889.

Meshorer, Ya'akov. *Jewish Coins of the Second Temple Period*, Tel-Aviv: 1967.

— 'A New Type of Coins of Agrippa II', *IEJ* 21 (1971), pp.164–65.

— *Ancient Jewish Coinage*. Vol. 2: *Herod the Great through Bar Cochba*. Dix Hills, NY: 1982.

— 'The Coins of Caesarea Paneas', *INJ* 8 (1984–85), pp.37–58, plates 7–15.

— *The Coinage of Aelia Capitolina*. Jerusalem, 1989.

— 'Ancient Jewish Coinage – Addendum I', *INJ* 11 (1990–91), pp.104–32, pls 17–32.

Meyer, Hugo. *Antinoos. Die archäologischen Denkmäler unter Einbeziehung des Numatismatischen und Epigraphischen Materials sowie der Literarischen Nachrichten. ein Beitrag zur Kunst- und Kulturgeschichte der Hadrianisch-frühantoninischen Zeit*. München: 1991.

Meyshan, Josef. 'An Unknown Portrait Coin of Agrippa I', *INJ* 1 (1963), pp.66–67.

Millar, Fergus. *The Roman Near East 31 BC-AD 337*. Cambridge, MA: 1993.

Millar, Fergus, and Segal, Erich (eds). *Caesar Augustus: Seven Aspects*. Oxford: 1984.

Miller, Conrad. *Itineraria Romana. Römische Reisewege an der Hand der Tabula Peutingeriana*. Stuttgart: 1917.

Milne, J. Grafton. *A History of Egypt Under Roman Rule*. London: 1898.

Mitchell, Stephen. 'Imperial Building in the Eastern Roman Provinces', *Harvard Studies in Classical Philology* 91 (1987): pp.333–65.

Moore, Wayne. 'Coins of the Iturean Dynasts of Chalcis sub Libano', unpublished manuscript: 1990.

Murray, Robert. *Symbols of Church and Kingdom: A Study in Early Syriac Tradition*. Cambridge: 1975.

Nagy, Rebbeca Martin, et al. (eds). *Sepphoris in Galilee: Crosscurrents of Culture*. Raleigh, N.C.: 1996

Nau, F. 'Les Suffragants d'Antioche au *milieu* au IVe Siécle', in *Revue de L'Orient Chrétien*. 2nd Series 14 (1909).

Negev, A. 'The Inscription of the Emperor Julian at Ma'ayan Barukh', *IEJ* 19 (1969), pp.170–73.

Netzer, E. 'An Architectural and Archaeological Analysis of Building in the Herodian Period at Herodium and Jericho.' Ph.D. Thesis: Hebrew University, 1977.

Neubauer, Adolph. *La Géographie du Talmud*. Paris: 1868.

Newbold, Captain. 'On the Lake Phiala – the Jordan and Its Sources', *The Journal of the Royal Asiatic Society* 16 (1856), pp.8–31.

Newby, P.H. *Saladin in His Time*. New York: 1983.

Nickelsburg, George W.E. 'Enoch, Levi, and Peter: Recipients of Revelation in Upper Galilee', *Journal of Biblical Literature* 100:4 (December, 1981), pp.575–600.

— *I Enoch: A Commentary on the Book of I Enoch Chapters 1–36; 81–108*. Minneapolis: 2001.

North, Robert. 'Quirks of Jordan River Cartography', in Adnan Hadidi (ed.), *Studies in the History and Archaeology of Jordan* 2 (1985), pp.205–15.

O'Ballance, Edgar. *The Third Arab-Israeli War*. London: 1972.

Offord, Joseph. 'A Nabatean Inscription Concerning Philip, Tetrarch of Auranitis', *Palestine Exploration Fund Quarterly Statement 1919*, pp.82–85.

Oliphant, Laurence. *The Land of Gilead, With Excursions in the Lebanon*. Edinburgh: 1880.

Overman, J. Andrew, Olive, Jack, and Nelson, Michael. 'Discovering Herod's Shrine to Augustus: Mystery Temple Found at Omrit', *BAR* 29 (March/April 2003), 40–49, 67–68.

Parrot, André. *Samarie Capitale du Royaume d'Israel. Cahiers D'Archéologie Biblique* No 7. Neuchatel: 1955.

Paton, Lewis B. 'Survivals of Primitive Religion in Modern Palestine', *Annual of the American Schools of Oriental Research* 1, pp.51–65. Cambridge: 1925.

Perate, André. 'Note sur le Groupe de Paneas', *Mélanges d'Archéologie et d'Histoire* 5 (1885), pp.303–12.

Perdrizet, Paul, and Lefebvre, Gustave. *Les Graffites Grecs du Memnonion d'Abydos*. Paris: 1919.

Picard, C. 'Observations sur les Sculptures Berytiennes de Délos', *Berytus* 2 (1935), pp.11–24.

Porter, Josiah L. *Five Years in Damascus*. 2nd Edition, Revised. London: 1870.

Poussou, M. 'Voyage aux Sources du Jourdain', *Annales de la Propagation de la Foi* 61 (Nov. 1838), pp.130–39. Lyon: 1839.

Prawer, Joshua. *The World of the Crusaders*. New York: 1972.

— 'The Autobiography of Obadyah the Norman, a Convert to Judaism at the Time of the First Crusade', in Isadore Twersky (ed.), *Studies in Medieval Jewish History and Literature. Harvard Judaic Monographs* 2. Cambridge: 1979, pp.110–34.

— *The History of the Jews in the Latin Kingdom of Jerusalem*. Oxford: 1988.

Price, S.R.F. *Rituals and Power: the Roman Imperial Cult in Asia Minor*. Cambridge: 1984.

Prime, William C. *Tent Life in the Holy Land*. New York: 1857.

Pringle, Denys. *The Churches of the Crusader Kingdom: A Corpus*. Vol. 1: A-K. Cambridge: 1993.

— *Secular Buildings in the Crusader Kingdom of Jerusalem*. Cambridge: 1997.

Qedar, Sh. 'Two Lead Weights of Herod Antipas and Agrippa II and the Early History of Tiberias', *INJ* 9 (1986–87), pp.29–35.

— 'A Coin of Agrippa II Commemorating the Roman Victory over the Jews', *Schweizer Munzblatter* 154 (May, 1989), pp.33–36.

Rafeq, Abdul-Karim. *The Province of Damascus 1723–83*. Beirut: 1966.

Rakicic, Mark. 'The *Lagobolon* of Pan on the Coinage of Antigonus Gonatas', *The Celator* 10:3 (March, 1996), pp.6–12.

Reed, Jonathan. 'Galileans, 'Israelite Village Communities', and the Sayings Gospel Q', pp.87–108 in Eric Meyers (ed.), *Galilee Through the Centuries: Confluence of Cultures.* Winona Lake, Indiana: 1999.

Reifenberg, A. 'Unpublished and Unusual Jewish Coins', *IEJ* 1 (1950–1951), p.176–78, pl. 32.

Reisner, G.A., Fisher, Clarence S., and Lyon, David G. *Harvard Excavations at Samaria 1908–1910. Harvard Semitic Series.* 2 Vols. Cambridge: 1924.

Relandi, Hadriani. *Palaestina ex Monumentis Veteribus Illustrata (Book III: 918–22).* Trajecti Batavorum: 1714.

Rey, E.-G. *Recherches Geographique et Historiques sur la Domination des Latins en Orient.* Paris: 1877.
— *Les Familles d'Outre-Mer de du Cange.* Paris: 1869.

Richardson, L., Jr. *A New Topographical Dictionary of Ancient Rome.* Baltimore and London: 1992.

Richardson, Robert. *Travels along the Mediterranean.* Vol. 2. London: 1822.

Ridder, A. de. *Collection de Clercq. Catalogue publié par les soins de l'Académie des Inscriptions et Belles-Lettres* 4: *Les Marbres, les vases peints et les ivoires.* Paris: 1906.

Rix, Herbert. *Tent and Testament. A Camping Tour in Palestine.* London: 1907.

Robert, Louis. *Hellenica. Recueil d'Epigraphie de Numismatique et d'Antiquitiés Greques* 4. Paris: 1948.
— *Hellenica. Recueil d'Epigraphie de Numismatique et d'Antiquitiés Greques* 11–12. Paris: 1960.

Robinson, Edward. 'Researches in Palestine', in *Bibliotheca Sacra: or Tracts and Essays on Topics connected with Biblical Literature and Theology* 1. New York and London: 1843, pp.4–88.
— *Later Biblical Researches in Palestine and the Adjacent Regions. A Journal of Travels in the Year 1852.* 2nd Edition. Boston: 1857.

Rohricht, Reinhold. *Bibliotheca Geographica Palaestinae. Chronologisches Verzeichnis der von 333 bis 1878 Verfassten Literatur uber das Heilige Land mit dem Versuch Einer Kartographie.* Revised and Updated by David H.K. Amiran. London: 1989. First published 1890.

Roller, Duane W. *The Building Program of Herod the Great.* Berkeley: 1998.

Roman, Yadin. 'The Making of a Border', *Eretz Magazine.*

Rosenberger, M. *City Coins of Palestine.* Vol. 1. Jerusalem: 1972; Vol. 2. Jerusalem: 1975.

Rousseau, John J., and Arav, Rami. *Jesus and His World: An Archaeological and Cultural Dictionary.* Minneapolis: 1995.

Runciman, Steven. *A History of the Crusades.* Vol. 2: *The Kingdom of Jerusalem and the Frankish East 1100–1187.* Cambridge: 1951.

Russell, James. 'A Roman Military Diploma from Rough Cilicia', *Bonner Jahrbücher* 195 (1995), pp.67–133.
— 'The Archaeological Context of Magic in the Early Byzantine Period', in Henry Mcguire (ed.), *Byzantine Magic. Dumbarton Oaks Research Library and Collection.* Washington, D.C., 1995.
— 'The Persian Invasions of Syria/Palestine and Asia Minor in the Reign of Heraclius: Archaeological, Numismatic and Epigraphic Evidence', in *The Dark Centuries of Byzantium (7th–9th c.). National Hellenic Research Foundation, Institute for Byzantine Research, International Symposium* 9. Athens: 2001.

Russell, Kenneth W. 'The Earthquake of May 19, A.D. 363', *Bulletin of the American Schools of Oriental Research* 238 (Spring, 1980), pp.47–64.
— 'The Earthquake Chronology of Palestine and Northwest Arabia from the 2nd through the Mid-8th Century A.D', *Bulletin of the American Schools of Oriental Research* 260 (Fall/November 1985), pp.37–59.
— 'Excavating and Rebuilding the Temple of Hercules', *ACOR Newsletter* 5 (November, 1991), pp.1–3.

Saldarini, Anthony. 'The Social World of Christain Jews and Jewish-Christians', in Hayim Lapin (ed.), *Religious and Ethnic Communities in Later Roman Palestine. Studies and Texts in Jewish History and Culture* 5 (1998), pp.115–54.

— *Matthew's Christian-Jewish Community.* Chicago: 1994.

Salibi, Kamal S. *Syria Under Islam. Empire on Trial 634–1097.* Delmar, NY: 1977.

Sandys, George. *Sandys Travels.* 7th Edition. London: 1673.

Scheiber, Alexander. 'The Origins of 'Obadyah, the Norman Proselyte', *The Journal of Jewish Studies* 5.1 (1954), pp.32–35.

Schick, Robert. *The Christian Communities of Palestine from Byzantine to Islamic Rule. A Historical and Archaeological Study.* Princeton: 1995.

Schlumberger, Gustave. *Numismatique de l'Orient Latin* (Reprint of 1878 Edition). Graz-Austria: 1964.

Schürer, Emil. *The History of the Jewish People in the Age of Jesus Christ.* Vol. 2. New York: 1972.

Schwartz, Daniel R. *Agrippa I: The Last King of Judea. Texte und Studien zum Antiken Judentum.* 23. Tübingen: 1990.

— 'Caesarea and Its 'Isactium: Epigraphy, Numismatics and Herodian Chronology', pp.167–81; 'Texts, Coins, Fashions and Dates: Josephus' Vita and Agrippa II's Death', pp.243–82. *Studies in the Jewish Background of Christianity. Wissenschaftliche Untersuchungen zum Neuen Testament.* Tübingen: 1992.

Sear, David R. *Greek Coins and Their Values.* Vol. 2: Asia and North Africa. London: 1975.

Seetzen, Jasper Ulrich. *A Brief Account of the Countries Adjoining the Lake of Tiberias, the Jordan, and the Dead Sea.* Bath: 1810.

— *Reisen durch Syrien, Palästina, Phönicien, die Transjordan-Länder, Arabia Petraea und Unter-Aegypten.* Edited by F. Kruse. Berlin: 1854.

Seyrig, Henri. 'Antiquités Syriennes', *Syria* 13 (1932), pp.50–64.

— 'Antiquites Syriennes', *Syria* 27 (1950), pp.229–52.

— 'Antiquités Syriennes', *Syria* 42 (1965), pp.25–34.

Shaked, Idan. 'Banias, the "Officers' Pool"'. *ESI* 13 (1993), pp.7–8.

Sourdel, Dominique. *Les Cultes du Hauran à l'Époque Romaine.* Institut Français d'Archéologie de Beyrouth. Bibliothèque archéologique et historique 53. Paris: 1952.

Sperber, Daniel. *Roman Palestine, 200–400: Money and Prices.* Ramat-Gan, Israel: 1974.

Stavrou, Theofanis G., and Weisensel, Peter. *Russian Travelers to the Christian East from the Twelfth to the Twentieth Centuries.* Columbus, Ohio: 1986.

Stein, Alla. 'The Undated Coins of Agrippa II under Nero', *INJ* 8 (1984–1985), pp.9–11.

Stern, Menachem. *Greek and Latin Authors on Jews and Judaism.* Vols 1–2. Jerusalem: 1974, 1980.

Stevenson, Willian B. *The Crusaders in the East. A Brief History of the Wars of Islam with the Latins in Syria During the Twelfth and Thirteenth Centuries.* Cambridge: 1907.

Strack, H.L., and Stemberger, G. *Introduction to the Talmud and Midrash.* Edinburgh: 1991.

Strickert, Fred. 'The Coins of Philip', in Rami Arav and Richard A. Freund, (eds) *Bethsaida: A City by the North Shore of the Sea of Galilee.* Vol. 1. *Bethsaida Excavations Project.* Kirksville, MO: 1995.

Sullivan, Phillip B. 'A Note on the Flavian Accession', *The Classical Journal* 49 (1953), pp.67–70.

Sullivan, Richard D. *Near Eastern Royalty and Rome, 100–30 BC.* Toronto: 1990.

Sussman, J. 'The Inscription in the Synagogue at Rehob', pp.146–53 in Lee I. Levine (ed.), *Ancient Synagogues Revealed.* Jerusalem: 1981.

Tardieu, M. *Les Paysages Reliques: Routes et Haltes Syriennes.* Louvain: 1990.

Taylor, Bayard. *The Lands of the Saracen; or, Pictures of Palestine, Asia Minor, Sicily, and Spain.* New York: 1857.

The Cambridge Medieval History. Vol. 2. Cambridge: 1913.

The Encyclopaedia of Islam. New Edition. Leiden: 1960.

Thompson, Charles. *Travels through Turkey in Asia, the Holy Land, Arabia, Egypt and Other Parts of the World.* Glasgow: 1798.

Thomson, William M. *The Land and the Book.* Vol. 2: *Central Palestine and Phoenicia.* Hartford, CT: 1911.

— 'The Sources of the Jordan, the Lake el-Huleh, and the Adjacent Country', *Bibliotheca Sacra and Theological Review* 3 (Andover: 1846), pp.184–207.

Toynbee, Jocelyn M.C. *The Hadrianic School. A Chapter in the History of Greek Art*. Cambridge: 1934.

Trattner, Ernest, *Understanding the Talmud*, New York: 1955.

Travlos, John N. *Pictorial Dictionary of Ancient Athens*. London: 1971.

Tristram, H.B. *The Land of Israel: A Journal of Travels in Palestine, Undertaken with Special Reference to its Physical Character*. London: 1866.

Trombley, Frank Richard. *The Survival of Paganism in the Byzantine Empire during the Pre-Iconoclastic Period (540–727)*. Ph.D. Dissertation, UCLA: 1981.

— *Hellenic Religion and Christianization* C. 370–529. 2 Vols. Leiden: 1993.

Tsafrir, Yoram. 'The Maps Used by Theodosius: on the Pilgrim Maps of the Holy Land and Jerusalem in the sixth Century C.E.' *Dumbarton Oaks Papers*, No 40 (1986), pp.129–45.

— (ed.). *Ancient Churches Revealed*. Jerusalem: 1993.

— 'The Fate of Pagan Cult Places in Palestine: the Archaeological Evidence with Empasis on Bet Shean', in Hayim Lapin (ed.), *Religious and Ethnic Communities in Later Roman Palestine. Studies and Texts in Jewish History and Culture* 5 (1998), pp.197–218.

Twain, Mark (Samuel L. Clemens). *The Innocents Abroad, or The New Pilgrims' Progress*. Hartford, Conn.: 1870.

Tzaferis, Vassilios. 'Cults and Deities Worshiped at Caesarea Philippi-Banias', in Eugene Ulrich et al., *Priests, Prophets and Scribes. Essays on the Formation of Heritage of Second Temple Judaism in Honour of Joseph Blenkinsopp*. Sheffield: 1992.

Tzaferis, Vassilios, and Avner, Rina. 'Banias – 1990', *ESI* 10 (1991), pp.1–2.

Tzaferis, Vassilios, and Israeli, Shoshana. 'Banias – 1993', *ESI* 16 (1997), pp.9–11.

Tzaferis, Vassilios, and Israeli, Shoshana. 'Banias – 1994', *ESI* 16 (1997), pp.11–14.

Tzaferis, Vassilios, and Peleg, M. 'Banias Excavation Project– 1988', *ESI* 7–8 (1988–1989), pp.10–11.

Urman, Dan. *The Golan. A Profile of a Region during the Roman and Byzantine Periods. BAR International Series* 269. Oxford: 1985.

Velde, C.W.M. van de. *Narrative of a Journey through Syria and Palestine in 1851 and 1852*. Vol. 2. Edinburgh: 1854.

— *Le Pays d'Israel*. Paris: 1857.

Van Dyke, Henry. *Out-of-Doors in the Holy Land*. New York: 1908.

Van Egmont, J. A., and Heymon, John. *Travels through Part of Europe, Asia Minor, the Islands of the Archipelago, Syria, Palestine, Egypt, Mount Sinai, Etc.* 2 Vols London: 1769.

Von Matt, Leonard. *Early Christian Art in Rome*. Commentary by Enrico Josi. New York: Universe Books, 1961.

Walbank, Frank W. *A Historical Commentary on Polybius*, Vols 1–3. Oxford: 1957.

Watzinger, Carl. *Denkmäler Palästinas. Eine Einführung in die Archäologie des Heiligen Landes*. Leipzig: 1935.

Wechter, Pinchas. 'The History of the Jews in Egypt and Syria under the Rule of the Mamluks', *The Jewish Quarterly Review* 36 (1945), pp.201–5.

Whigham, Peter, and Jay, Peter. *The Poems of Meleager*. Berkeley and Los Angeles: 1975.

White, L. Michael, 'Crisis Management and Boundary Maintenance: The Social Location of the Matthean Community', pp.211–57 in Balch, David L. *Social History in the Matthean Community: Cross Disciplinary Approaches*. Minneapolis: 1991.

Wilkinson, John. *Jerusalem Pilgrims Before the Crusades*. Jerusalem: 1977.

— (ed.). *Jerusalem Pilgrimage 1099–1185*. London: 1988.

Wilpert, Joseph. 'Alte Kopie der Statue von Paneas', pp.296–301 in M. Abramić and V. Hoffilller (eds), *Strena Buliciana. Commentationes Gratulatoriae Francisco Bulić*. Zagreb: 1924.

Wilson, Charles. 'Geography of the Bible', pp.52–56 in Edward H. Plumptre (ed.), *The Bible Educator*, Vol. 3. 2nd Edition. London: 1884. Continued in Vol 4: pp.247–54.

Wilson, Edward L. *In Scripture Lands*. London: 1891.

Wilson, John. *The Lands of the Bible Visited and Described*, Vol. 2. Edinburgh: 1847.

Wortabet, Gregory M. *Syria, and the Syrians: or, Turkey in the Dependencies*, Vol. 1. London: 1856.

Wright, Thomas (ed.). *Early Travels in Palestine, Comprising the Narratives of Arculf, Willibald, Bernard, Saewulf, Sigurd, Benjamin of Tudela, Sir John Maundeville, De La Brocquière, and Maundrell*. New York: 1968. [First published 1848.]

Wycherley, R.E. *The Stones of Athens*. Princeton: 1978.

Zeyadeh, Ali. 'Urban Transformation in the Decapolis Cities of Jordan', *ARAM Periodical* 4 (1992), pp.101–15.

Ziadeh, Nicola. 'Urban Life in Syria Under the Early Mamluks. Publication of the Faculty of Arts and Sciences', *Oriental Series* 24. Beirut: 1953.

INDEX OF PLACES

INDEX OF PEOPLE

GENERAL INDEX